Skip·Beat!

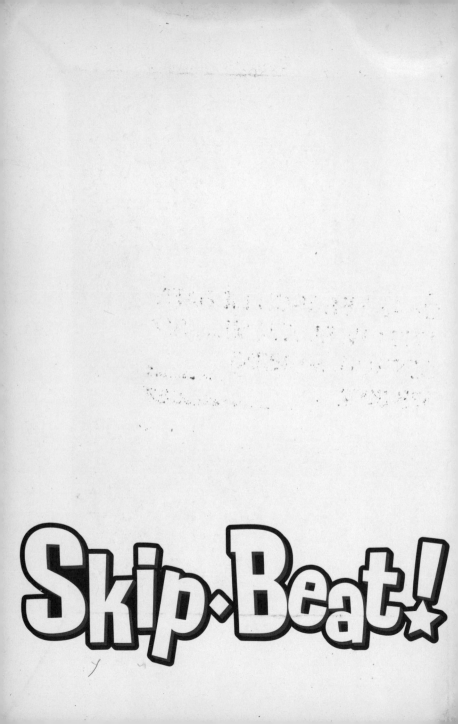

14

Story & Art by Yoshiki Nakamura

Skip·Beat!

Volume 14

CONTENTS

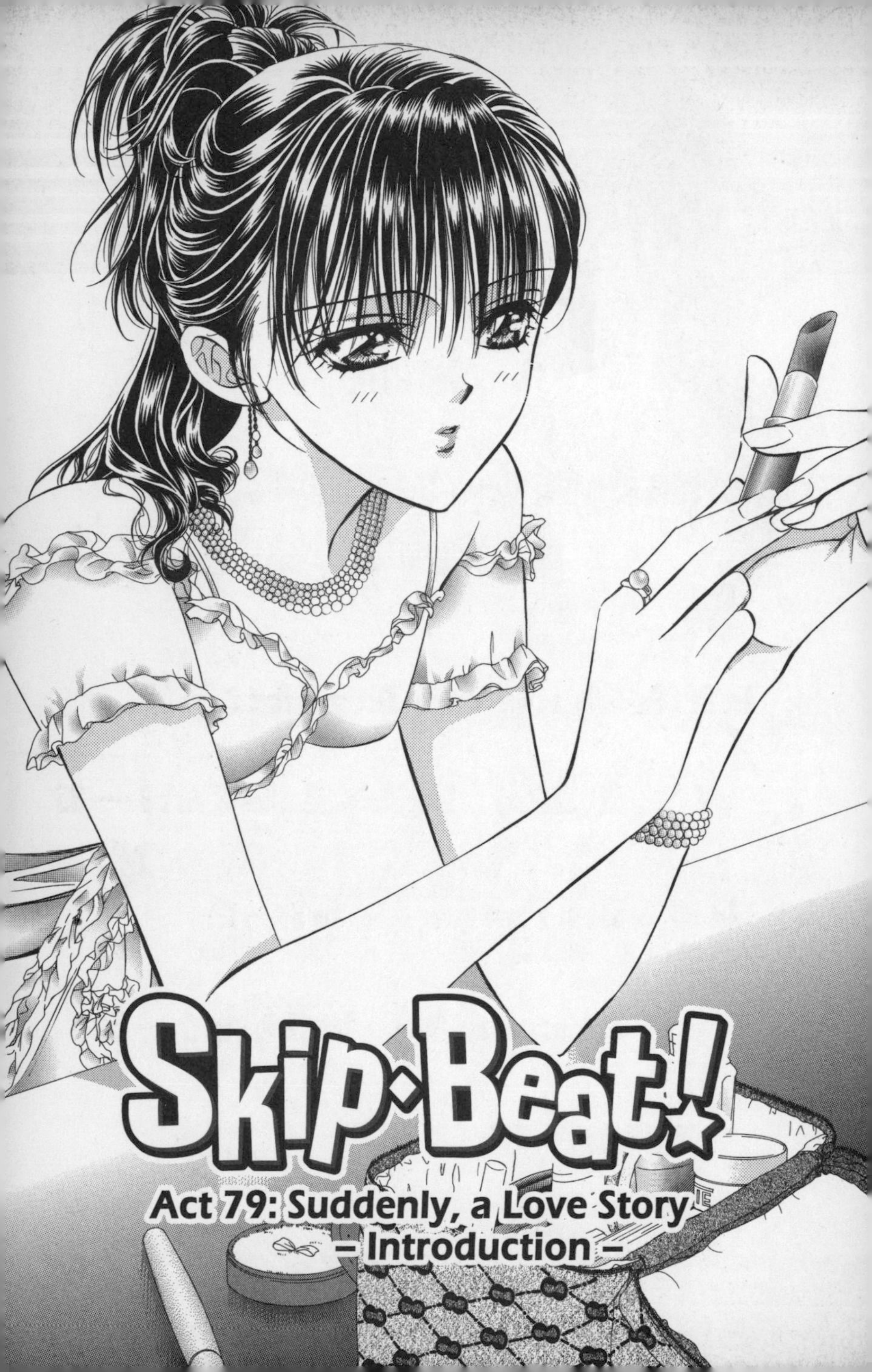
Skip·Beat!
Act 79: Suddenly, a Love Story
– Introduction –

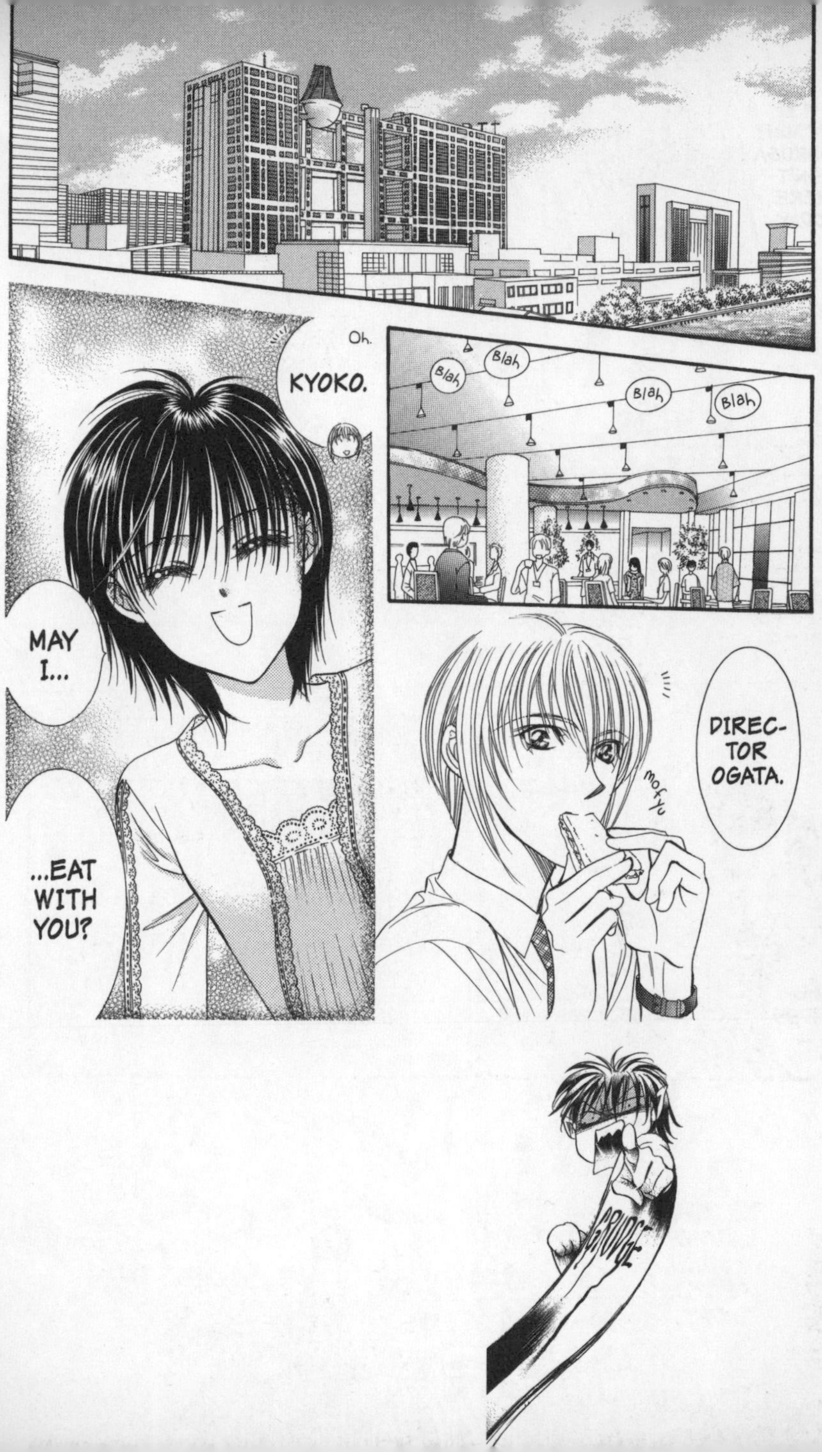

Blah
Blah
Blah
Blah
mofyu
DIREC-TOR OGATA.
Oh.
KYOKO.
MAY I...
...EAT WITH YOU?
GRUDGE

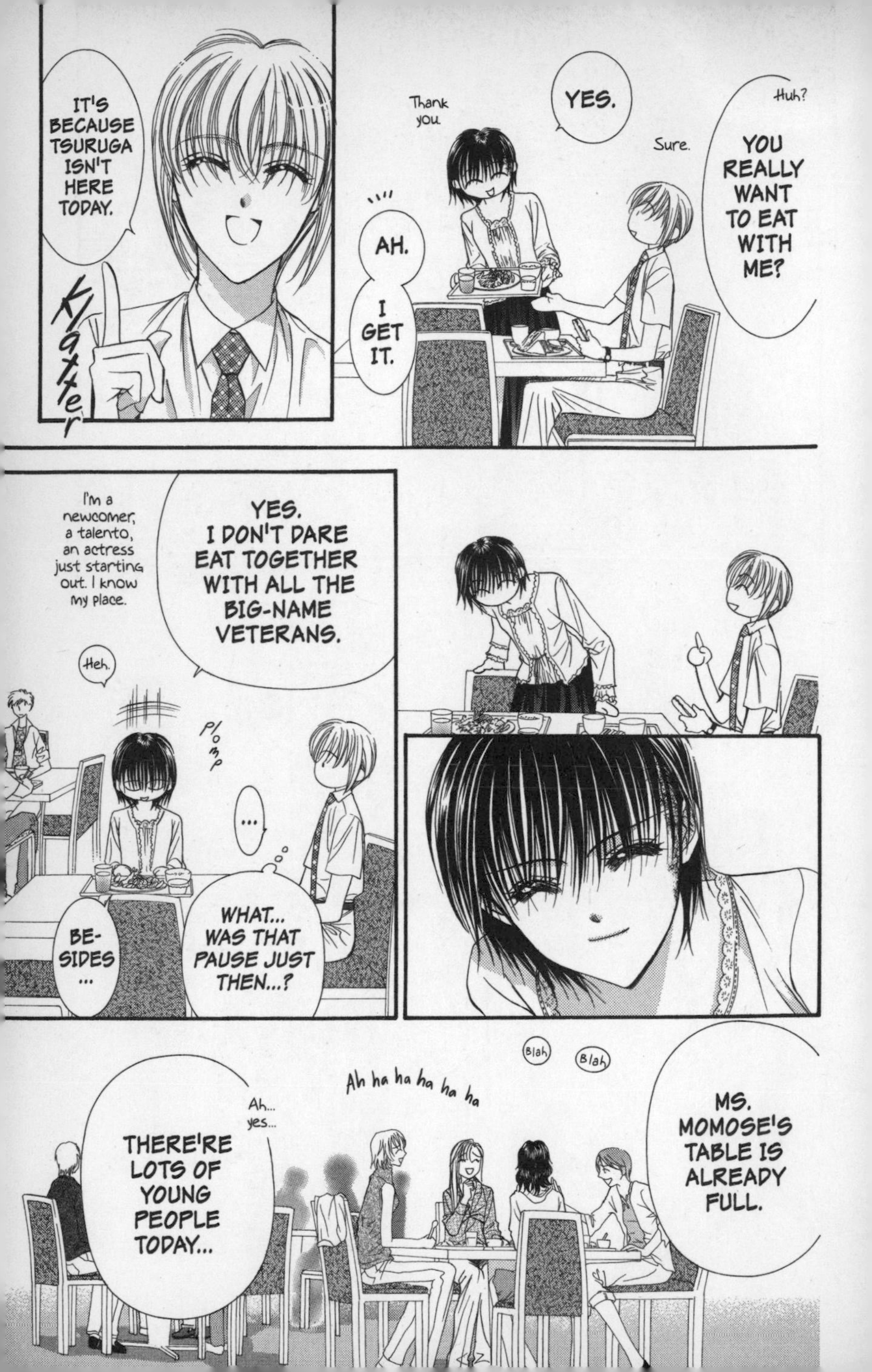
Huh?
YOU REALLY WANT TO EAT WITH ME?
Sure.
YES.
Thank you.
AH. I GET IT.
IT'S BECAUSE TSURUGA ISN'T HERE TODAY.
Klatter
YES. I DON'T DARE EAT TOGETHER WITH ALL THE BIG-NAME VETERANS.
I'm a newcomer, a talento, an actress just starting out. I know my place.
Heh.
Plomp
...
WHAT... WAS THAT PAUSE JUST THEN...?
BE-SIDES...
MS. MOMOSE'S TABLE IS ALREADY FULL.
Blah
Blah
Ah ha ha ha ha ha
Ah... yes...
THERE'RE LOTS OF YOUNG PEOPLE TODAY...

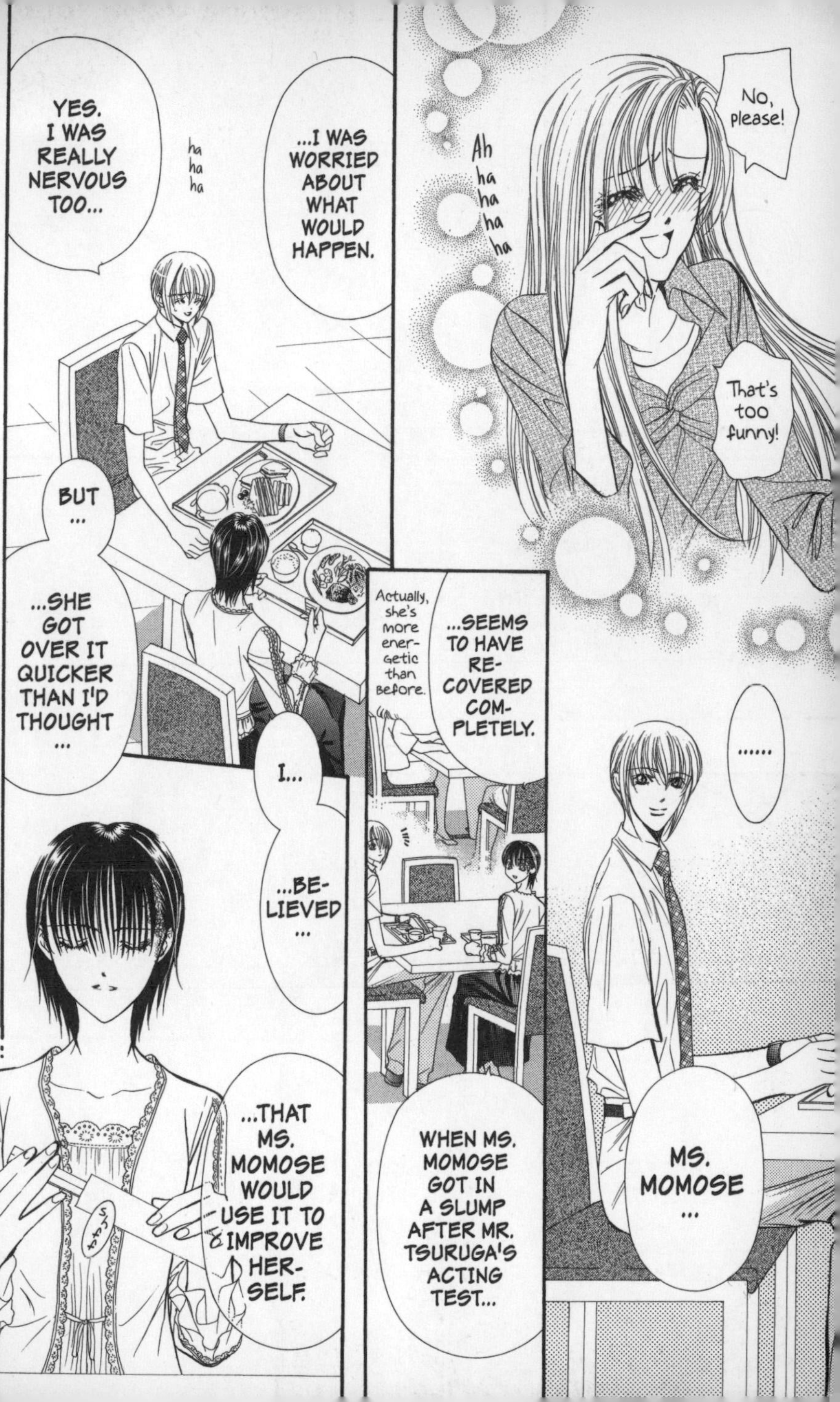
No, please!
Ah ha ha ha ha
That's too funny!
......
MS. MOMOSE ...
WHEN MS. MOMOSE GOT IN A SLUMP AFTER MR. TSURUGA'S ACTING TEST...
...SEEMS TO HAVE RE-COVERED COM-PLETELY.
Actually, she's more ener-getic than before.
...I WAS WORRIED ABOUT WHAT WOULD HAPPEN.
ha ha ha
YES. I WAS REALLY NERVOUS TOO...
BUT ...
...SHE GOT OVER IT QUICKER THAN I'D THOUGHT ...
I...
...BE-LIEVED ...
...THAT MS. MOMOSE WOULD USE IT TO IMPROVE HER-SELF.

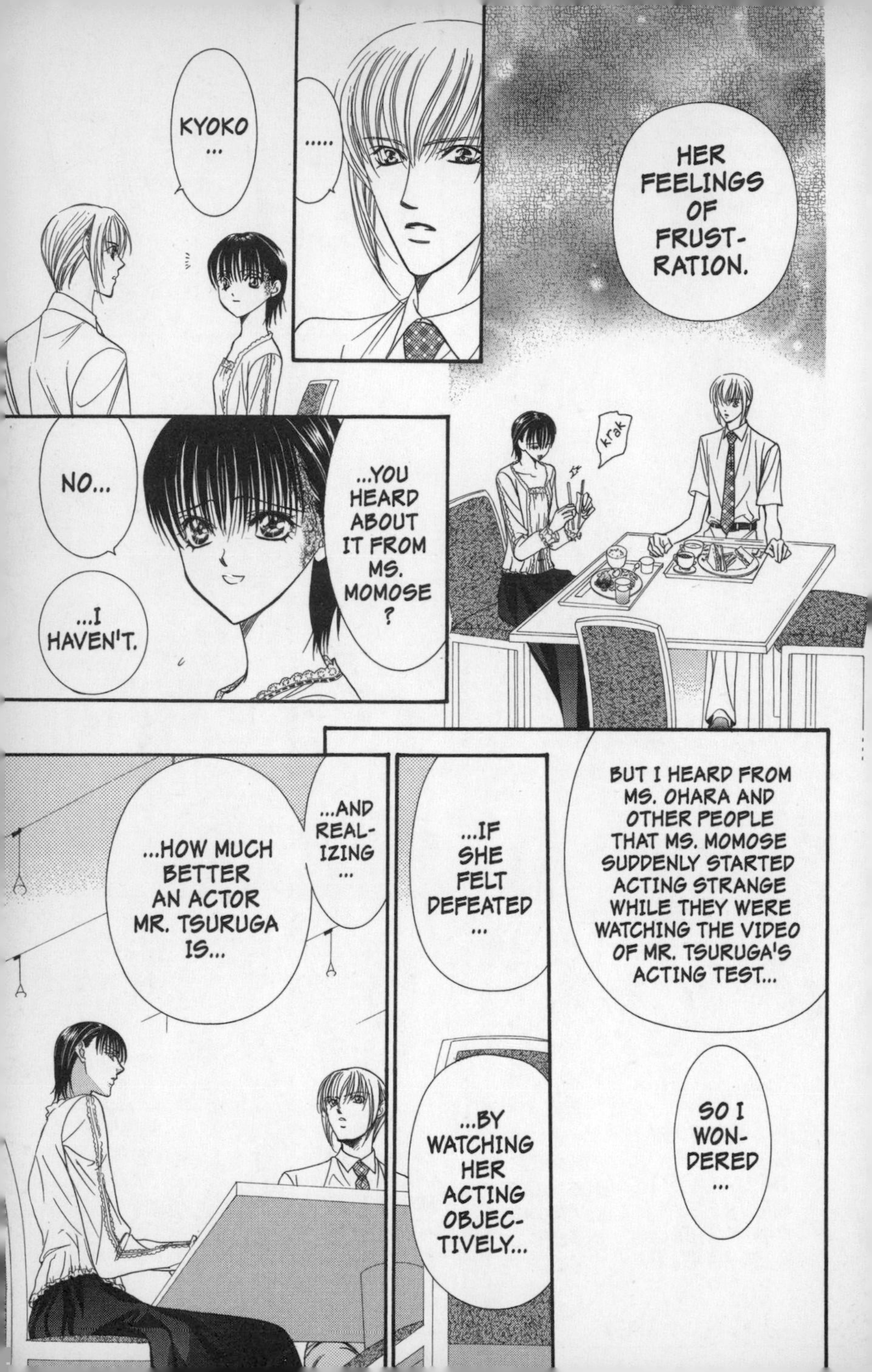
HER FEELINGS OF FRUSTRATION.
krak
.....
KYOKO ...
...YOU HEARD ABOUT IT FROM MS. MOMOSE?
NO...
...I HAVEN'T.
BUT I HEARD FROM MS. OHARA AND OTHER PEOPLE THAT MS. MOMOSE SUDDENLY STARTED ACTING STRANGE WHILE THEY WERE WATCHING THE VIDEO OF MR. TSURUGA'S ACTING TEST...
SO I WONDERED ...
...IF SHE FELT DEFEATED ...
...BY WATCHING HER ACTING OBJECTIVELY...
...AND REALIZING ...
...HOW MUCH BETTER AN ACTOR MR. TSURUGA IS...

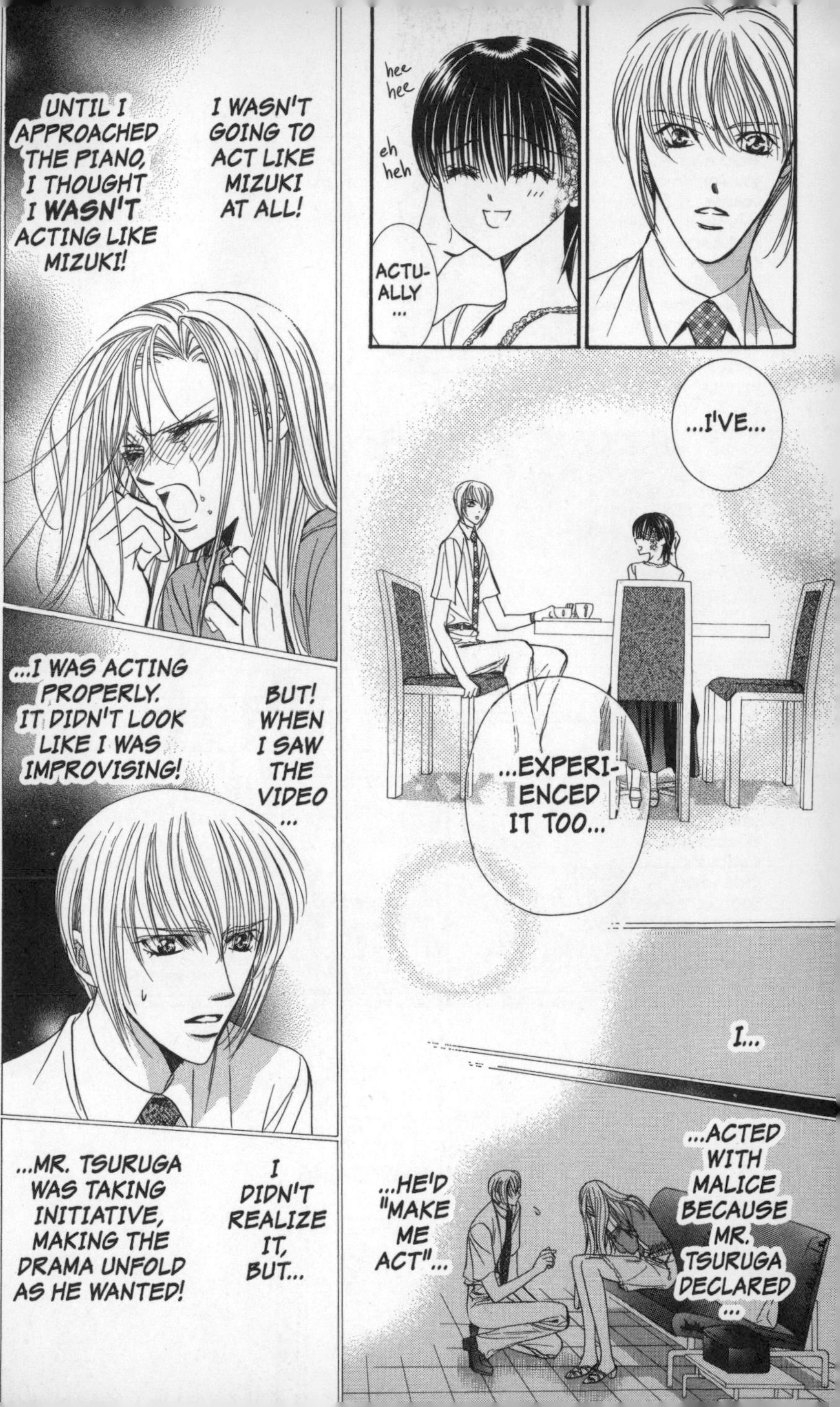
hee hee
eh heh
ACTU-ALLY ...
...I'VE...
...EXPERI-ENCED IT TOO...
I...
...ACTED WITH MALICE BECAUSE MR. TSURUGA DECLARED ...
...HE'D "MAKE ME ACT"...
I WASN'T GOING TO ACT LIKE MIZUKI AT ALL!
UNTIL I APPROACHED THE PIANO, I THOUGHT I WASN'T ACTING LIKE MIZUKI!
BUT! WHEN I SAW THE VIDEO ...
...I WAS ACTING PROPERLY. IT DIDN'T LOOK LIKE I WAS IMPROVISING!
I DIDN'T REALIZE IT, BUT...
...MR. TSURUGA WAS TAKING INITIATIVE, MAKING THE DRAMA UNFOLD AS HE WANTED!

Skip•Beat! 14

Hello everybody. Thank you for reading this volume of Skip•Beat this time around too. In the previous volume, the main story involving DARK MOON finally ended. However, it's not completely over yet...it is still forced to appear as part of Kyoko and Ren's work.

And in this volume, I was able to begin a new arc, "Suddenly, a Love Story"... those of you who only read the manga volumes...please brace yourself...this arc...is long...about the same as the DARK MOON arc... the one who's drawing it can't help mumbling "It...wasn't supposed to be this way..." ...when I realized that there was no way it would finish in the scheduled number of chapters, my panic is obvious in the subtitle when the chapters were published in the magazine:

Suddenly, a Love Story
– Introduction –
This part

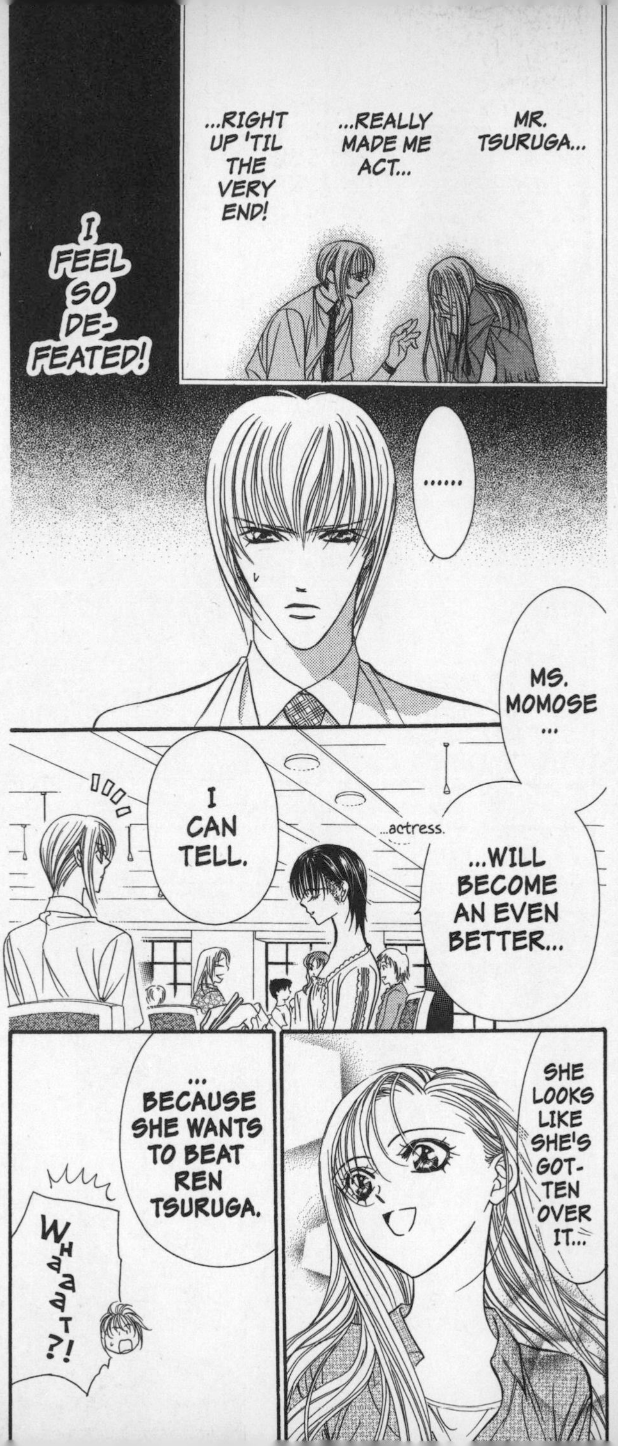
MR. TSURUGA...
...REALLY MADE ME ACT...
...RIGHT UP 'TIL THE VERY END!
I FEEL SO DE-FEATED!
......
MS. MOMOSE ...
...WILL BECOME AN EVEN BETTER...
...actress.
I CAN TELL.
SHE LOOKS LIKE SHE'S GOT-TEN OVER IT...
... BECAUSE SHE WANTS TO BEAT REN TSURUGA.
WHaaaT?!

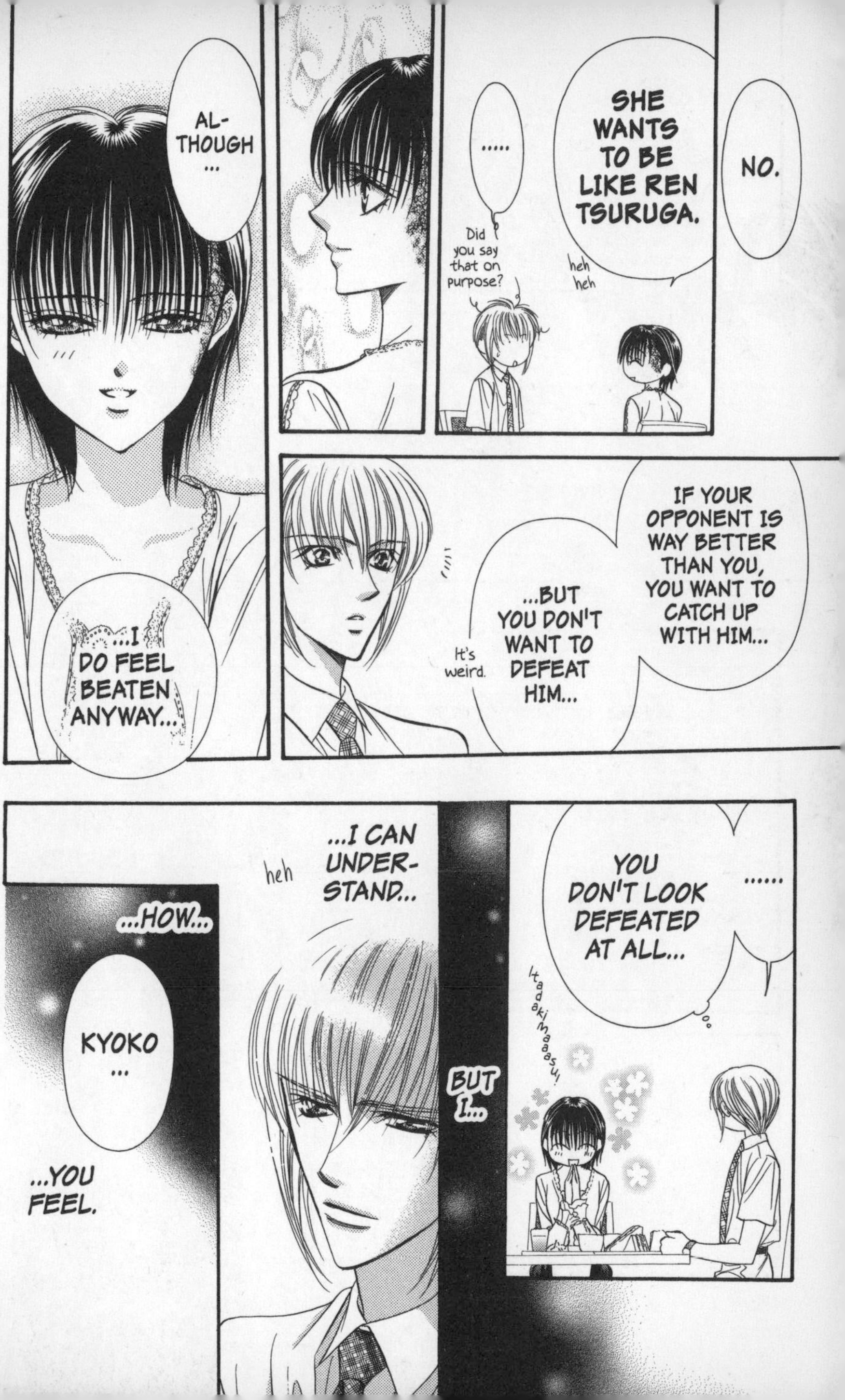
NO.
SHE WANTS TO BE LIKE REN TSURUGA.
heh heh
.....
Did you say that on purpose?
IF YOUR OPPONENT IS WAY BETTER THAN YOU, YOU WANT TO CATCH UP WITH HIM...
...BUT YOU DON'T WANT TO DEFEAT HIM...
It's weird.
AL-THOUGH ...
...I DO FEEL BEATEN ANYWAY...
......
YOU DON'T LOOK DEFEATED AT ALL...
Itadakimaaasu!
...I CAN UNDER-STAND...
heh
BUT I...
...HOW...
KYOKO ...
...YOU FEEL.

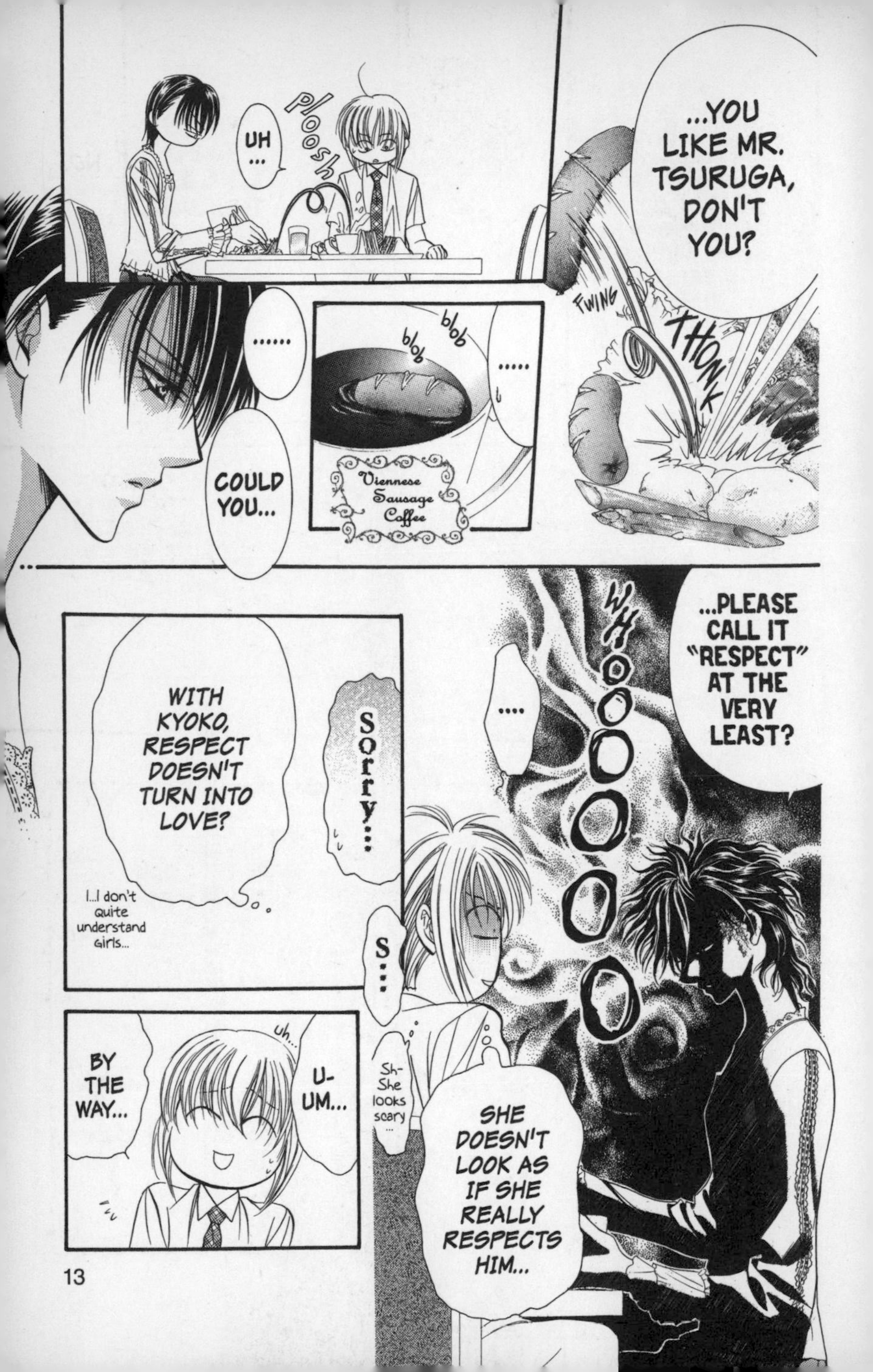
...YOU LIKE MR. TSURUGA, DON'T YOU?
FWING
THONK
UH ...
Ploosh
.....
blob
blob
Viennese Sausage Coffee
......
COULD YOU...
...PLEASE CALL IT "RESPECT" AT THE VERY LEAST?
WHOOOOOOO
....
Sorry...
S...
Sh-She looks scary ...
SHE DOESN'T LOOK AS IF SHE REALLY RESPECTS HIM...
WITH KYOKO, RESPECT DOESN'T TURN INTO LOVE?
I...I don't quite understand girls...
uh...
U-UM...
BY THE WAY...

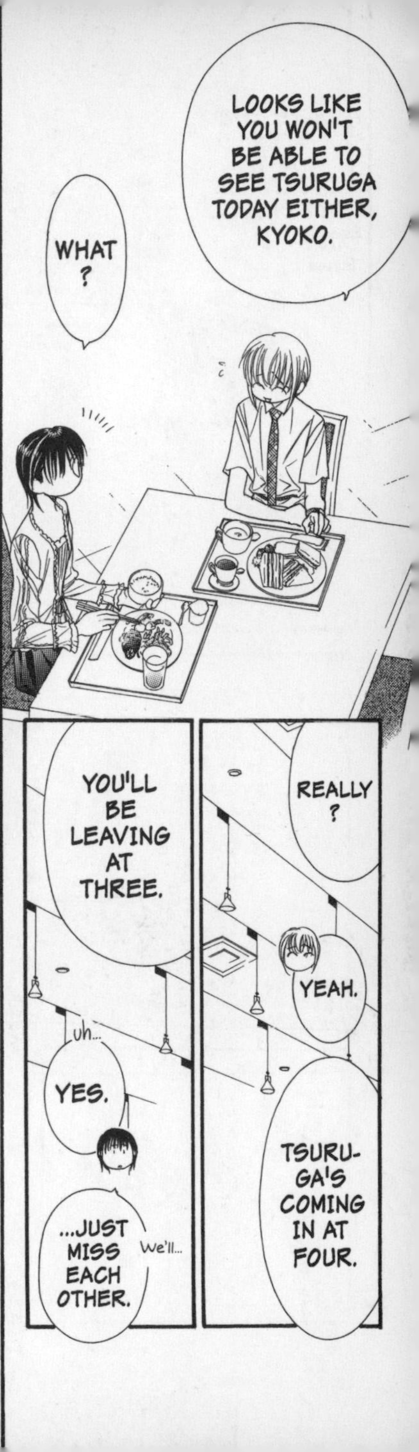
LOOKS LIKE YOU WON'T BE ABLE TO SEE TSURUGA TODAY EITHER, KYOKO.
WHAT?
REALLY?
YEAH.
TSURU-GA'S COMING IN AT FOUR.
YOU'LL BE LEAVING AT THREE.
uh...
YES.
We'll...
...JUST MISS EACH OTHER.
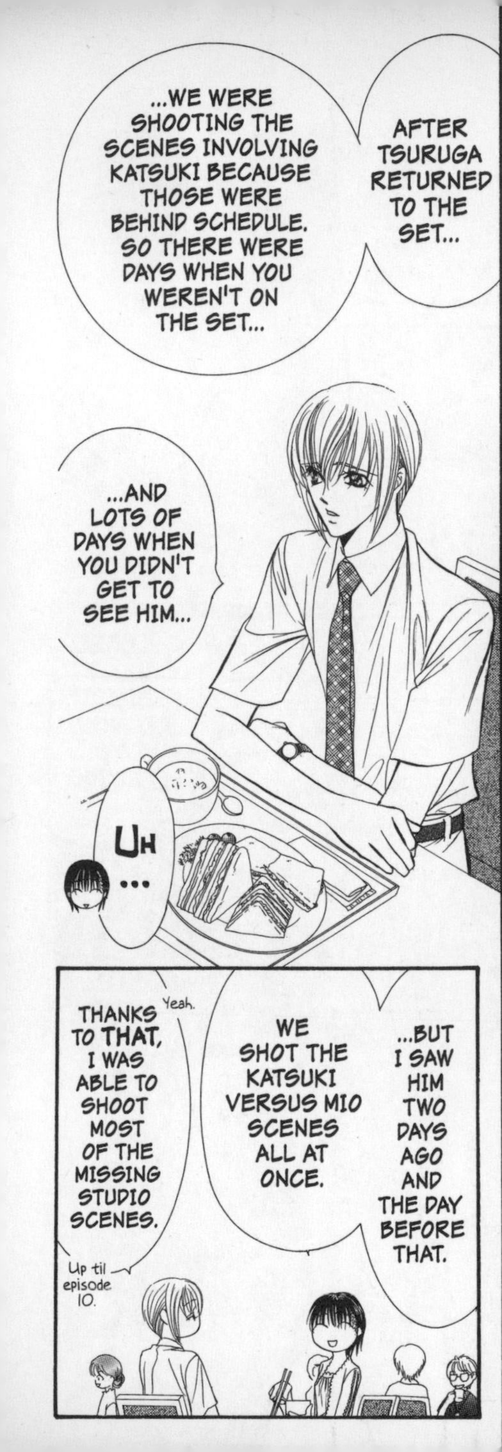
AFTER TSURUGA RETURNED TO THE SET...
...WE WERE SHOOTING THE SCENES INVOLVING KATSUKI BECAUSE THOSE WERE BEHIND SCHEDULE. SO THERE WERE DAYS WHEN YOU WEREN'T ON THE SET...
...AND LOTS OF DAYS WHEN YOU DIDN'T GET TO SEE HIM...
UH...
...BUT I SAW HIM TWO DAYS AGO AND THE DAY BEFORE THAT.
WE SHOT THE KATSUKI VERSUS MIO SCENES ALL AT ONCE.
Yeah.
THANKS TO THAT, I WAS ABLE TO SHOOT MOST OF THE MISSING STUDIO SCENES.
Up til episode 10.

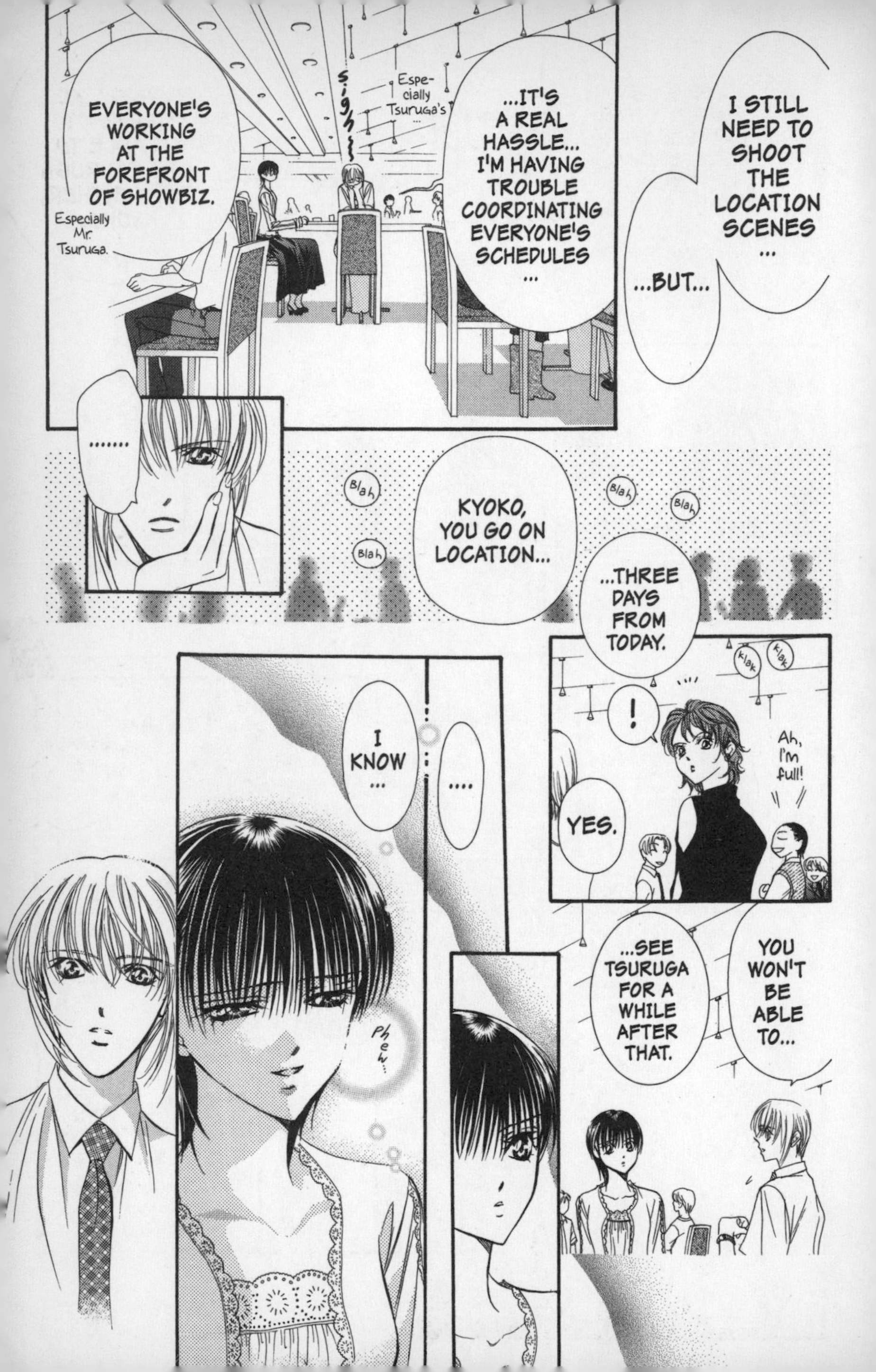
I STILL NEED TO SHOOT THE LOCATION SCENES...
...BUT...
...IT'S A REAL HASSLE... I'M HAVING TROUBLE COORDINATING EVERYONE'S SCHEDULES...
sigh~
Especially Tsuruga's...
EVERYONE'S WORKING AT THE FOREFRONT OF SHOWBIZ.
Especially Mr. Tsuruga.
Blah
Blah
KYOKO, YOU GO ON LOCATION...
...THREE DAYS FROM TODAY.
Blah
Blah
....
klak
klak
!
Ah, I'm full!
YES.
YOU WON'T BE ABLE TO...
...SEE TSURUGA FOR A WHILE AFTER THAT.
....
I KNOW...
Phew...

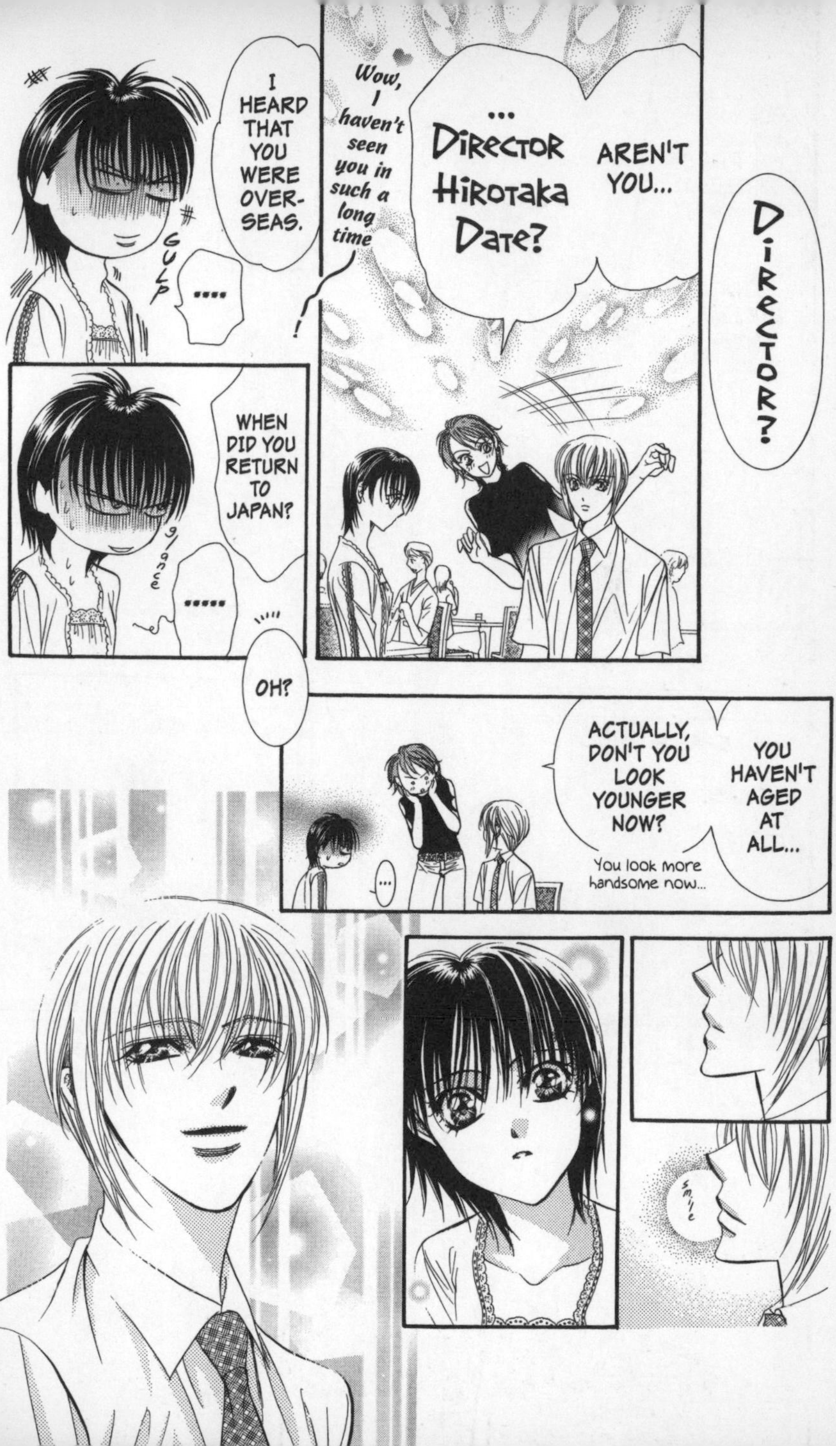
DIRECTOR?
AREN'T YOU...
...DIRECTOR HIROTAKA DATE?
Wow, I haven't seen you in such a long time
I HEARD THAT YOU WERE OVERSEAS.
....
GULP
WHEN DID YOU RETURN TO JAPAN?
.....
glance
OH?
YOU HAVEN'T AGED AT ALL...
ACTUALLY, DON'T YOU LOOK YOUNGER NOW?
You look more handsome now...
...
smile

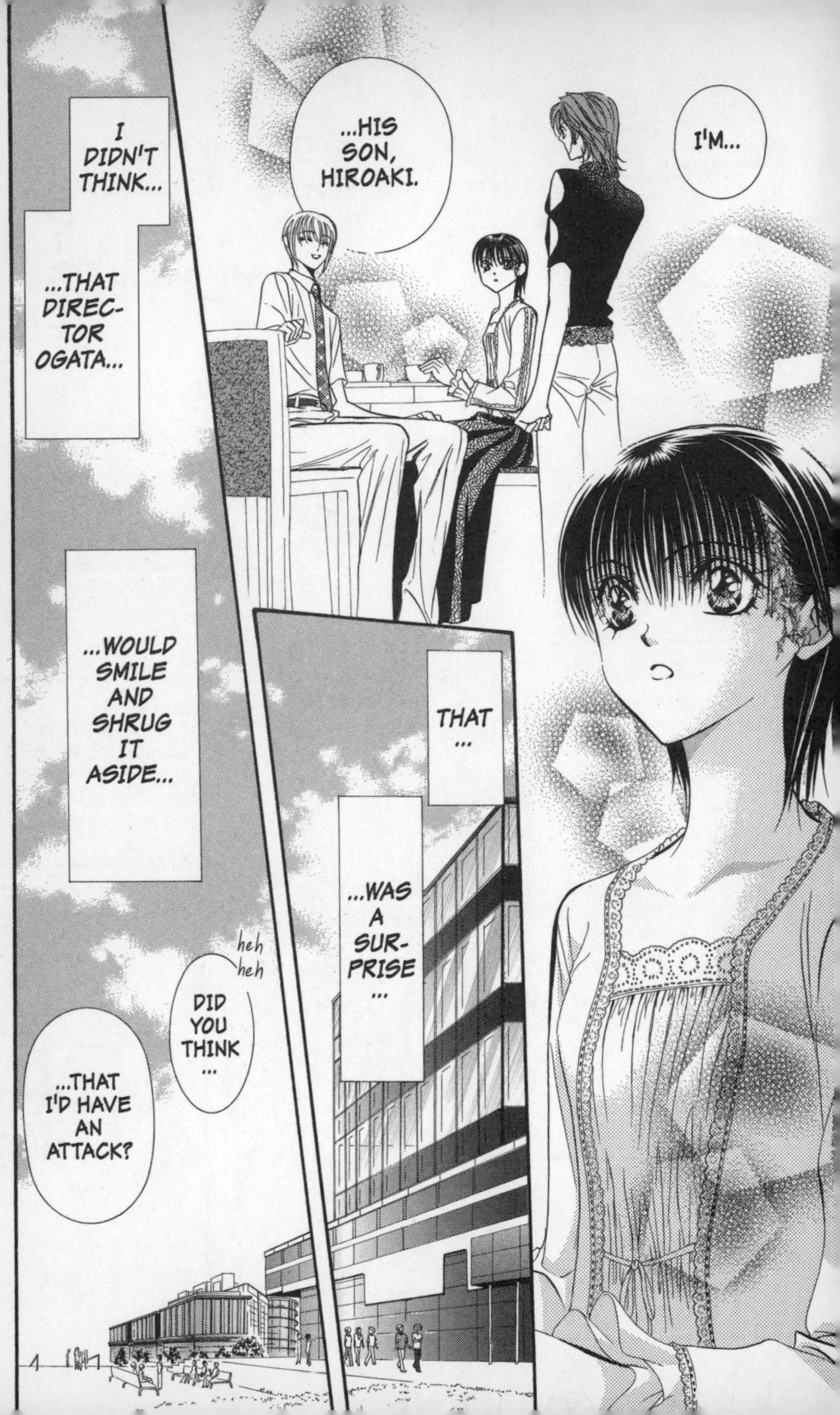
I'M...
...HIS SON, HIROAKI.
I DIDN'T THINK...
...THAT DIRECTOR OGATA...
...WOULD SMILE AND SHRUG IT ASIDE...
THAT...
...WAS A SURPRISE...
heh heh
DID YOU THINK...
...THAT I'D HAVE AN ATTACK?

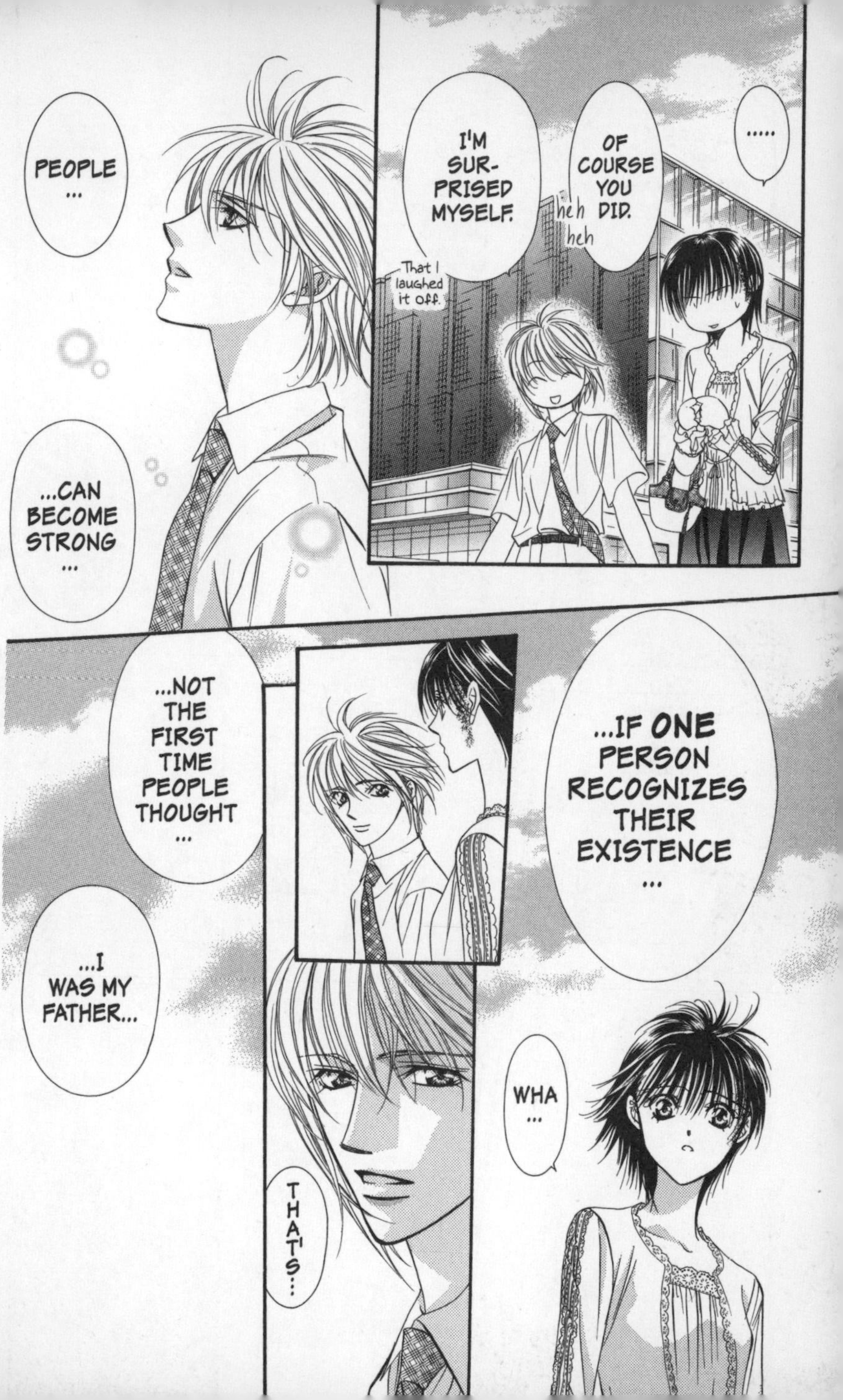
.....
OF COURSE YOU DID.
heh heh
I'M SUR-PRISED MYSELF.
That I laughed it off.
PEOPLE ...
...CAN BECOME STRONG ...
...IF ONE PERSON RECOGNIZES THEIR EXISTENCE ...
...NOT THE FIRST TIME PEOPLE THOUGHT ...
...I WAS MY FATHER...
WHA ...
THAT'S...

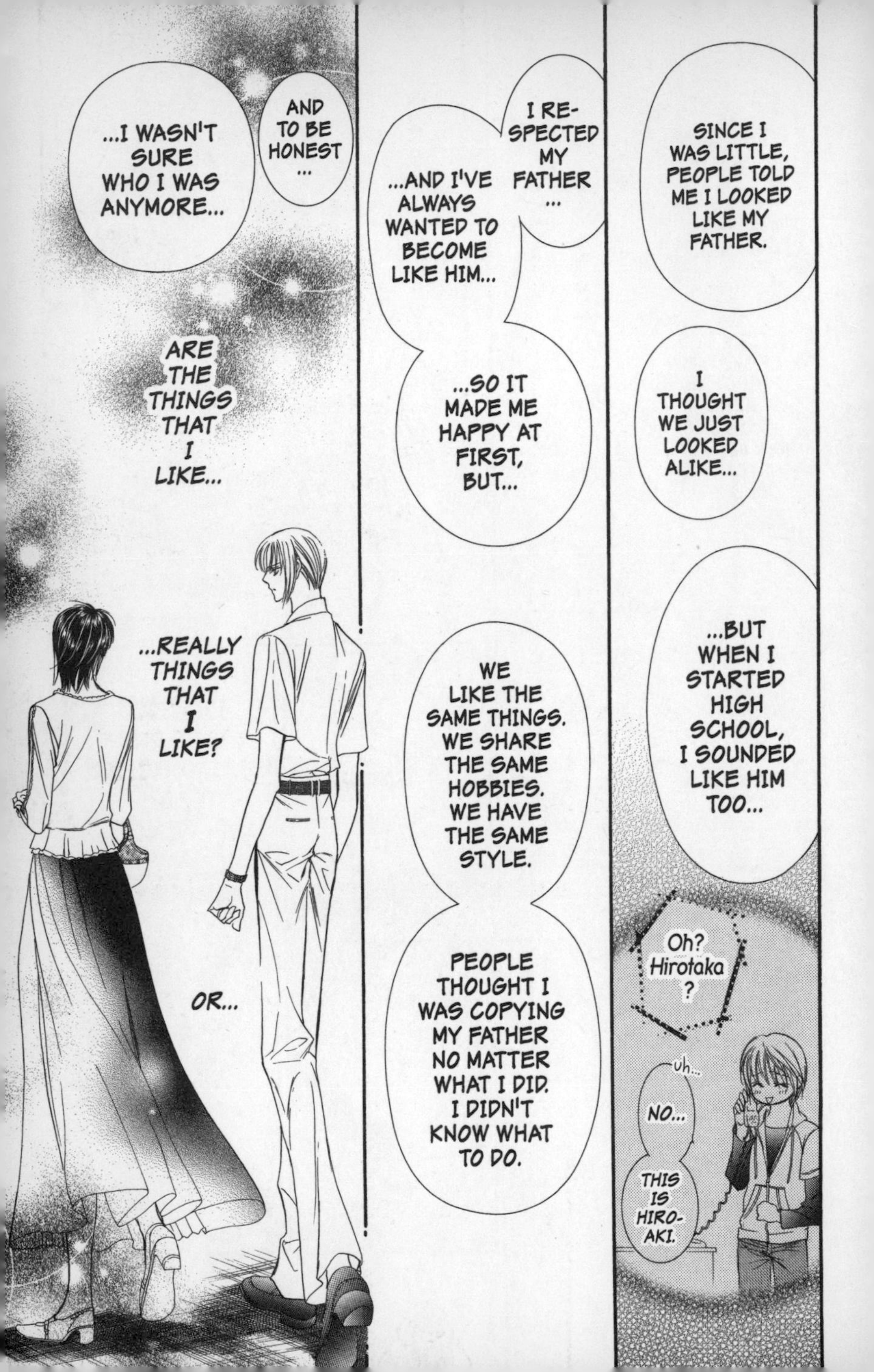
SINCE I WAS LITTLE, PEOPLE TOLD ME I LOOKED LIKE MY FATHER.
I THOUGHT WE JUST LOOKED ALIKE...
...BUT WHEN I STARTED HIGH SCHOOL, I SOUNDED LIKE HIM TOO...
Oh? Hirotaka?
uh...
NO...
THIS IS HIRO-AKI.
I RE-SPECTED MY FATHER...
...AND I'VE ALWAYS WANTED TO BECOME LIKE HIM...
...SO IT MADE ME HAPPY AT FIRST, BUT...
WE LIKE THE SAME THINGS. WE SHARE THE SAME HOBBIES. WE HAVE THE SAME STYLE.
PEOPLE THOUGHT I WAS COPYING MY FATHER NO MATTER WHAT I DID. I DIDN'T KNOW WHAT TO DO.
AND TO BE HONEST...
...I WASN'T SURE WHO I WAS ANYMORE...
ARE THE THINGS THAT I LIKE...
...REALLY THINGS THAT I LIKE?
OR...

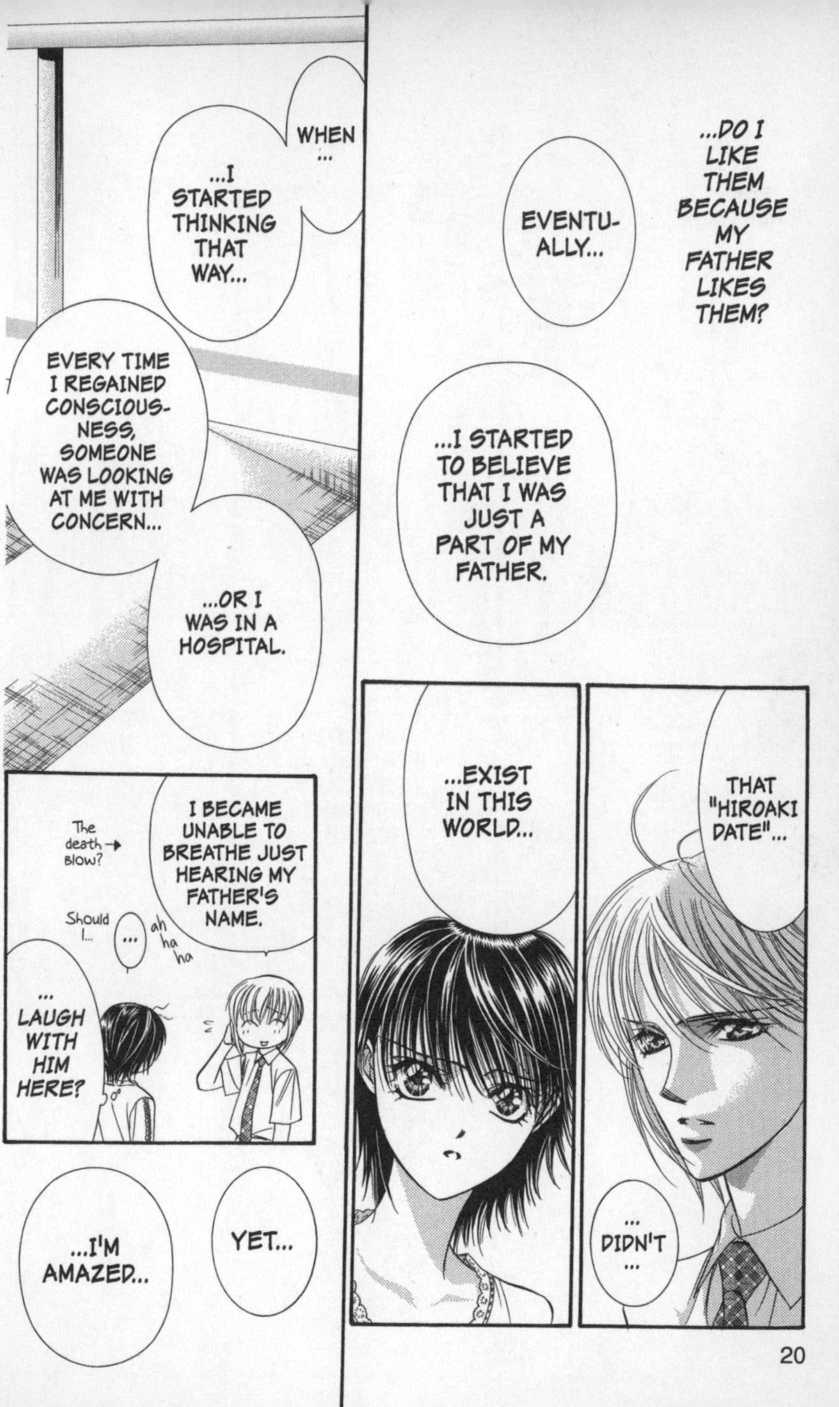
...DO I LIKE THEM BECAUSE MY FATHER LIKES THEM?
EVENTU-ALLY...
...I STARTED TO BELIEVE THAT I WAS JUST A PART OF MY FATHER.
THAT "HIROAKI DATE"...
...DIDN'T...
...EXIST IN THIS WORLD...
WHEN...
...I STARTED THINKING THAT WAY...
EVERY TIME I REGAINED CONSCIOUS-NESS, SOMEONE WAS LOOKING AT ME WITH CONCERN...
...OR I WAS IN A HOSPITAL.
I BECAME UNABLE TO BREATHE JUST HEARING MY FATHER'S NAME.
The death blow?
ah ha ha
...
Should I...
...LAUGH WITH HIM HERE?
YET...
...I'M AMAZED...

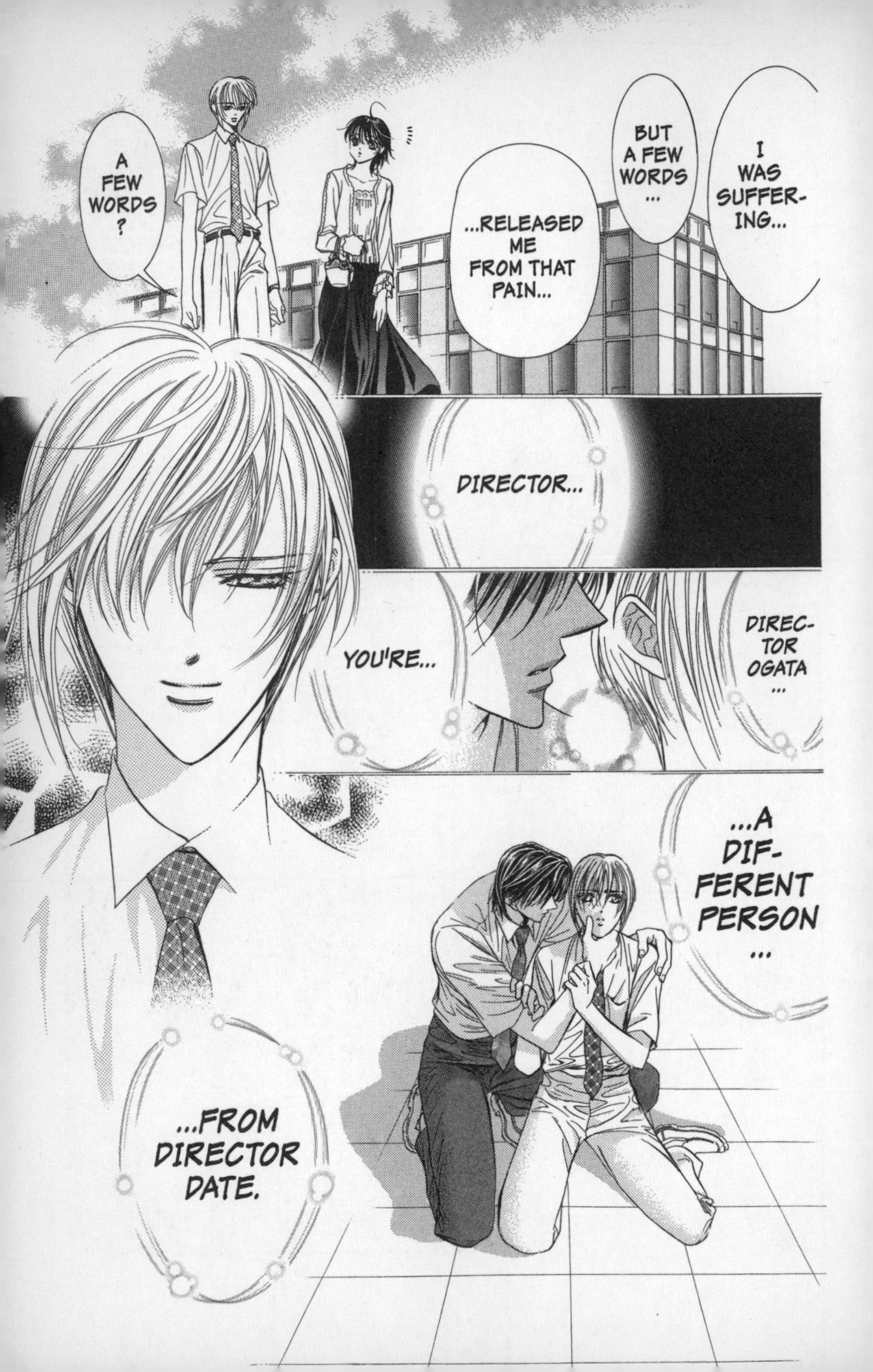
I WAS SUFFER-ING...
BUT A FEW WORDS...
...RELEASED ME FROM THAT PAIN...
A FEW WORDS?
DIRECTOR...
DIREC-TOR OGATA...
YOU'RE...
...A DIF-FERENT PERSON...
...FROM DIRECTOR DATE.

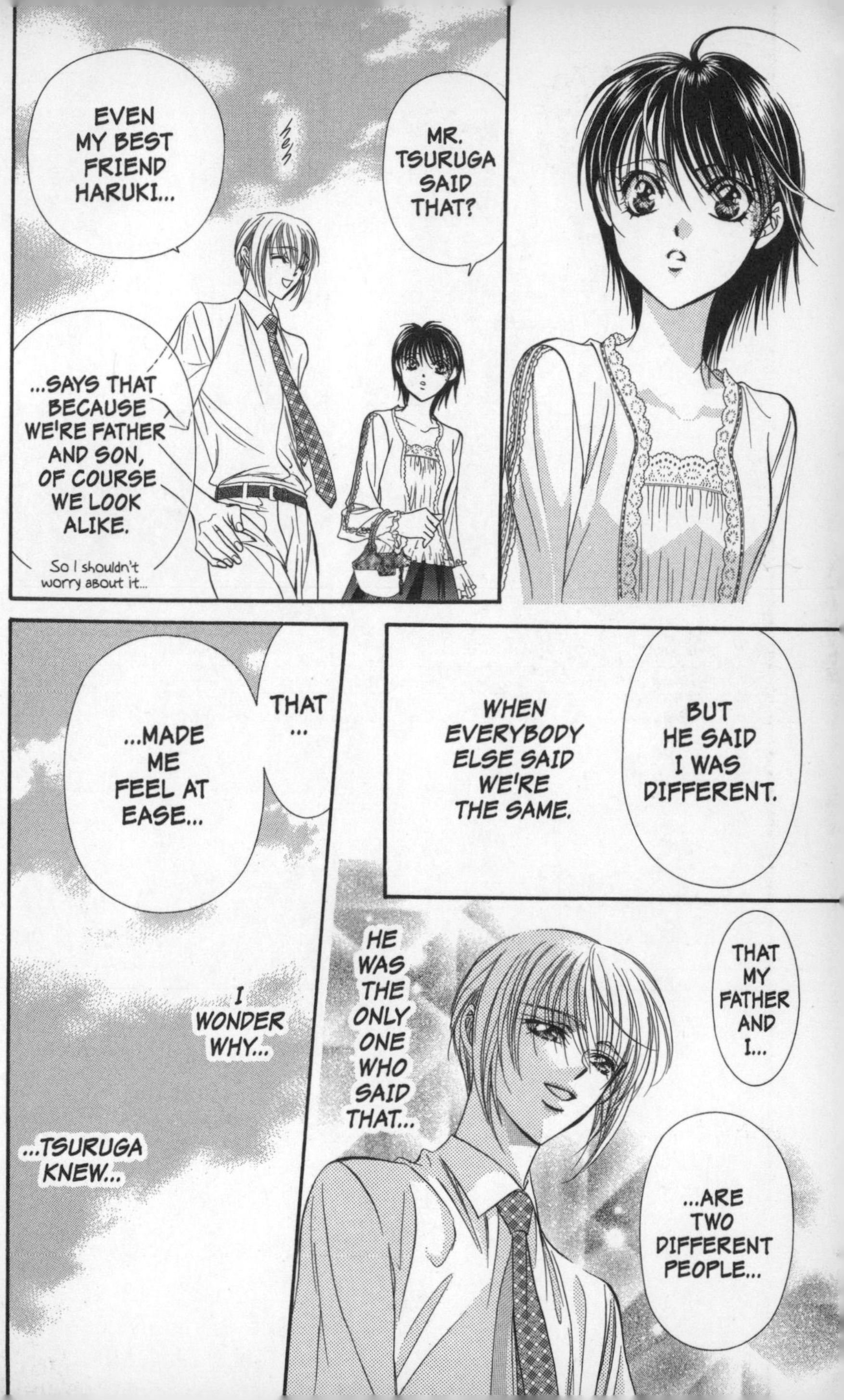
MR. TSURUGA SAID THAT?
EVEN MY BEST FRIEND HARUKI...
...SAYS THAT BECAUSE WE'RE FATHER AND SON, OF COURSE WE LOOK ALIKE.
So I shouldn't worry about it...
BUT HE SAID I WAS DIFFERENT.
WHEN EVERYBODY ELSE SAID WE'RE THE SAME.
THAT ...
...MADE ME FEEL AT EASE...
THAT MY FATHER AND I...
...ARE TWO DIFFERENT PEOPLE...
HE WAS THE ONLY ONE WHO SAID THAT...
I WONDER WHY...
...TSURUGA KNEW...

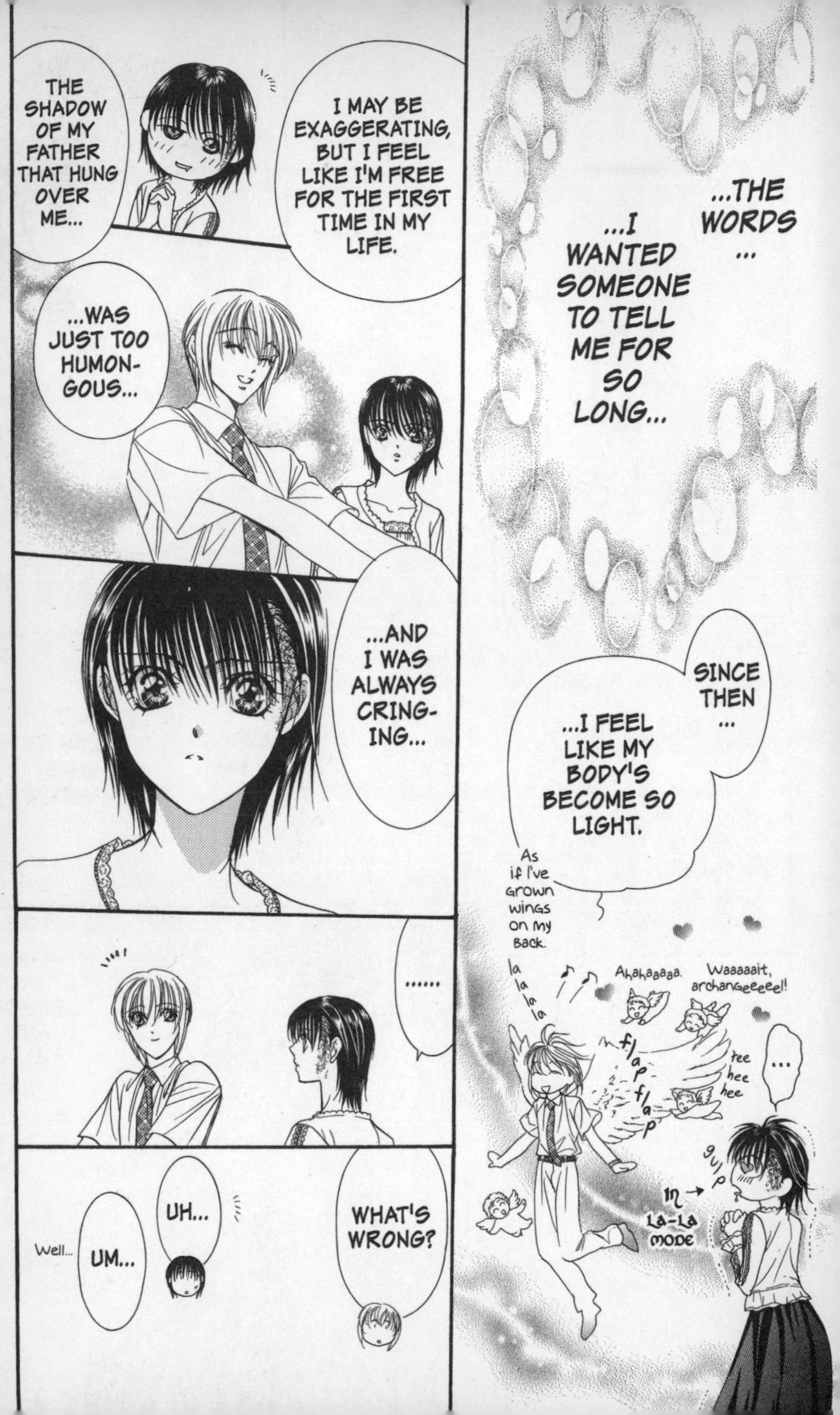
...THE WORDS ...
...I WANTED SOMEONE TO TELL ME FOR SO LONG...
SINCE THEN ...
...I FEEL LIKE MY BODY'S BECOME SO LIGHT.
As if I've grown wings on my back.
la la la la
Ahahaaaaa.
Waaaaait, archangeeeeel!
flap flap
tee hee hee
...
gulp
In → La-La mode
I MAY BE EXAGGERATING, BUT I FEEL LIKE I'M FREE FOR THE FIRST TIME IN MY LIFE.
THE SHADOW OF MY FATHER THAT HUNG OVER ME...
...WAS JUST TOO HUMON-GOUS...
...AND I WAS ALWAYS CRING-ING...
......
WHAT'S WRONG?
UH...
UM...
Well...

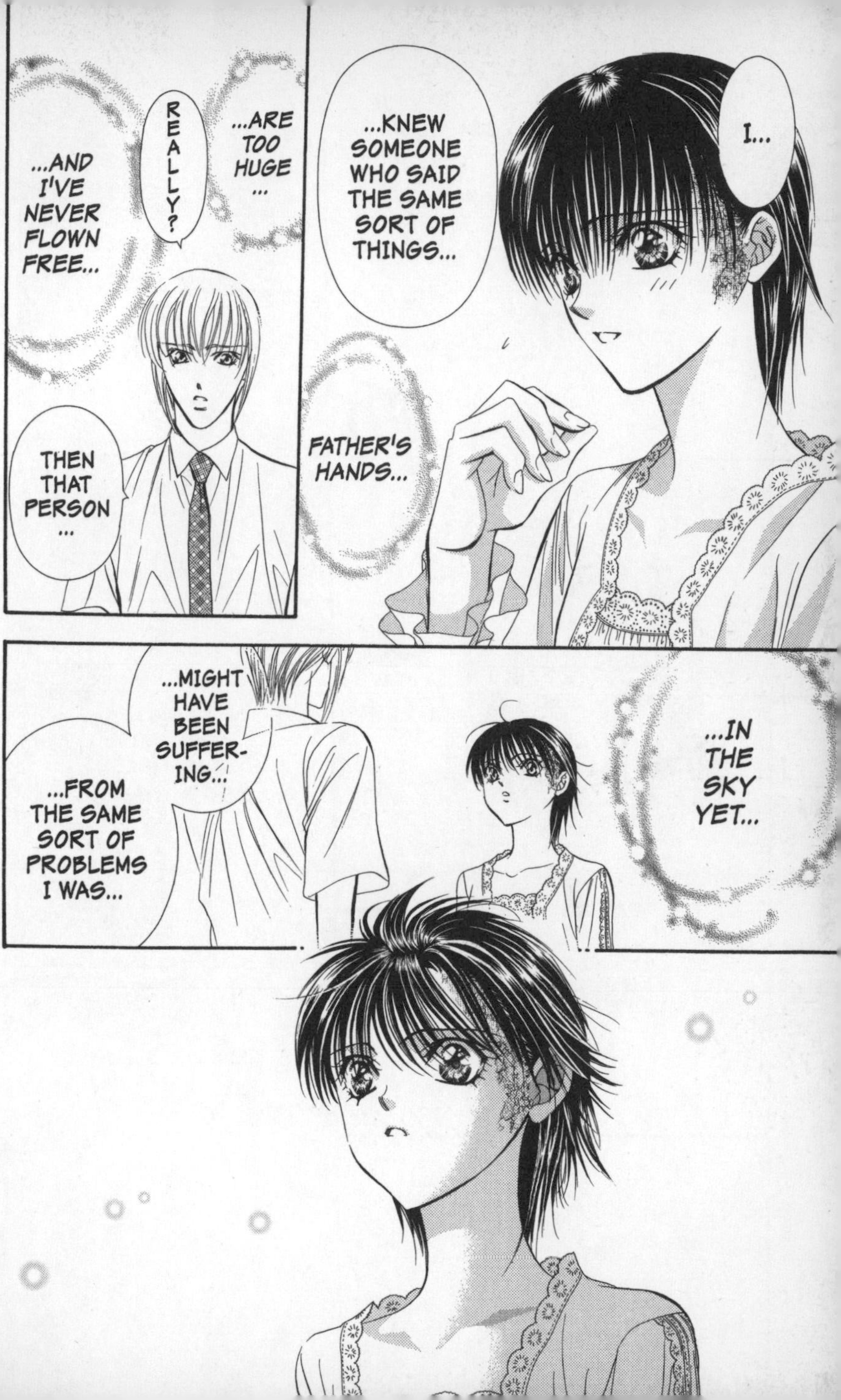
I...
...KNEW SOMEONE WHO SAID THE SAME SORT OF THINGS...
FATHER'S HANDS...
...ARE TOO HUGE...
REALLY?
...AND I'VE NEVER FLOWN FREE...
THEN THAT PERSON...
...IN THE SKY YET...
...MIGHT HAVE BEEN SUFFER-ING...
...FROM THE SAME SORT OF PROBLEMS I WAS...

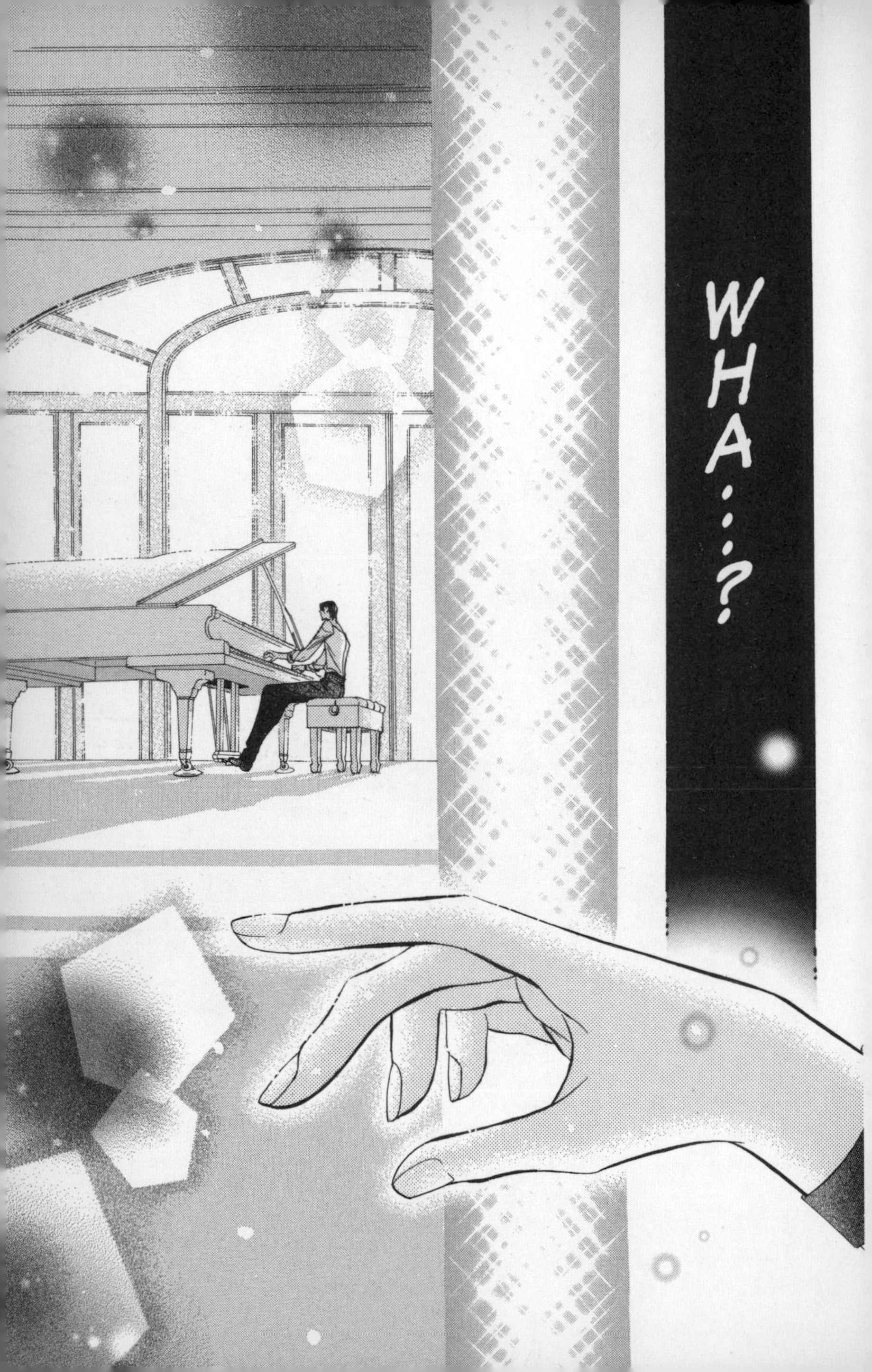
WHA...?

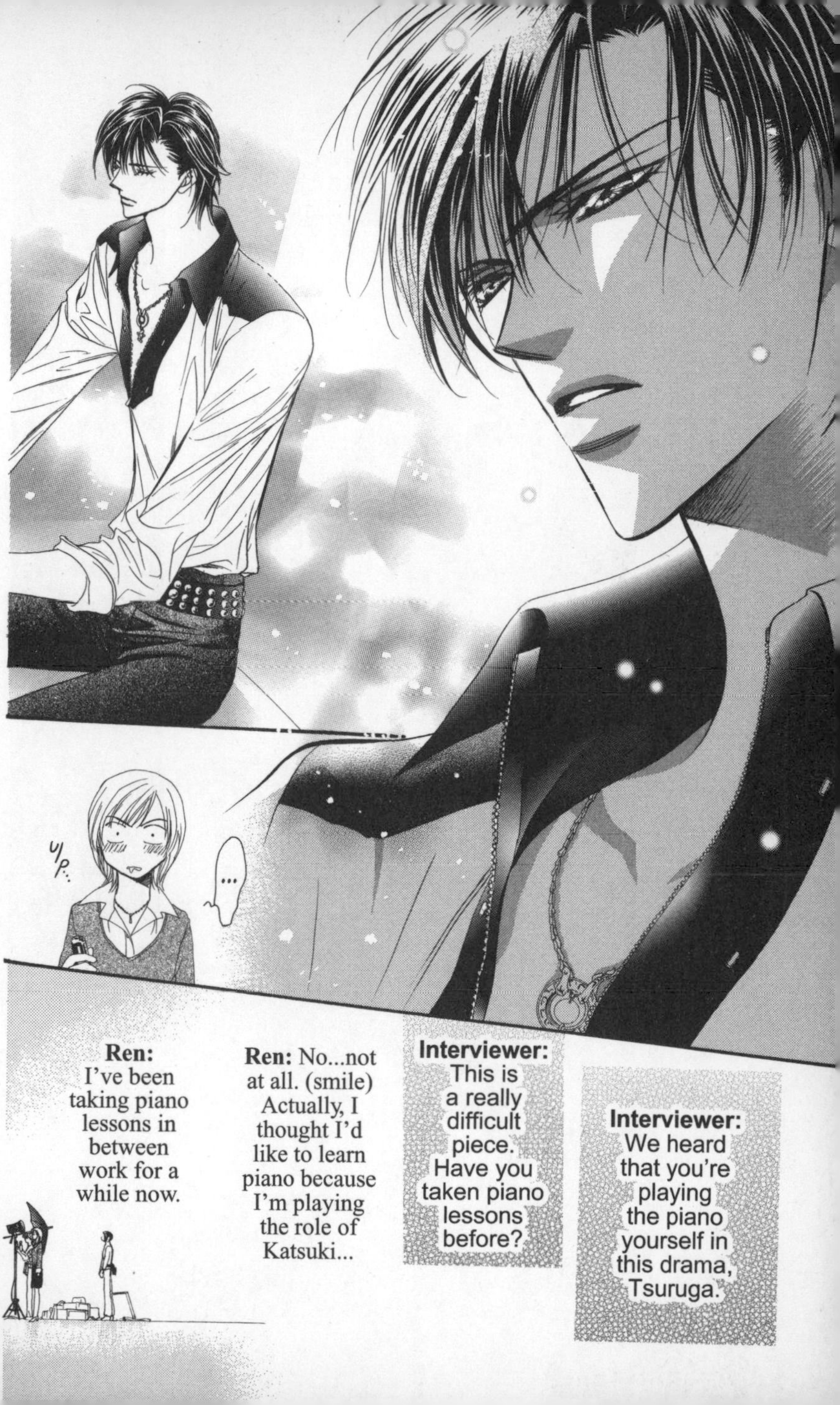
...
ulp...
Interviewer: We heard that you're playing the piano yourself in this drama, Tsuruga.
Interviewer: This is a really difficult piece. Have you taken piano lessons before?
Ren: No...not at all. (smile) Actually, I thought I'd like to learn piano because I'm playing the role of Katsuki...
Ren: I've been taking piano lessons in between work for a while now.

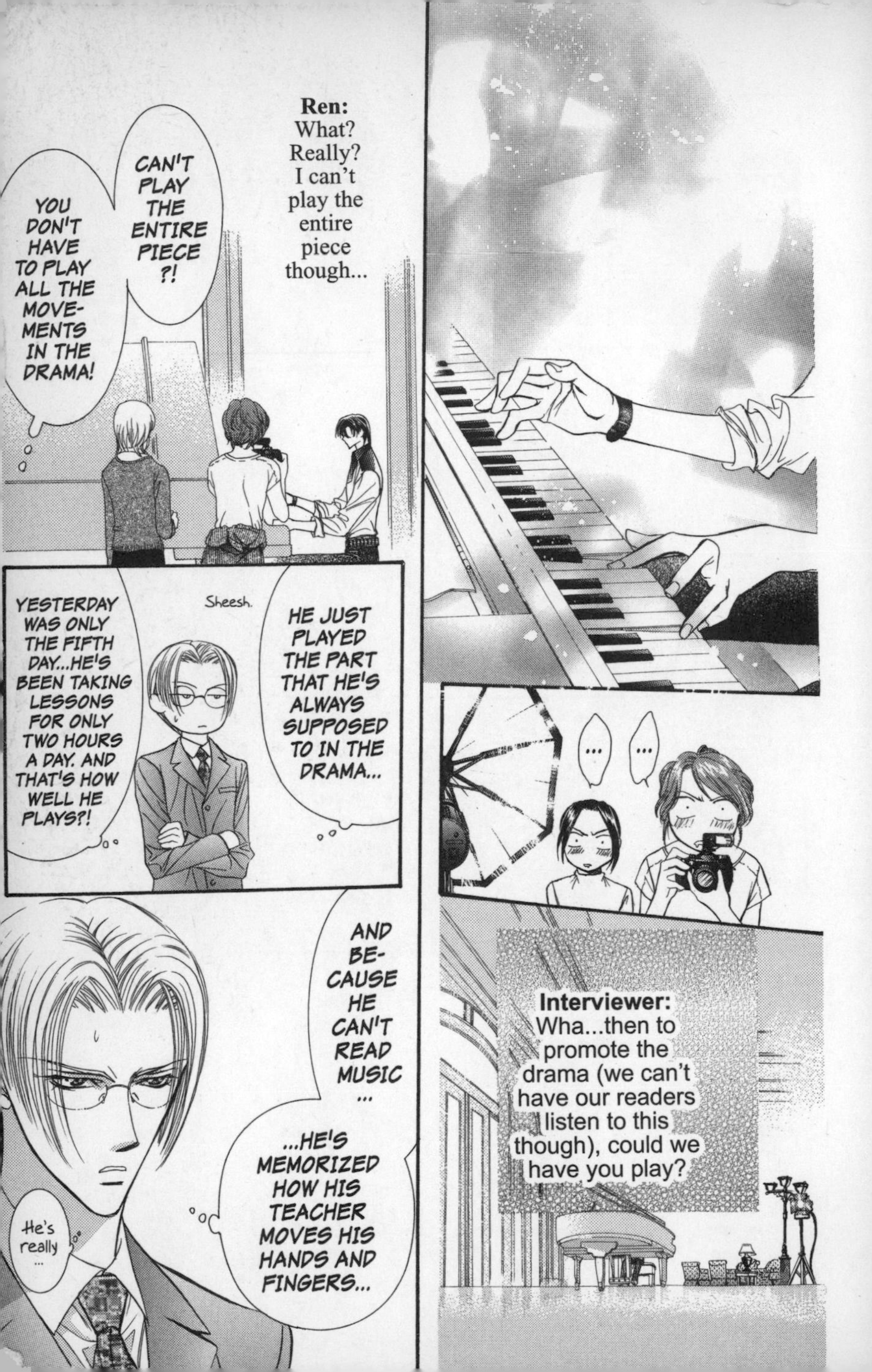
...
...
Interviewer: Wha...then to promote the drama (we can't have our readers listen to this though), could we have you play?
Ren: What? Really? I can't play the entire piece though...
CAN'T PLAY THE ENTIRE PIECE ?!
YOU DON'T HAVE TO PLAY ALL THE MOVE-MENTS IN THE DRAMA!
HE JUST PLAYED THE PART THAT HE'S ALWAYS SUPPOSED TO IN THE DRAMA...
Sheesh.
YESTERDAY WAS ONLY THE FIFTH DAY...HE'S BEEN TAKING LESSONS FOR ONLY TWO HOURS A DAY. AND THAT'S HOW WELL HE PLAYS?!
AND BE-CAUSE HE CAN'T READ MUSIC ...
...HE'S MEMORIZED HOW HIS TEACHER MOVES HIS HANDS AND FINGERS...
He's really ...

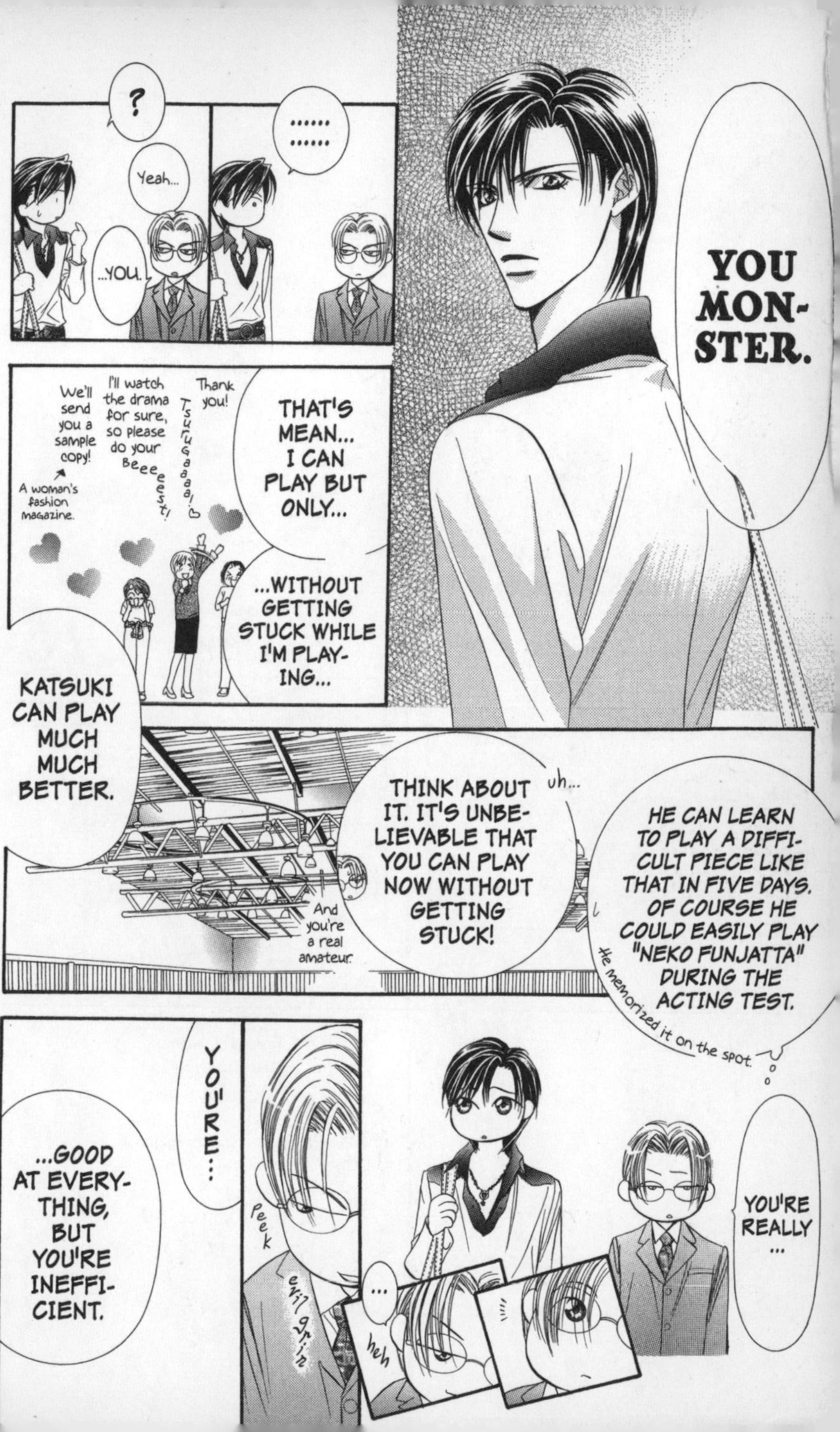
YOU MONSTER.
......
......
?
Yeah...
...YOU.
THAT'S MEAN... I CAN PLAY BUT ONLY...
...WITHOUT GETTING STUCK WHILE I'M PLAYING...
Thank you!
Tsurugaaaa!
I'll watch the drama for sure, so please do your Beeeeeest!
We'll send you a sample copy!
A woman's fashion magazine.
KATSUKI CAN PLAY MUCH MUCH BETTER.
HE CAN LEARN TO PLAY A DIFFICULT PIECE LIKE THAT IN FIVE DAYS. OF COURSE HE COULD EASILY PLAY "NEKO FUNJATTA" DURING THE ACTING TEST.
He memorized it on the spot.
uh...
THINK ABOUT IT. IT'S UNBELIEVABLE THAT YOU CAN PLAY NOW WITHOUT GETTING STUCK!
And you're a real amateur.
YOU'RE REALLY ...
YOU'RE...
Peek
...
heh
evil grin
...GOOD AT EVERYTHING, BUT YOU'RE INEFFICIENT.

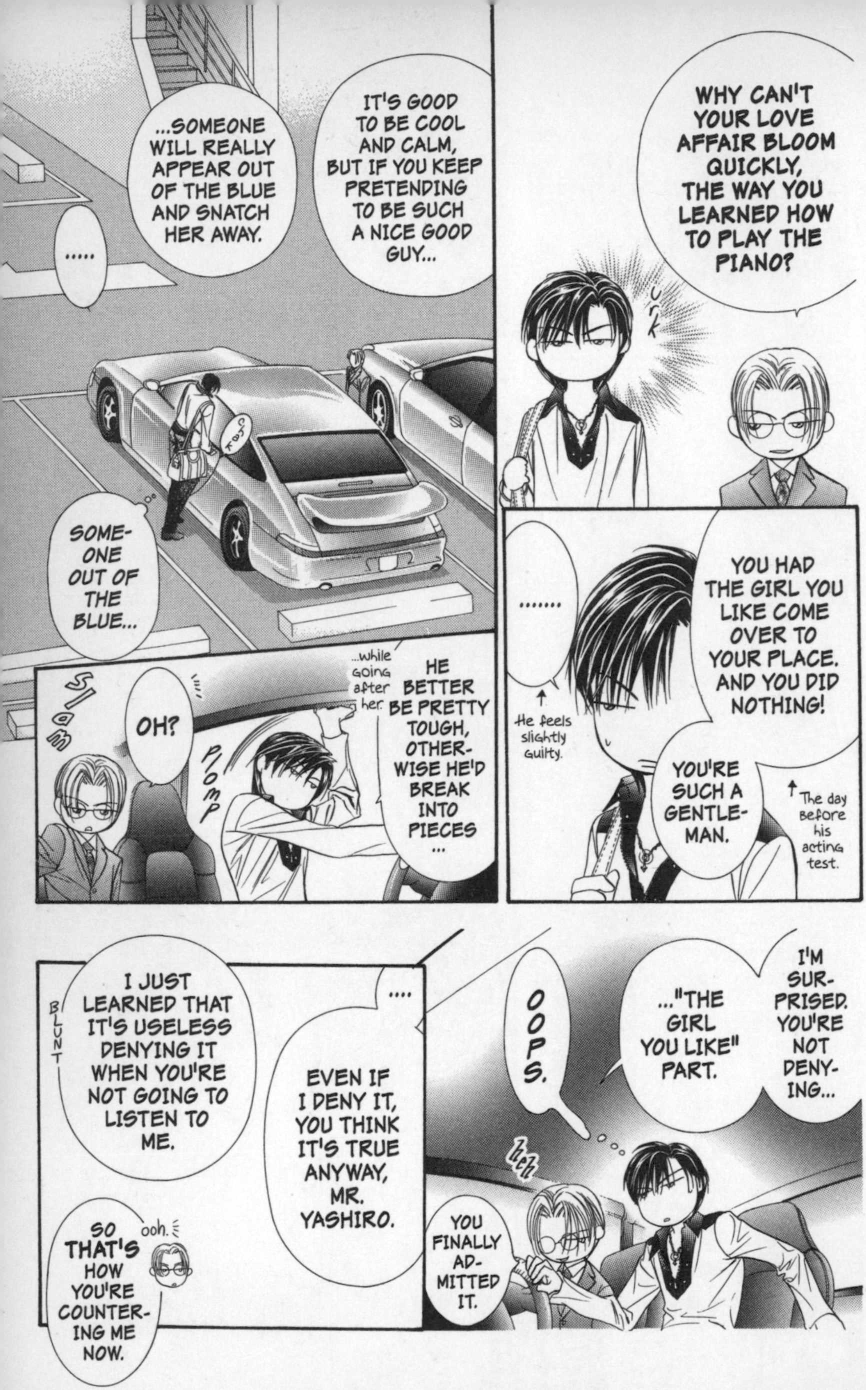

WHY CAN'T YOUR LOVE AFFAIR BLOOM QUICKLY, THE WAY YOU LEARNED HOW TO PLAY THE PIANO?
URK
YOU HAD THE GIRL YOU LIKE COME OVER TO YOUR PLACE. AND YOU DID NOTHING!
YOU'RE SUCH A GENTLEMAN.
The day before his acting test.
....
He feels slightly guilty.
IT'S GOOD TO BE COOL AND CALM, BUT IF YOU KEEP PRETENDING TO BE SUCH A NICE GOOD GUY...
...SOMEONE WILL REALLY APPEAR OUT OF THE BLUE AND SNATCH HER AWAY.
.....
SOME-ONE OUT OF THE BLUE...
HE BETTER BE PRETTY TOUGH, OTHER-WISE HE'D BREAK INTO PIECES ...
...while going after her.
PLOMP
OH?
SLAM
I'M SUR-PRISED. YOU'RE NOT DENY-ING...
..."THE GIRL YOU LIKE" PART.
OOPS.
HEH
YOU FINALLY AD-MITTED IT.
....
EVEN IF I DENY IT, YOU THINK IT'S TRUE ANYWAY, MR. YASHIRO.
I JUST LEARNED THAT IT'S USELESS DENYING IT WHEN YOU'RE NOT GOING TO LISTEN TO ME.
BLUNT
ooh.
SO THAT'S HOW YOU'RE COUNTER-ING ME NOW.

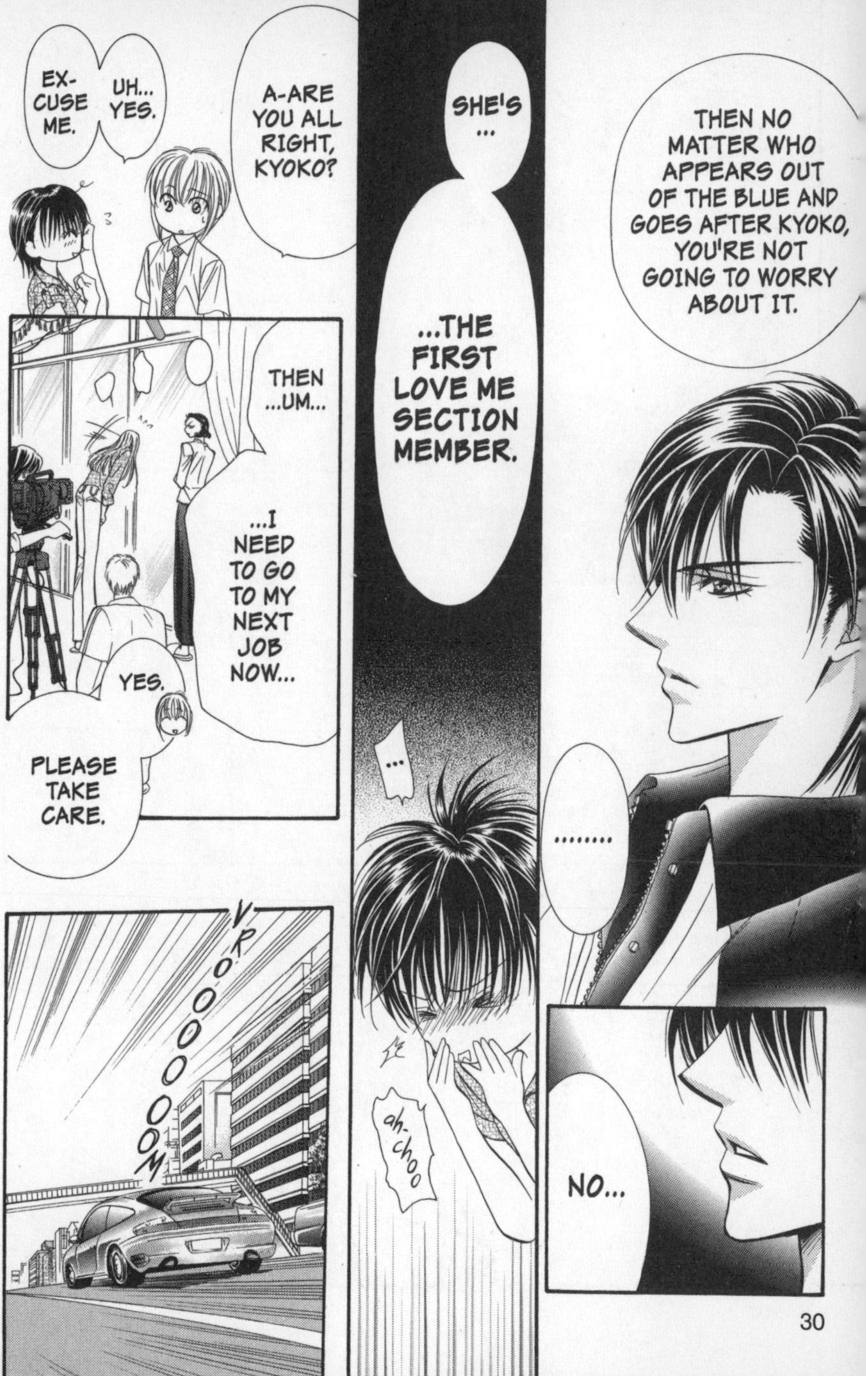
THEN NO MATTER WHO APPEARS OUT OF THE BLUE AND GOES AFTER KYOKO, YOU'RE NOT GOING TO WORRY ABOUT IT.
....
NO...
SHE'S ...
...THE FIRST LOVE ME SECTION MEMBER.
...
ah-choo
A-ARE YOU ALL RIGHT, KYOKO?
UH... YES.
EX-CUSE ME.
THEN ...UM...
...I NEED TO GO TO MY NEXT JOB NOW...
YES.
PLEASE TAKE CARE.
VROOOOOOOOOOM

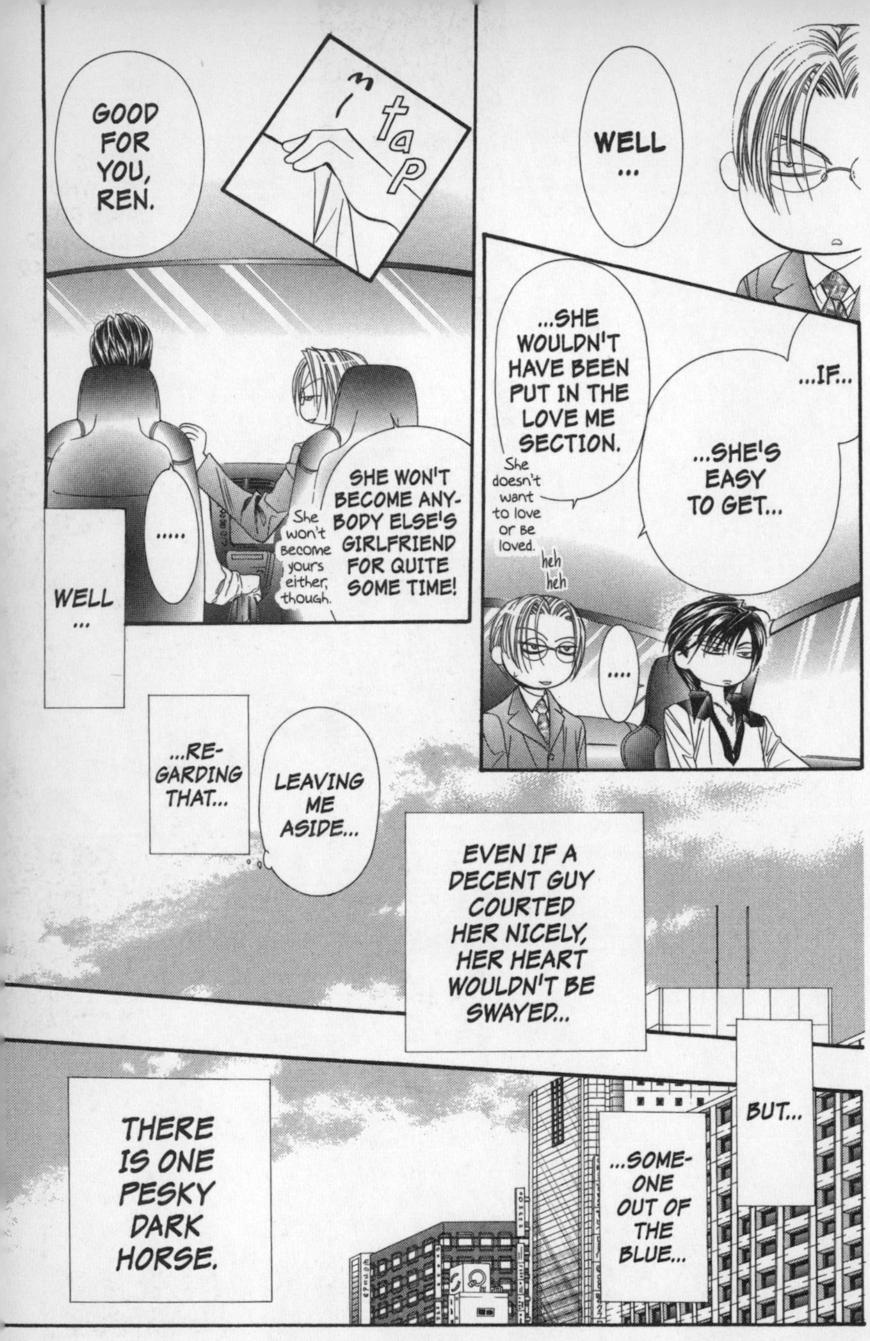
WELL ...
...IF...
...SHE'S EASY TO GET...
...SHE WOULDN'T HAVE BEEN PUT IN THE LOVE ME SECTION.
She doesn't want to love or be loved.
heh heh
....
GOOD FOR YOU, REN.
tap
SHE WON'T BECOME ANY-BODY ELSE'S GIRLFRIEND FOR QUITE SOME TIME!
She won't become yours either, though.
.....
WELL ...
LEAVING ME ASIDE...
...RE-GARDING THAT...
EVEN IF A DECENT GUY COURTED HER NICELY, HER HEART WOULDN'T BE SWAYED...
BUT...
...SOME-ONE OUT OF THE BLUE...
THERE IS ONE PESKY DARK HORSE.

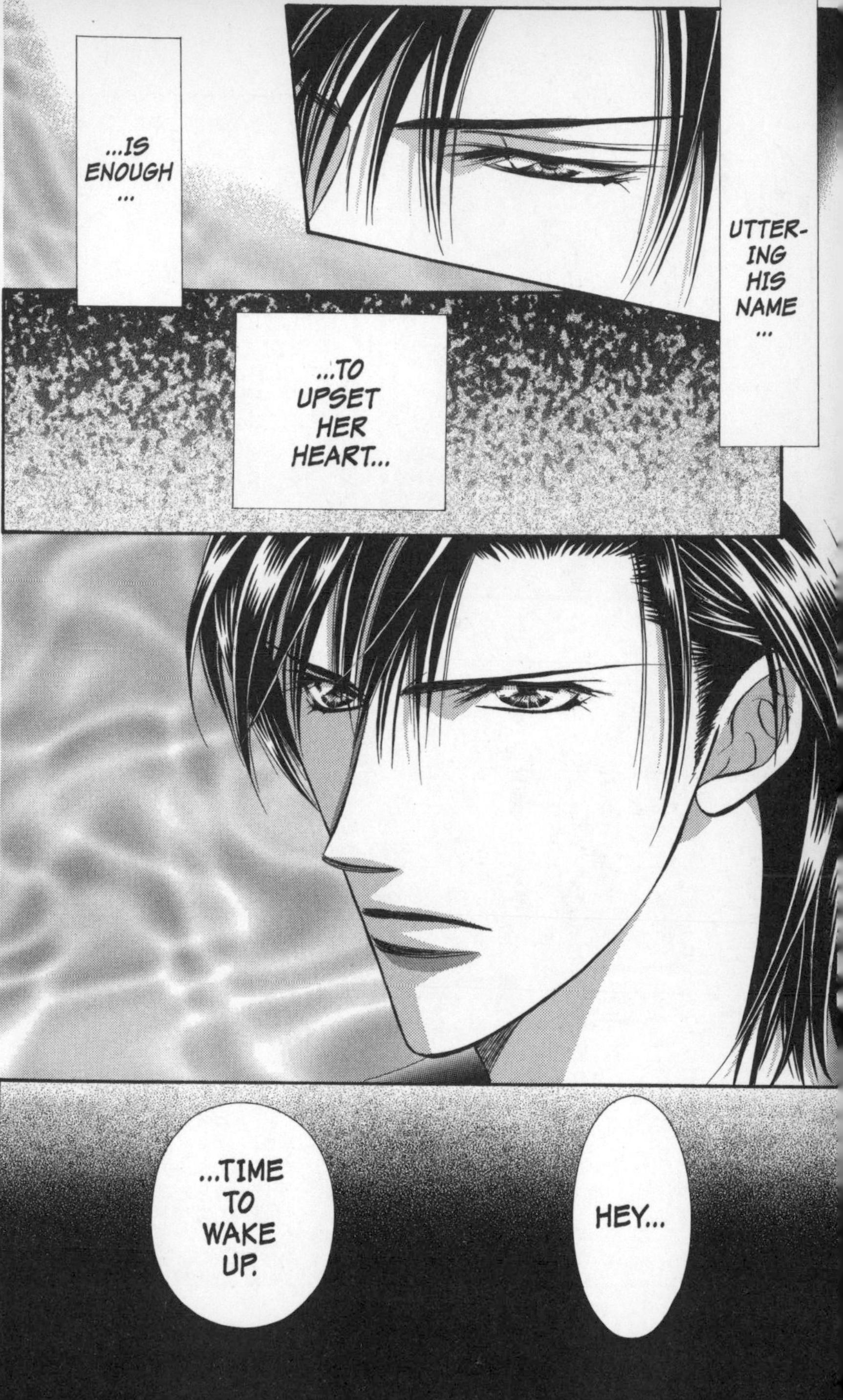
UTTERING HIS NAME...
...IS ENOUGH...
...TO UPSET HER HEART...
HEY...
...TIME TO WAKE UP.

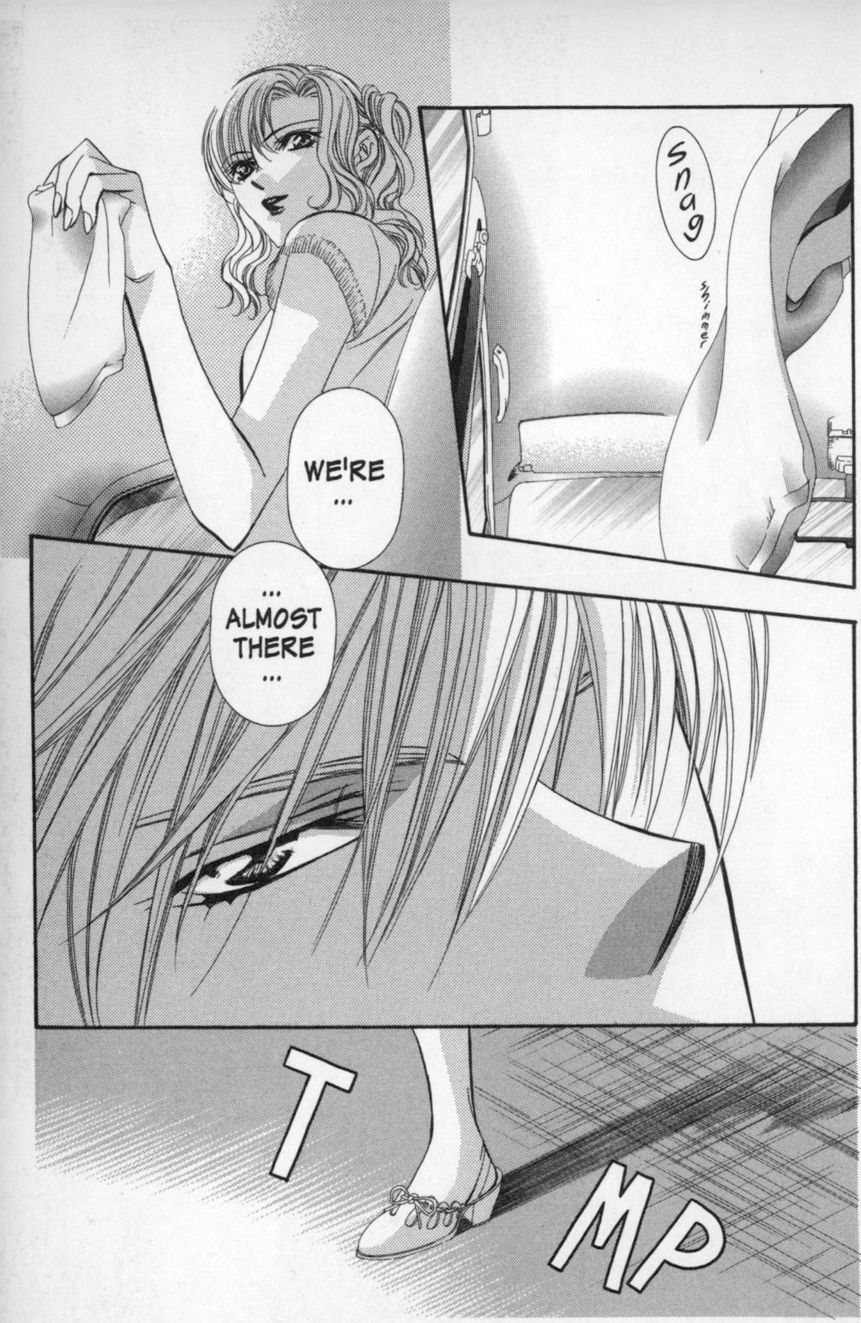
Snag
shimmer
WE'RE ...
... ALMOST THERE ...
TMP

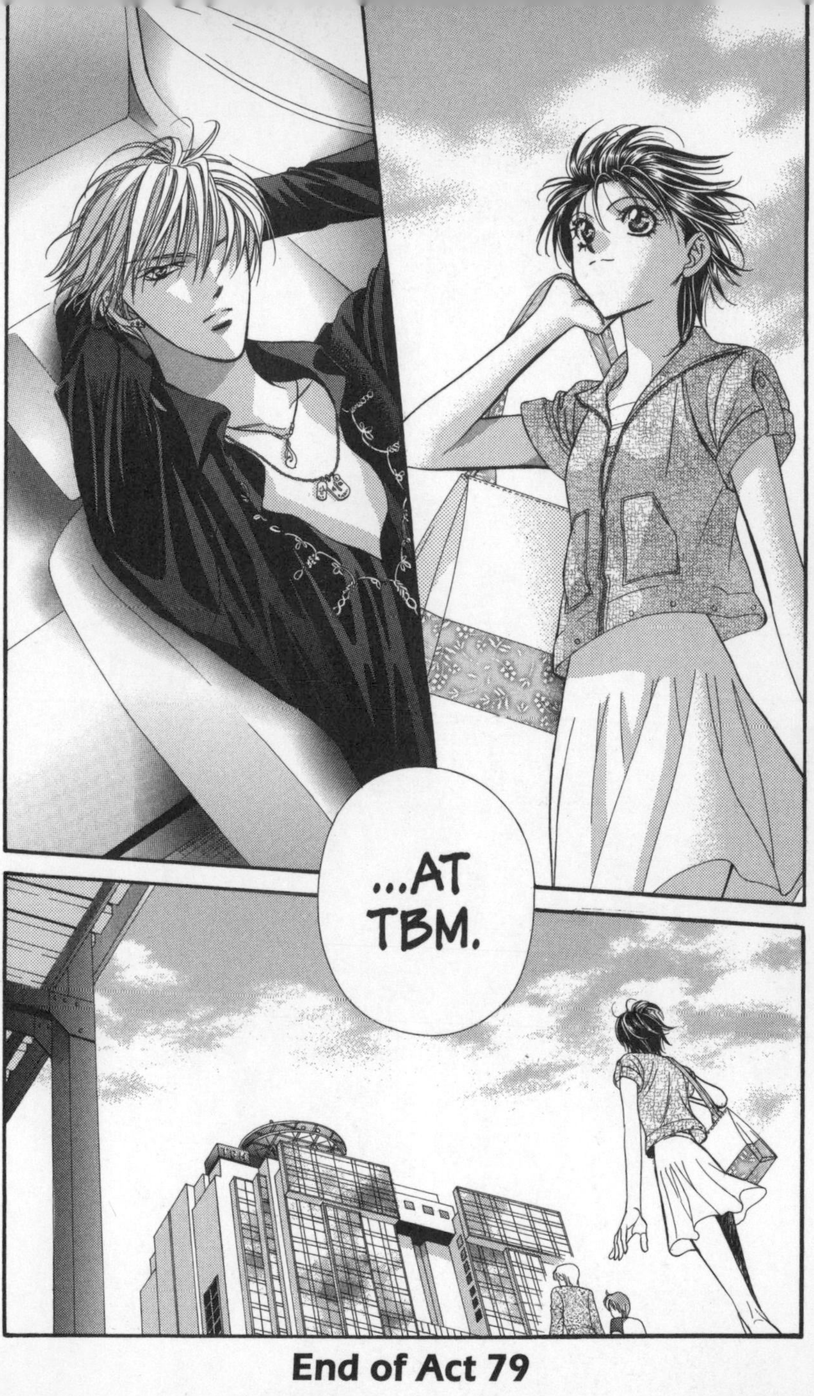
...AT TBM.

End of Act 79

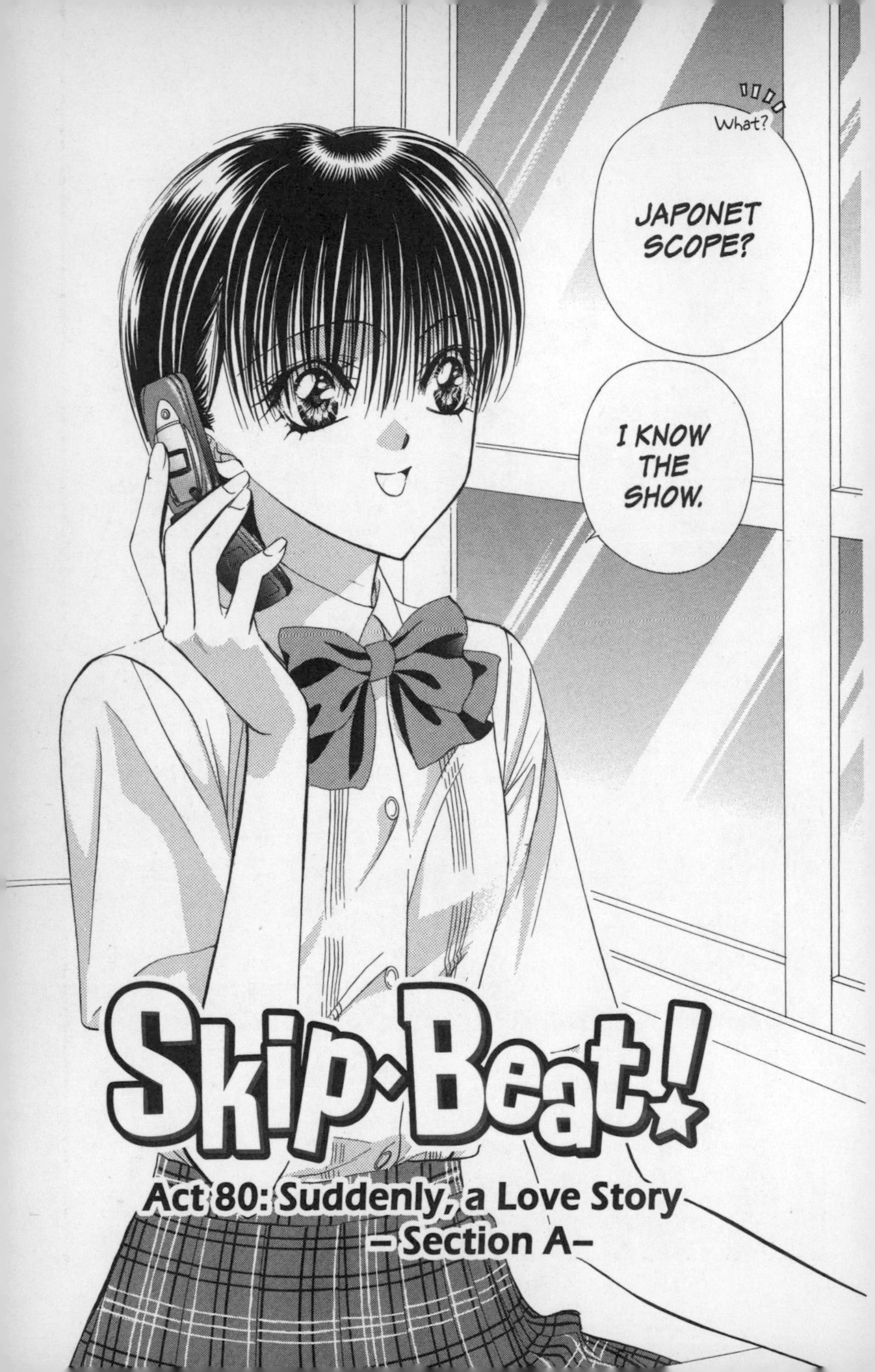
What?
JAPONET SCOPE?
I KNOW THE SHOW.
Skip·Beat!
Act 80: Suddenly, a Love Story
– Section A–

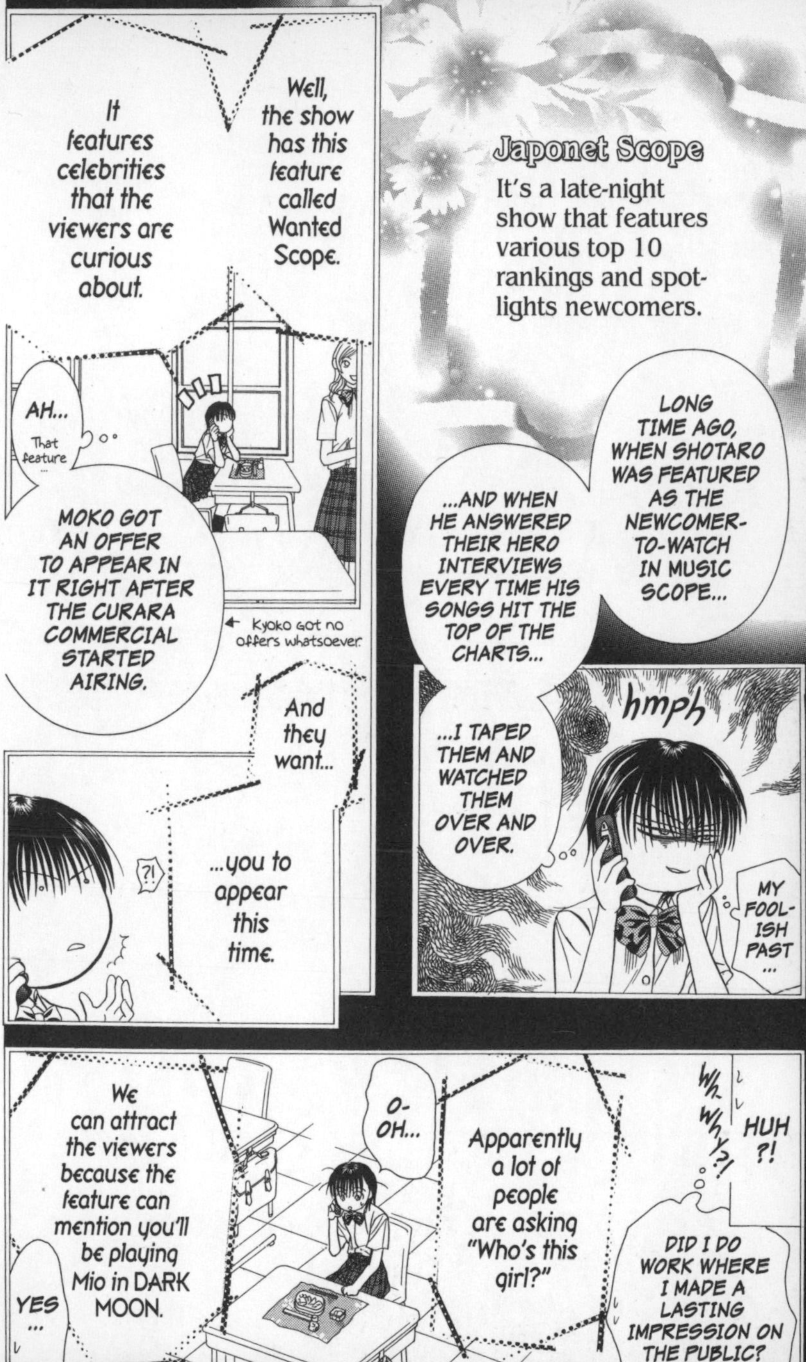
Japonet Scope
It's a late-night show that features various top 10 rankings and spot-lights newcomers.
LONG TIME AGO, WHEN SHOTARO WAS FEATURED AS THE NEWCOMER-TO-WATCH IN MUSIC SCOPE...
...AND WHEN HE ANSWERED THEIR HERO INTERVIEWS EVERY TIME HIS SONGS HIT THE TOP OF THE CHARTS...
hmph
...I TAPED THEM AND WATCHED THEM OVER AND OVER.
MY FOOL-ISH PAST...
Well, the show has this feature called Wanted Scope.
It features celebrities that the viewers are curious about.
AH...
That feature...
MOKO GOT AN OFFER TO APPEAR IN IT RIGHT AFTER THE CURARA COMMERCIAL STARTED AIRING.
← Kyoko got no offers whatsoever.
And they want...
?!
...you to appear this time.
Wh-why?!
HUH?!
DID I DO WORK WHERE I MADE A LASTING IMPRESSION ON THE PUBLIC?
Apparently a lot of people are asking "Who's this girl?"
O-OH...
We can attract the viewers because the feature can mention you'll be playing Mio in DARK MOON.
YES...

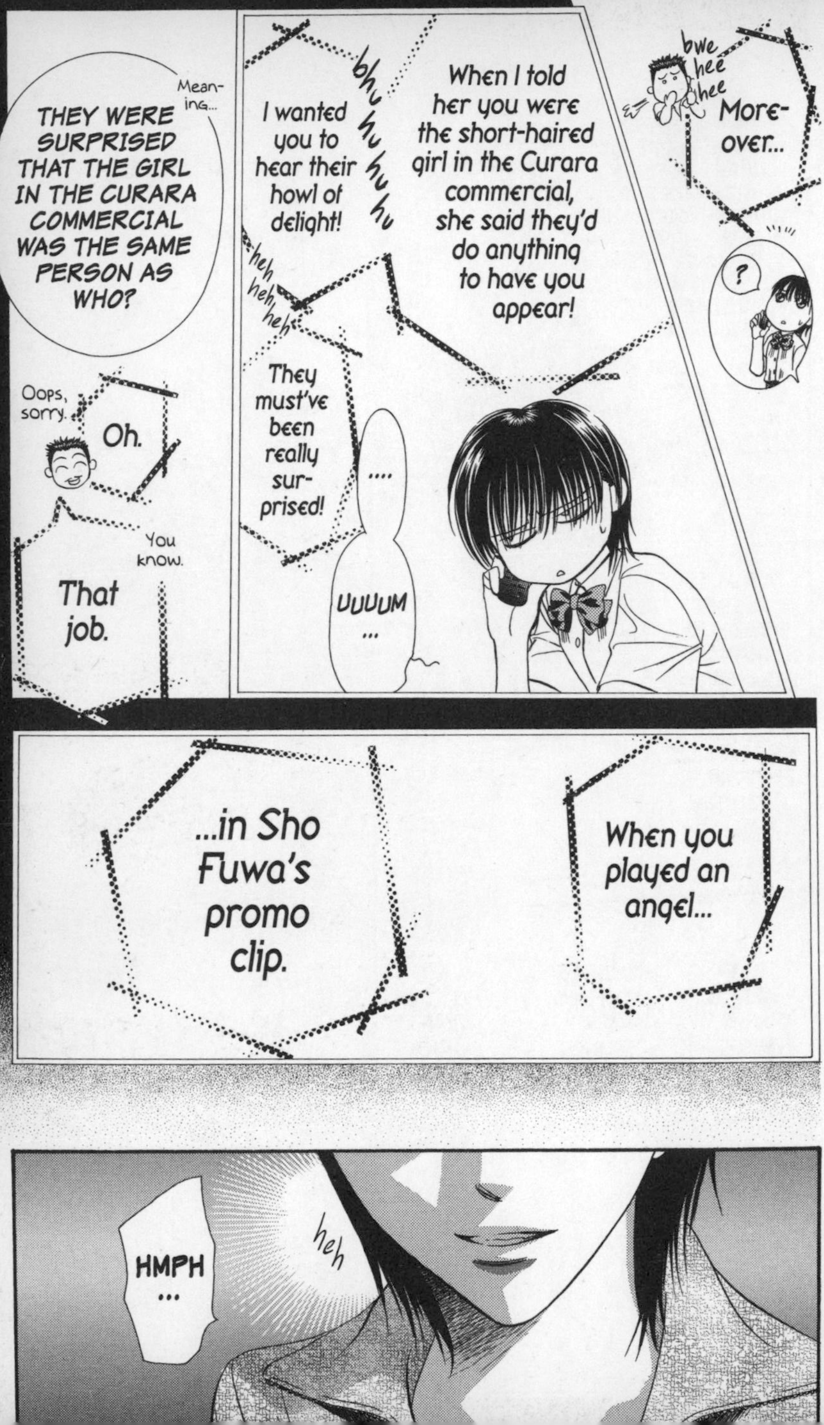
bwe hee hee
More-over...
?
When I told her you were the short-haired girl in the Curara commercial, she said they'd do anything to have you appear!
bhu hu hu hu hu
I wanted you to hear their howl of delight!
heh heh heh
They must've been really sur-prised!
....
UUUUM ...
Mean-ing...
THEY WERE SURPRISED THAT THE GIRL IN THE CURARA COMMERCIAL WAS THE SAME PERSON AS WHO?
Oops, sorry.
Oh.
You know.
That job.
When you played an angel...
...in Sho Fuwa's promo clip.
heh
HMPH ...

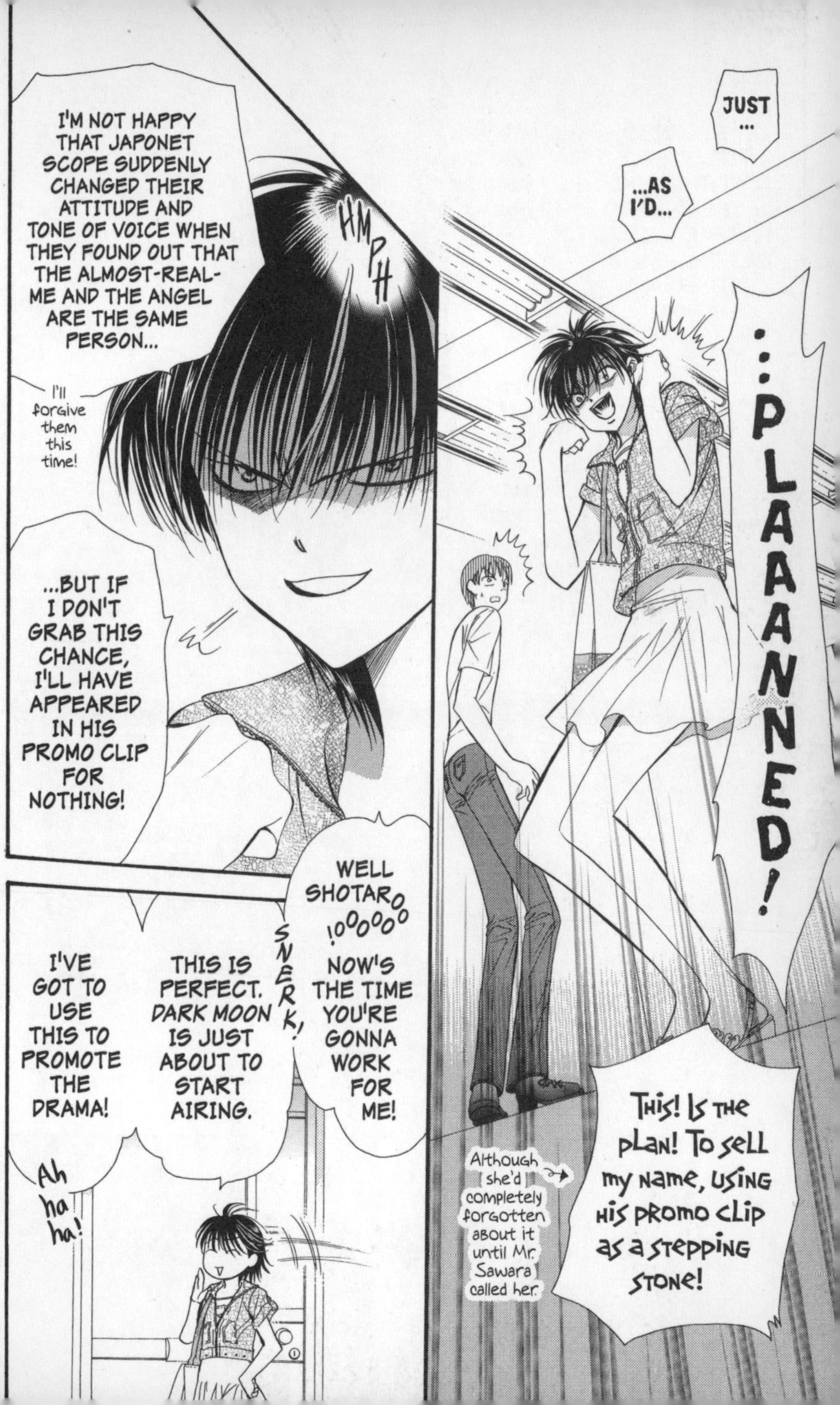
JUST...
...AS I'D...
...PLAANNED!
This! Is the plan! To sell my name, using his promo clip as a stepping stone!
Although she'd completely forgotten about it until Mr. Sawara called her.
I'M NOT HAPPY THAT JAPONET SCOPE SUDDENLY CHANGED THEIR ATTITUDE AND TONE OF VOICE WHEN THEY FOUND OUT THAT THE ALMOST-REAL-ME AND THE ANGEL ARE THE SAME PERSON...
HMPH
I'll forgive them this time!
...BUT IF I DON'T GRAB THIS CHANCE, I'LL HAVE APPEARED IN HIS PROMO CLIP FOR NOTHING!
WELL SHOTAROOO !OOOOOO NOW'S THE TIME YOU'RE GONNA WORK FOR ME!
SNERK!
THIS IS PERFECT. DARK MOON IS JUST ABOUT TO START AIRING.
I'VE GOT TO USE THIS TO PROMOTE THE DRAMA!
Ah ha ha!

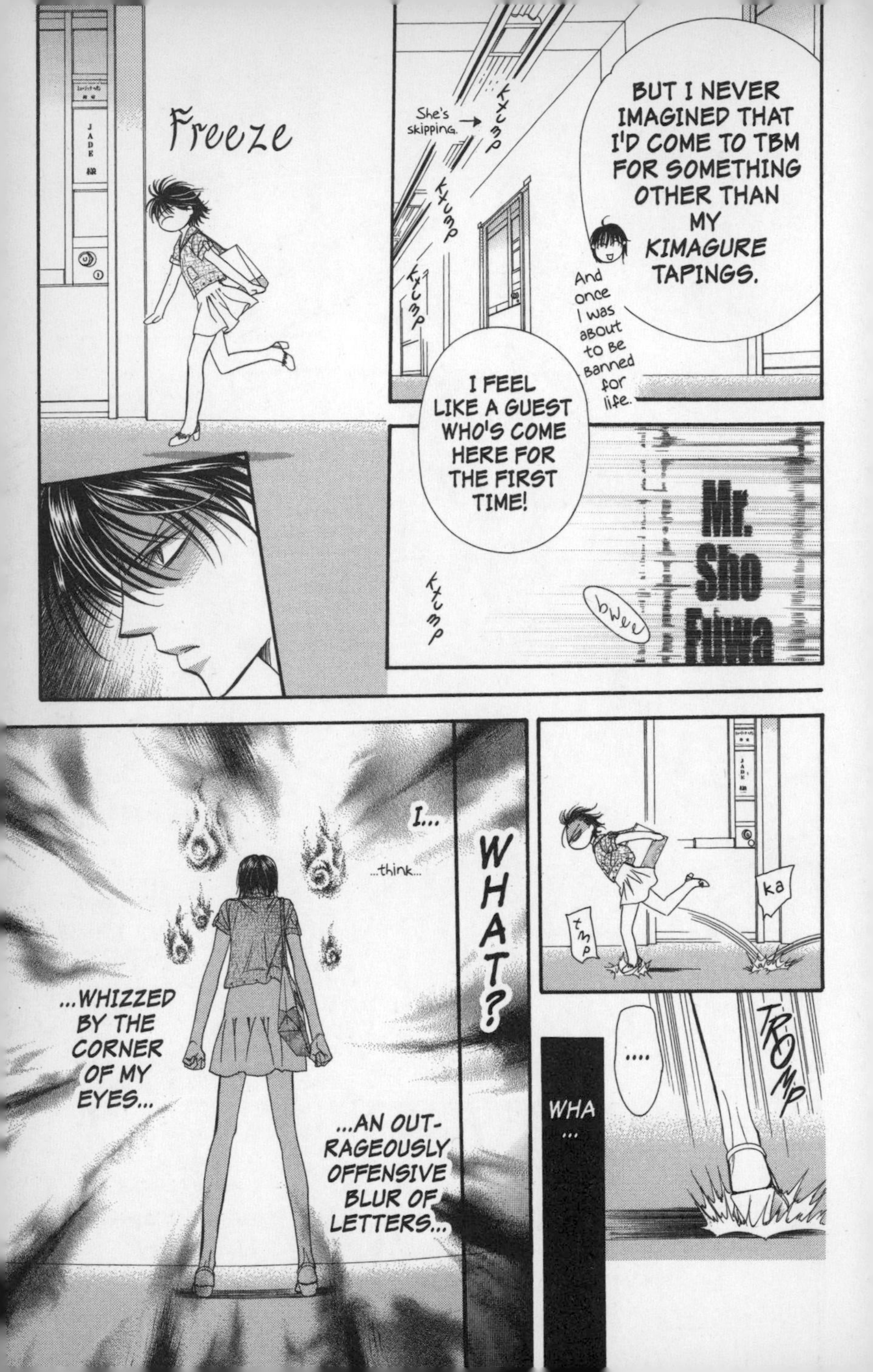
She's skipping.
KTUMP
KTUMP
KTUMP
BUT I NEVER IMAGINED THAT I'D COME TO TBM FOR SOMETHING OTHER THAN MY KIMAGURE TAPINGS.
And once I was about to be banned for life.
I FEEL LIKE A GUEST WHO'S COME HERE FOR THE FIRST TIME!
Freeze
Mr. Sho Fuwa
bwee
KTUMP
ka
tmp
TROMP
....
WHA...
WHAT?
I...
...think...
...WHIZZED BY THE CORNER OF MY EYES...
...AN OUT-RAGEOUSLY OFFENSIVE BLUR OF LETTERS...

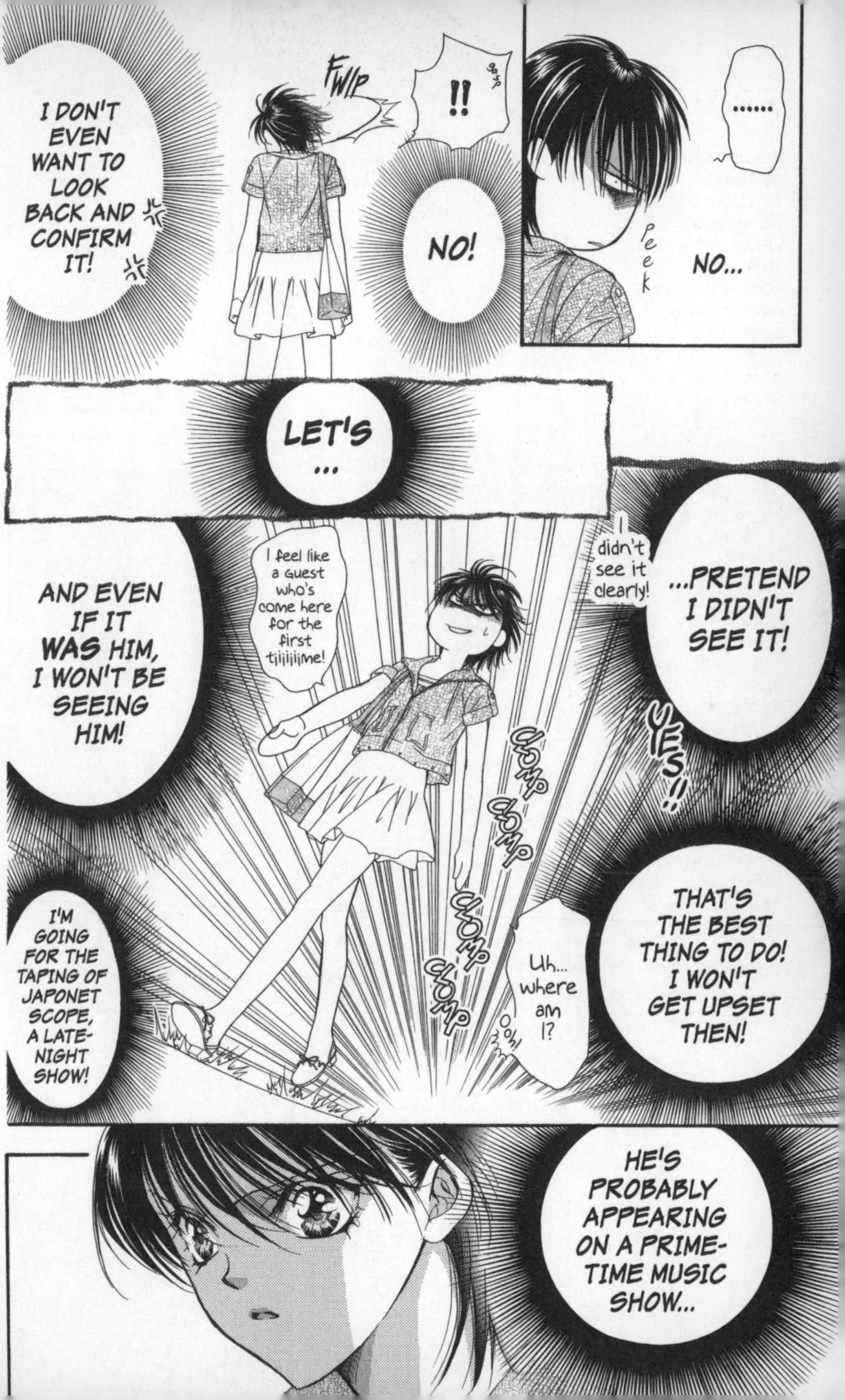
......
Peek
NO...
gasp
!!
FWIP
NO!
I DON'T EVEN WANT TO LOOK BACK AND CONFIRM IT!
LET'S ...
...PRETEND I DIDN'T SEE IT!
YES!!
I didn't see it clearly!
I feel like a guest who's come here for the first tiiiiiiime!
AND EVEN IF IT WAS HIM, I WON'T BE SEEING HIM!
THAT'S THE BEST THING TO DO! I WON'T GET UPSET THEN!
Uh... where am I?
Ooh!
CLOMP CLOMP CLOMP CLOMP
I'M GOING FOR THE TAPING OF JAPONET SCOPE, A LATE-NIGHT SHOW!
HE'S PROBABLY APPEARING ON A PRIME-TIME MUSIC SHOW...

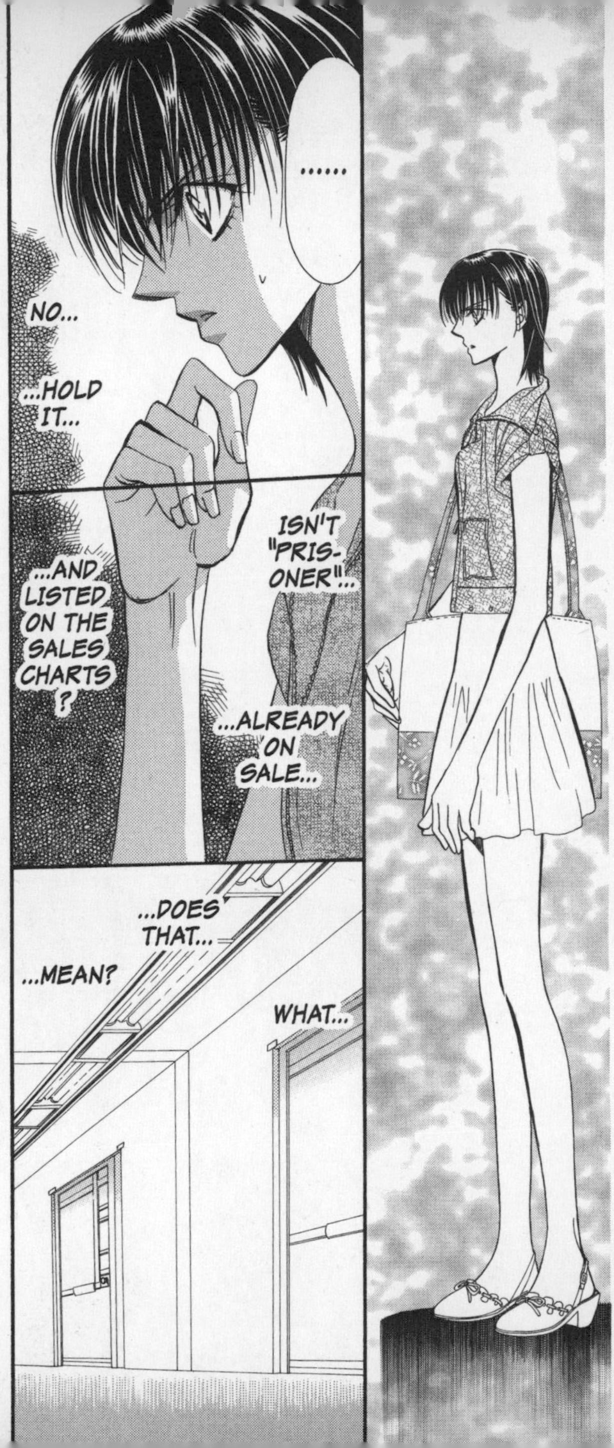
......
NO...
...HOLD IT...
ISN'T "PRISONER"...
...ALREADY ON SALE...
...AND LISTED ON THE SALES CHARTS?
WHAT...
...DOES THAT...
...MEAN?

PRISONER

It must have been obvious...

To my dear readers whom I confused...I apologize...to be honest...I thought six chapters would be enough...oh dear... I...do this a lot...really...and to be honest again...uh...I've got to mention PRISONER...

I dragged out PRISONER to begin the "Suddenly, ..." arc...but I confess...I had absolutely no intention of following up on how the CD was doing sales-wise, or how people perceived Kyoko's performance in the promo clip... when the promo clip arc was over, that was it for me...I don't want to look back on the past... cuz...that happened back in Volume 8, you know...? What am I doing, bringing up such an old episode... My dear readers would feel that way too...

-Continued-

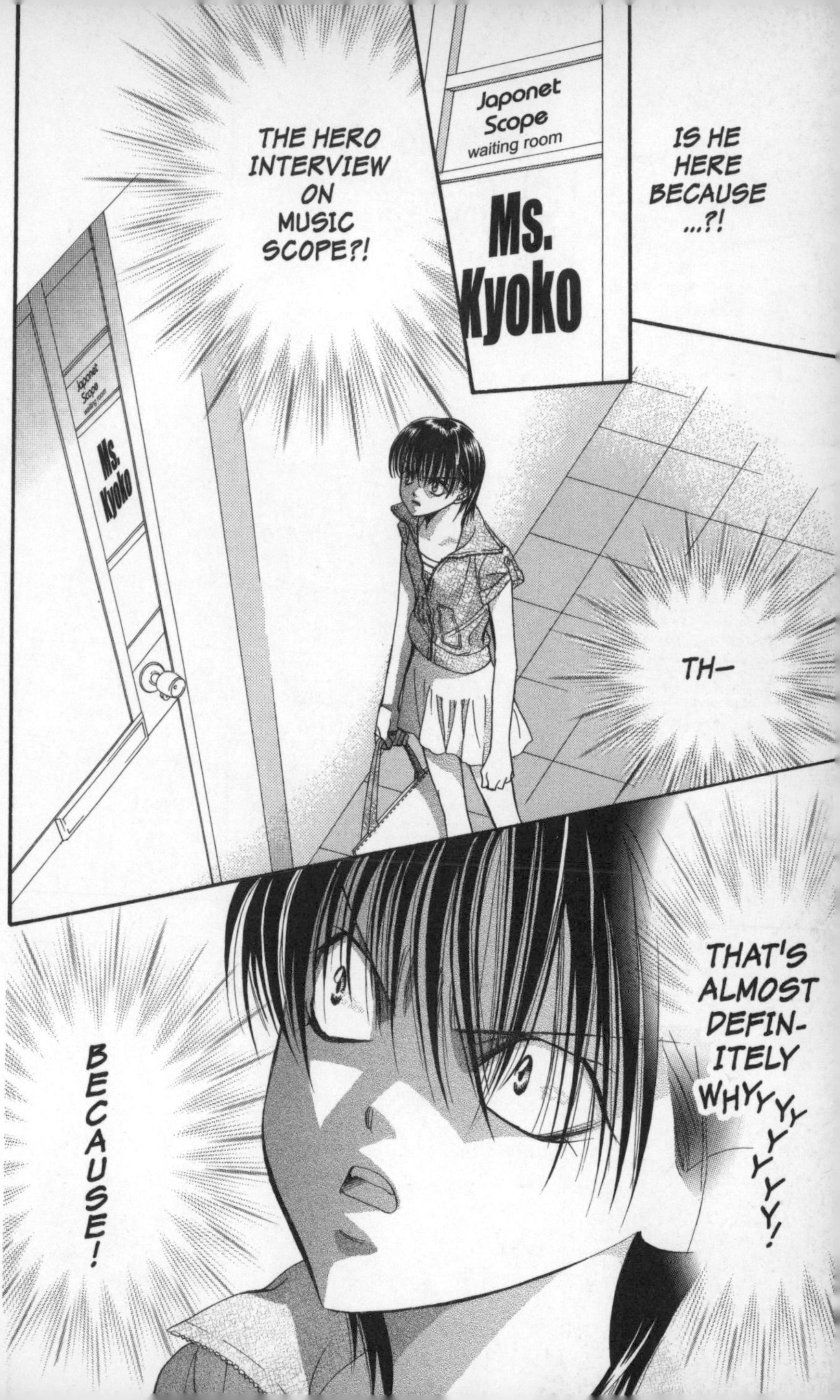
IS HE HERE BECAUSE ...?!
Japonet Scope waiting room
Ms. Kyoko
THE HERO INTERVIEW ON MUSIC SCOPE?!
Japonet Scope waiting room
Ms. Kyoko
TH—
THAT'S ALMOST DEFIN-ITELY WHYYYYYYYY!
BECAUSE!

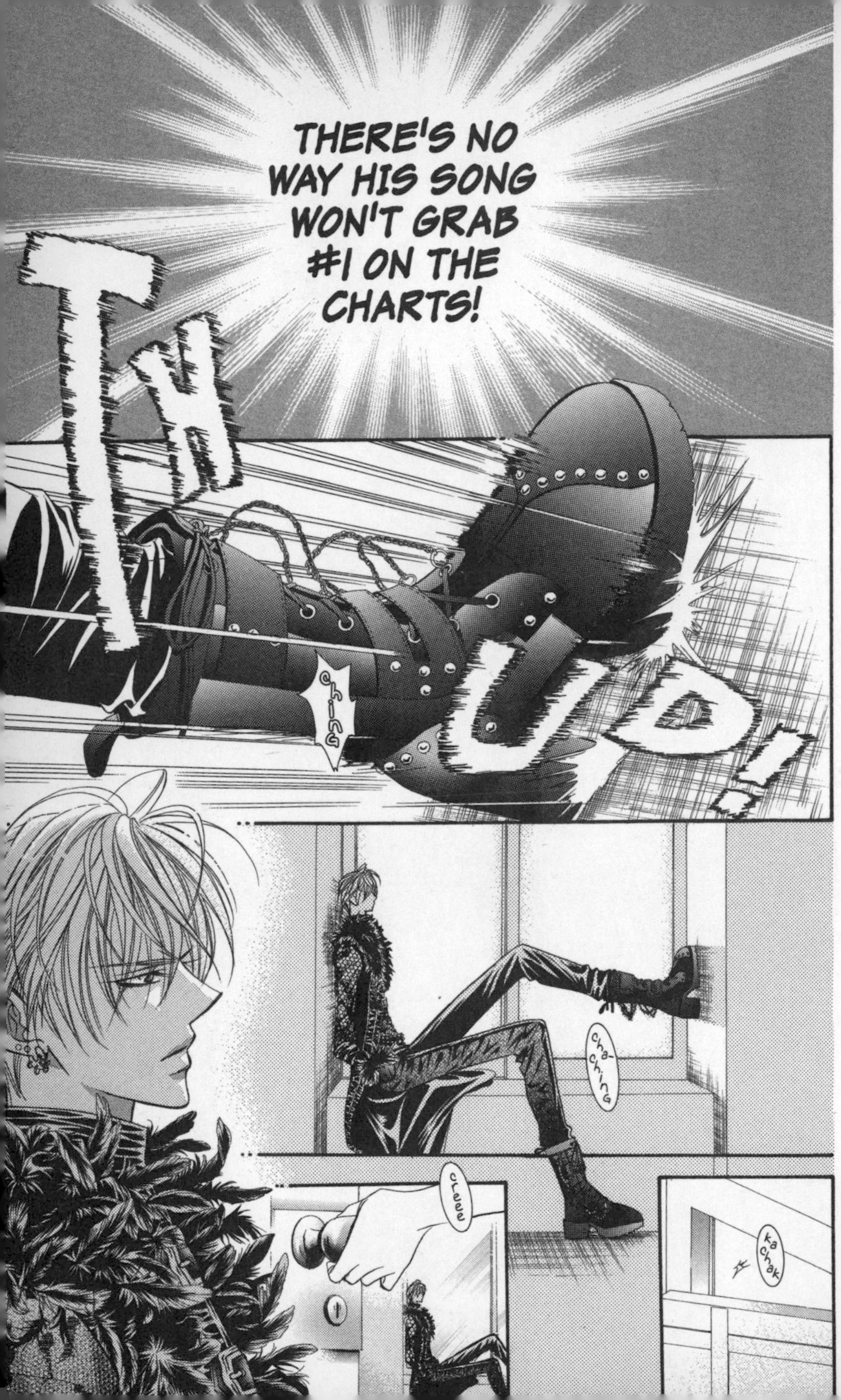
THERE'S NO WAY HIS SONG WON'T GRAB #1 ON THE CHARTS!
THUD!
ching
Cha-ching
creee
ka chak

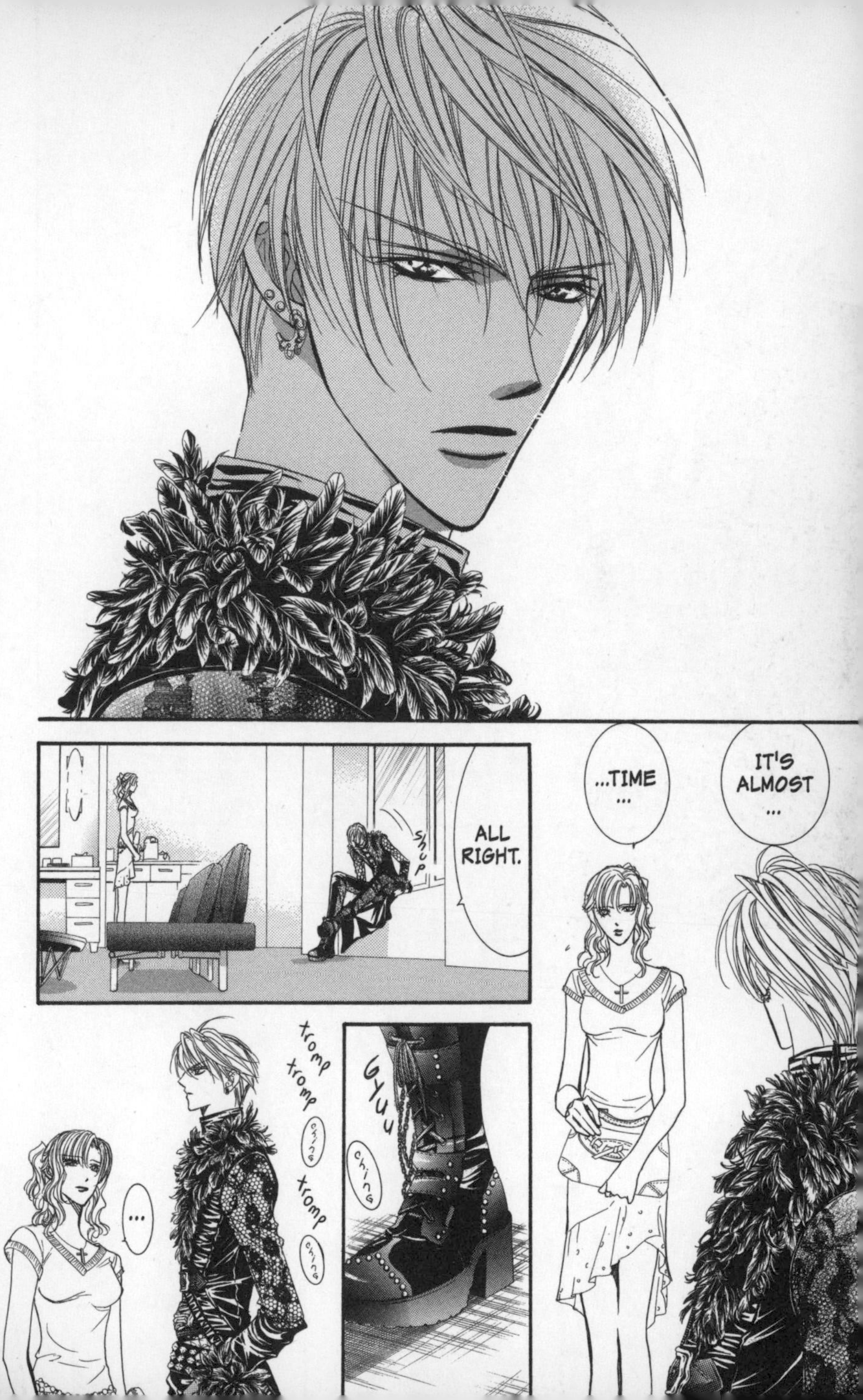
IT'S ALMOST ...
...TIME ...
ALL RIGHT.
SHUP
GYUU
ching
tromp
tromp
ching
tromp
ching
...

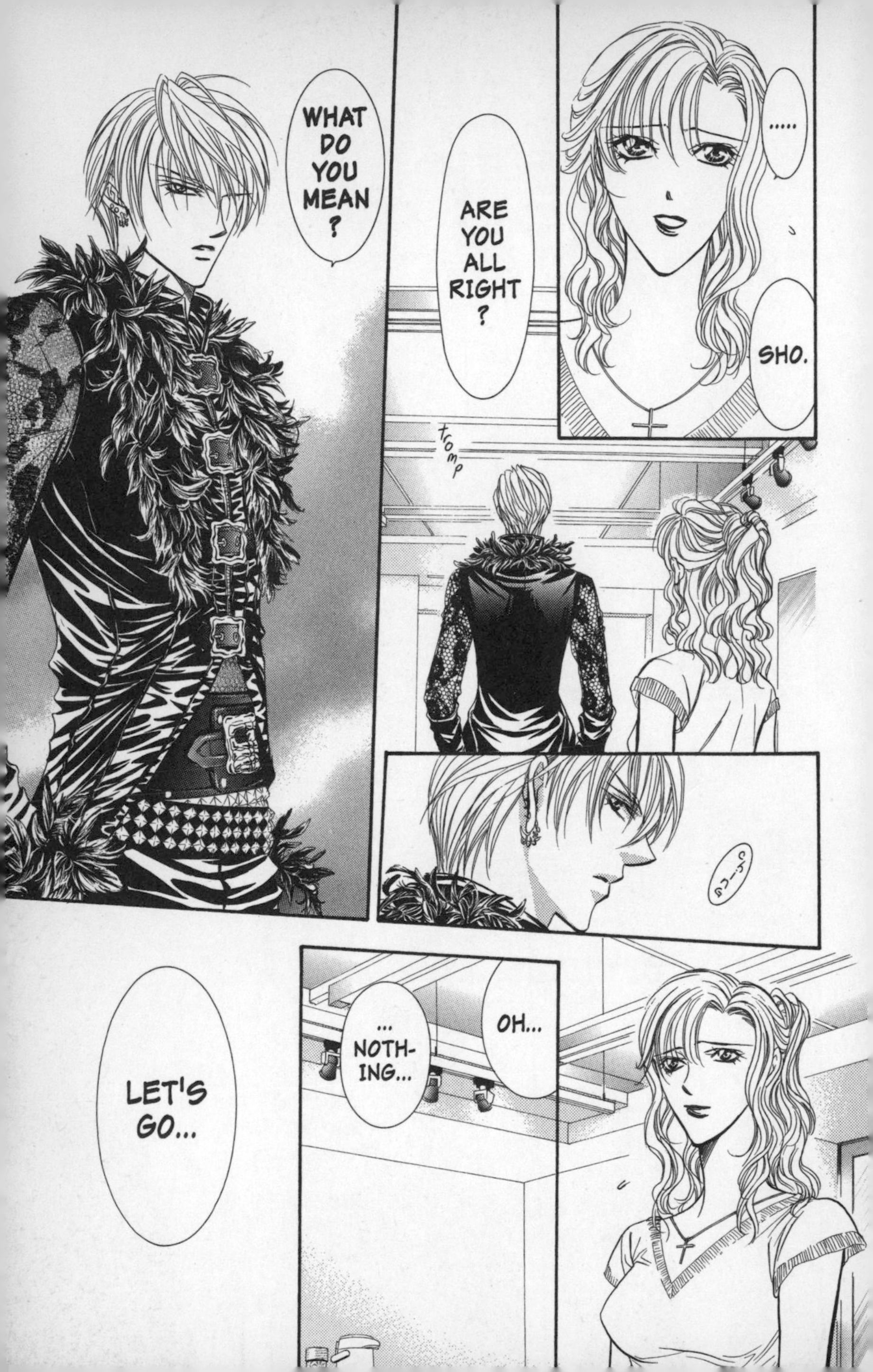
.....
SHO.
ARE YOU ALL RIGHT?
tromp
WHAT DO YOU MEAN?
OH...
...NOTHING...
LET'S GO...

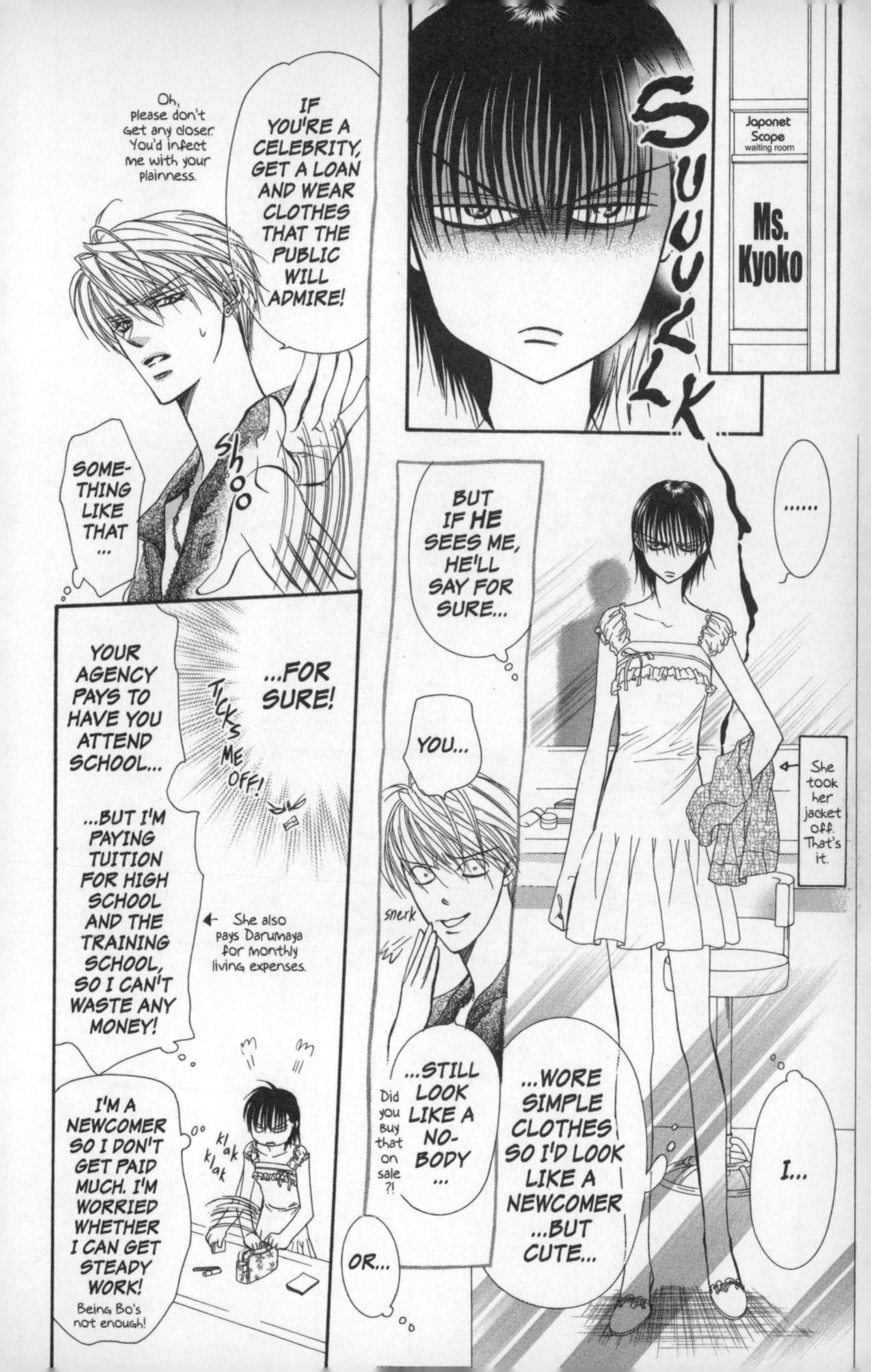
SUUULK
Japonet Scope waiting room
Ms. Kyoko
......
She took her jacket off. That's it.
I...
...WORE SIMPLE CLOTHES SO I'D LOOK LIKE A NEWCOMER ...BUT CUTE...
OR...
BUT IF HE SEES ME, HE'LL SAY FOR SURE...
YOU...
snerk
...STILL LOOK LIKE A NO-BODY ...
Did you buy that on sale?!
IF YOU'RE A CELEBRITY, GET A LOAN AND WEAR CLOTHES THAT THE PUBLIC WILL ADMIRE!
Oh, please don't get any closer. You'd infect me with your plainness.
Shoo
SOME-THING LIKE THAT ...
...FOR SURE!
TICKS ME OFF!
YOUR AGENCY PAYS TO HAVE YOU ATTEND SCHOOL...
...BUT I'M PAYING TUITION FOR HIGH SCHOOL AND THE TRAINING SCHOOL, SO I CAN'T WASTE ANY MONEY!
She also pays Darumaya for monthly living expenses.
I'M A NEWCOMER SO I DON'T GET PAID MUCH. I'M WORRIED WHETHER I CAN GET STEADY WORK!
Being Bo's not enough!
klak klak

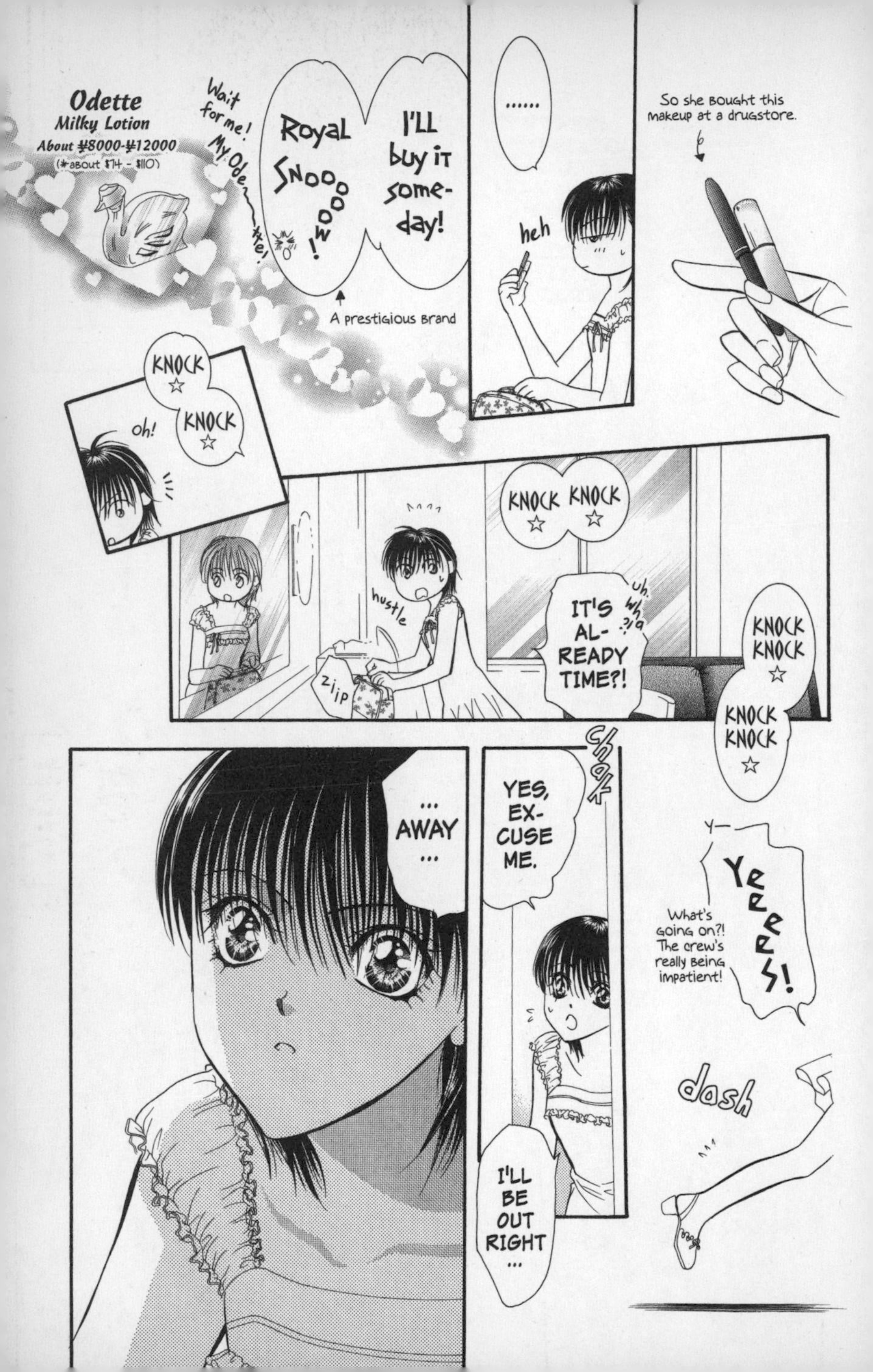
So she bought this makeup at a drugstore.
......
heh
I'LL buy it someday!
Royal Snooooow!
A prestigious brand
Odette
Milky Lotion
About ¥8000-¥12000
(*about $74 - $110)
Wait for me! My Ode~tte!
KNOCK ☆ KNOCK ☆
oh!
KNOCK ☆ KNOCK ☆
uh, wha?!
IT'S AL-READY TIME?!
hustle
zip
KNOCK KNOCK ☆
KNOCK KNOCK ☆
Y— Yeeees!
What's going on?! The crew's really being impatient!
dash
Chak
YES, EX-CUSE ME.
I'LL BE OUT RIGHT ...
... AWAY ...

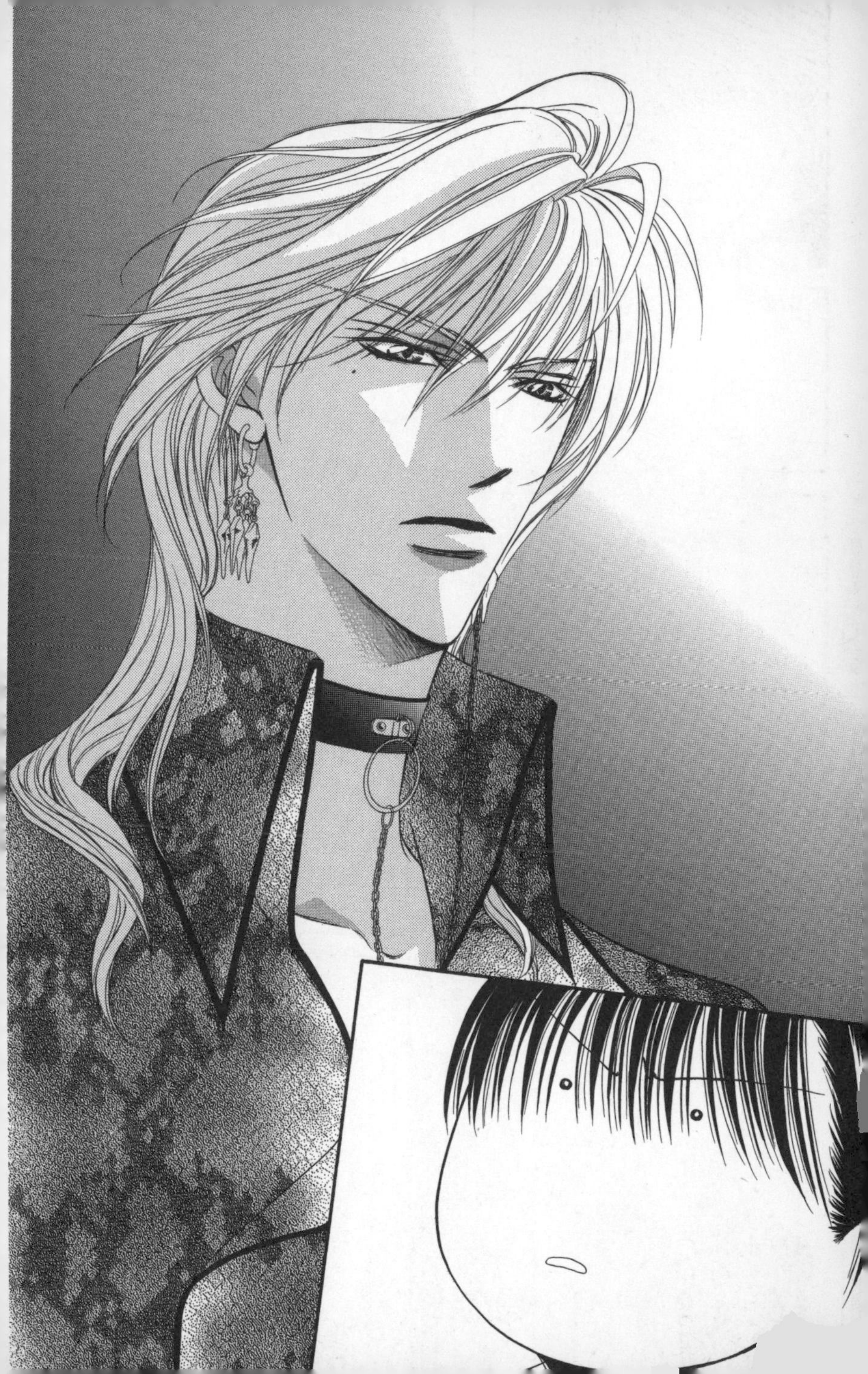

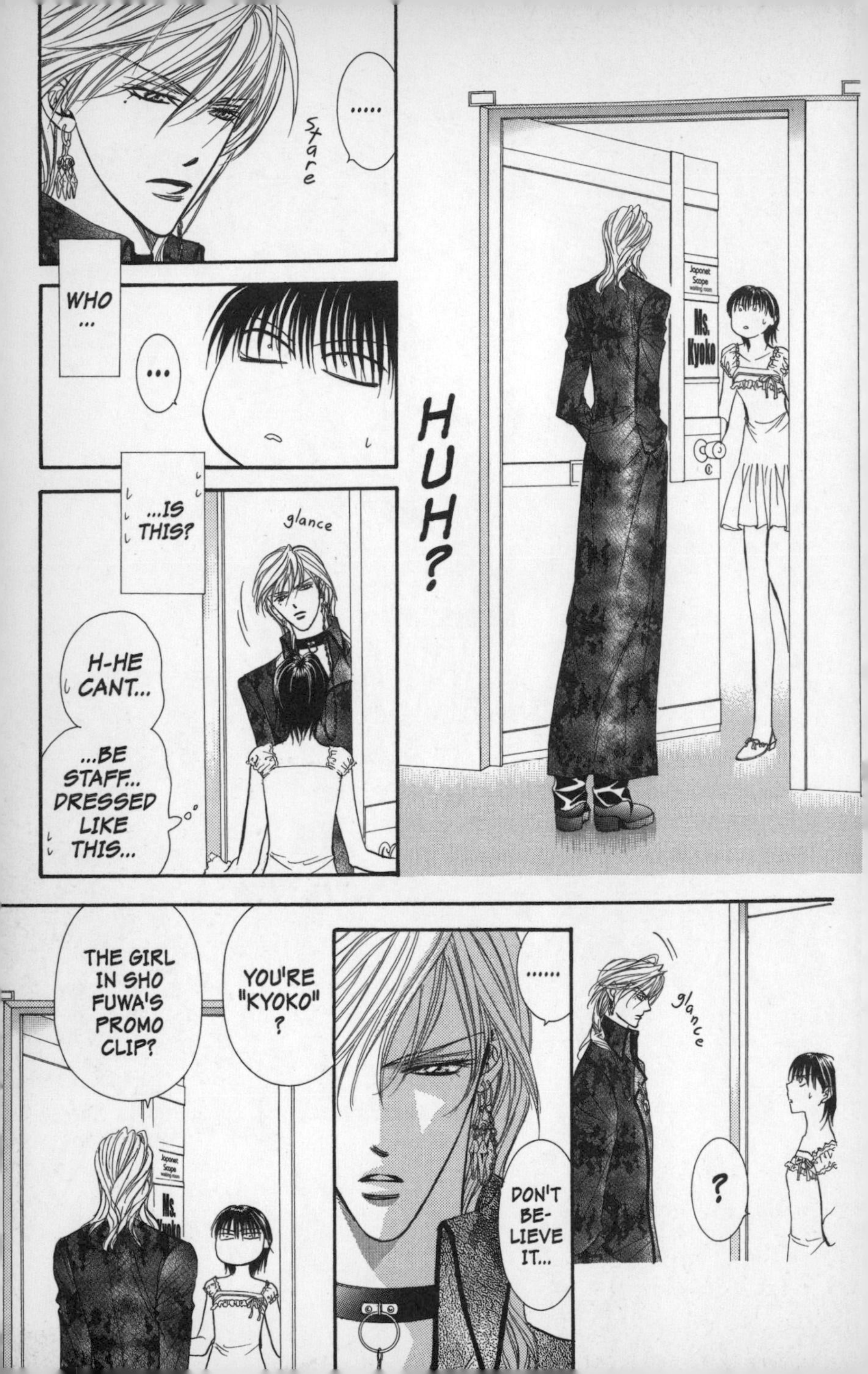
HUH?
Japonet Scope waiting room
Ms. Kyoko
.....
Stare
WHO...
...
...IS THIS?
glance
H-HE CANT...
...BE STAFF... DRESSED LIKE THIS...
glance
?
......
DON'T BE-LIEVE IT...
YOU'RE "KYOKO"?
THE GIRL IN SHO FUWA'S PROMO CLIP?
Japonet Scope waiting room
Ms. Kyoko

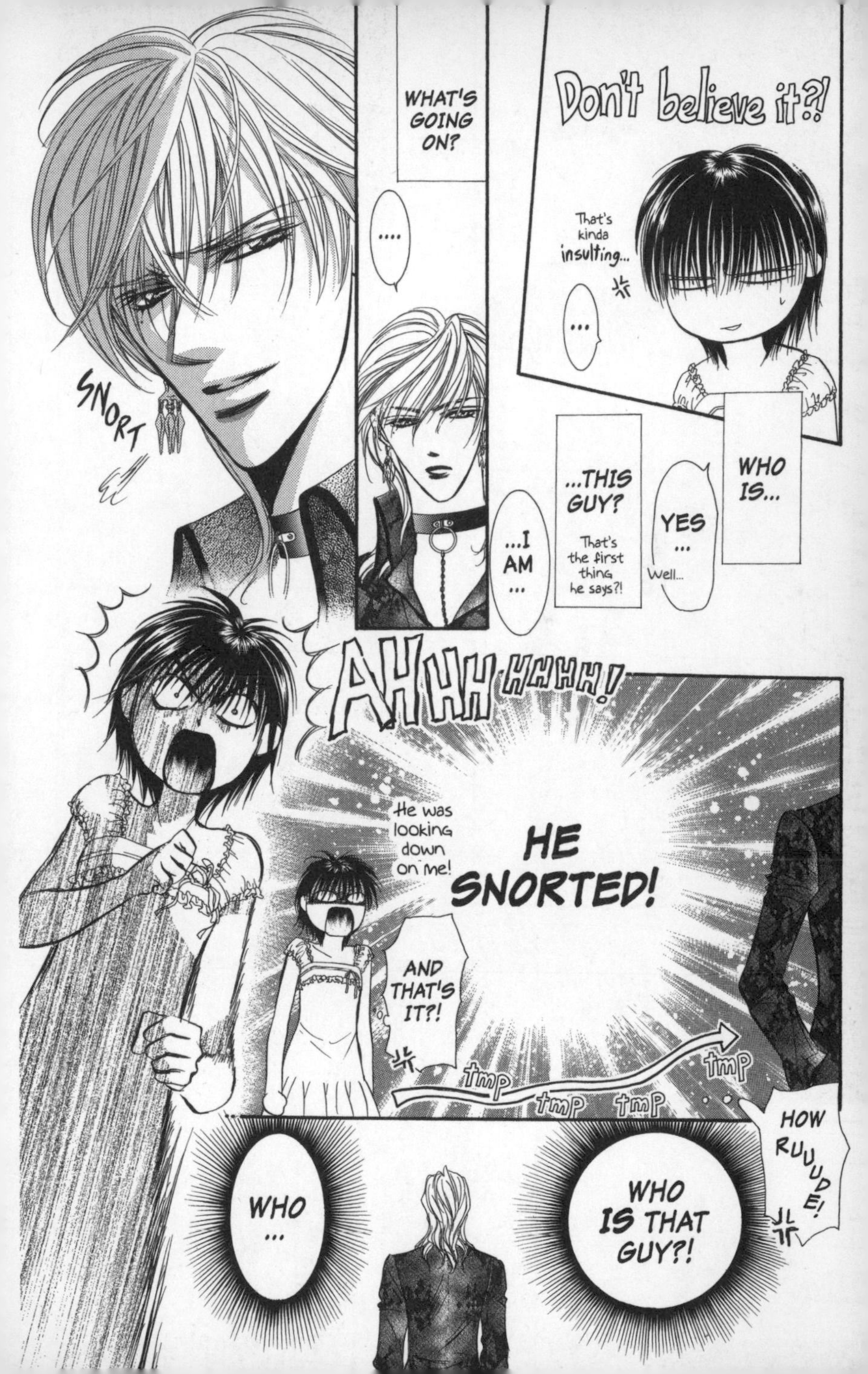
Don't believe it?!
That's kinda insulting...
...
WHO IS...
YES ...
Well...
...THIS GUY?
That's the first thing he says?!
...I AM ...
WHAT'S GOING ON?
....
SNORT
AHHHHHHH!
HE SNORTED!
He was looking down on me!
AND THAT'S IT?!
tmp
tmp
tmp
tmp
HOW RUUUDE!
WHO IS THAT GUY?!
WHO ...

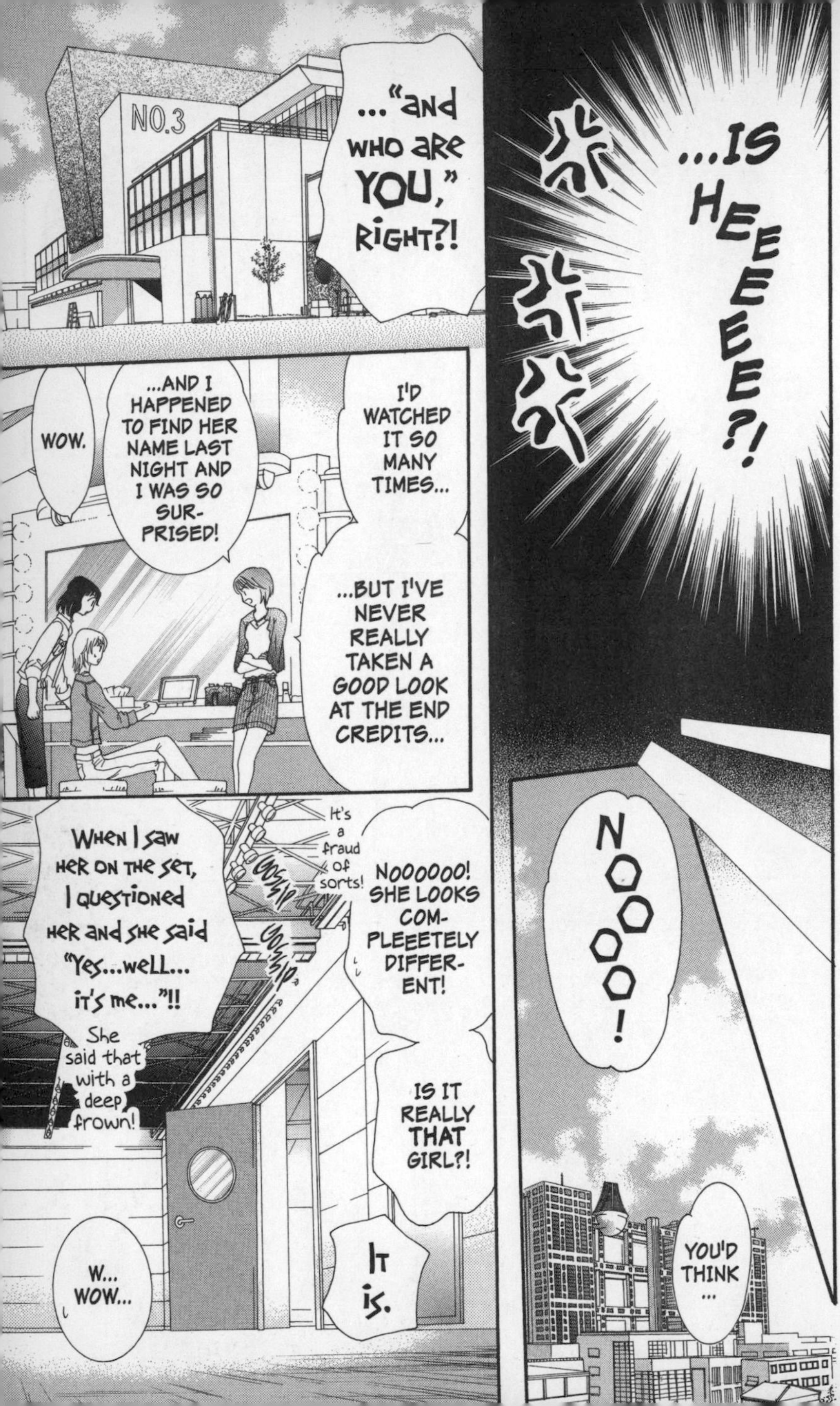
...IS HEEEEEE?!
NOOOO!
YOU'D THINK...
..."and who are YOU," right?!
I'D WATCHED IT SO MANY TIMES...
...BUT I'VE NEVER REALLY TAKEN A GOOD LOOK AT THE END CREDITS...
...AND I HAPPENED TO FIND HER NAME LAST NIGHT AND I WAS SO SURPRISED!
WOW.
NOOOOOO! SHE LOOKS COMPLEEETELY DIFFERENT!
It's a fraud of sorts!
When I saw her on the set, I questioned her and she said "Yes...well... it's me..."!!
She said that with a deep frown!
IS IT REALLY THAT GIRL?!
It is.
W... WOW...

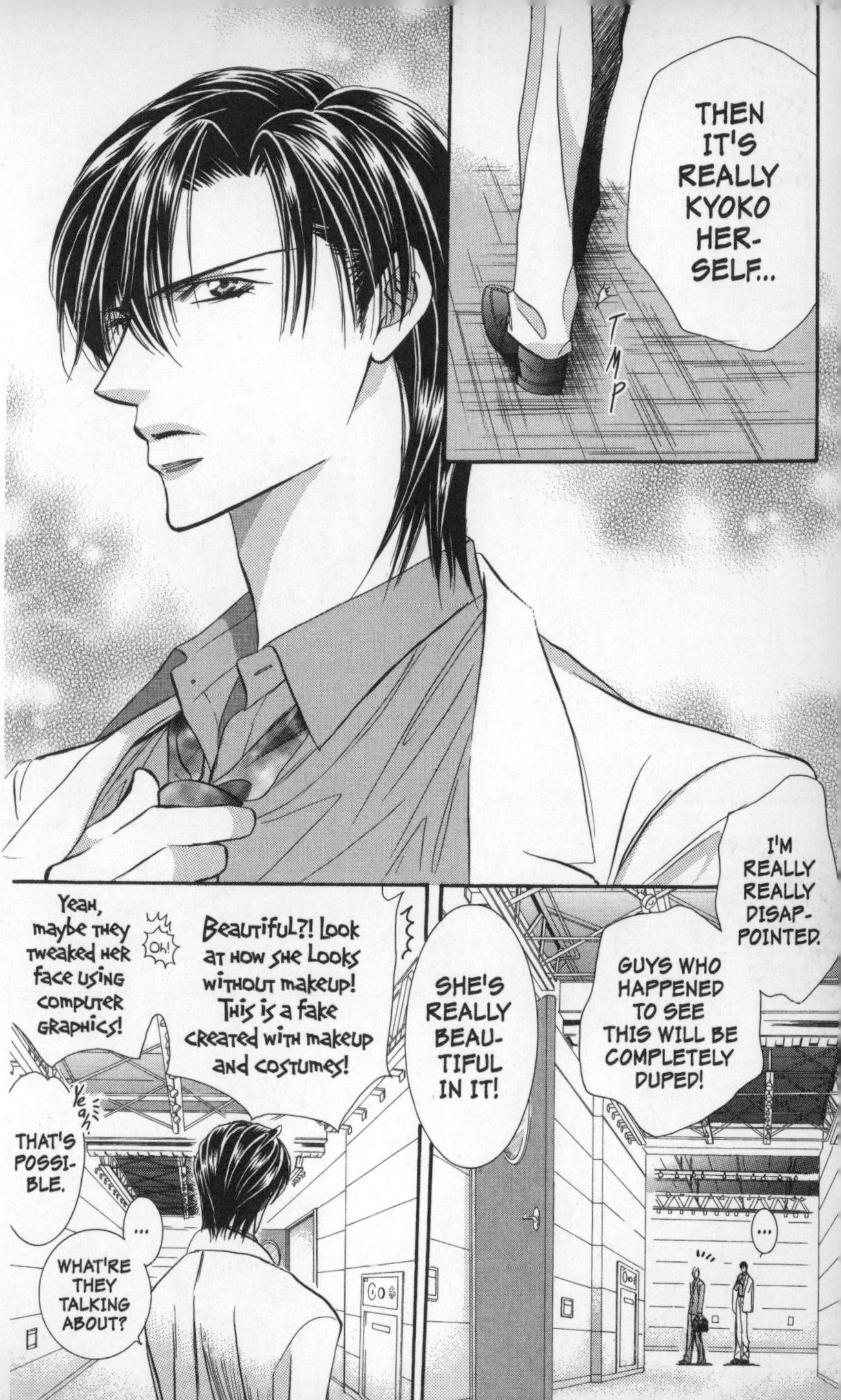
THEN IT'S REALLY KYOKO HER-SELF...
TMP
I'M REALLY REALLY DISAP-POINTED.
GUYS WHO HAPPENED TO SEE THIS WILL BE COMPLETELY DUPED!
SHE'S REALLY BEAU-TIFUL IN IT!
...
Beautiful?! Look at how she Looks without makeup! This is a fake created with makeup and costumes!
Oh!
Yeah, maybe they tweaked her face using computer graphics!
Yeah
THAT'S POSSI-BLE.
...
WHAT'RE THEY TALKING ABOUT?

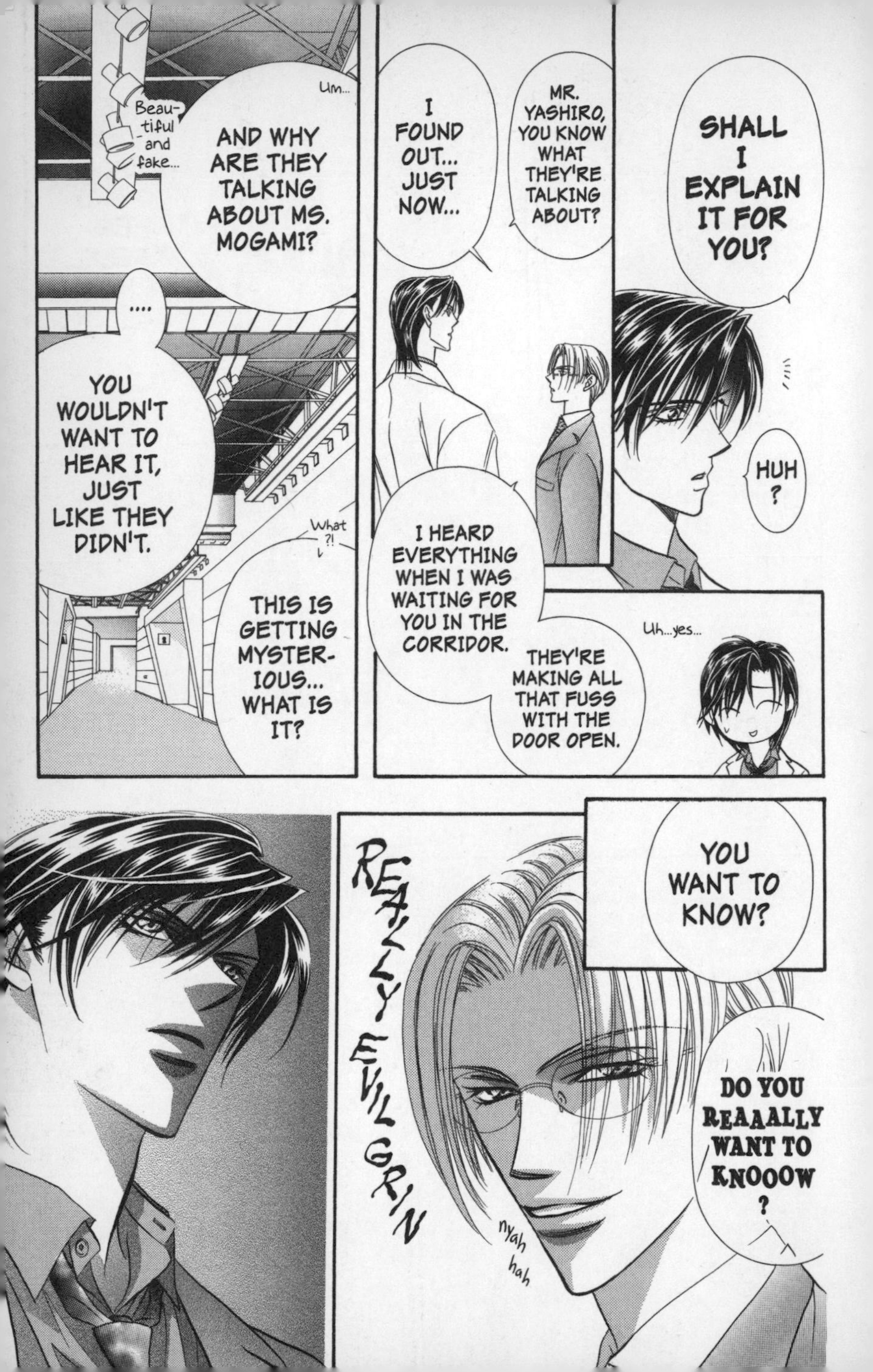
SHALL I EXPLAIN IT FOR YOU?
HUH?
MR. YASHIRO, YOU KNOW WHAT THEY'RE TALKING ABOUT?
I FOUND OUT... JUST NOW...
I HEARD EVERYTHING WHEN I WAS WAITING FOR YOU IN THE CORRIDOR.
Uh...yes...
THEY'RE MAKING ALL THAT FUSS WITH THE DOOR OPEN.
Um...
AND WHY ARE THEY TALKING ABOUT MS. MOGAMI?
Beau-tiful and fake...
....
YOU WOULDN'T WANT TO HEAR IT, JUST LIKE THEY DIDN'T.
What?!
THIS IS GETTING MYSTERIOUS... WHAT IS IT?
YOU WANT TO KNOW?
DO YOU REAAALLY WANT TO KNOOOW?
REALLY EVIL GRIN
nyah hah

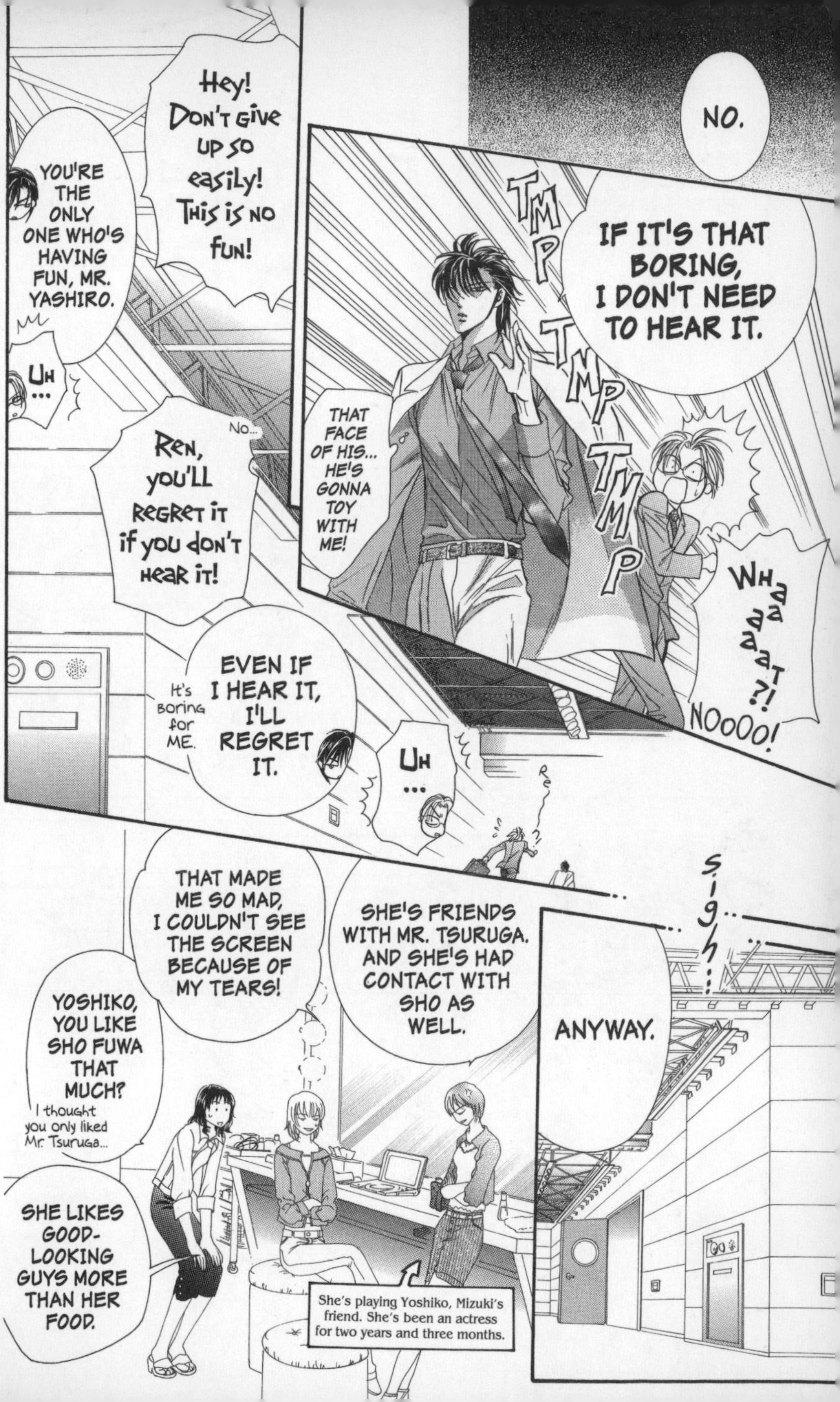
NO.
IF IT'S THAT BORING, I DON'T NEED TO HEAR IT.
TMP TMP TMP TMP
THAT FACE OF HIS... HE'S GONNA TOY WITH ME!
Whaaaaat?! NOOOO!
Hey! Don't give up so easily! This is no fun!
YOU'RE THE ONLY ONE WHO'S HAVING FUN, MR. YASHIRO.
Uh...
No...
Ren, you'll regret it if you don't hear it!
EVEN IF I HEAR IT, I'LL REGRET IT.
It's boring for ME.
Uh...
Re...
Sigh...
ANYWAY.
SHE'S FRIENDS WITH MR. TSURUGA. AND SHE'S HAD CONTACT WITH SHO AS WELL.
THAT MADE ME SO MAD, I COULDN'T SEE THE SCREEN BECAUSE OF MY TEARS!
YOSHIKO, YOU LIKE SHO FUWA THAT MUCH?
I thought you only liked Mr. Tsuruga...
SHE LIKES GOOD-LOOKING GUYS MORE THAN HER FOOD.
She's playing Yoshiko, Mizuki's friend. She's been an actress for two years and three months.

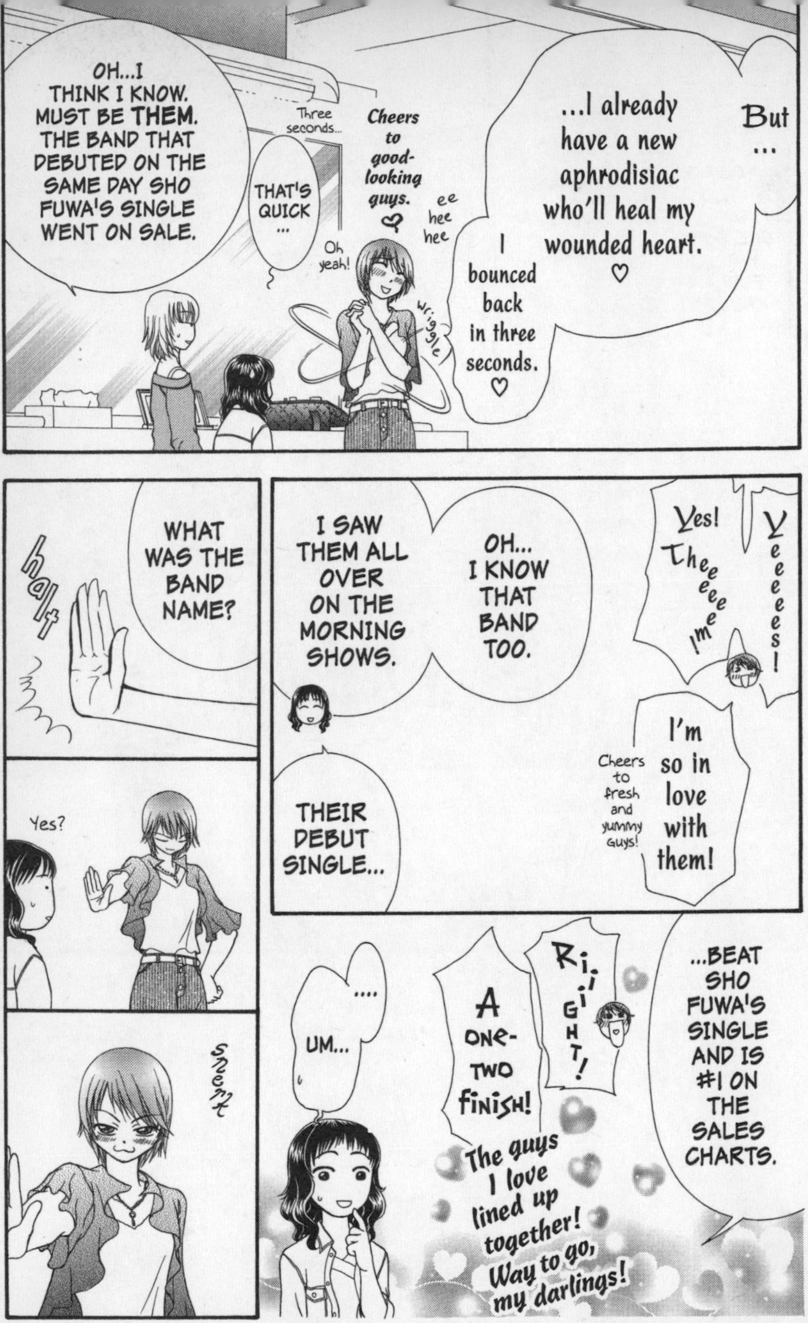
But ...
...I already have a new aphrodisiac who'll heal my wounded heart. ♡
I bounced back in three seconds. ♡
ee hee hee
wriggle
Cheers to good-looking guys. ♡
Oh yeah!
Three seconds...
THAT'S QUICK ...
OH...I THINK I KNOW. MUST BE THEM. THE BAND THAT DEBUTED ON THE SAME DAY SHO FUWA'S SINGLE WENT ON SALE.
Yes! Theeeee I'm
Yeeeeees!
I'm so in love with them!
Cheers to fresh and yummy guys!
OH... I KNOW THAT BAND TOO.
I SAW THEM ALL OVER ON THE MORNING SHOWS.
THEIR DEBUT SINGLE...
...BEAT SHO FUWA'S SINGLE AND IS #1 ON THE SALES CHARTS.
Riiiiiight!
A ONE-TWO finish!
The guys I love lined up together! Way to go, my darlings!
....
UM...
WHAT WAS THE BAND NAME?
halt
Yes?
snort

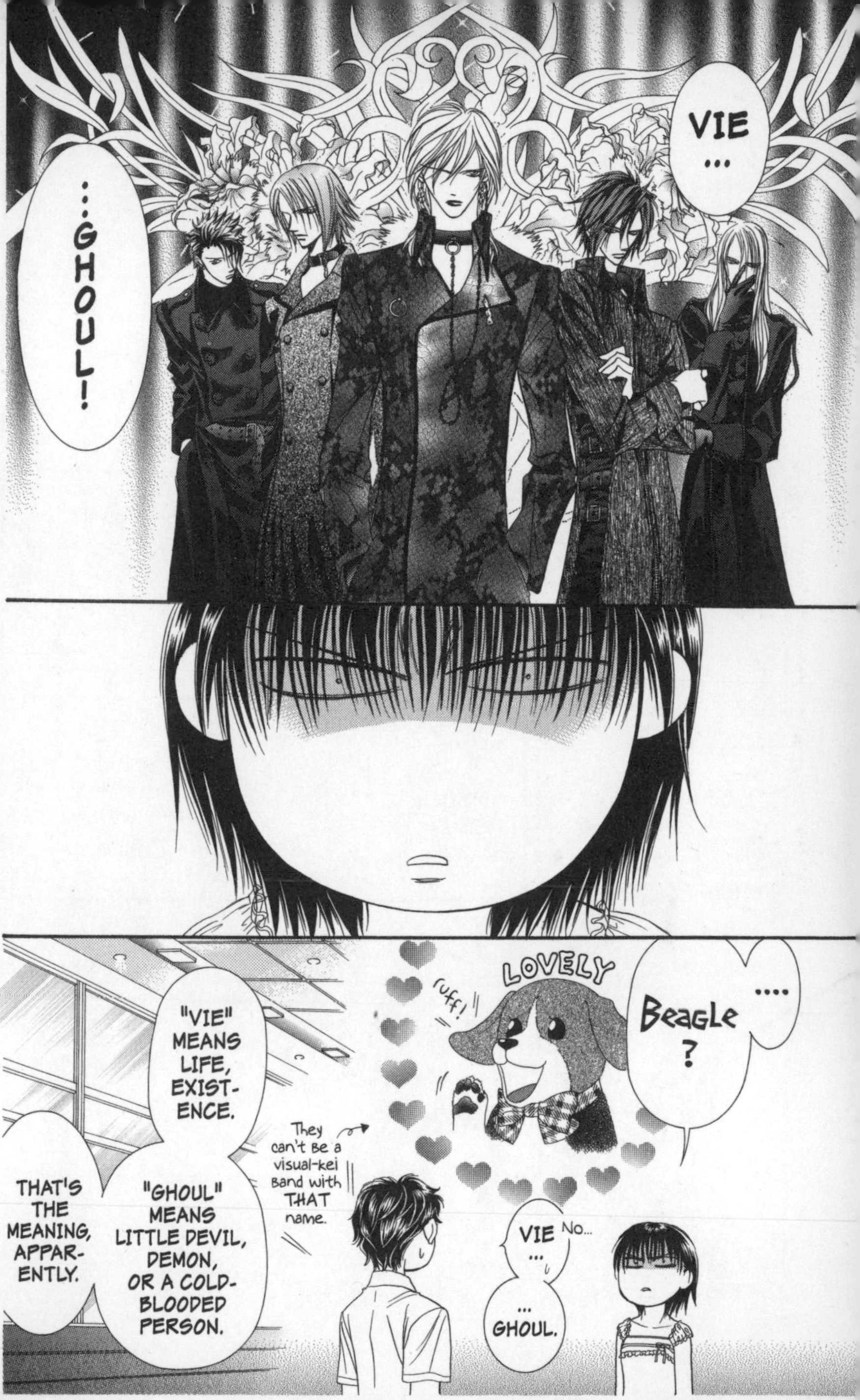
VIE ...
...GHOUL!
.... Beagle?
LOVELY
ruff!
They can't be a visual-kei band with THAT name.
VIE ...
... GHOUL.
No...
"VIE" MEANS LIFE, EXISTENCE.
"GHOUL" MEANS LITTLE DEVIL, DEMON, OR A COLD-BLOODED PERSON.
THAT'S THE MEANING, APPARENTLY.

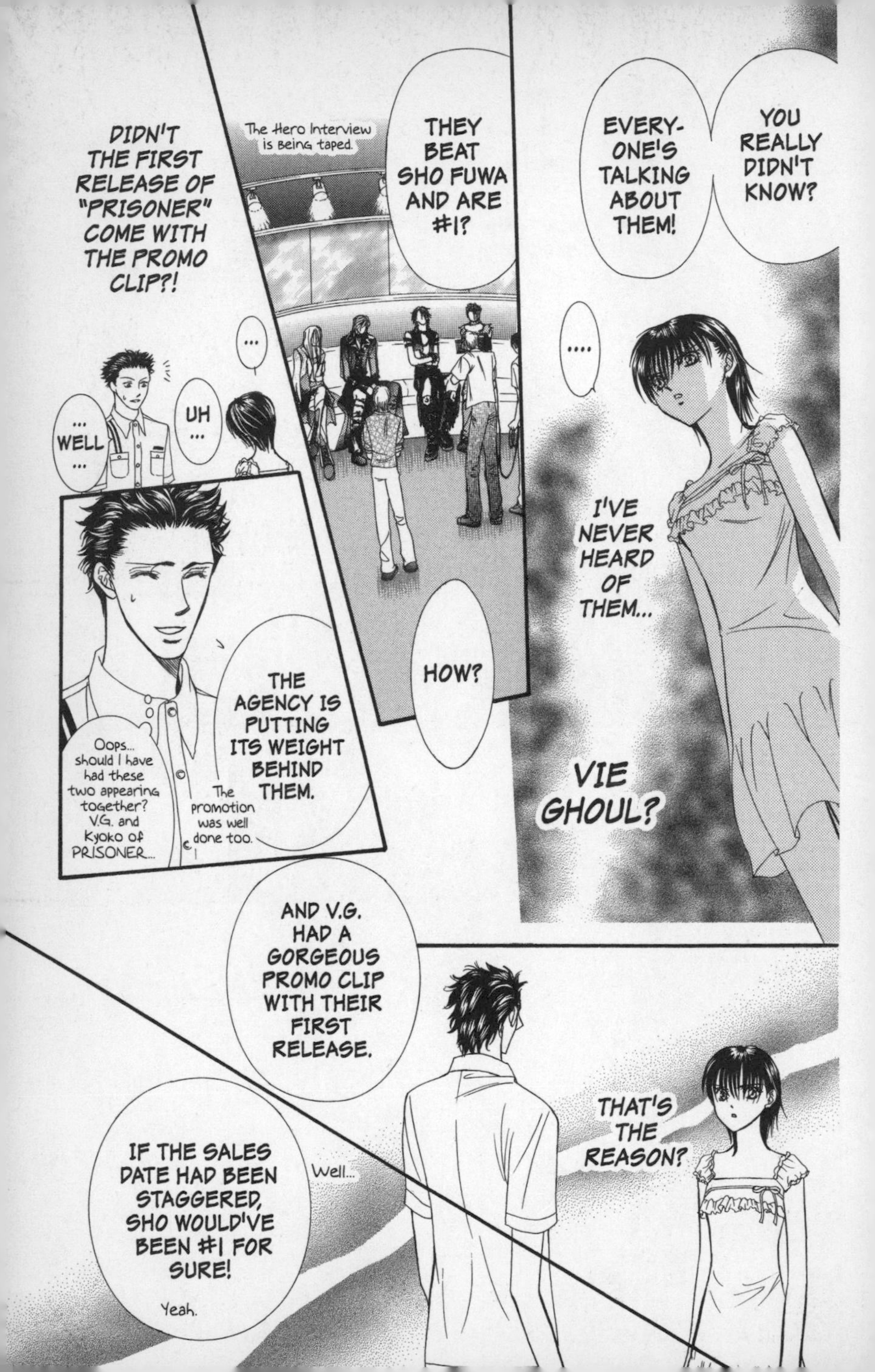
YOU REALLY DIDN'T KNOW?
EVERY-ONE'S TALKING ABOUT THEM!
....
I'VE NEVER HEARD OF THEM...
VIE GHOUL?
The Hero Interview is being taped.
THEY BEAT SHO FUWA AND ARE #1?
...
HOW?
DIDN'T THE FIRST RELEASE OF "PRISONER" COME WITH THE PROMO CLIP?!
UH ...
... WELL ...
THE AGENCY IS PUTTING ITS WEIGHT BEHIND THEM.
The promotion was well done too.
Oops... should I have had these two appearing together? V.G. and Kyoko of PRISONER...
AND V.G. HAD A GORGEOUS PROMO CLIP WITH THEIR FIRST RELEASE.
THAT'S THE REASON?
Well...
IF THE SALES DATE HAD BEEN STAGGERED, SHO WOULD'VE BEEN #1 FOR SURE!
Yeah.

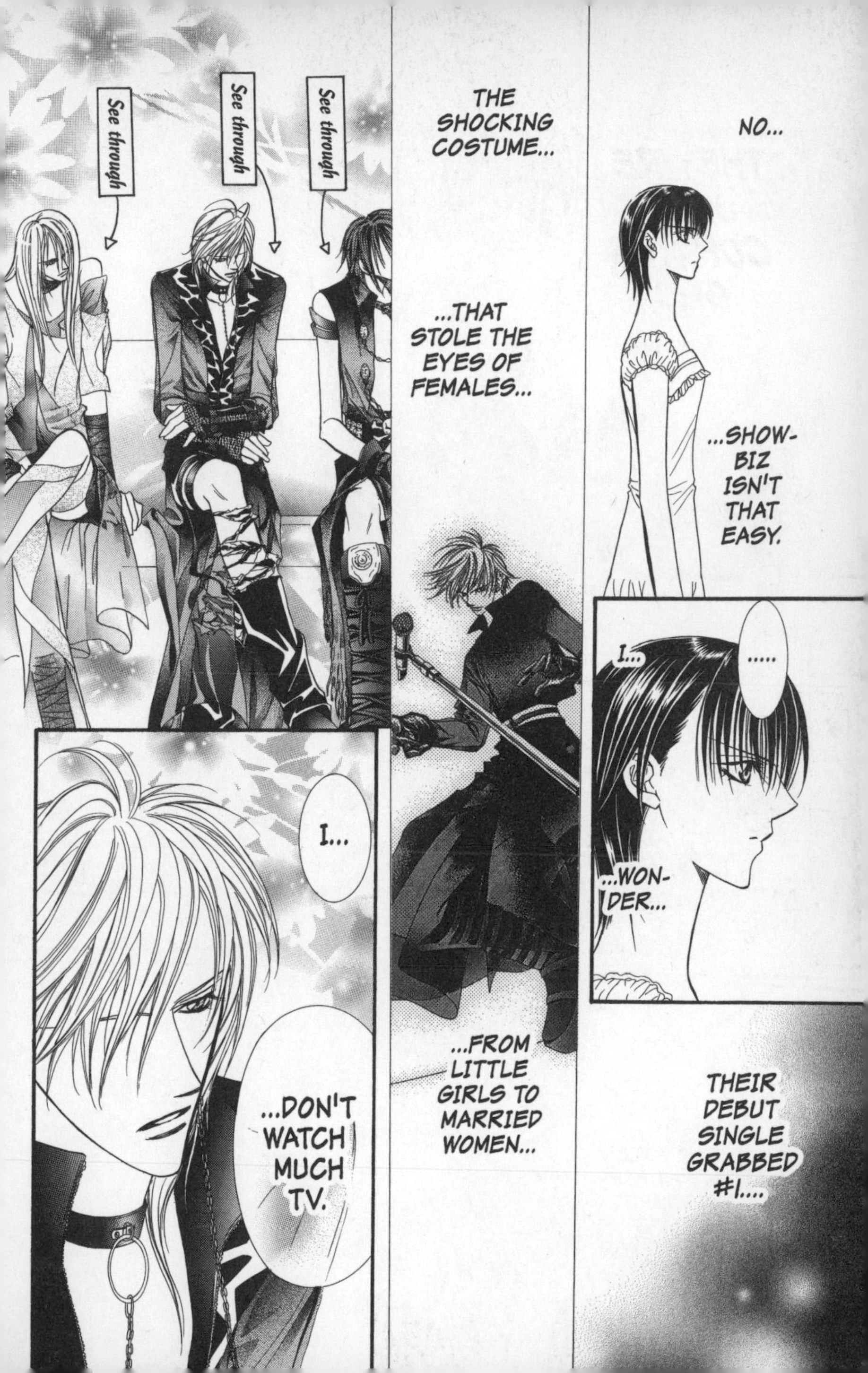
NO...
...SHOW-BIZ ISN'T THAT EASY.
.....
I...
...WON-DER...
THEIR DEBUT SINGLE GRABBED #1....
THE SHOCKING COSTUME...
...THAT STOLE THE EYES OF FEMALES...
...FROM LITTLE GIRLS TO MARRIED WOMEN...
See through
See through
See through
I...
...DON'T WATCH MUCH TV.

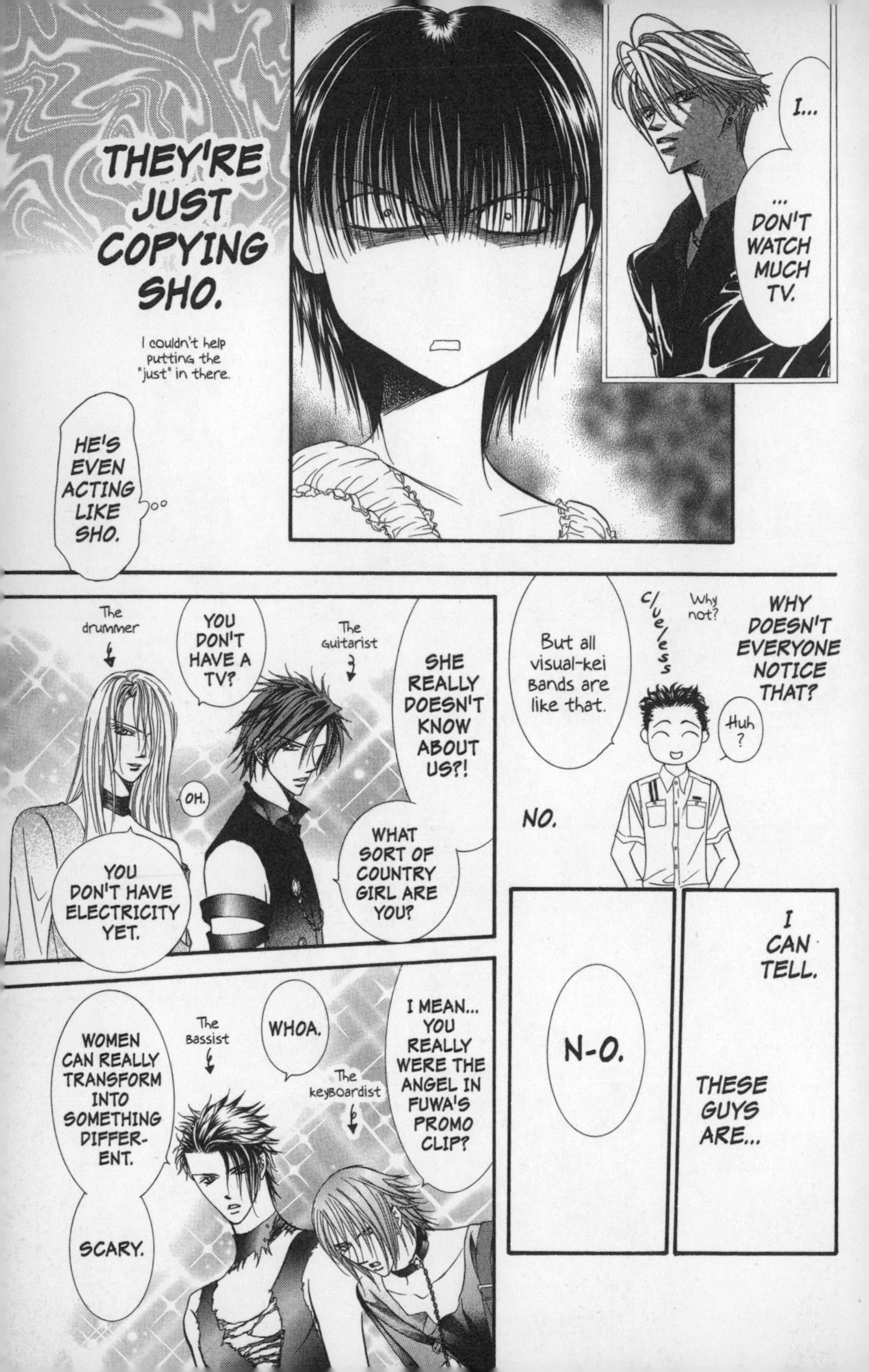
I...
...DON'T WATCH MUCH TV.
THEY'RE JUST COPYING SHO.
I couldn't help putting the "just" in there.
HE'S EVEN ACTING LIKE SHO.
WHY DOESN'T EVERYONE NOTICE THAT?
Why not?
Clueless
Huh?
But all visual-kei Bands are like that.
NO.
SHE REALLY DOESN'T KNOW ABOUT US?!
WHAT SORT OF COUNTRY GIRL ARE YOU?
The Guitarist
YOU DON'T HAVE A TV?
The drummer
OH.
YOU DON'T HAVE ELECTRICITY YET.
I CAN TELL.
THESE GUYS ARE...
N-O.
I MEAN... YOU REALLY WERE THE ANGEL IN FUWA'S PROMO CLIP?
The keyBoardist
WHOA.
The Bassist
WOMEN CAN REALLY TRANSFORM INTO SOMETHING DIFFER-ENT.
SCARY.

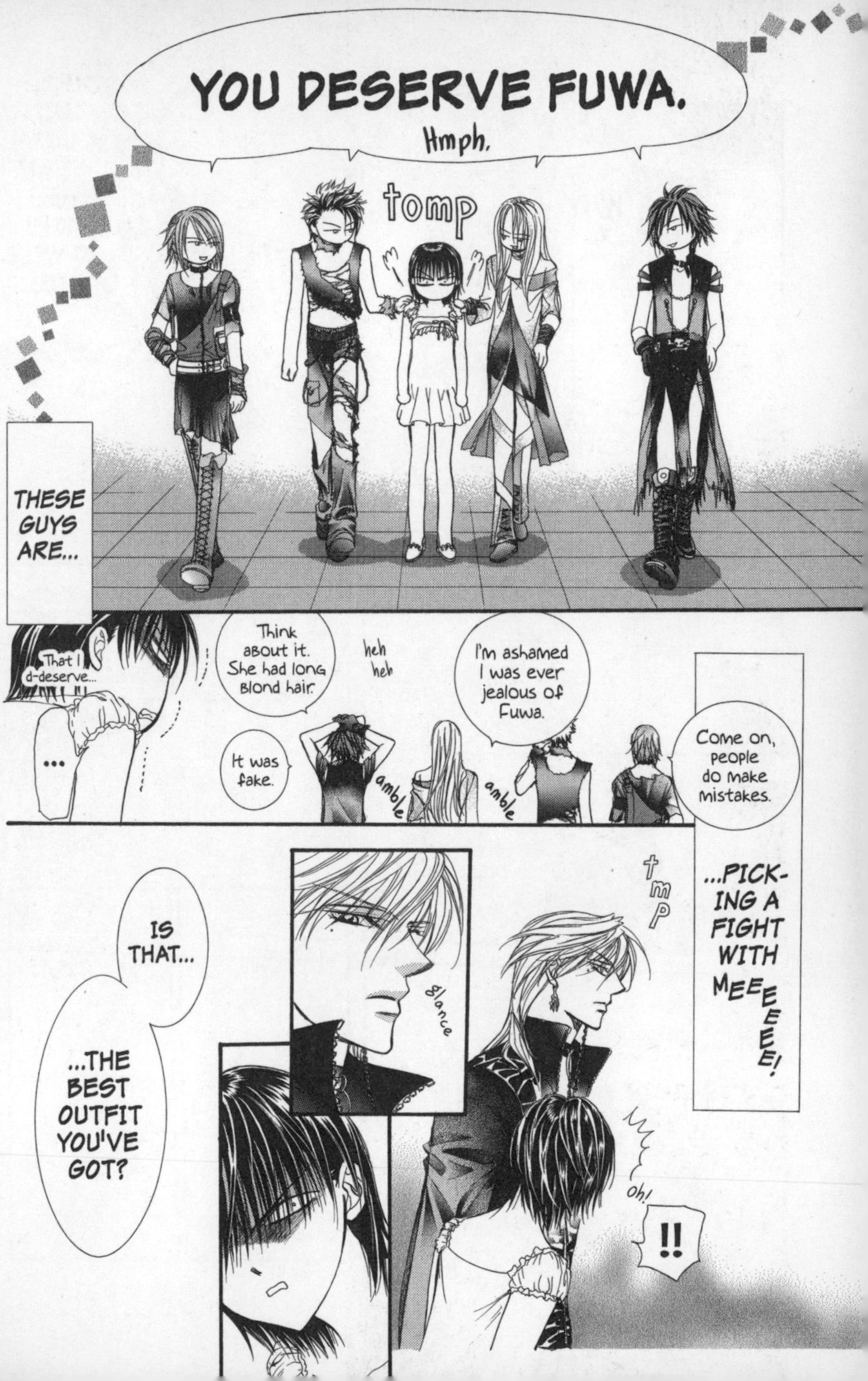
YOU DESERVE FUWA.
Hmph.
tomp
THESE GUYS ARE...
Come on, people do make mistakes.
I'm ashamed I was ever jealous of Fuwa.
heh heh
Think about it. She had long blond hair.
It was fake.
amble
amble
That I d-deserve...
...
...PICKING A FIGHT WITH MEEEEEEE!
tmp
glance
IS THAT...
...THE BEST OUTFIT YOU'VE GOT?
oh!
!!

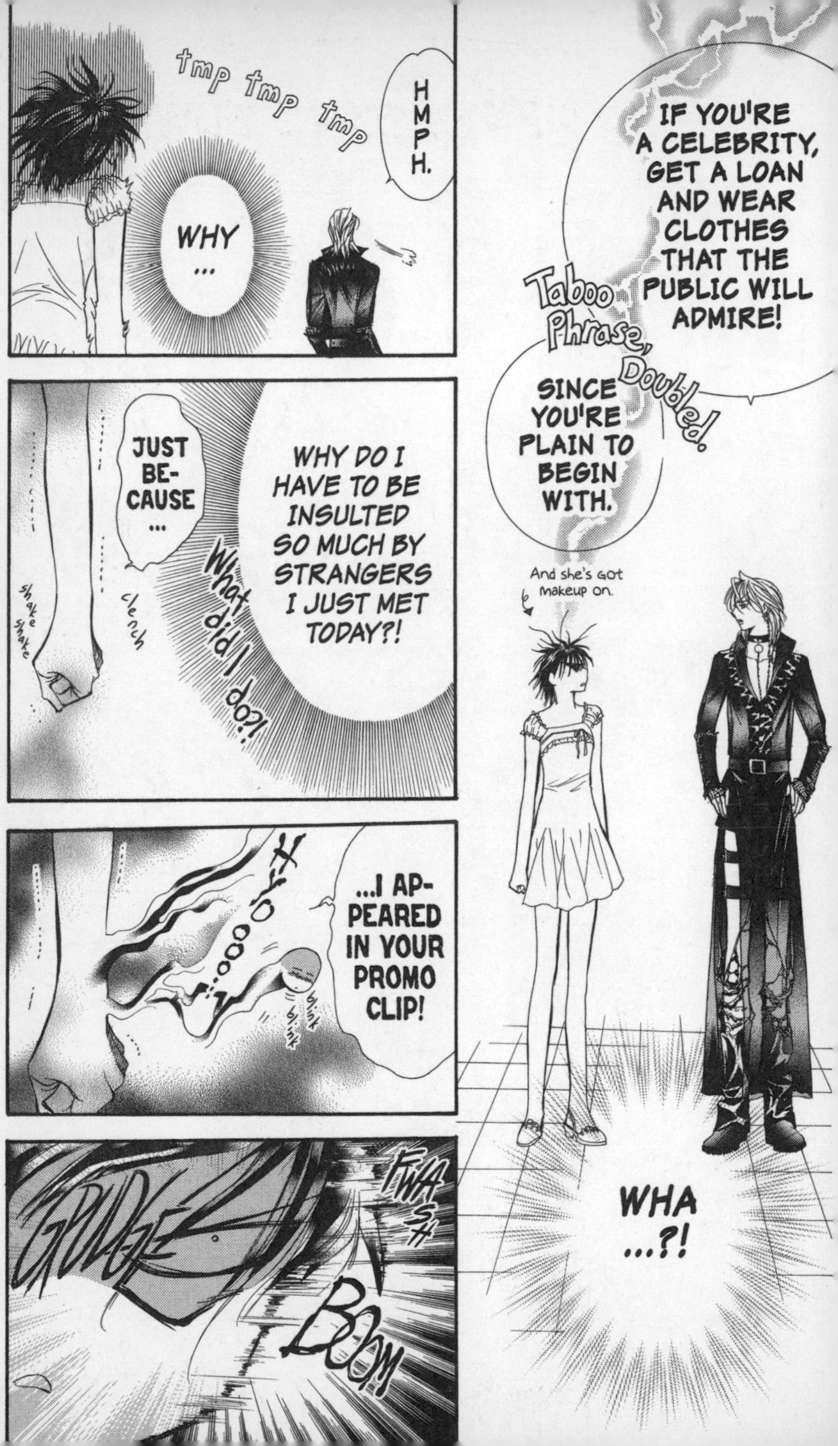
IF YOU'RE A CELEBRITY, GET A LOAN AND WEAR CLOTHES THAT THE PUBLIC WILL ADMIRE!
Taboo Phrase, Doubled!
SINCE YOU'RE PLAIN TO BEGIN WITH.
And she's got makeup on.
WHA ...?!
HMPH.
tmp tmp tmp
WHY ...
WHY DO I HAVE TO BE INSULTED SO MUCH BY STRANGERS I JUST MET TODAY?!
What did I do?!
JUST BE-CAUSE ...
clench
shake shake
...I AP-PEARED IN YOUR PROMO CLIP!
Hyoooo...
blink blink
FWASH
BOOM

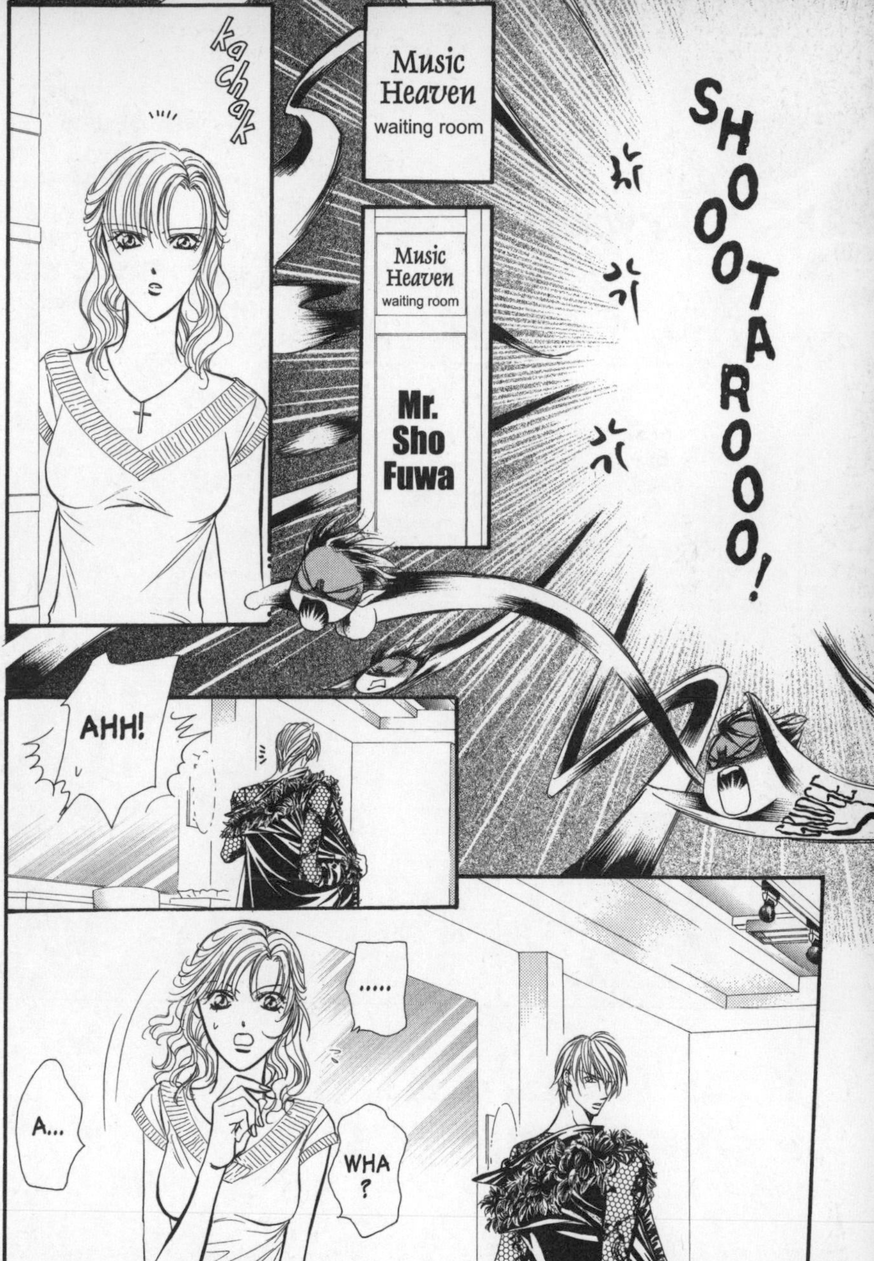
Music Heaven waiting room
Music Heaven waiting room
Mr. Sho Fuwa
SHOOOTAROOOO!
ka chak
AHH!
.....
WHA ?
A...

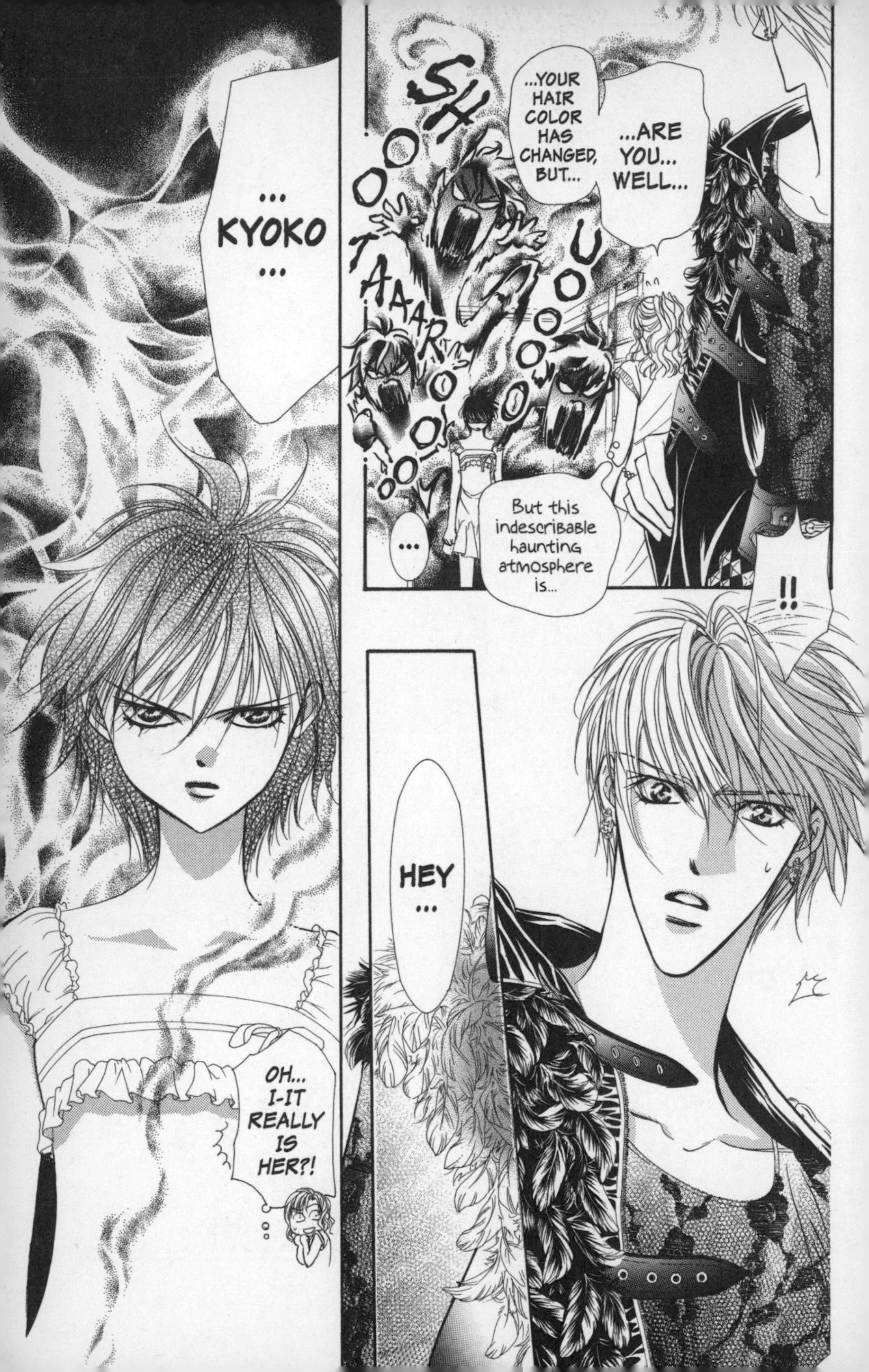
...ARE YOU... WELL...
...YOUR HAIR COLOR HAS CHANGED, BUT...
But this indescribable haunting atmosphere is...
...
!!
HEY ...
... KYOKO ...
OH... I-IT REALLY IS HER?!

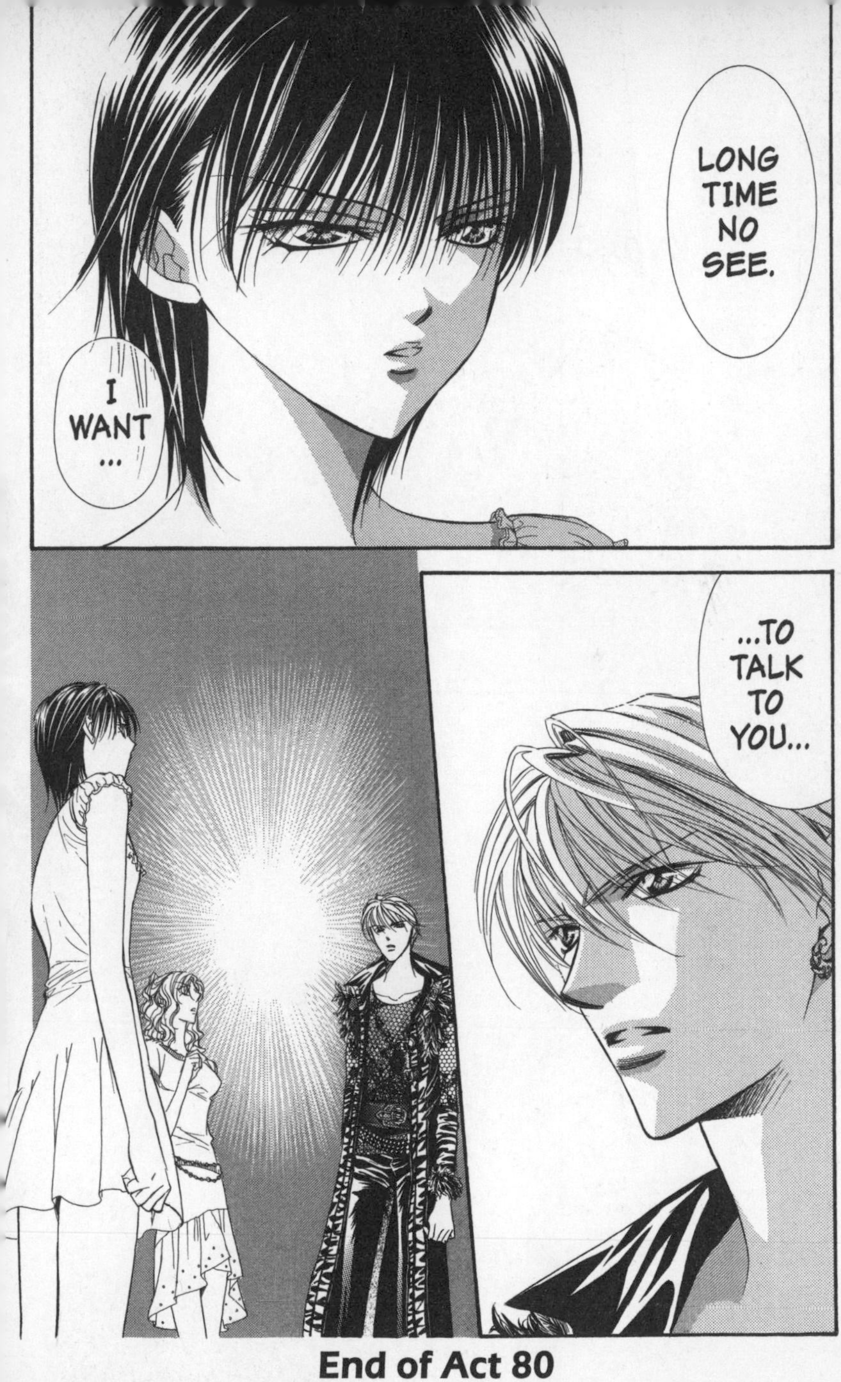
LONG TIME NO SEE.
I WANT...
...TO TALK TO YOU...

End of Act 80

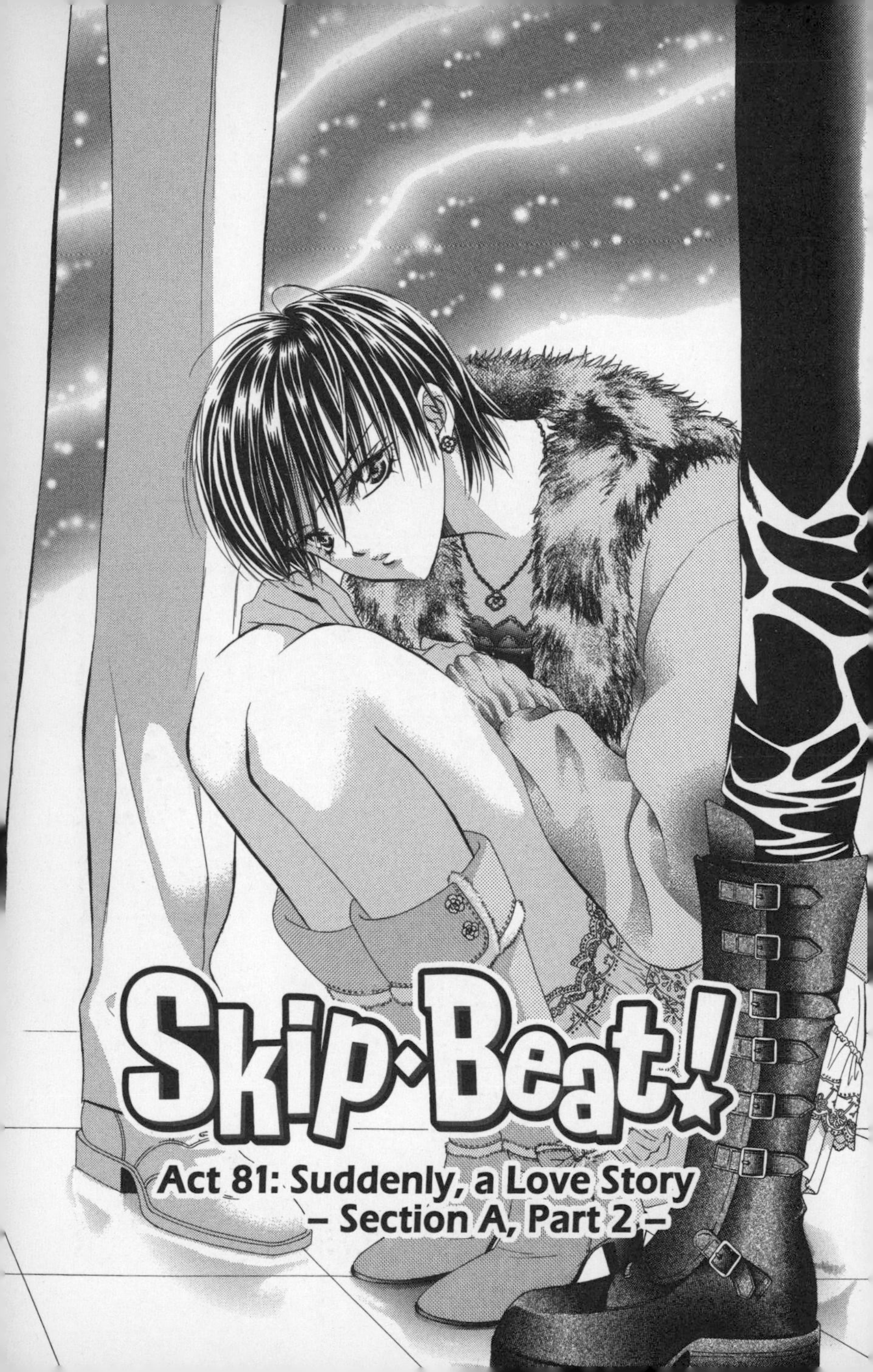
Skip·Beat!
Act 81: Suddenly, a Love Story
– Section A, Part 2 –

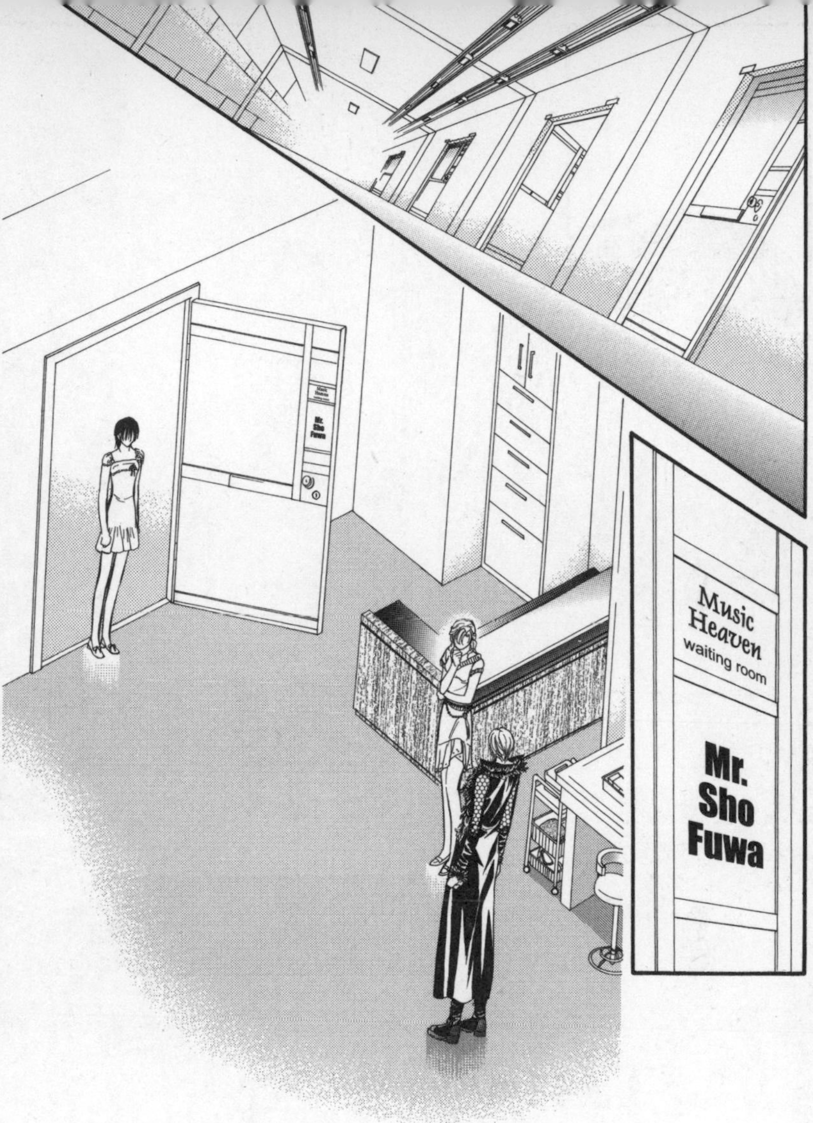
Music Heaven
waiting room
Mr. Sho Fuwa

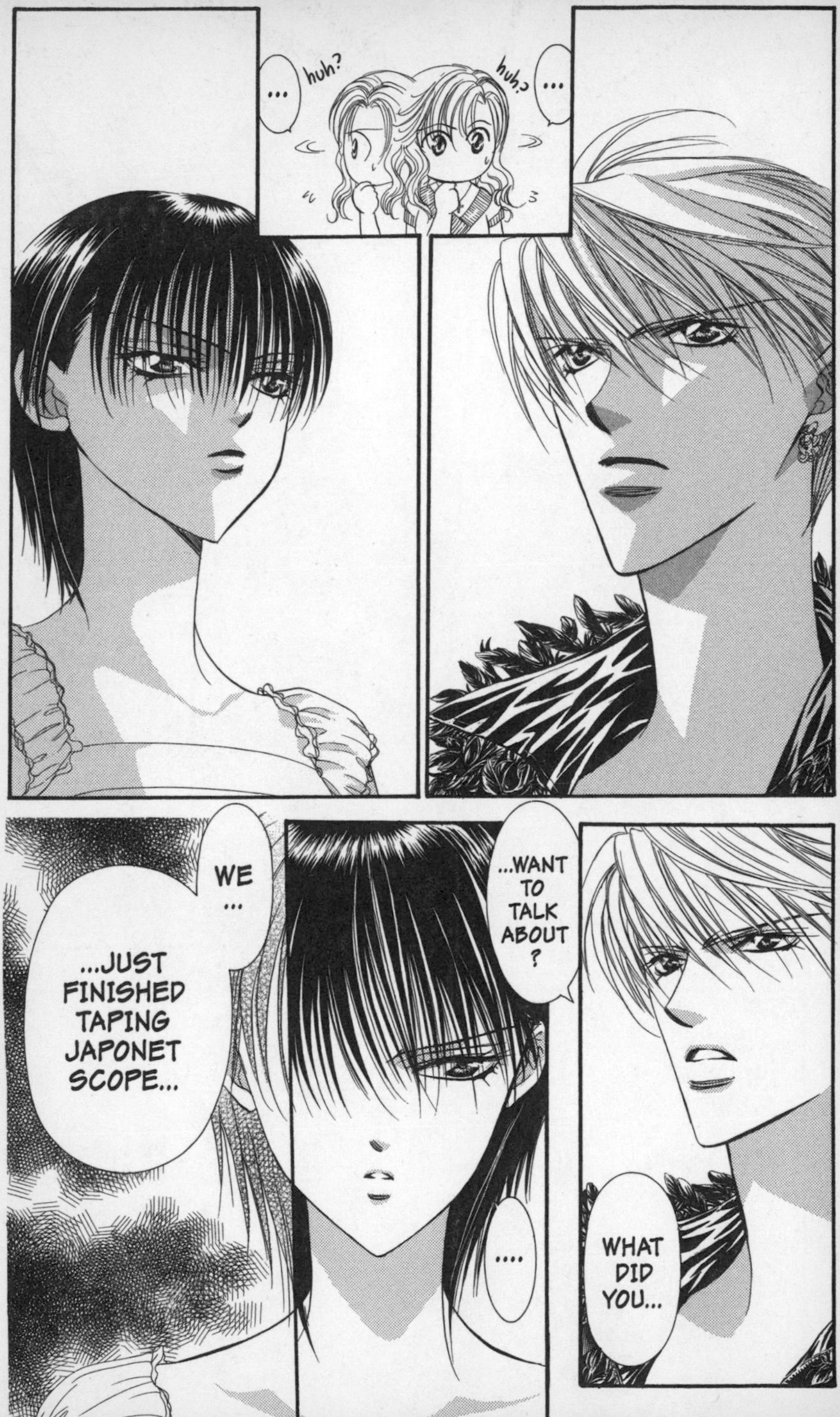
huh?
...
...
huh?
WHAT DID YOU...
...WANT TO TALK ABOUT?
....
WE ...
...JUST FINISHED TAPING JAPONET SCOPE...

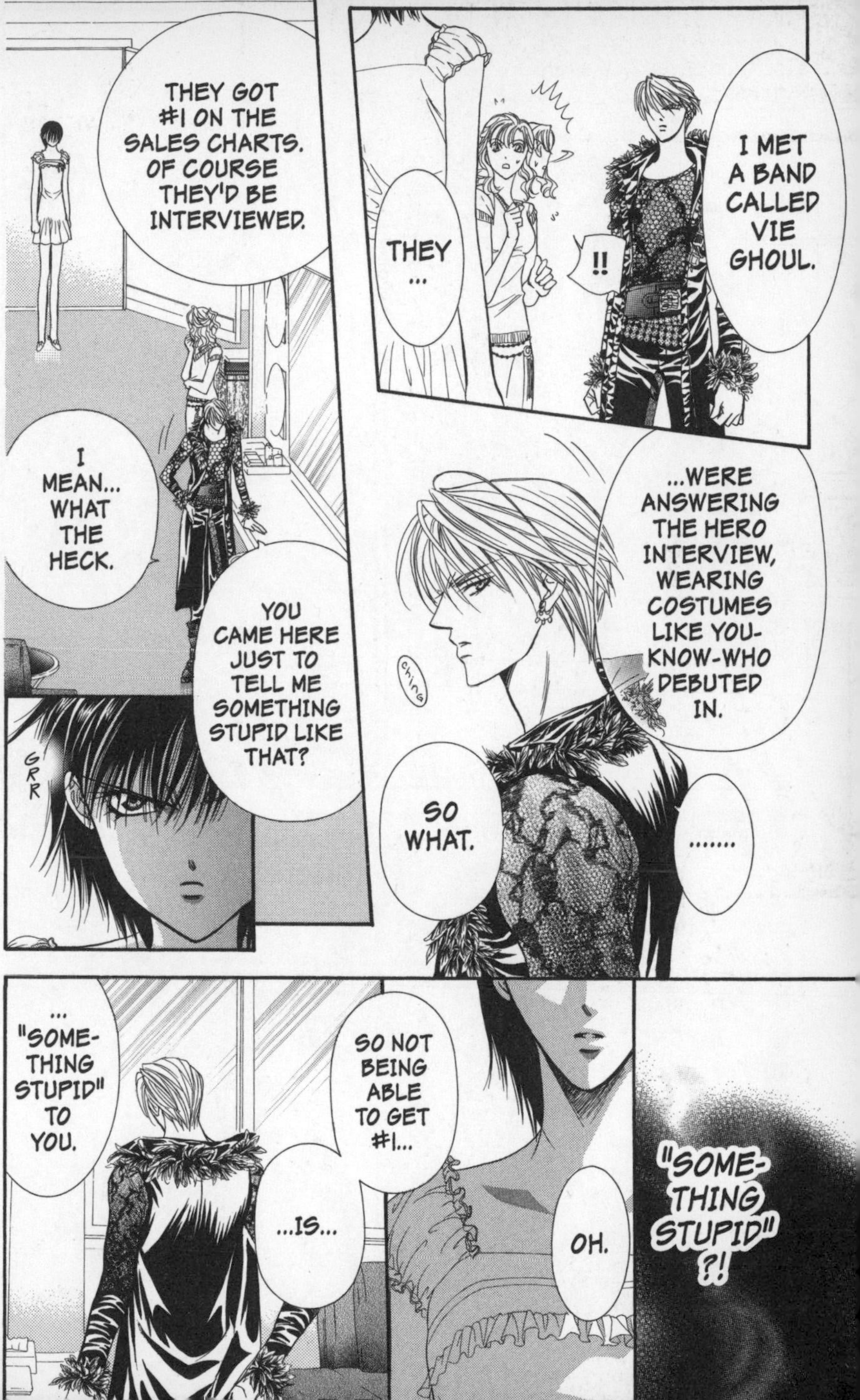
I MET A BAND CALLED VIE GHOUL.
!!
THEY ...
...WERE ANSWERING THE HERO INTERVIEW, WEARING COSTUMES LIKE YOU-KNOW-WHO DEBUTED IN.
ching
....
SO WHAT.
THEY GOT #1 ON THE SALES CHARTS. OF COURSE THEY'D BE INTERVIEWED.
I MEAN... WHAT THE HECK.
YOU CAME HERE JUST TO TELL ME SOMETHING STUPID LIKE THAT?
GRR
"SOME-THING STUPID"?!
OH.
SO NOT BEING ABLE TO GET #1...
...IS...
... "SOME-THING STUPID" TO YOU.

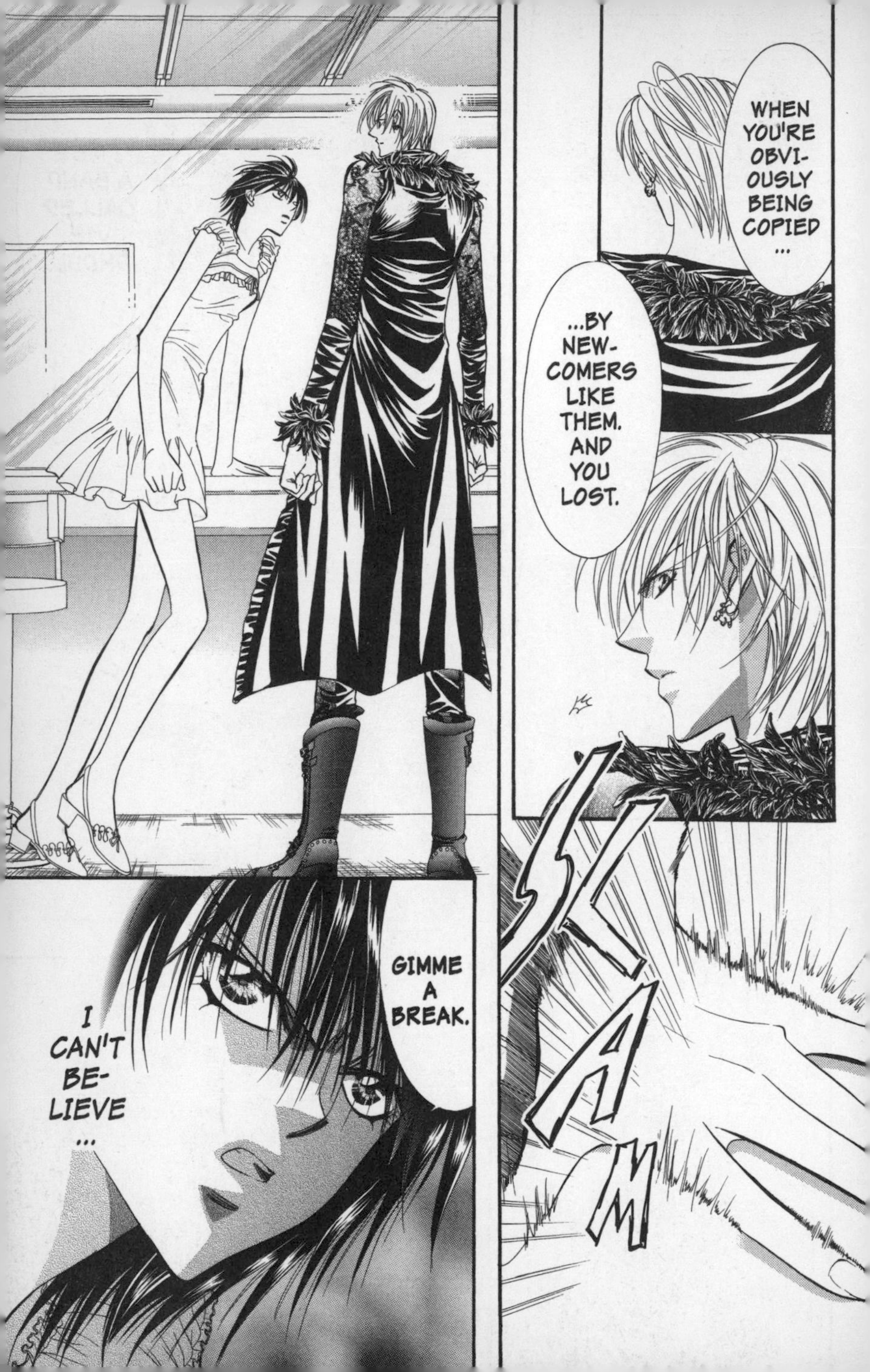
WHEN YOU'RE OBVIOUSLY BEING COPIED...
...BY NEWCOMERS LIKE THEM. AND YOU LOST.
SLAM
GIMME A BREAK.
I CAN'T BELIEVE...

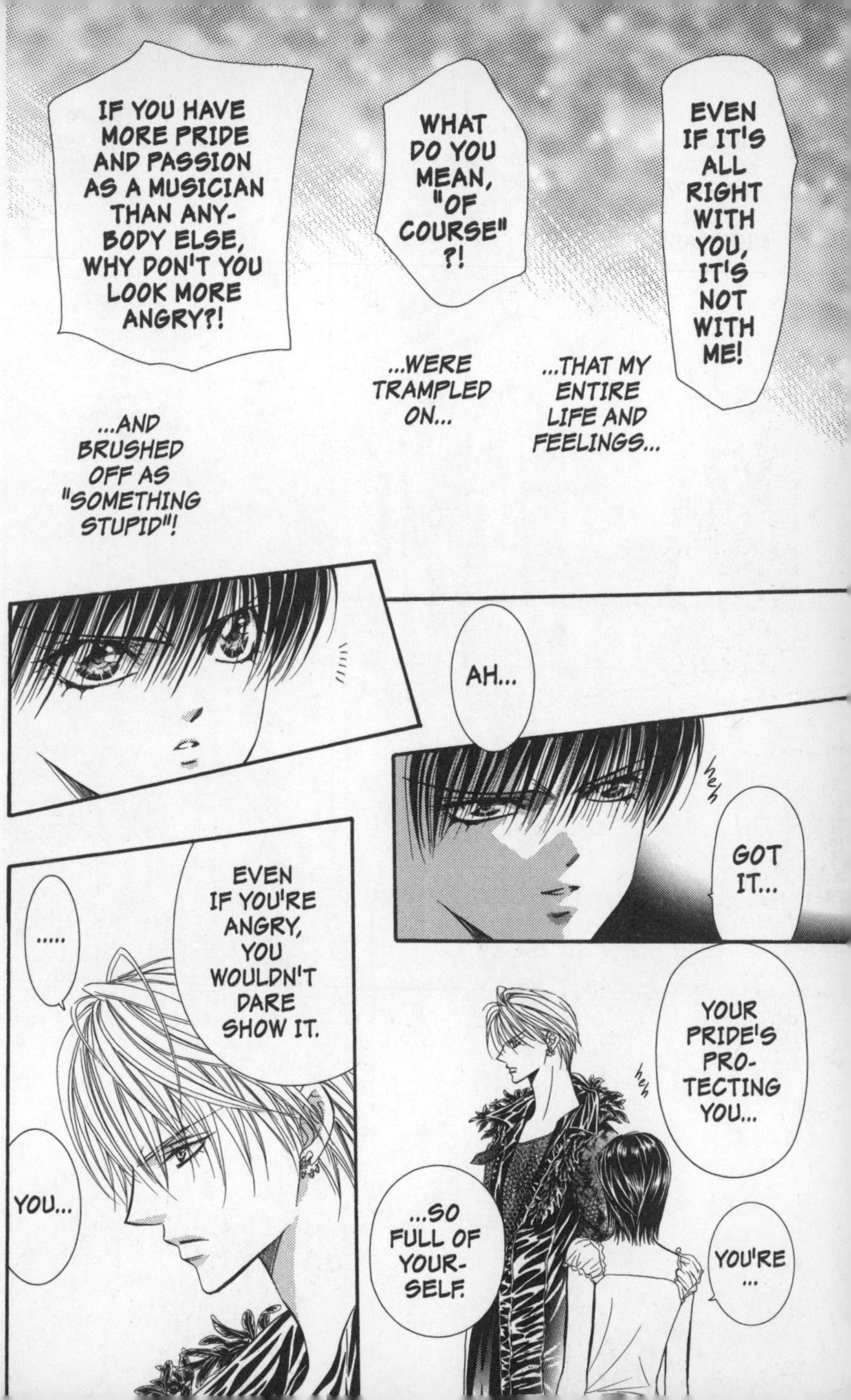
EVEN IF IT'S ALL RIGHT WITH YOU, IT'S NOT WITH ME!
...THAT MY ENTIRE LIFE AND FEELINGS...
...WERE TRAMPLED ON...
...AND BRUSHED OFF AS "SOMETHING STUPID"!
WHAT DO YOU MEAN, "OF COURSE"?!
IF YOU HAVE MORE PRIDE AND PASSION AS A MUSICIAN THAN ANY-BODY ELSE, WHY DON'T YOU LOOK MORE ANGRY?!
AH...
heh
GOT IT...
heh
YOUR PRIDE'S PRO-TECTING YOU...
YOU'RE...
...SO FULL OF YOUR-SELF.
EVEN IF YOU'RE ANGRY, YOU WOULDN'T DARE SHOW IT.
.....
YOU...

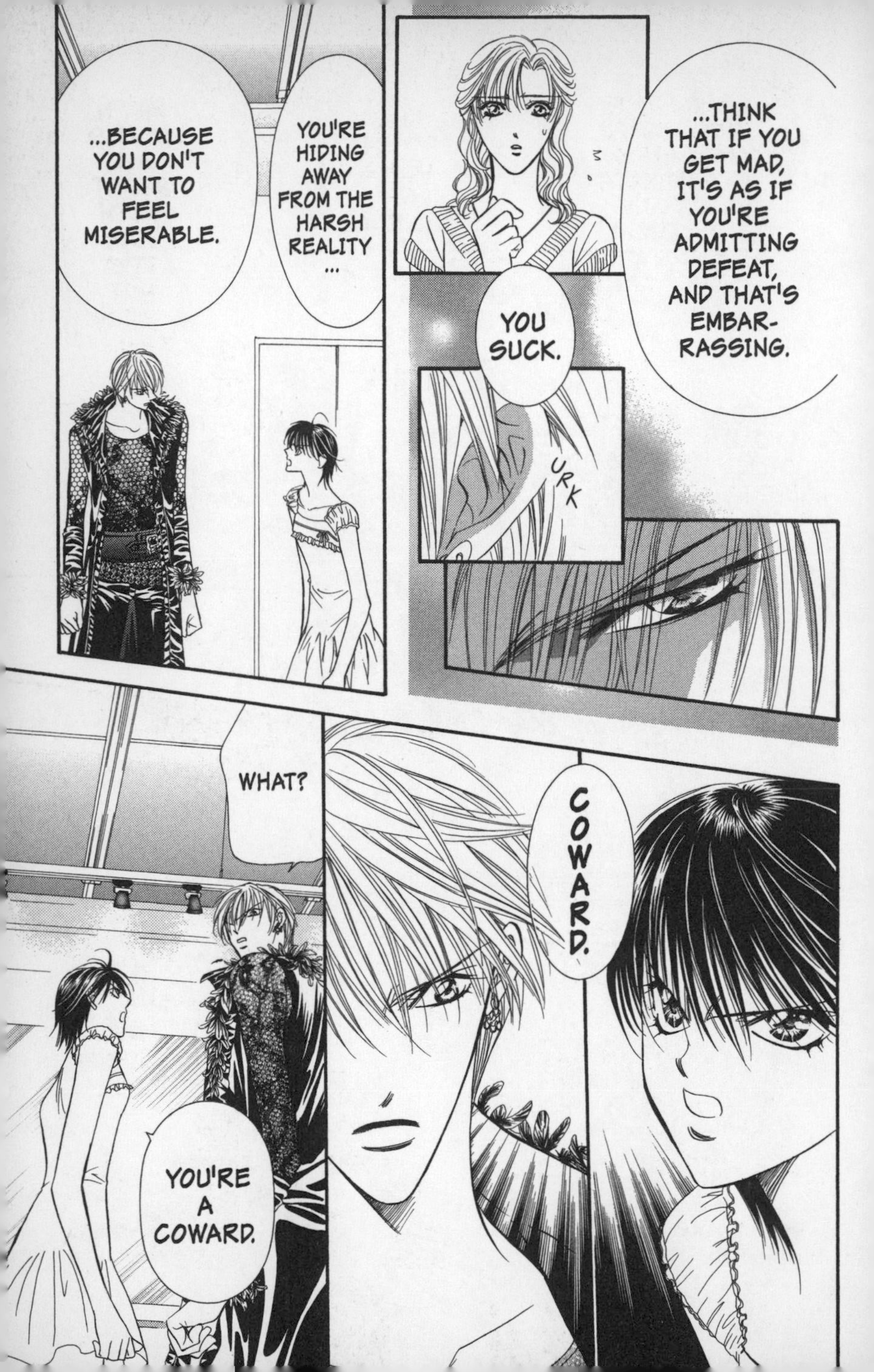
...THINK THAT IF YOU GET MAD, IT'S AS IF YOU'RE ADMITTING DEFEAT, AND THAT'S EMBARRASSING.
YOU SUCK.
URK
YOU'RE HIDING AWAY FROM THE HARSH REALITY ...
...BECAUSE YOU DON'T WANT TO FEEL MISERABLE.
COWARD.
WHAT?
YOU'RE A COWARD.

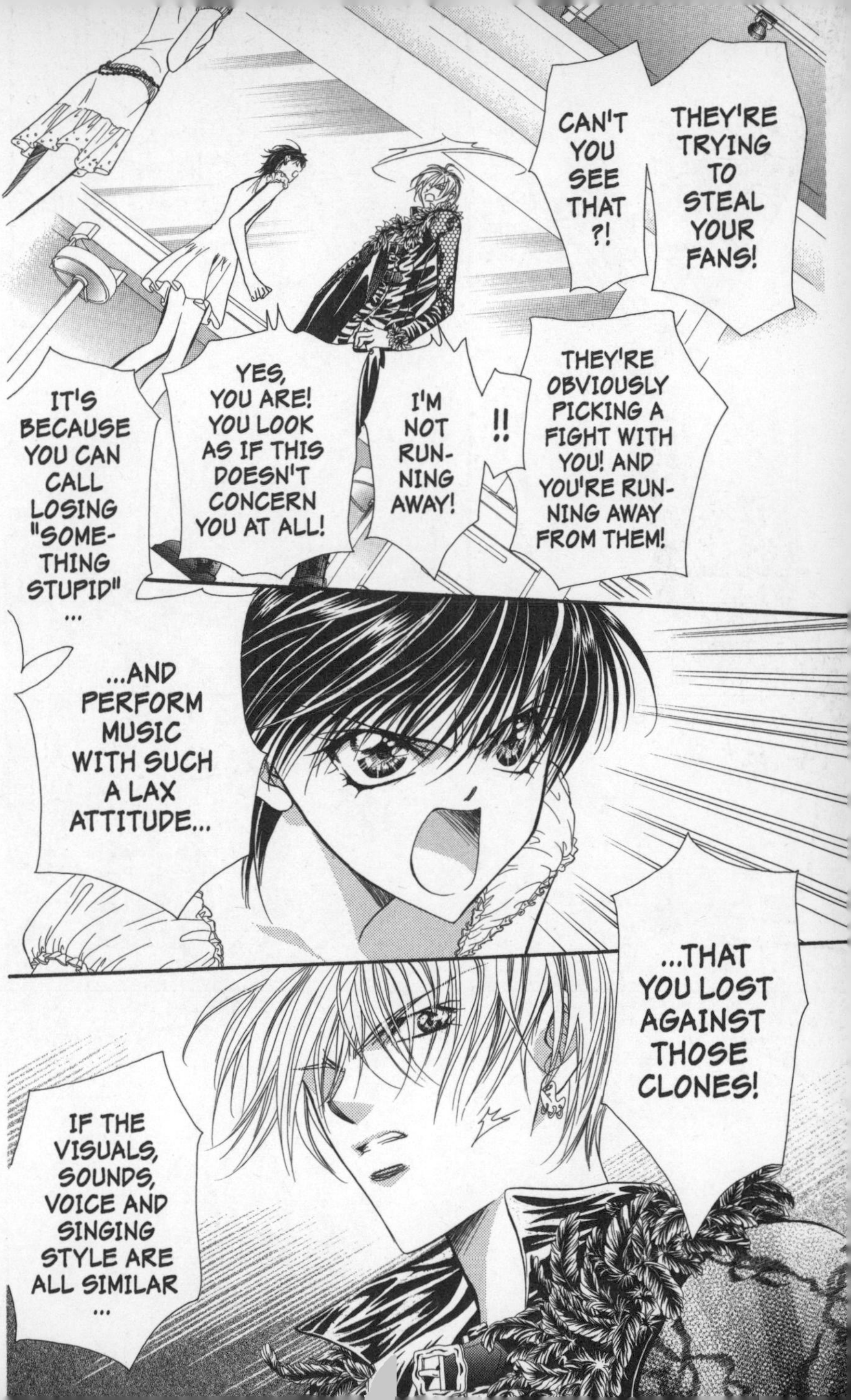
THEY'RE TRYING TO STEAL YOUR FANS!
CAN'T YOU SEE THAT?!
THEY'RE OBVIOUSLY PICKING A FIGHT WITH YOU! AND YOU'RE RUNNING AWAY FROM THEM!
!!
I'M NOT RUNNING AWAY!
YES, YOU ARE! YOU LOOK AS IF THIS DOESN'T CONCERN YOU AT ALL!
IT'S BECAUSE YOU CAN CALL LOSING "SOMETHING STUPID"...
...AND PERFORM MUSIC WITH SUCH A LAX ATTITUDE...
...THAT YOU LOST AGAINST THOSE CLONES!
IF THE VISUALS, SOUNDS, VOICE AND SINGING STYLE ARE ALL SIMILAR...

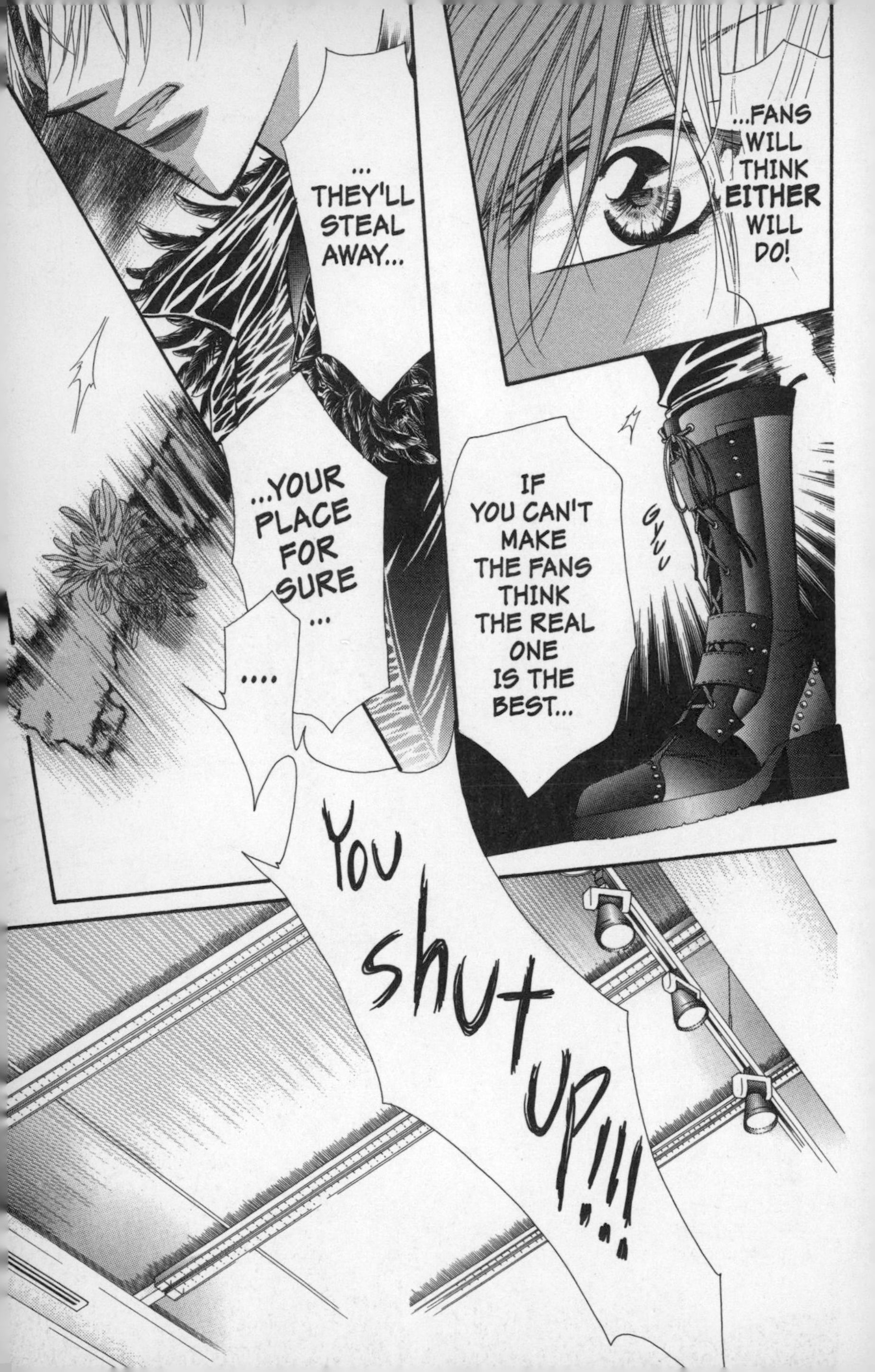
...FANS WILL THINK EITHER WILL DO!
... THEY'LL STEAL AWAY...
IF YOU CAN'T MAKE THE FANS THINK THE REAL ONE IS THE BEST...
GYUU
...YOUR PLACE FOR SURE ...
....
YOU SHUT UP!!!

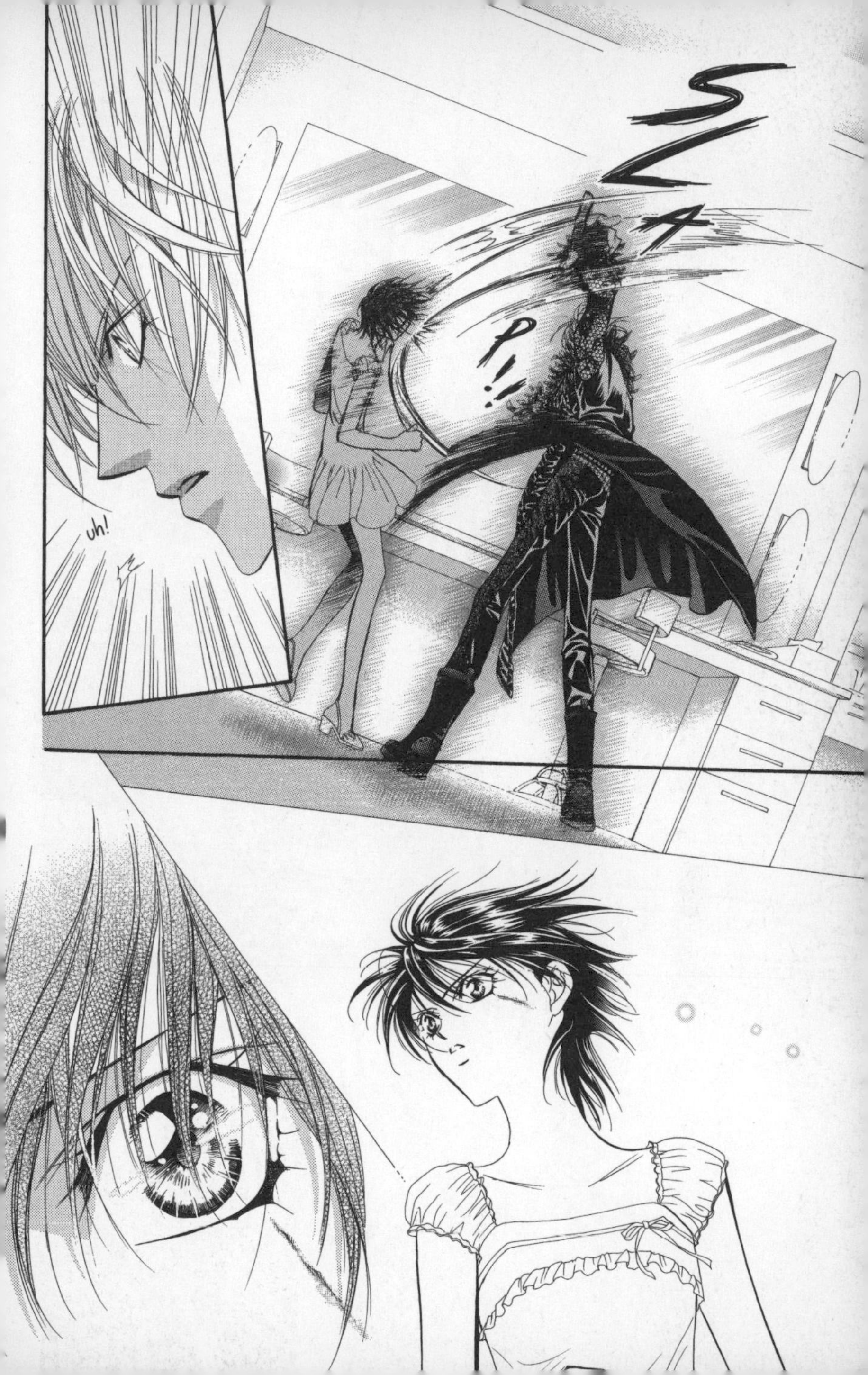
SZA
P!!
uh!

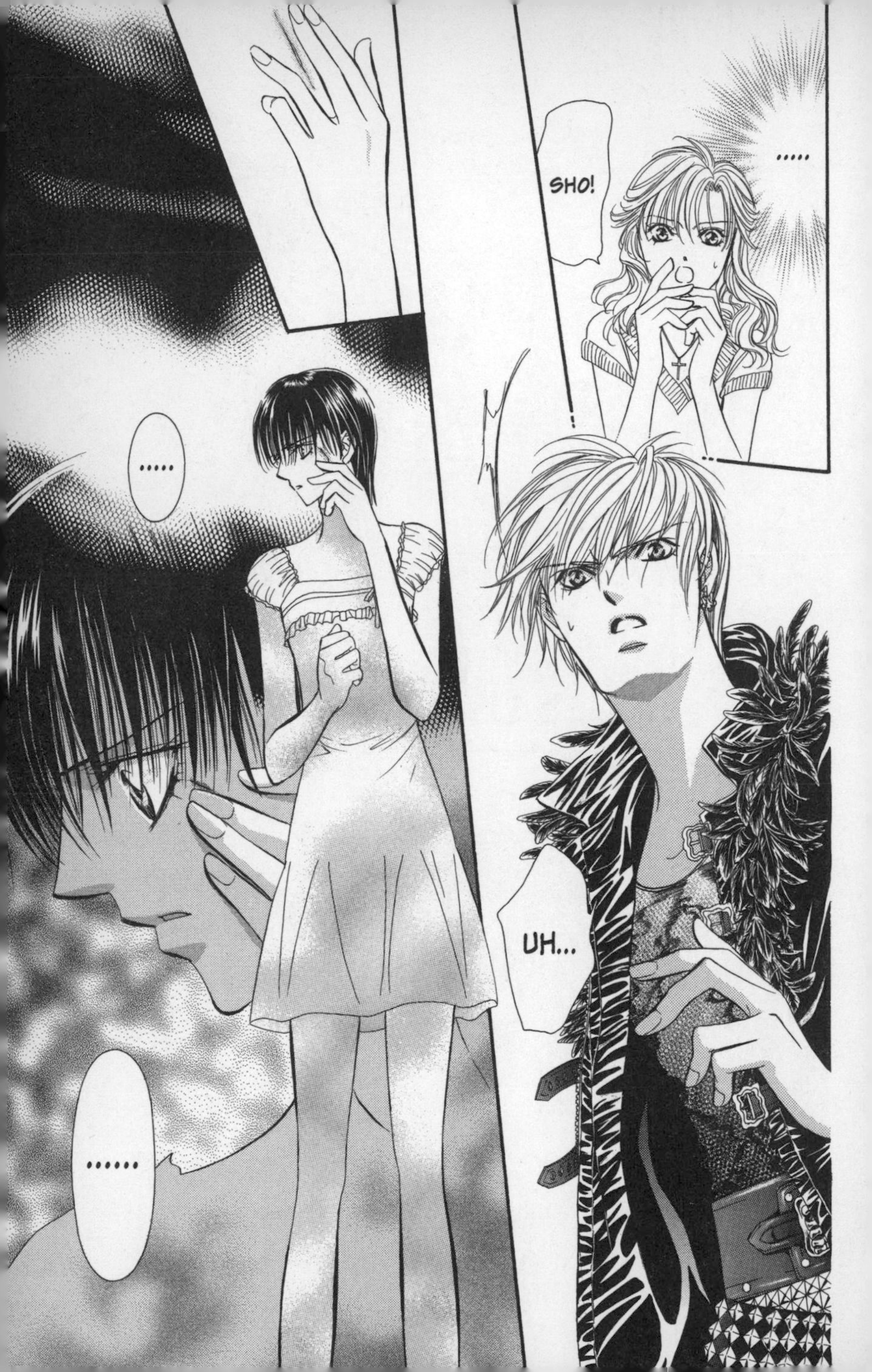
.....
SHO!
UH...
.....
......

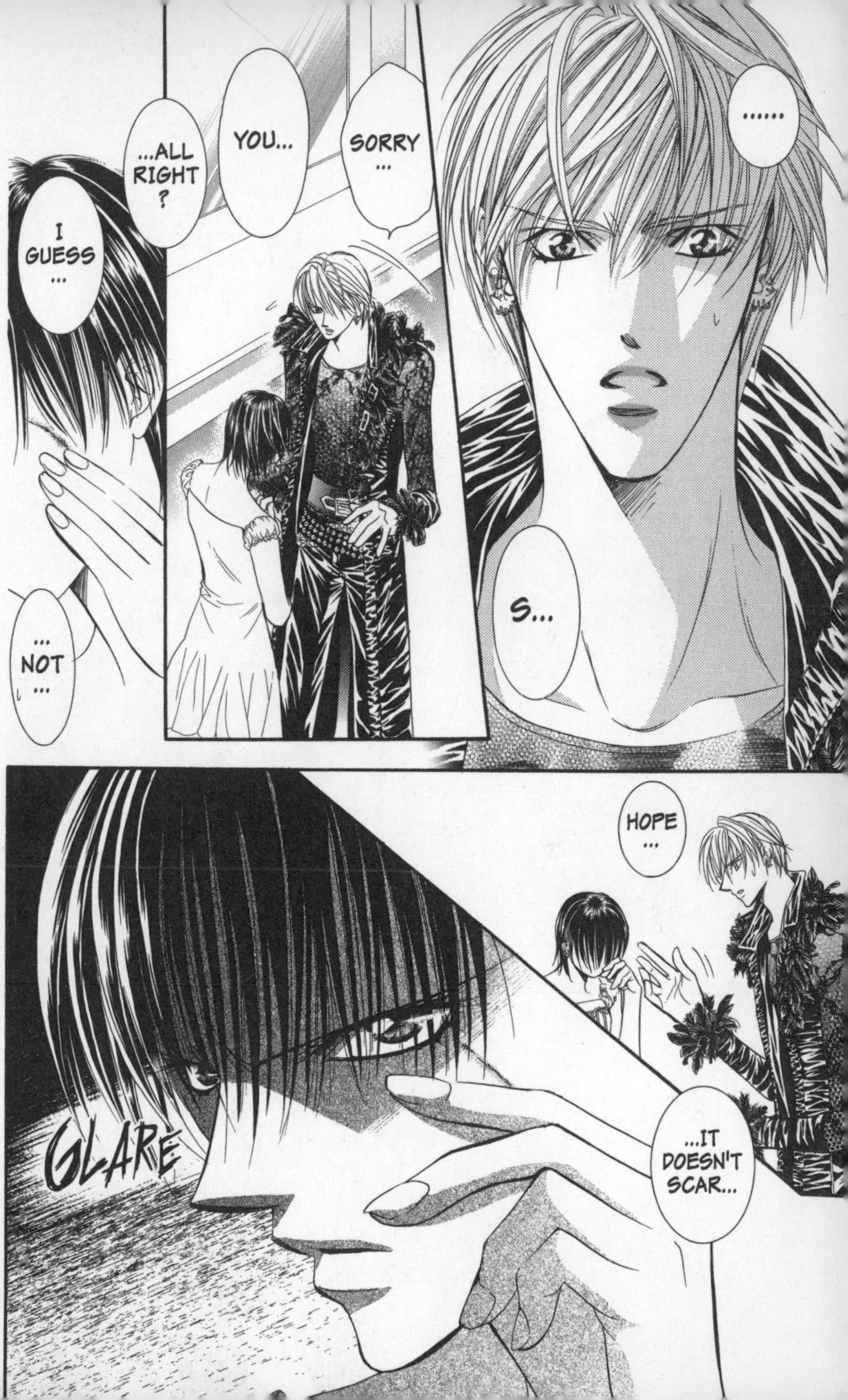
......
S...
SORRY ...
YOU...
...ALL RIGHT ?
I GUESS ...
... NOT ...
HOPE ...
...IT DOESN'T SCAR...
GLARE

I am NOT being spellbound...

I myself...was thinking" what the heck?" the most...so well...I still decided to use PRISONER because... um...there were a lot of readers who really wanted Ren to watch the angel Kyoko!...even during the DARK MOON arc, readers kept asking "When will Ren watch the promo clip?" And when the DARK MOON arc was over, readers hoped "Now Ren will finally watch the angel Kyoko, right?!" ...You people...want the man to watch the angel Kyoko that much?!

The ardent requests went on for so long, I gave in... ...because... as someone who's able to do work because the readers support me, I must do a service to the readers...but things won't turn out sweet as the readers fantasize...that's what I was thinking (then it's a not a service)...and I ended up drawing the scene where Ren watches the angel Kyoko...

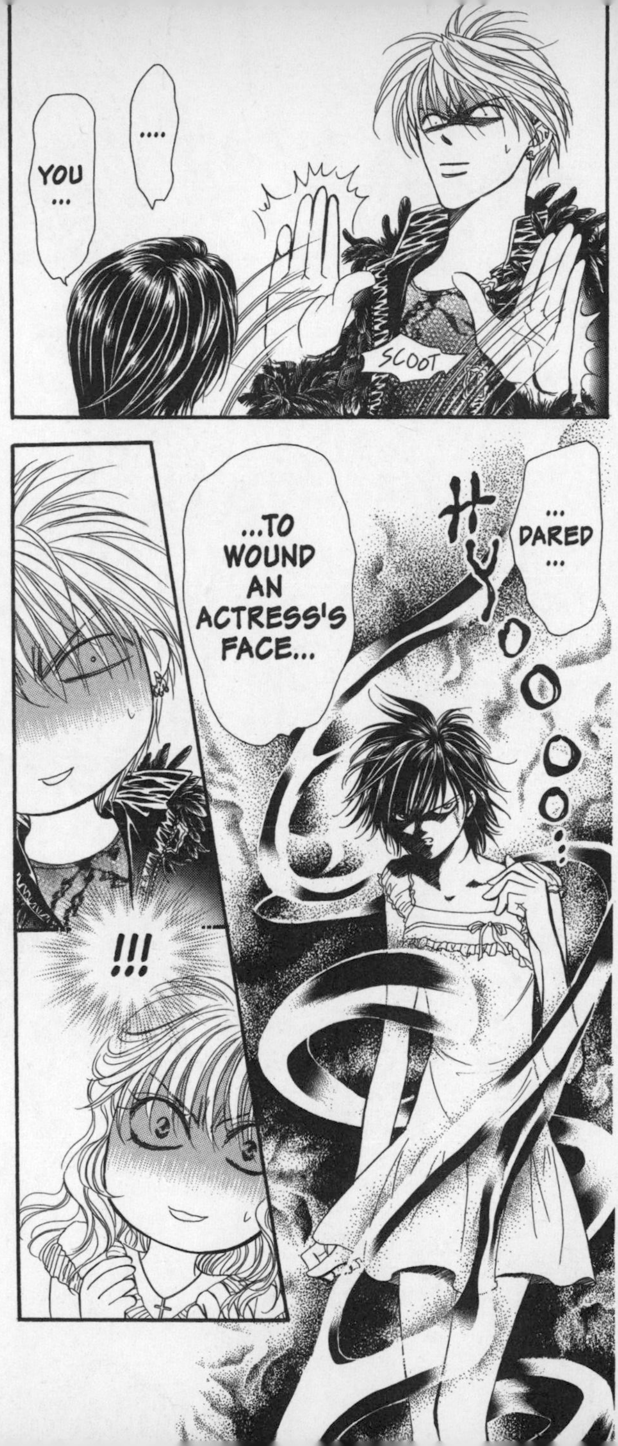
....
YOU ...
SCOOT
... DARED ...
...TO WOUND AN ACTRESS'S FACE...
HYOOOOO...
!!!

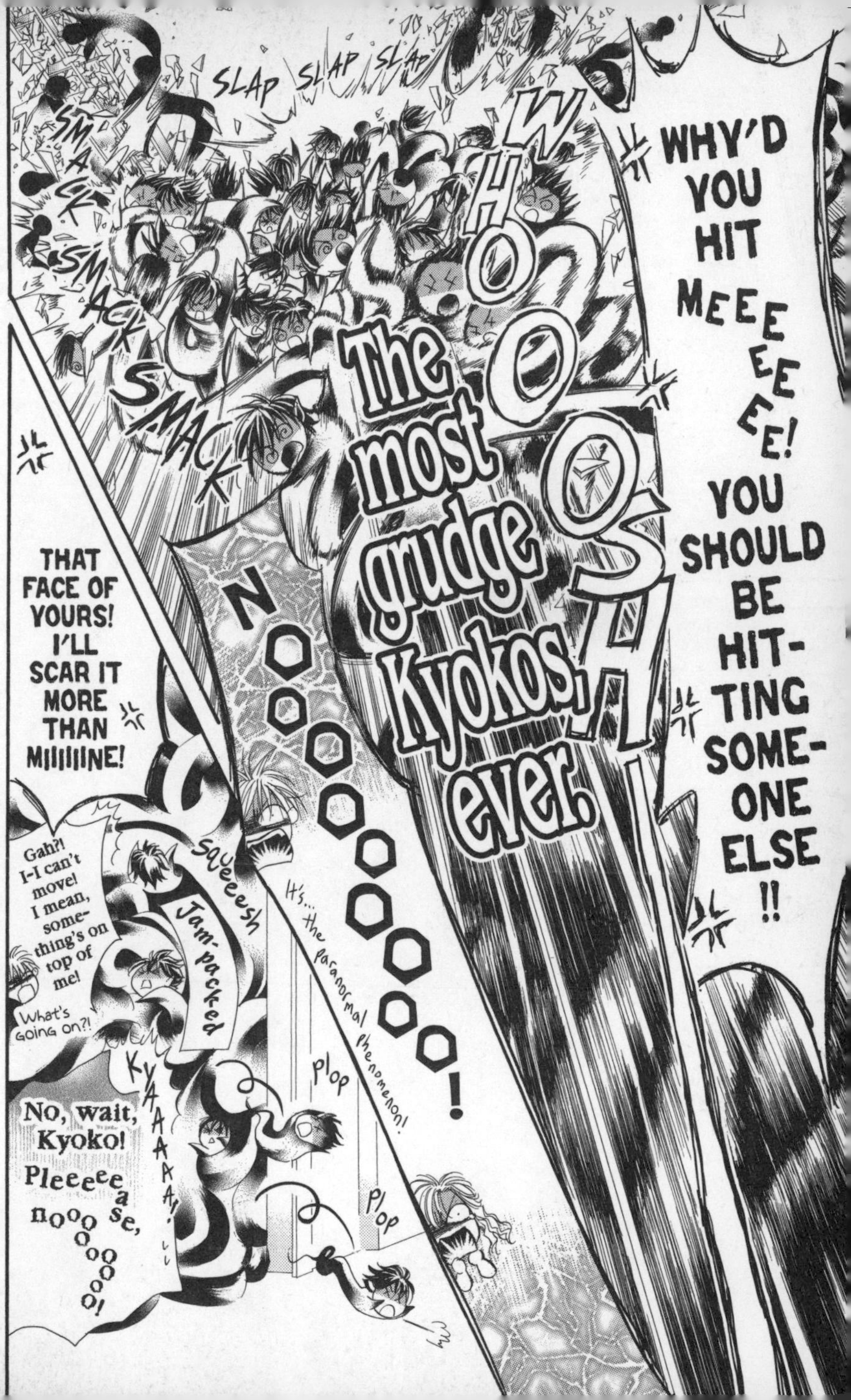
WHY'D YOU HIT MEEEEEEEE! YOU SHOULD BE HIT-TING SOME-ONE ELSE!!
WHOOOSH
SLAP SLAP SLAP
SMACK SMACK SMACK SMACK
The most grudge Kyokos, ever.
NOOOOOOOOOOO!
It's... the paranormal phenomenon!
plop
plop
THAT FACE OF YOURS! I'LL SCAR IT MORE THAN MIIIIIIINE!
Squeeeesh
Jam-packed
Gah?! I-I can't move! I mean, some-thing's on top of me!
What's going on?!
KYAAAAAA!
No, wait, Kyoko! Pleeeeease, noooooooooo!

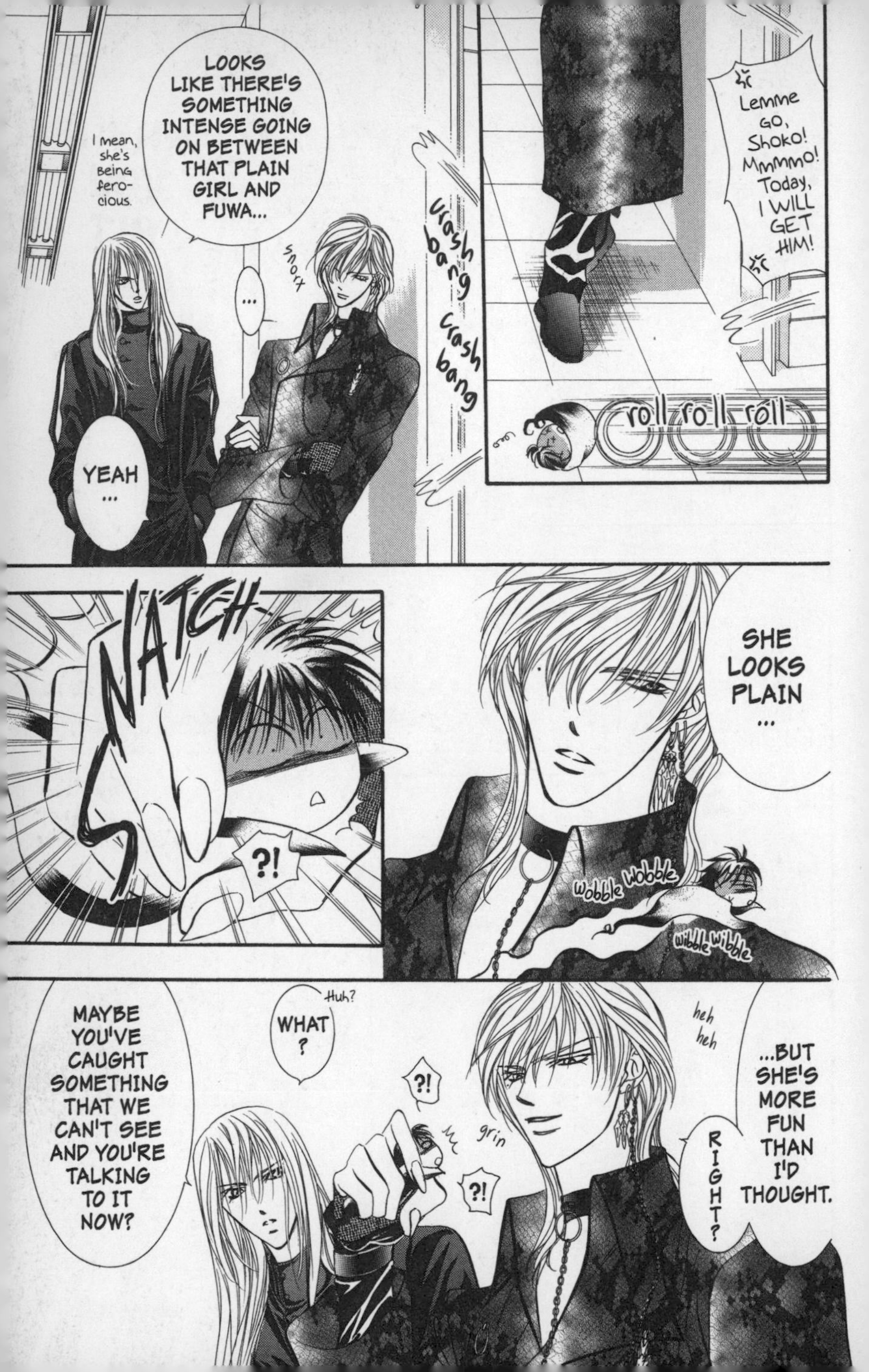
Lemme go, Shoko! Mmmmo! Today, I WILL GET HIM!
crash bang crash bang
roll roll roll
LOOKS LIKE THERE'S SOMETHING INTENSE GOING ON BETWEEN THAT PLAIN GIRL AND FUWA...
I mean, she's being fero-cious.
snorx
...
YEAH ...
SHE LOOKS PLAIN ...
wobble wobble
wibble wibble
NATCH
?!
heh heh
...BUT SHE'S MORE FUN THAN I'D THOUGHT.
RIGHT?
grin
?!
?!
WHAT?
Huh?
MAYBE YOU'VE CAUGHT SOMETHING THAT WE CAN'T SEE AND YOU'RE TALKING TO IT NOW?

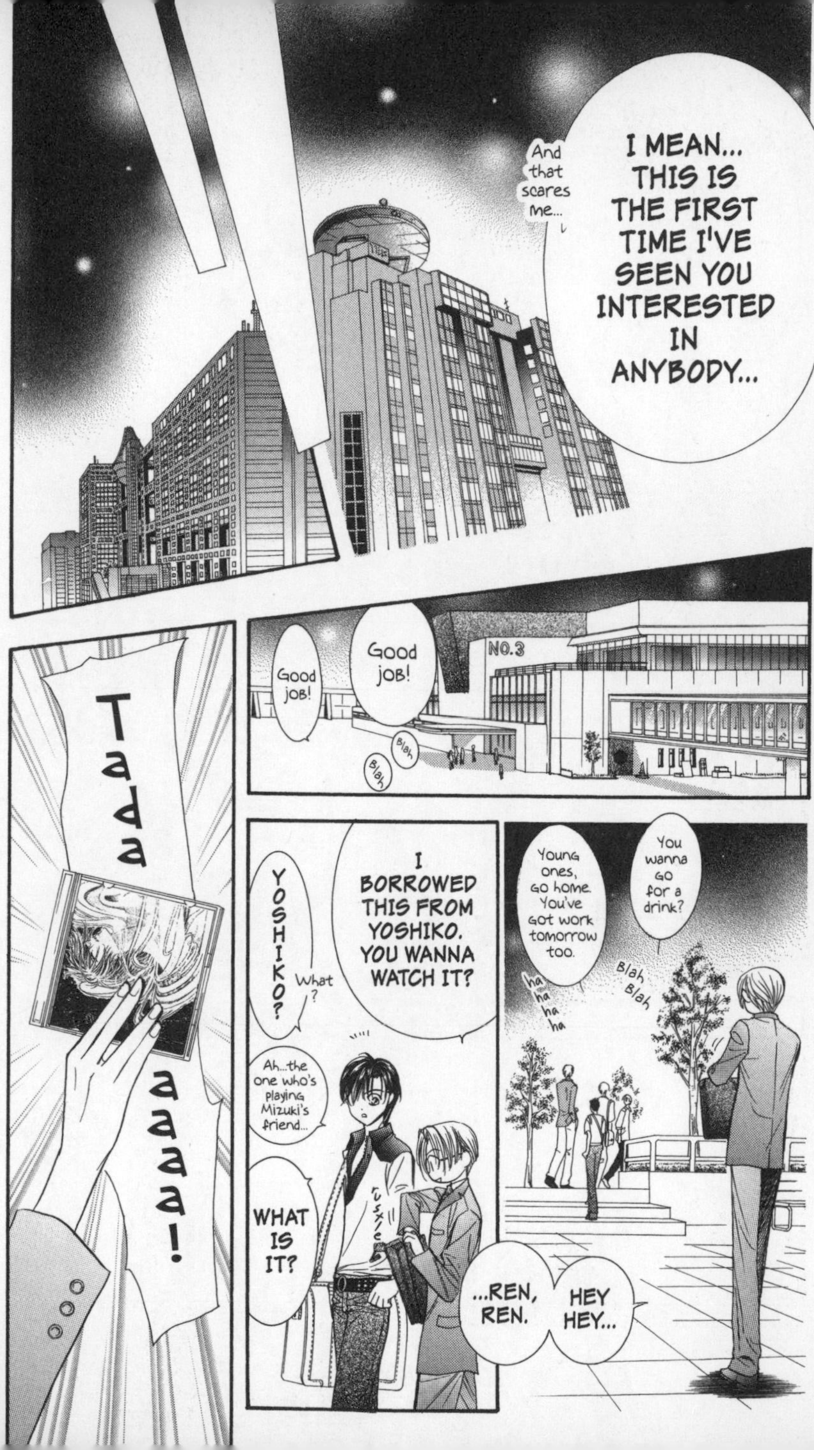
I MEAN... THIS IS THE FIRST TIME I'VE SEEN YOU INTERESTED IN ANYBODY...
And that scares me...
Good job!
Good job!
Blah
Blah
You wanna go for a drink?
Young ones, go home. You've got work tomorrow too.
ha ha ha ha ha
Blah Blah
HEY HEY...
...REN, REN.
I BORROWED THIS FROM YOSHIKO. YOU WANNA WATCH IT?
YOSHIKO?
What?
Ah...the one who's playing Mizuki's friend...
WHAT IS IT?
rustle
Tadaaaaaa!

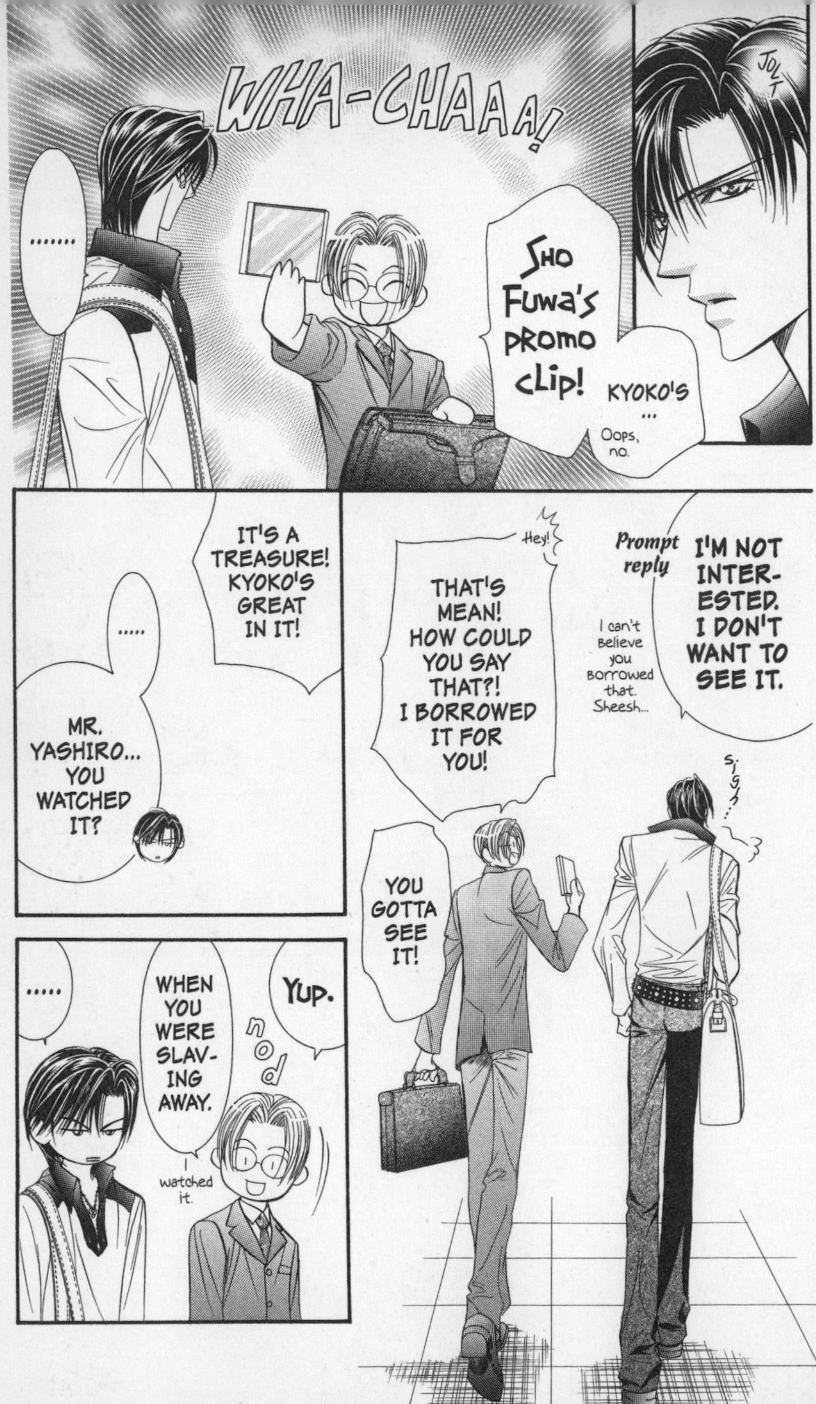
JOLT
WHA-CHAAAA!
....
SHO FUWA'S PROMO CLIP!
KYOKO'S ...
Oops, no.
Prompt reply
I'M NOT INTER-ESTED. I DON'T WANT TO SEE IT.
I can't believe you borrowed that. Sheesh...
Hey!
THAT'S MEAN! HOW COULD YOU SAY THAT?! I BORROWED IT FOR YOU!
sigh...
YOU GOTTA SEE IT!
IT'S A TREASURE! KYOKO'S GREAT IN IT!
.....
MR. YASHIRO... YOU WATCHED IT?
YUP.
nod
WHEN YOU WERE SLAV-ING AWAY.
I watched it.
.....

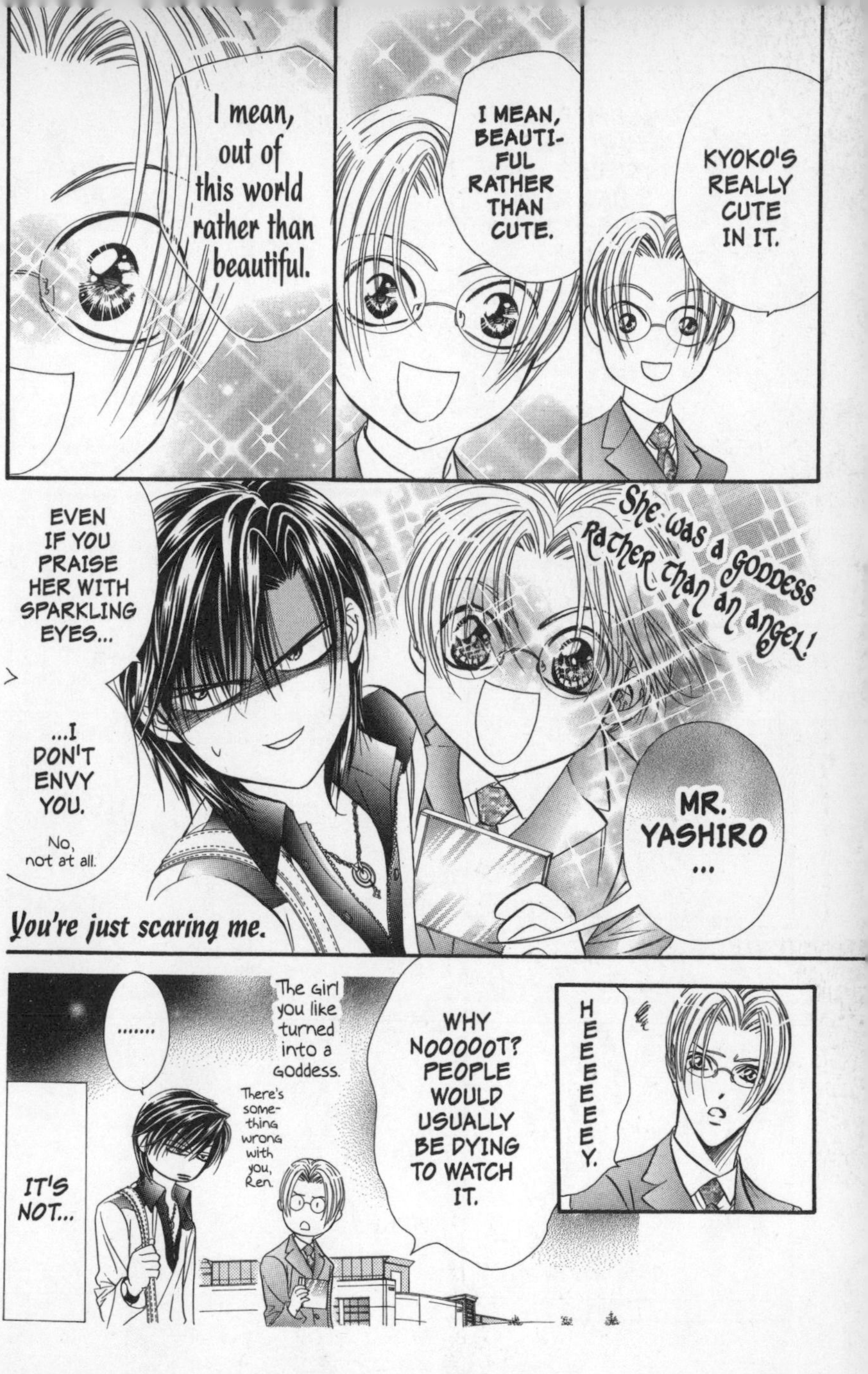
KYOKO'S REALLY CUTE IN IT.
I MEAN, BEAUTIFUL RATHER THAN CUTE.
I mean, out of this world rather than beautiful.
She was a goddess rather than an angel!
MR. YASHIRO ...
EVEN IF YOU PRAISE HER WITH SPARKLING EYES...
...I DON'T ENVY YOU.
No, not at all.
You're just scaring me.
HEEEEEEY.
WHY NOOOOOT? PEOPLE WOULD USUALLY BE DYING TO WATCH IT.
The girl you like turned into a goddess.
There's something wrong with you, Ren.
....
IT'S NOT...

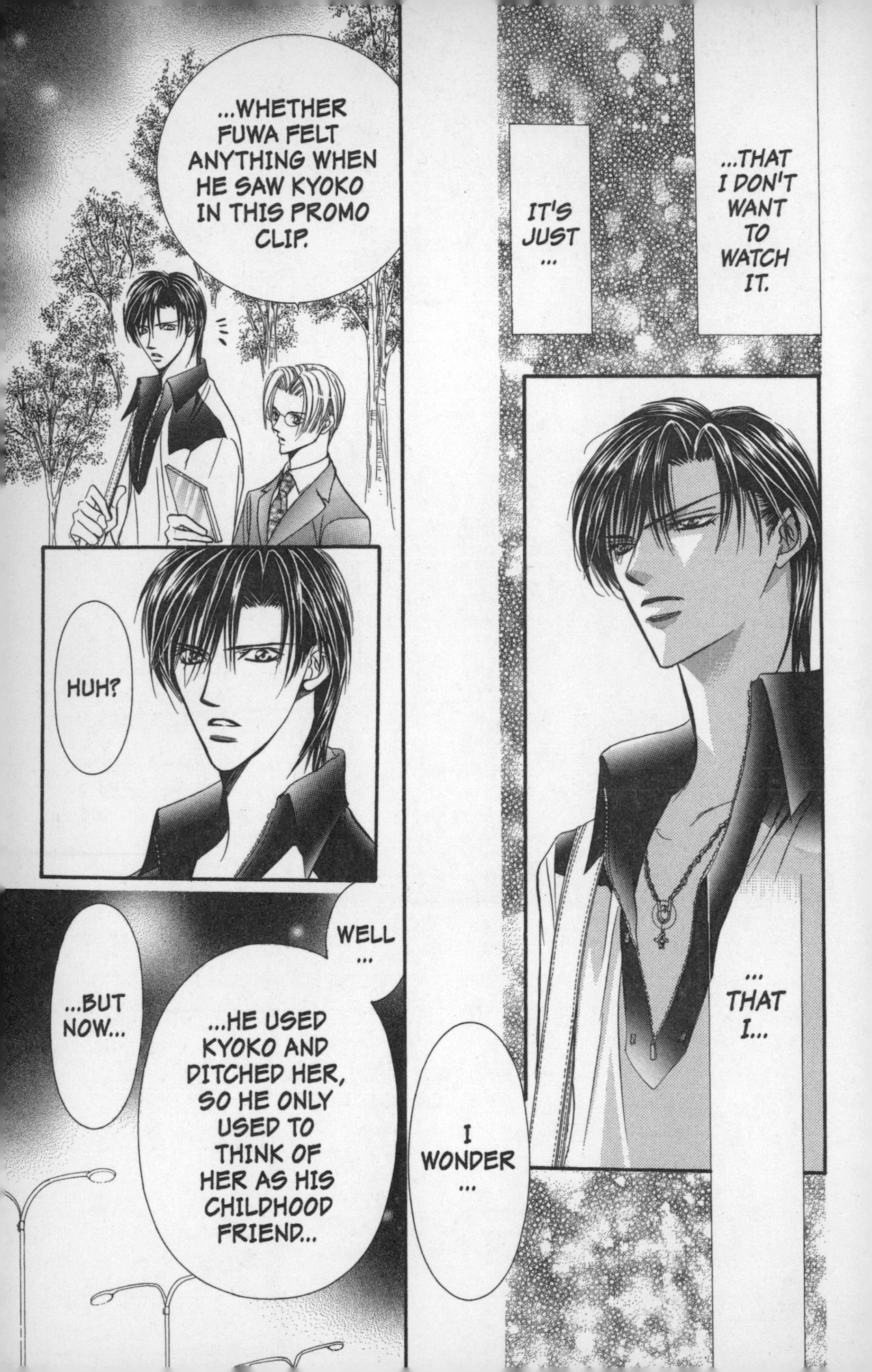
...WHETHER FUWA FELT ANYTHING WHEN HE SAW KYOKO IN THIS PROMO CLIP.
HUH?
WELL...
...HE USED KYOKO AND DITCHED HER, SO HE ONLY USED TO THINK OF HER AS HIS CHILDHOOD FRIEND...
...BUT NOW...
I WONDER...
IT'S JUST...
...THAT I DON'T WANT TO WATCH IT.
...THAT I...

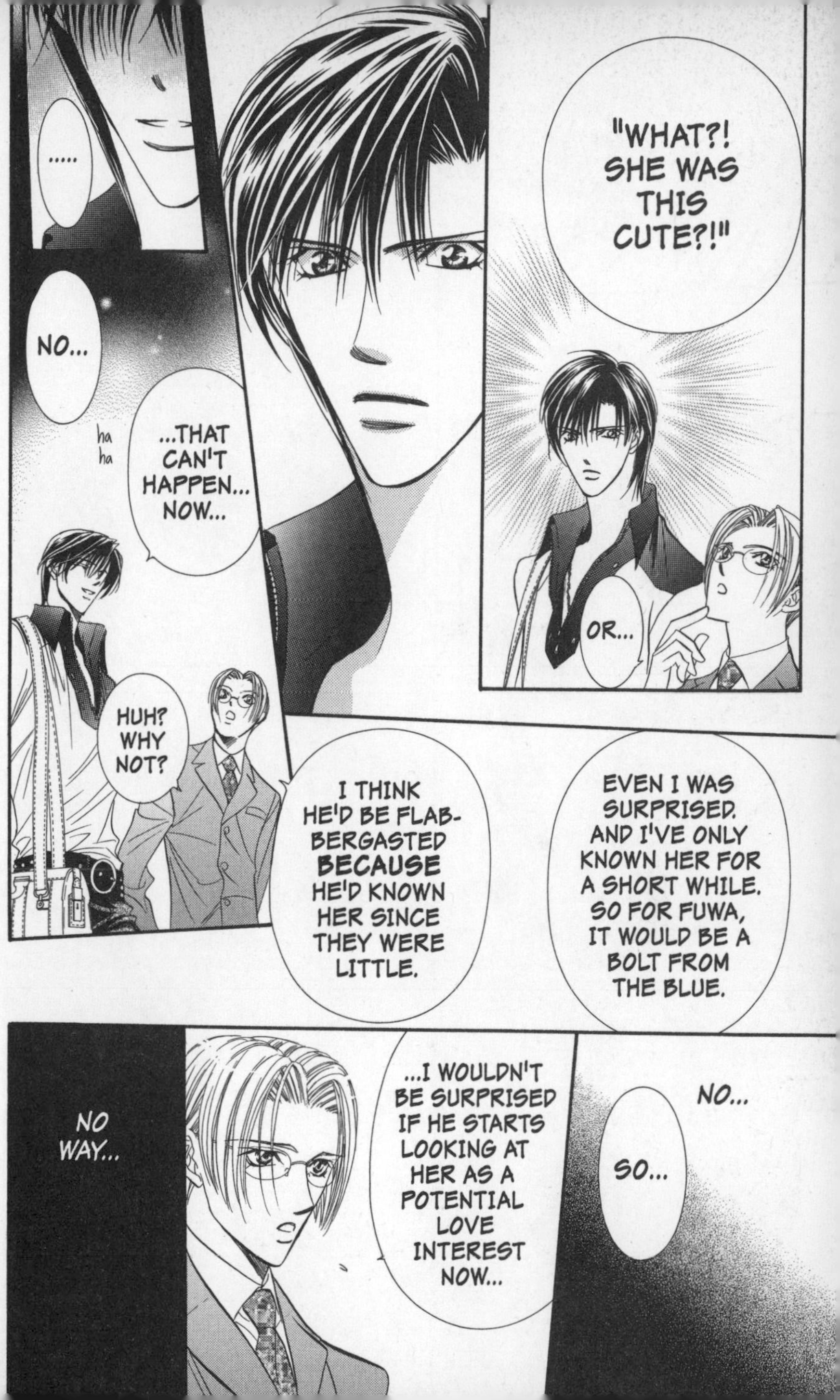
"WHAT?! SHE WAS THIS CUTE?!"
OR...
.....
NO...
ha ha
...THAT CAN'T HAPPEN... NOW...
HUH? WHY NOT?
EVEN I WAS SURPRISED. AND I'VE ONLY KNOWN HER FOR A SHORT WHILE. SO FOR FUWA, IT WOULD BE A BOLT FROM THE BLUE.
I THINK HE'D BE FLAB-BERGASTED **BECAUSE** HE'D KNOWN HER SINCE THEY WERE LITTLE.
NO...
SO...
...I WOULDN'T BE SURPRISED IF HE STARTS LOOKING AT HER AS A POTENTIAL LOVE INTEREST NOW...
NO WAY...

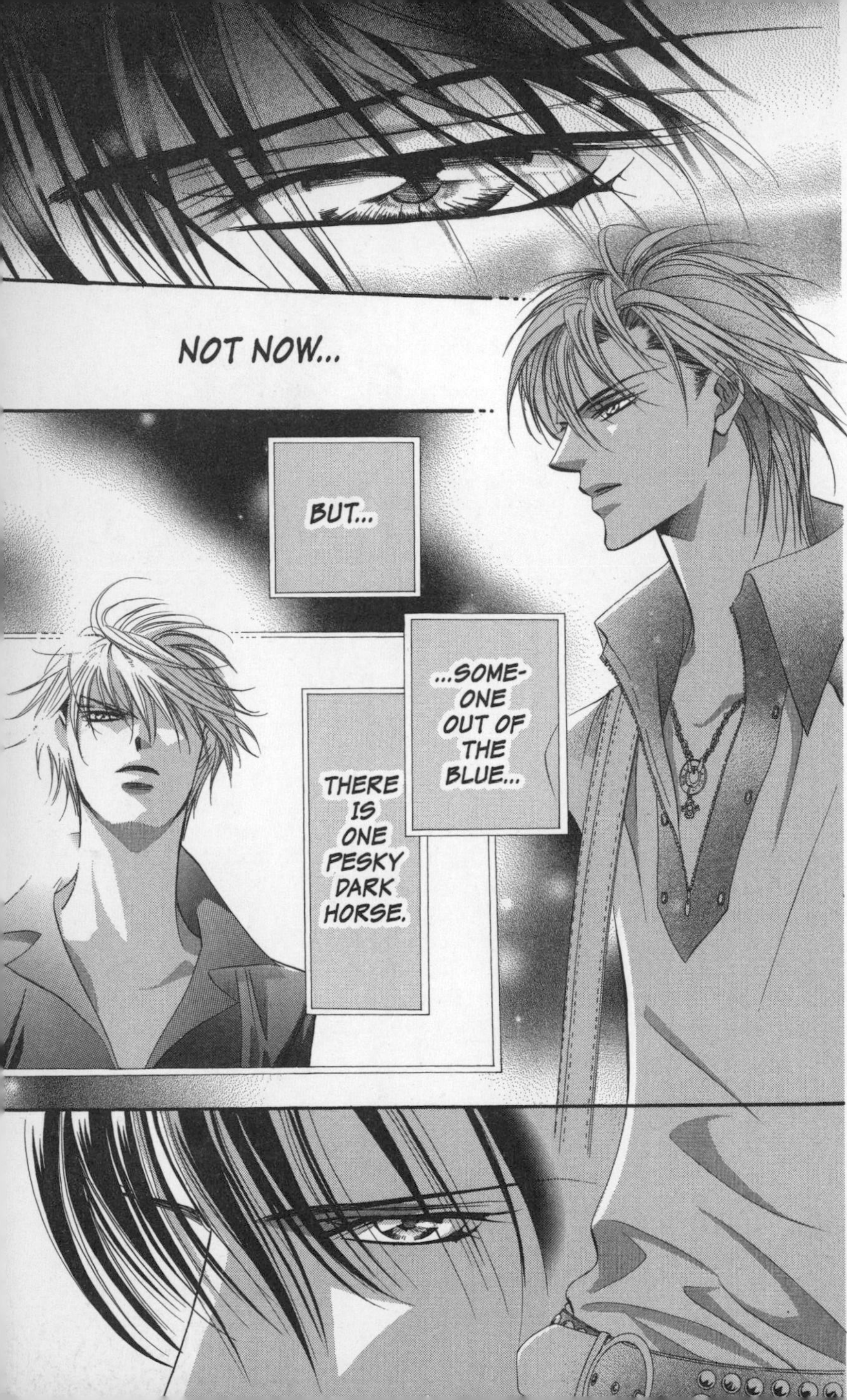
NOT NOW...
BUT...
...SOME-ONE OUT OF THE BLUE...
THERE IS ONE PESKY DARK HORSE.

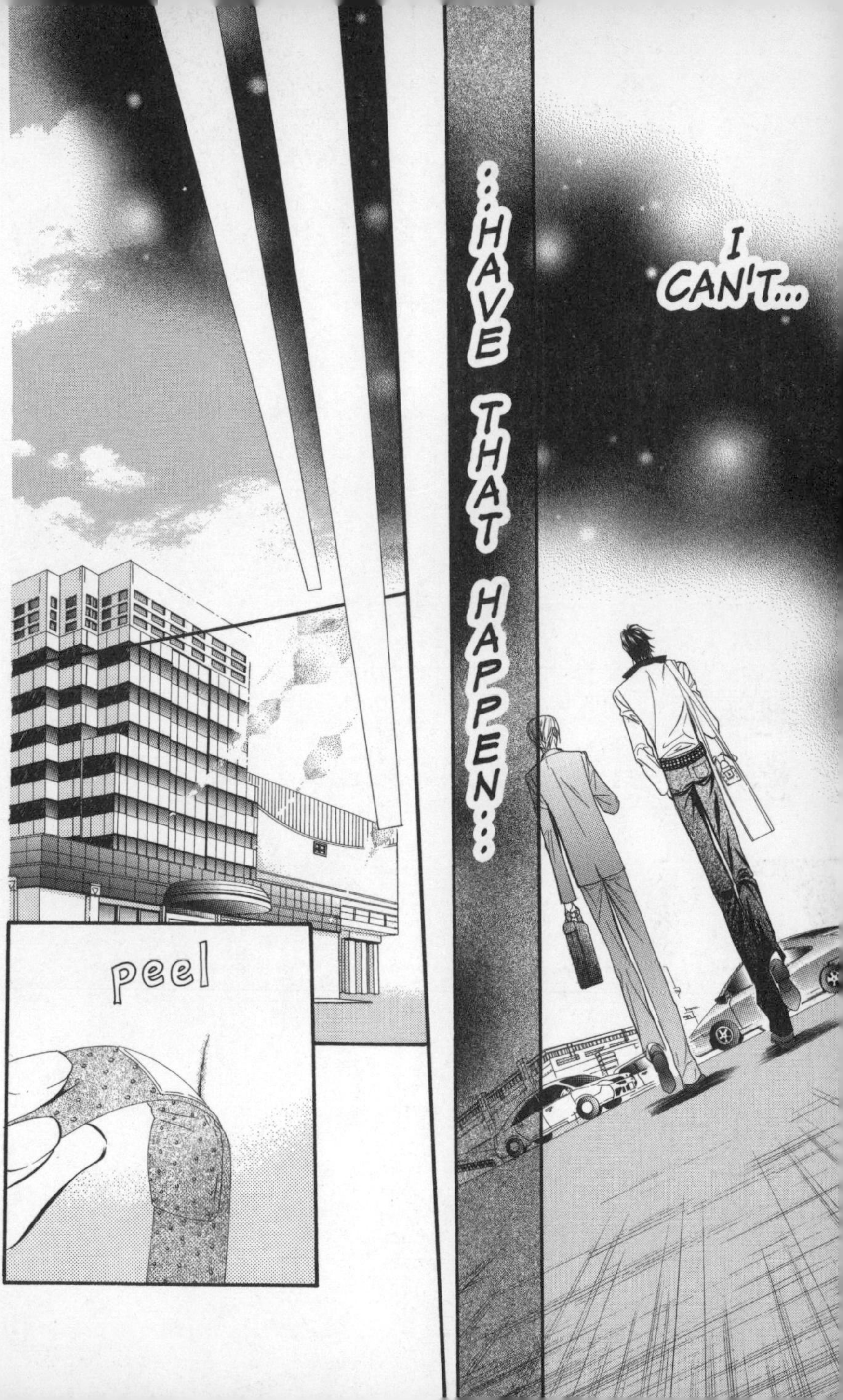
I CAN'T...
...HAVE THAT HAPPEN...
peel

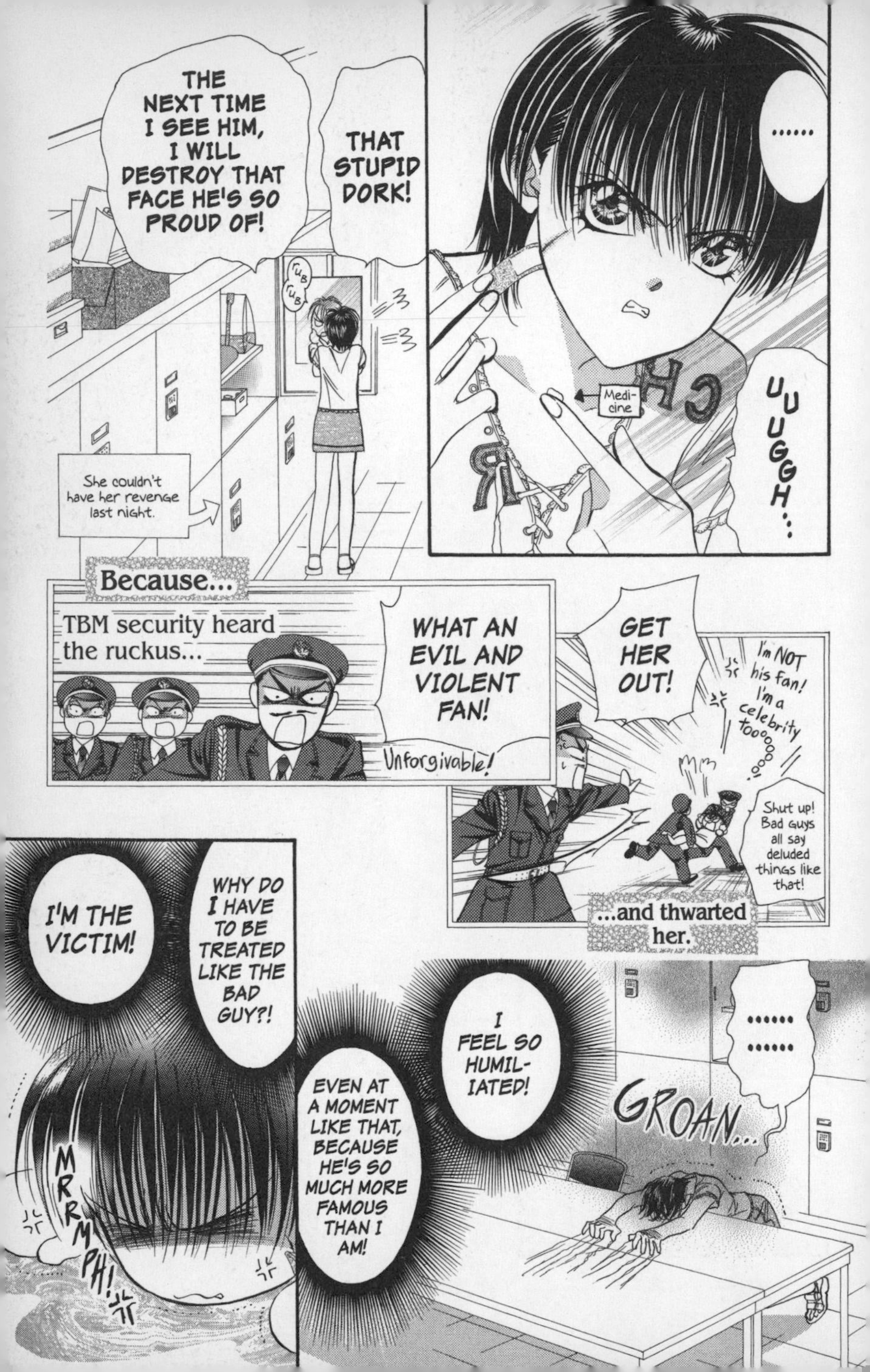
......
UUUGGH...
Medicine
THAT STUPID DORK!
THE NEXT TIME I SEE HIM, I WILL DESTROY THAT FACE HE'S SO PROUD OF!
rub rub
She couldn't have her revenge last night.
Because...
TBM security heard the ruckus...
WHAT AN EVIL AND VIOLENT FAN!
Unforgivable!
GET HER OUT!
I'm NOT his fan! I'm a celebrity toooooo!
Shut up! Bad guys all say deluded things like that!
...and thwarted her.
......
......
GROAN...
I FEEL SO HUMILIATED!
EVEN AT A MOMENT LIKE THAT, BECAUSE HE'S SO MUCH MORE FAMOUS THAN I AM!
WHY DO I HAVE TO BE TREATED LIKE THE BAD GUY?!
I'M THE VICTIM!
MRRMPH!

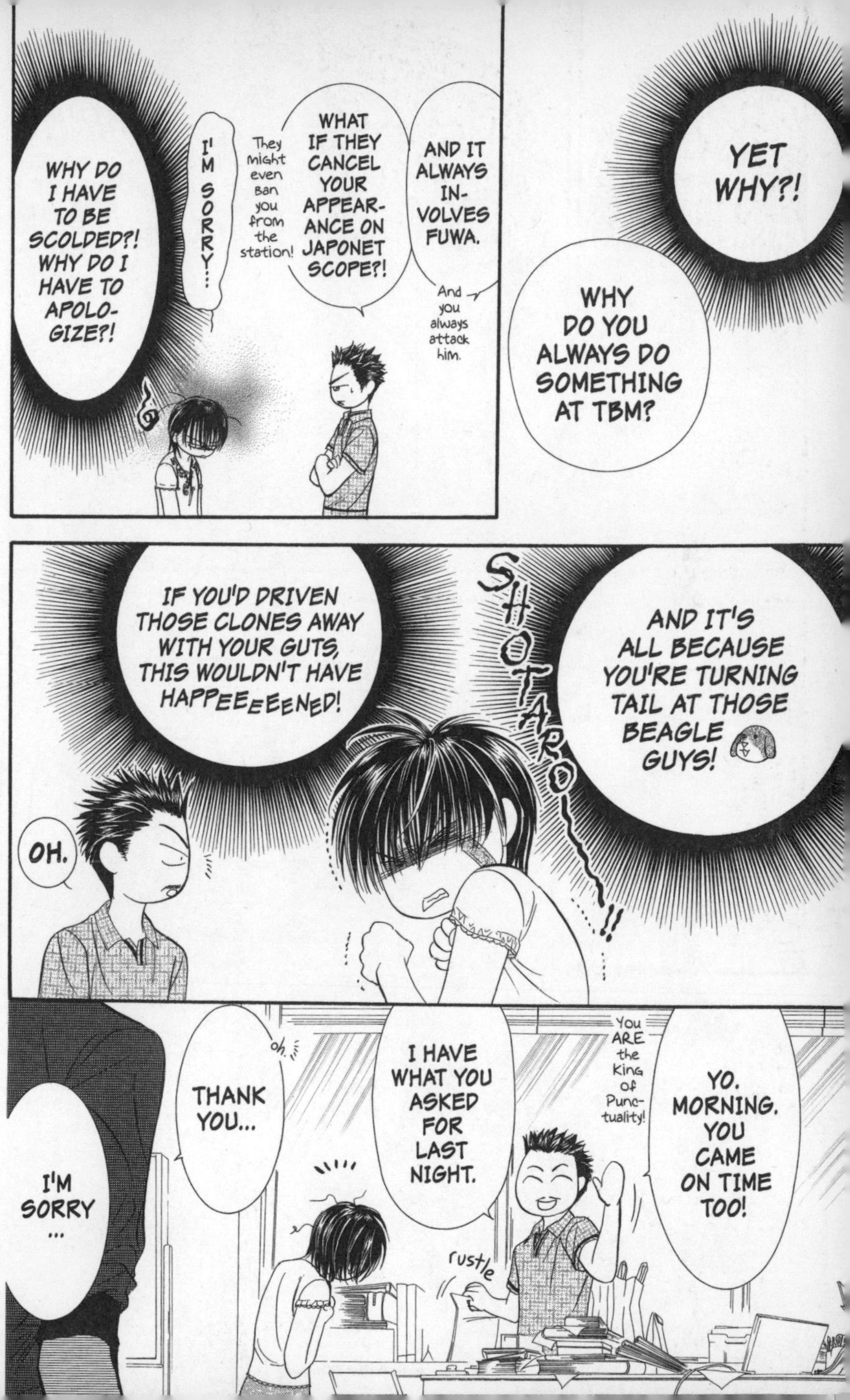
YET WHY?!
WHY DO YOU ALWAYS DO SOMETHING AT TBM?
AND IT ALWAYS IN-VOLVES FUWA.
And you always attack him.
WHAT IF THEY CANCEL YOUR APPEAR-ANCE ON JAPONET SCOPE?!
They might even ban you from the station!
I'M SORRY...
WHY DO I HAVE TO BE SCOLDED?! WHY DO I HAVE TO APOLO-GIZE?!
SHOTARO—!!
AND IT'S ALL BECAUSE YOU'RE TURNING TAIL AT THOSE BEAGLE GUYS!
IF YOU'D DRIVEN THOSE CLONES AWAY WITH YOUR GUTS, THIS WOULDN'T HAVE HAPPEEEEEENED!
OH.
YO. MORNING. YOU CAME ON TIME TOO!
You ARE the King of Punc-tuality!
I HAVE WHAT YOU ASKED FOR LAST NIGHT.
rustle
oh.
THANK YOU...
I'M SORRY...

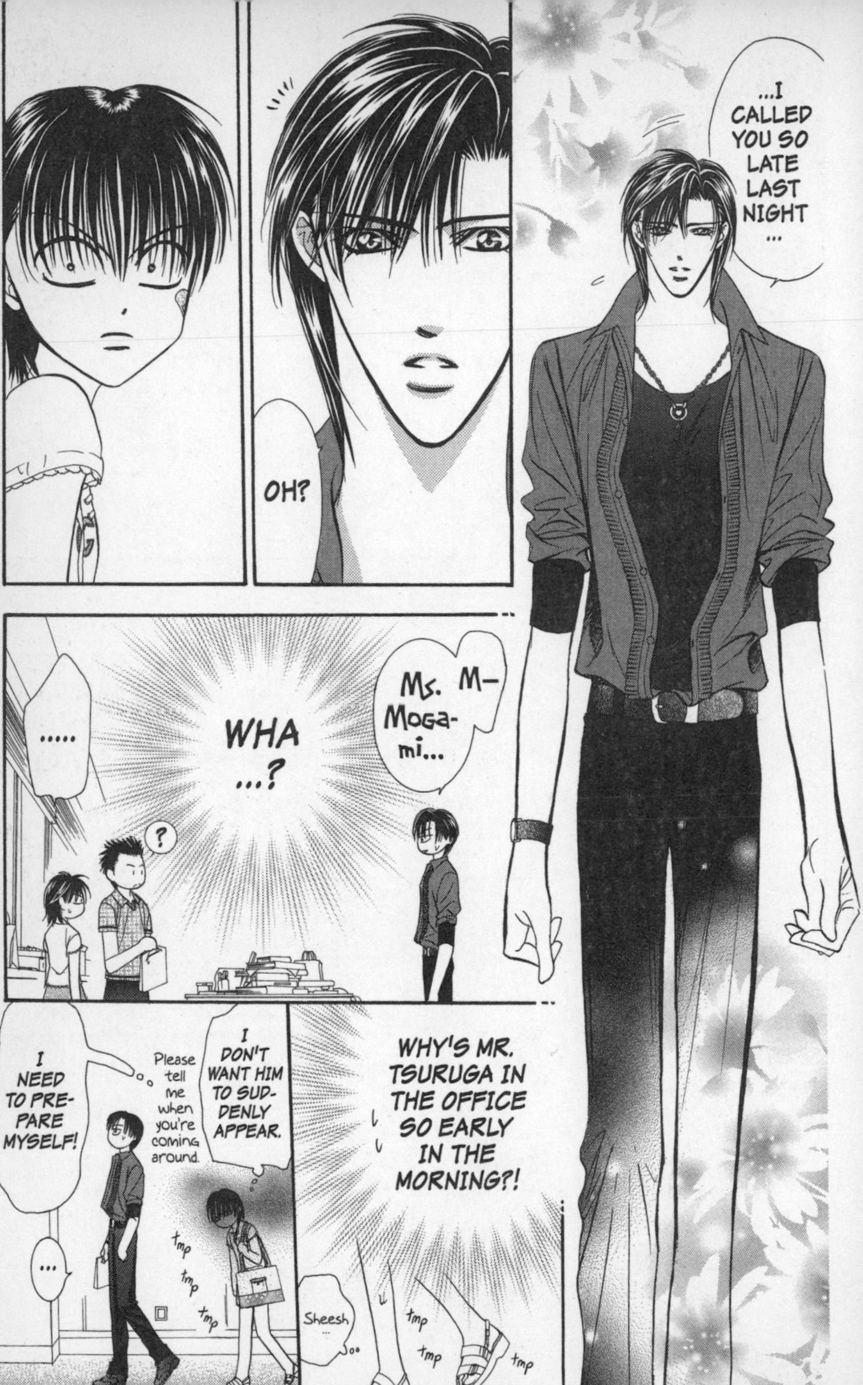
...I CALLED YOU SO LATE LAST NIGHT ...
OH?
Ms. M-Moga-mi...
WHA ...?
.....
?
WHY'S MR. TSURUGA IN THE OFFICE SO EARLY IN THE MORNING?!
Sheesh ...
tmp tmp tmp
I DON'T WANT HIM TO SUD-DENLY APPEAR.
Please tell me when you're coming around.
I NEED TO PRE-PARE MYSELF!
...
tmp tmp tmp

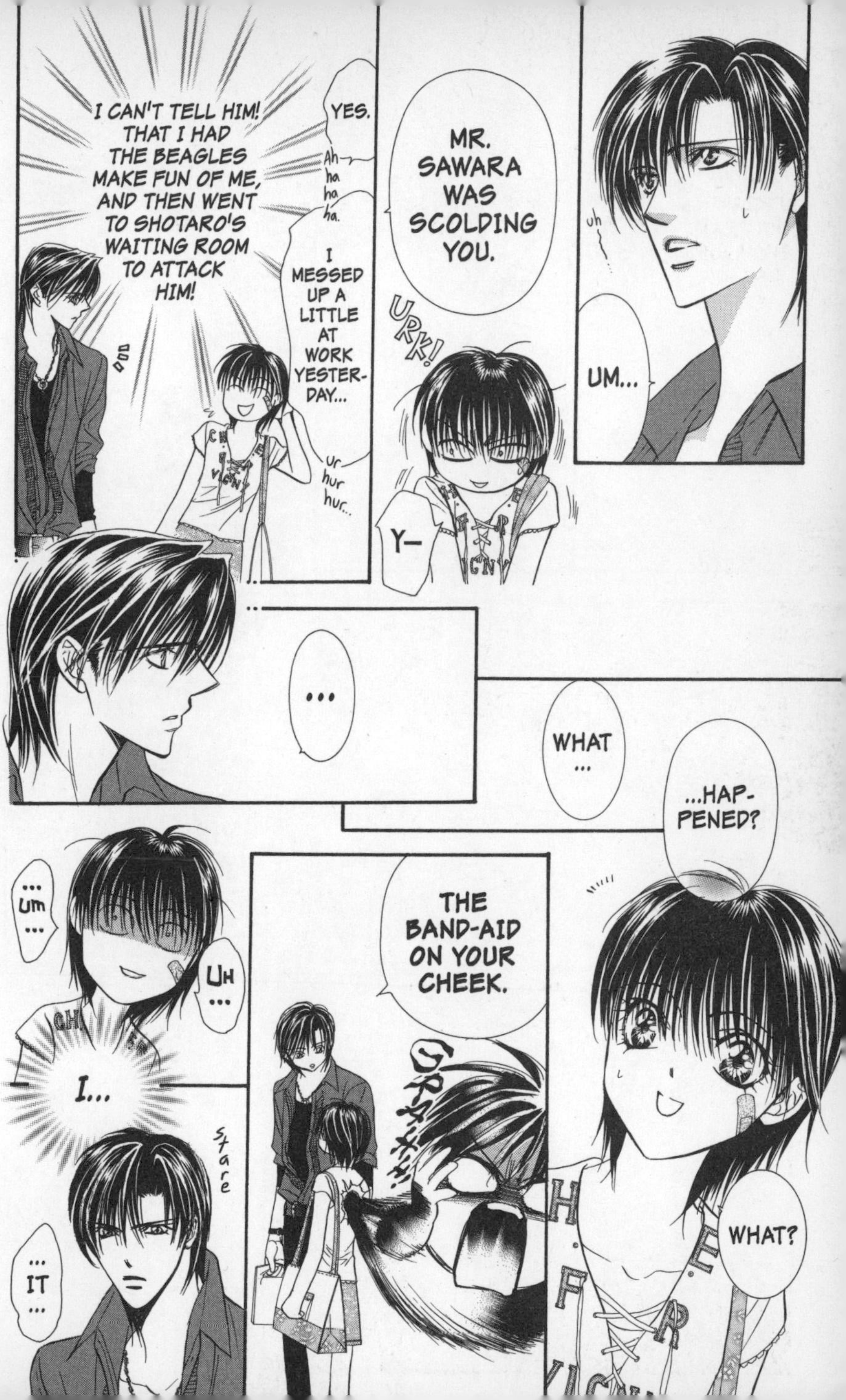
uh...
UM...
MR. SAWARA WAS SCOLDING YOU.
URK!
Y—
YES.
Ah ha ha ha.
I MESSED UP A LITTLE AT WORK YESTER-DAY...
Ur hur hur...
I CAN'T TELL HIM! THAT I HAD THE BEAGLES MAKE FUN OF ME, AND THEN WENT TO SHOTARO'S WAITING ROOM TO ATTACK HIM!
...
WHAT...
...HAP-PENED?
WHAT?
THE BAND-AID ON YOUR CHEEK.
...Um...
Uh...
I...
stare
...IT...

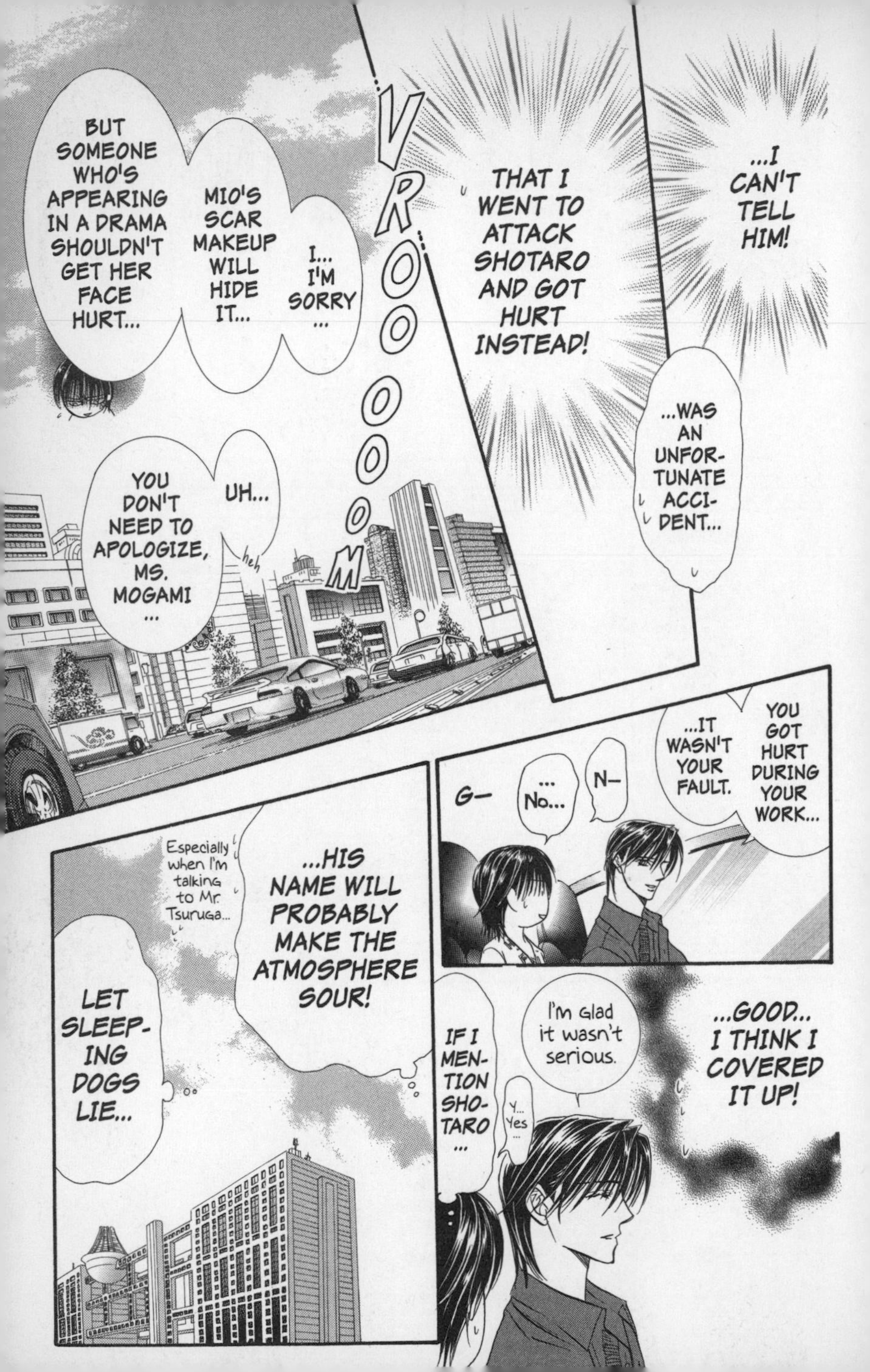
...I CAN'T TELL HIM!
...WAS AN UNFORTUNATE ACCIDENT...
THAT I WENT TO ATTACK SHOTARO AND GOT HURT INSTEAD!
VROOOOOOM
I... I'M SORRY...
MIO'S SCAR MAKEUP WILL HIDE IT...
BUT SOMEONE WHO'S APPEARING IN A DRAMA SHOULDN'T GET HER FACE HURT...
UH... heh
YOU DON'T NEED TO APOLOGIZE, MS. MOGAMI...
YOU GOT HURT DURING YOUR WORK...
...IT WASN'T YOUR FAULT.
N—
... No...
G—
...GOOD... I THINK I COVERED IT UP!
I'm Glad it wasn't serious.
Y... Yes...
IF I MENTION SHOTARO...
...HIS NAME WILL PROBABLY MAKE THE ATMOSPHERE SOUR!
Especially when I'm talking to Mr. Tsuruga...
LET SLEEPING DOGS LIE...

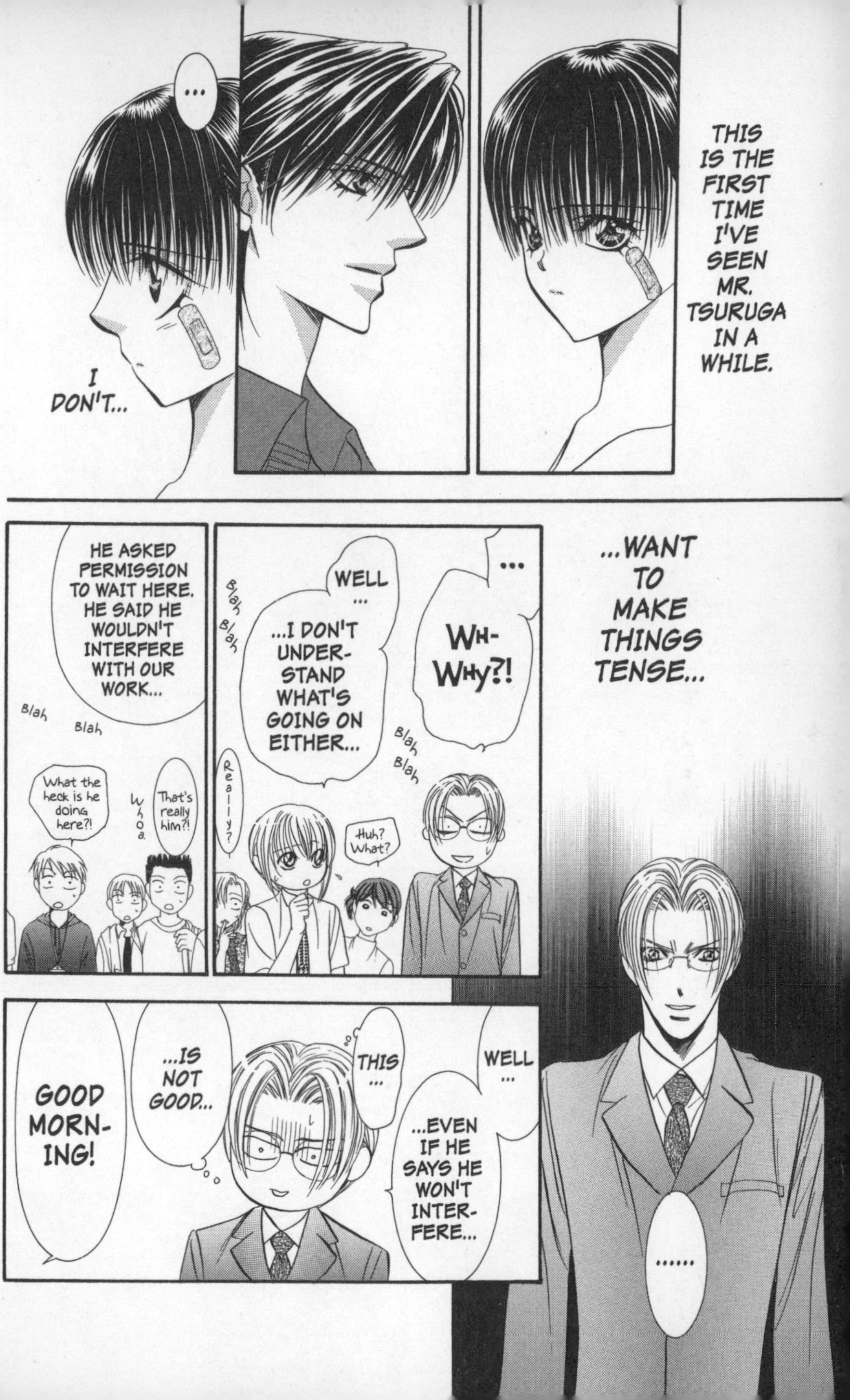
THIS IS THE FIRST TIME I'VE SEEN MR. TSURUGA IN A WHILE.
...
I DON'T...
...WANT TO MAKE THINGS TENSE...
......
...
WH- WHY?!
WELL ...
...I DON'T UNDERSTAND WHAT'S GOING ON EITHER...
Blah Blah
Blah Blah
Really?
Huh? What?
HE ASKED PERMISSION TO WAIT HERE. HE SAID HE WOULDN'T INTERFERE WITH OUR WORK...
Blah Blah
That's really him?!
Whoa.
What the heck is he doing here?!
WELL ...
...EVEN IF HE SAYS HE WON'T INTERFERE...
THIS ...
...IS NOT GOOD...
GOOD MORNING!

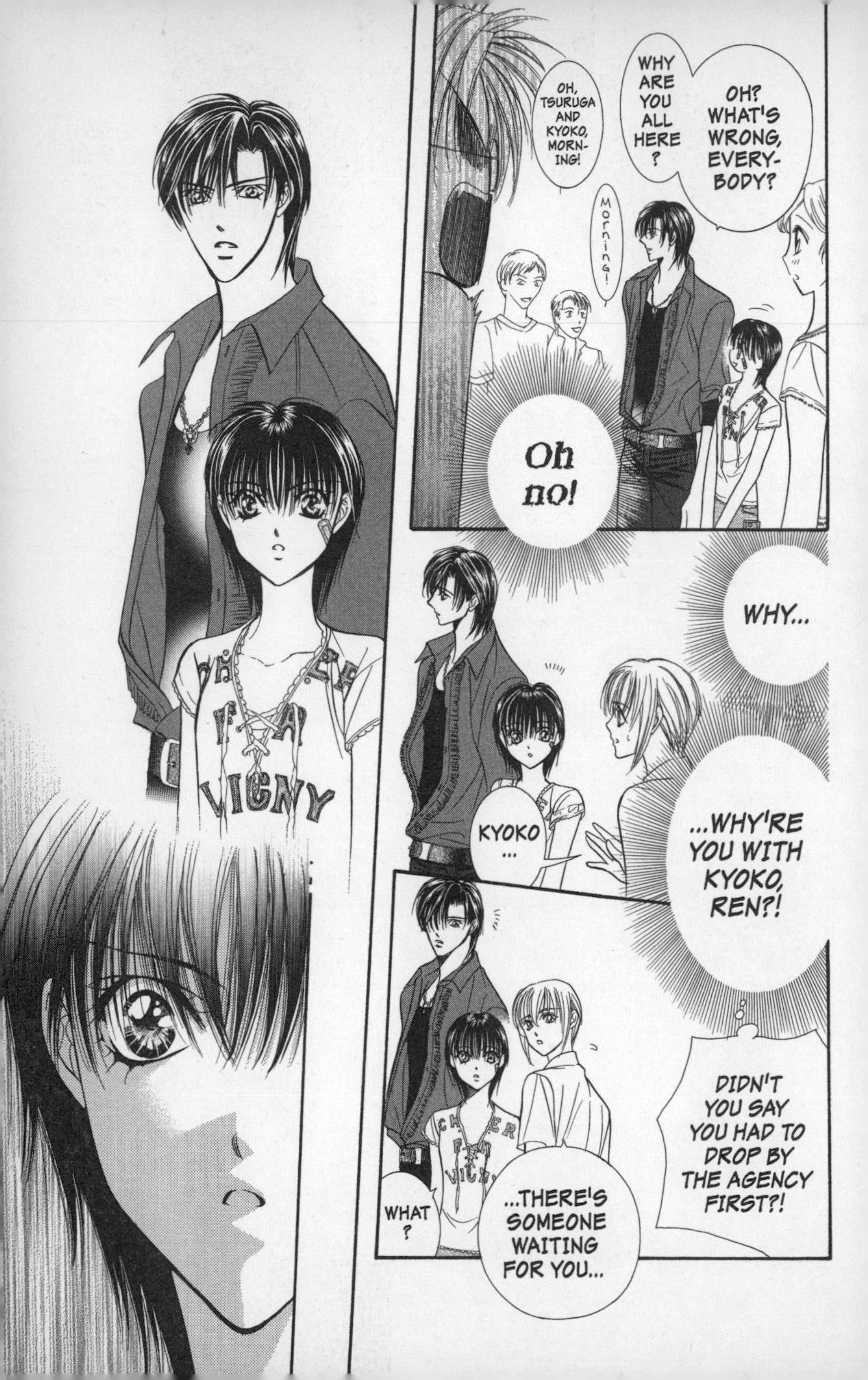

OH? WHAT'S WRONG, EVERYBODY?
WHY ARE YOU ALL HERE?
OH, TSURUGA AND KYOKO, MORNING!
Morning!
Oh no!
WHY...
...WHY'RE YOU WITH KYOKO, REN?!
KYOKO...
DIDN'T YOU SAY YOU HAD TO DROP BY THE AGENCY FIRST?!
...THERE'S SOMEONE WAITING FOR YOU...
WHAT?

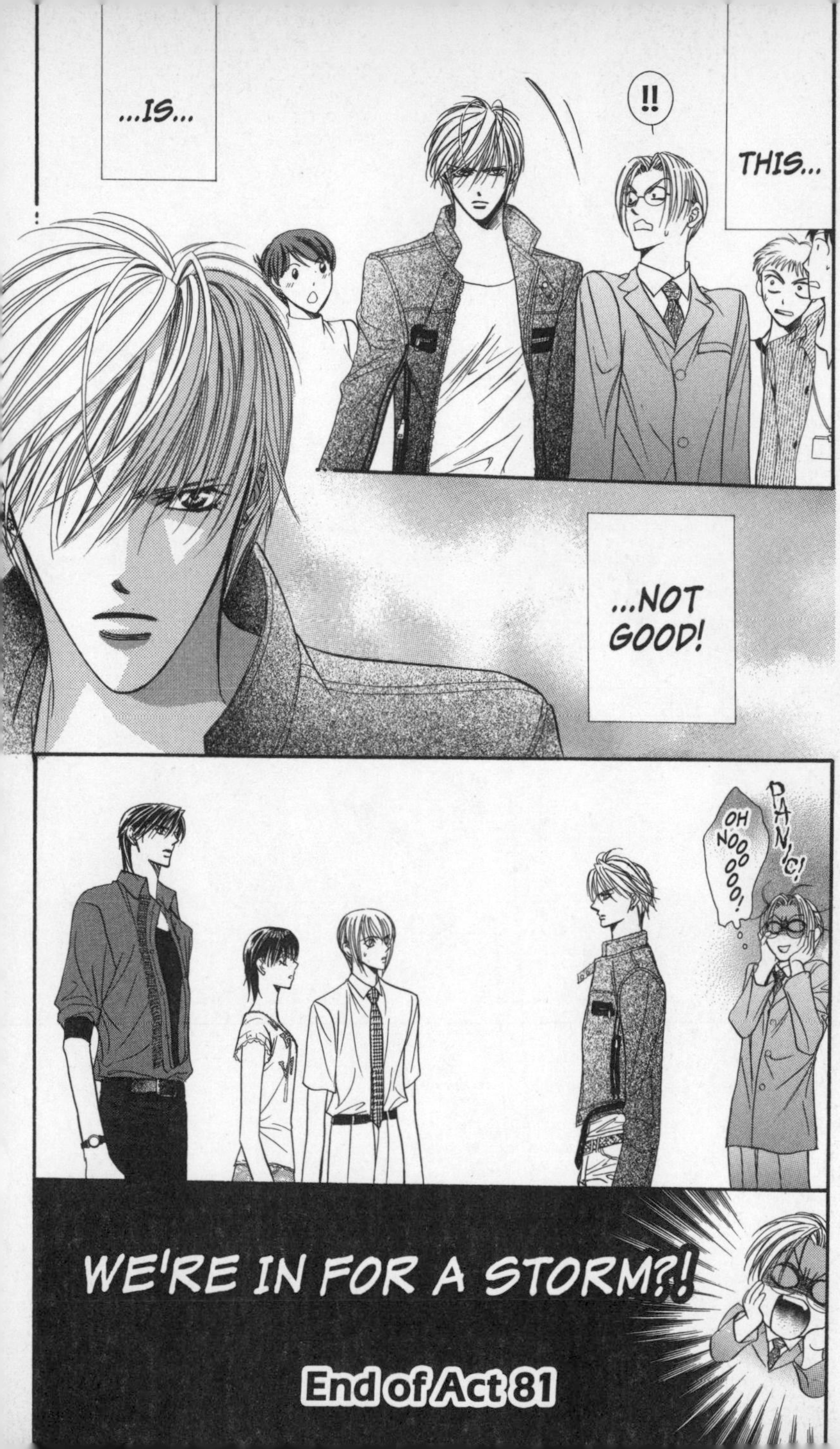
THIS...
!!
...IS...
...NOT GOOD!
PANIC!
OH NOOOOOOO!
WE'RE IN FOR A STORM?!
End of Act 81

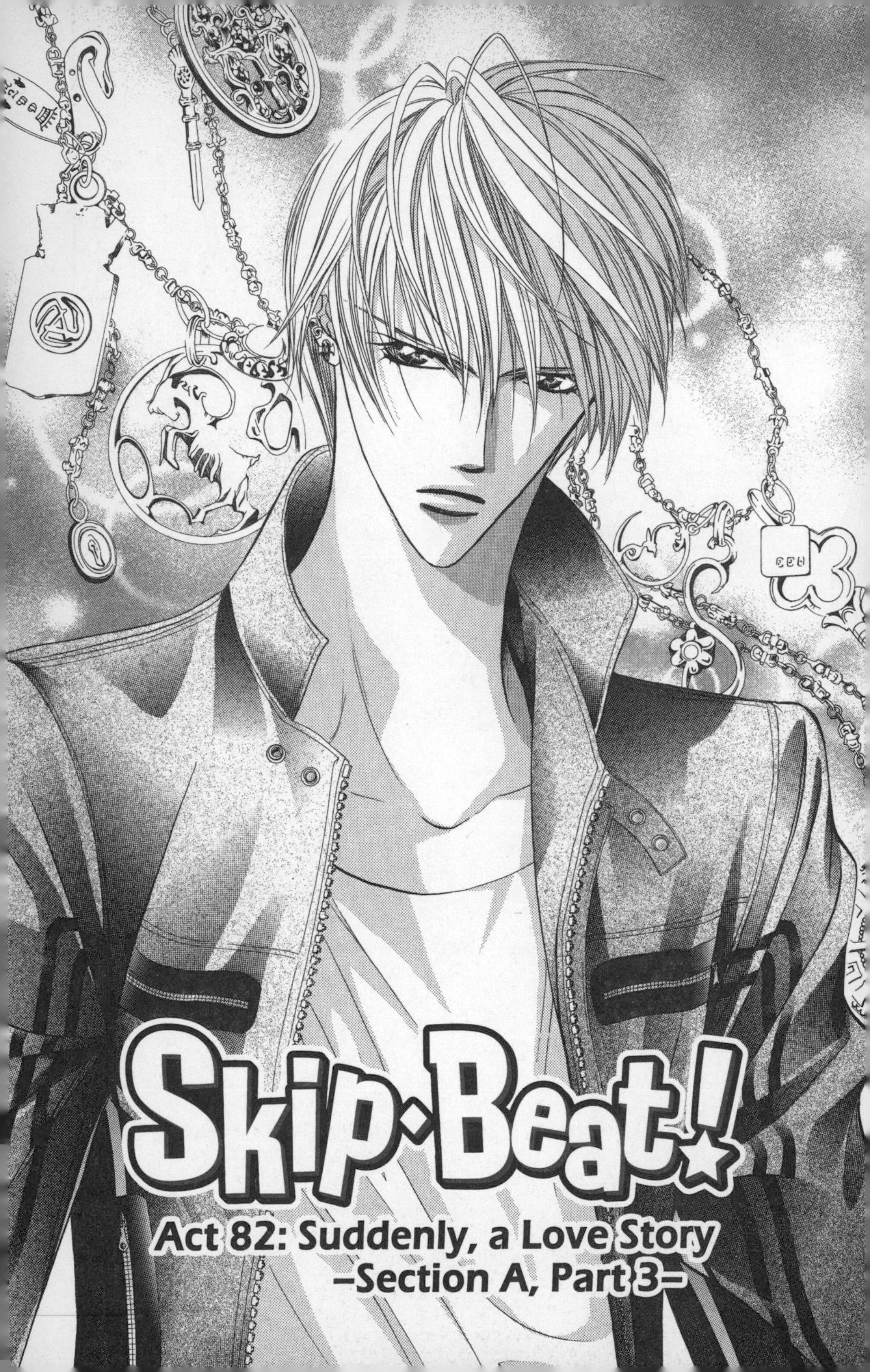
Skip·Beat!
Act 82: Suddenly, a Love Story
–Section A, Part 3–

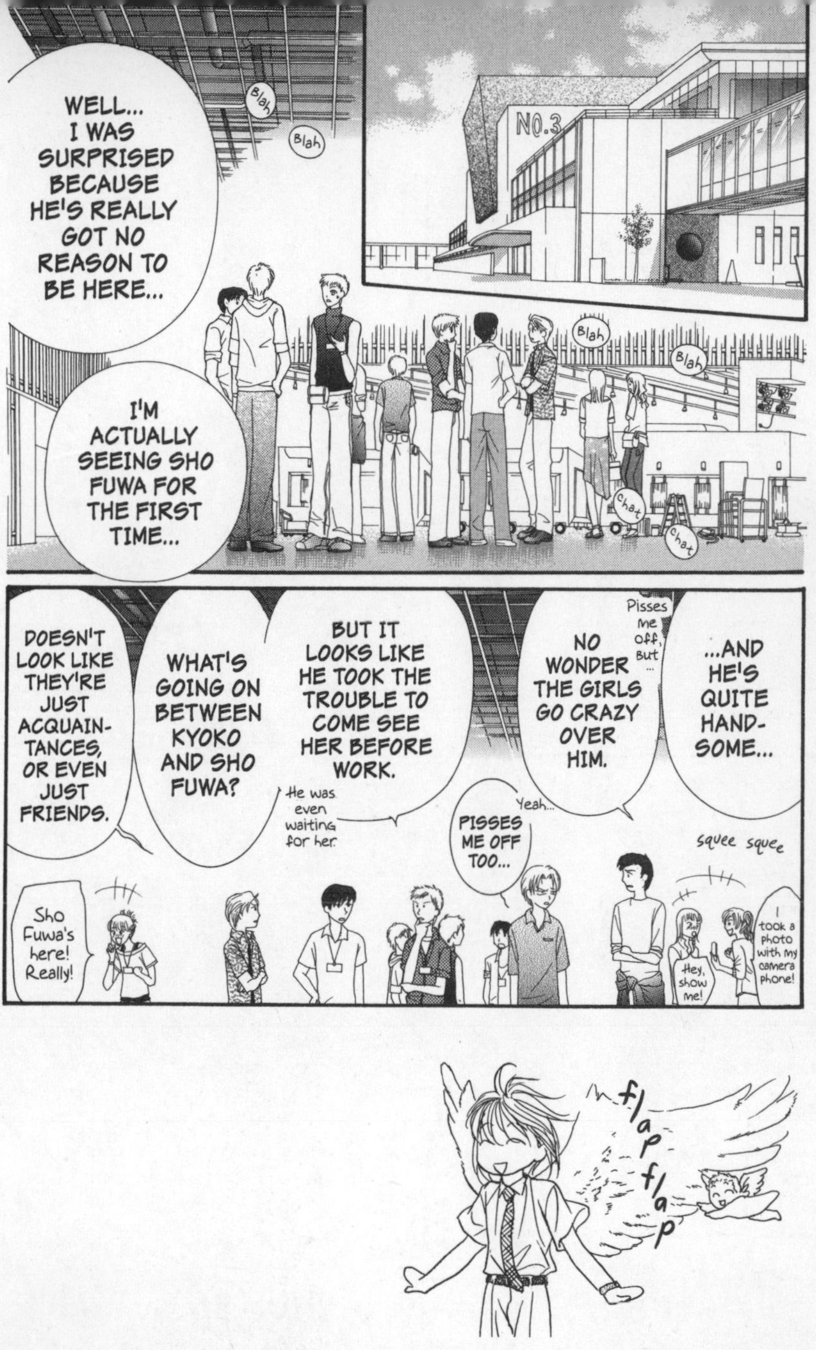
NO.3
WELL... I WAS SURPRISED BECAUSE HE'S REALLY GOT NO REASON TO BE HERE...
Blah Blah
I'M ACTUALLY SEEING SHO FUWA FOR THE FIRST TIME...
Blah Blah
Chat Chat
...AND HE'S QUITE HAND-SOME...
Pisses me off, but ...
NO WONDER THE GIRLS GO CRAZY OVER HIM.
Yeah...
PISSES ME OFF TOO...
BUT IT LOOKS LIKE HE TOOK THE TROUBLE TO COME SEE HER BEFORE WORK.
He was even waiting for her.
WHAT'S GOING ON BETWEEN KYOKO AND SHO FUWA?
DOESN'T LOOK LIKE THEY'RE JUST ACQUAIN-TANCES, OR EVEN JUST FRIENDS.
squee squee
I took a photo with my camera phone!
Hey, show me!
Sho Fuwa's here! Really!
flap flap

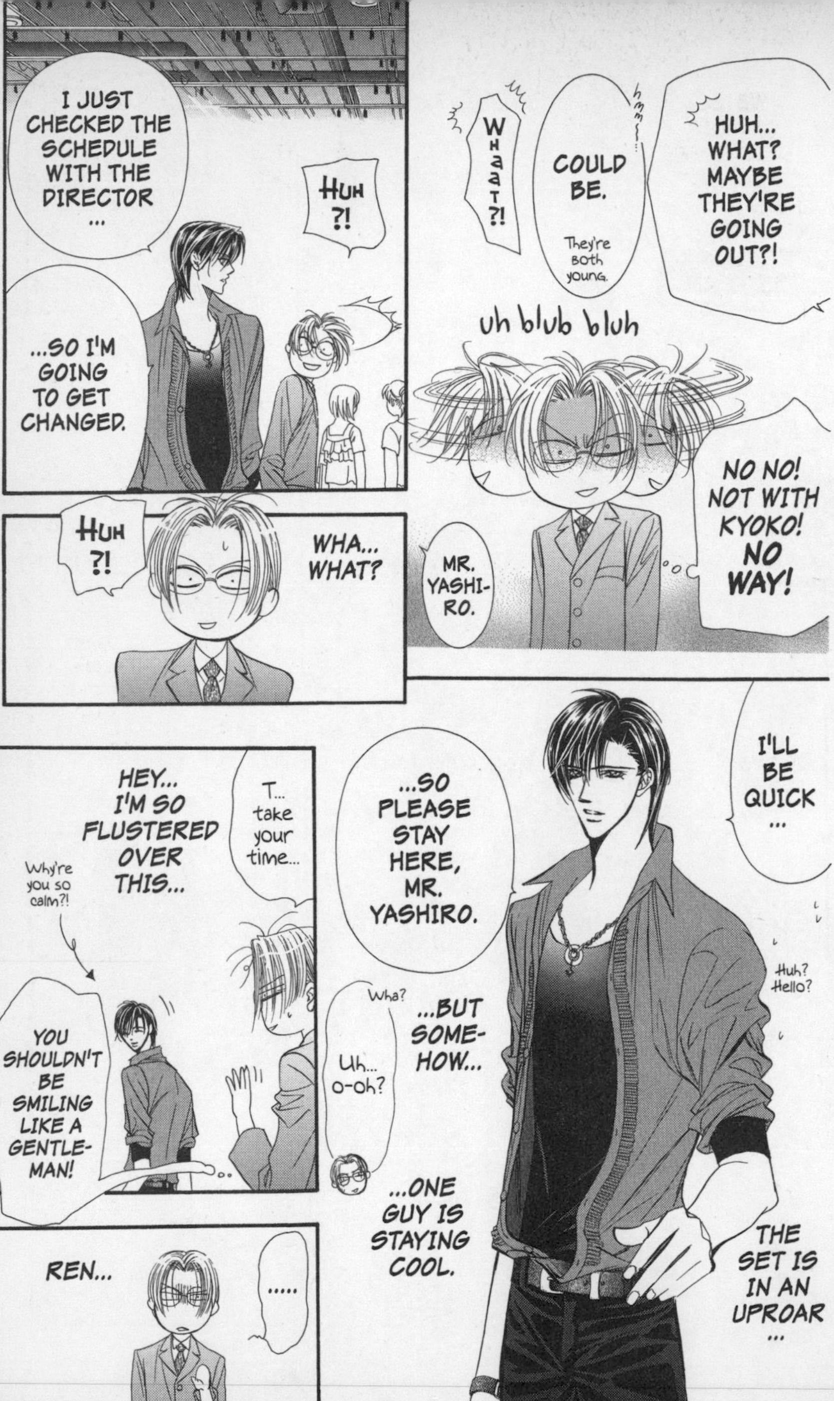
HUH... WHAT? MAYBE THEY'RE GOING OUT?!
hmm~...
COULD BE.
They're both young.
Whaaat?!
uh blub bluh
NO NO! NOT WITH KYOKO! NO WAY!
MR. YASHIRO.
I JUST CHECKED THE SCHEDULE WITH THE DIRECTOR...
HUH ?!
...SO I'M GOING TO GET CHANGED.
HUH ?!
WHA... WHAT?
I'LL BE QUICK...
...SO PLEASE STAY HERE, MR. YASHIRO.
Huh? Hello?
THE SET IS IN AN UPROAR...
...BUT SOMEHOW...
...ONE GUY IS STAYING COOL.
Wha?
Uh... o-oh?
T... take your time...
HEY... I'M SO FLUSTERED OVER THIS...
Why're you so calm?!
YOU SHOULDN'T BE SMILING LIKE A GENTLEMAN!
.....
REN...

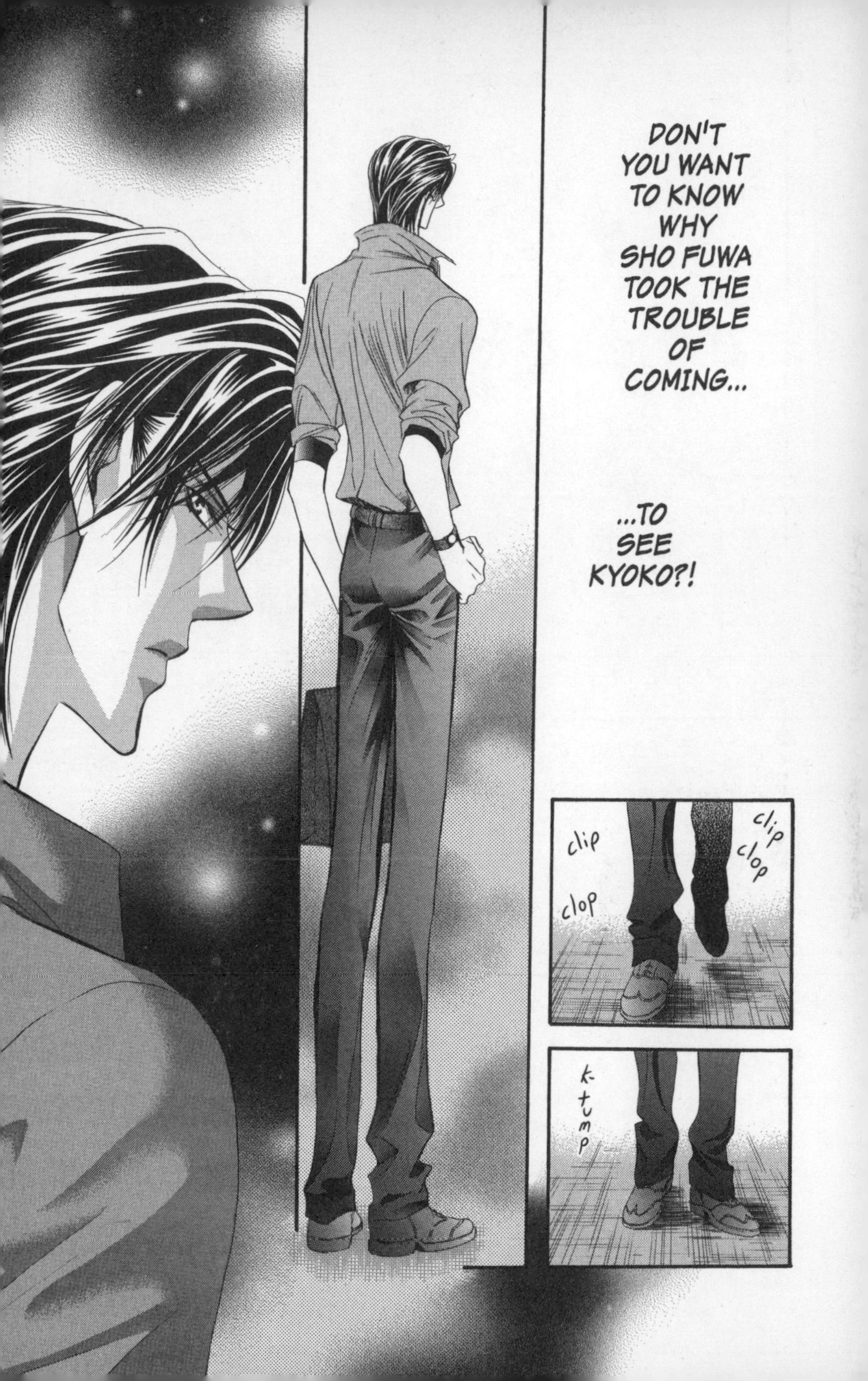
DON'T YOU WANT TO KNOW WHY SHO FUWA TOOK THE TROUBLE OF COMING...
...TO SEE KYOKO?!
clip clop
clip clop
k-tump

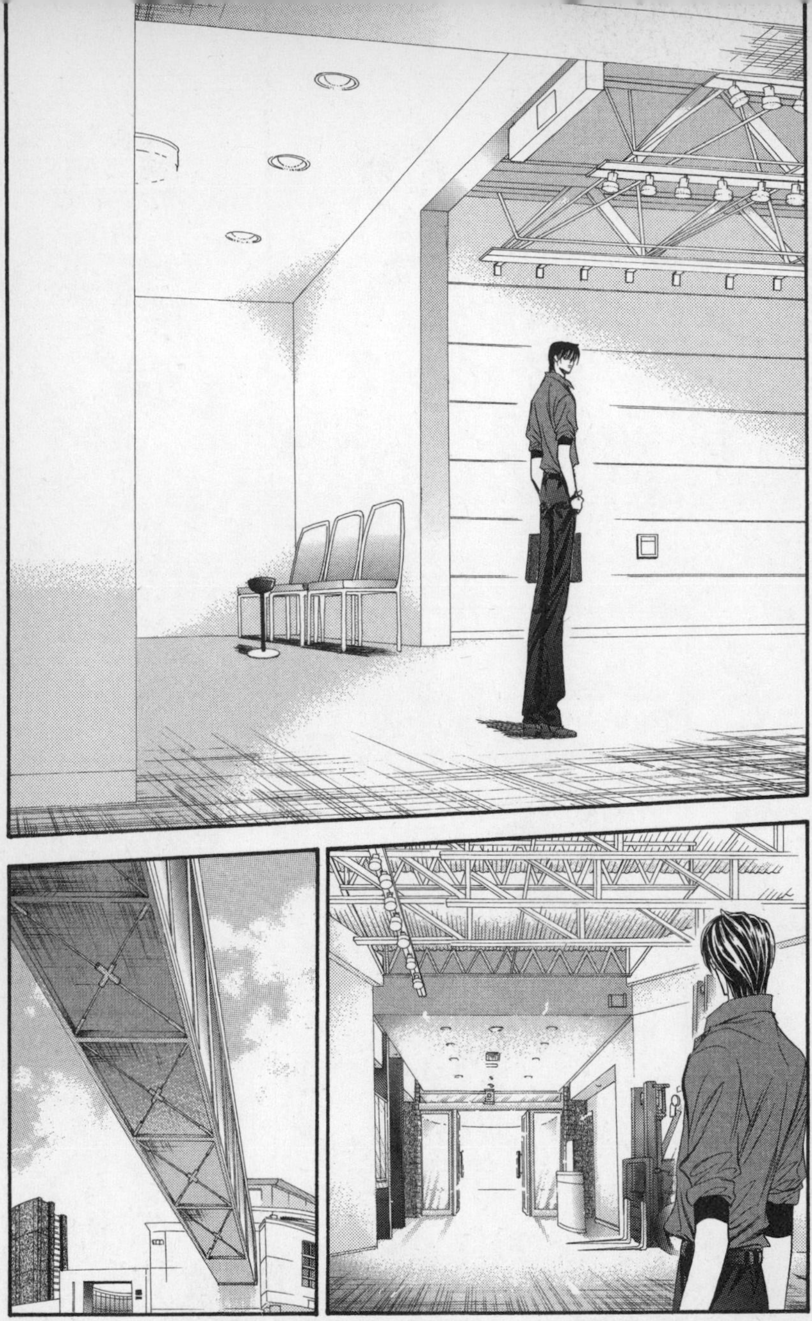

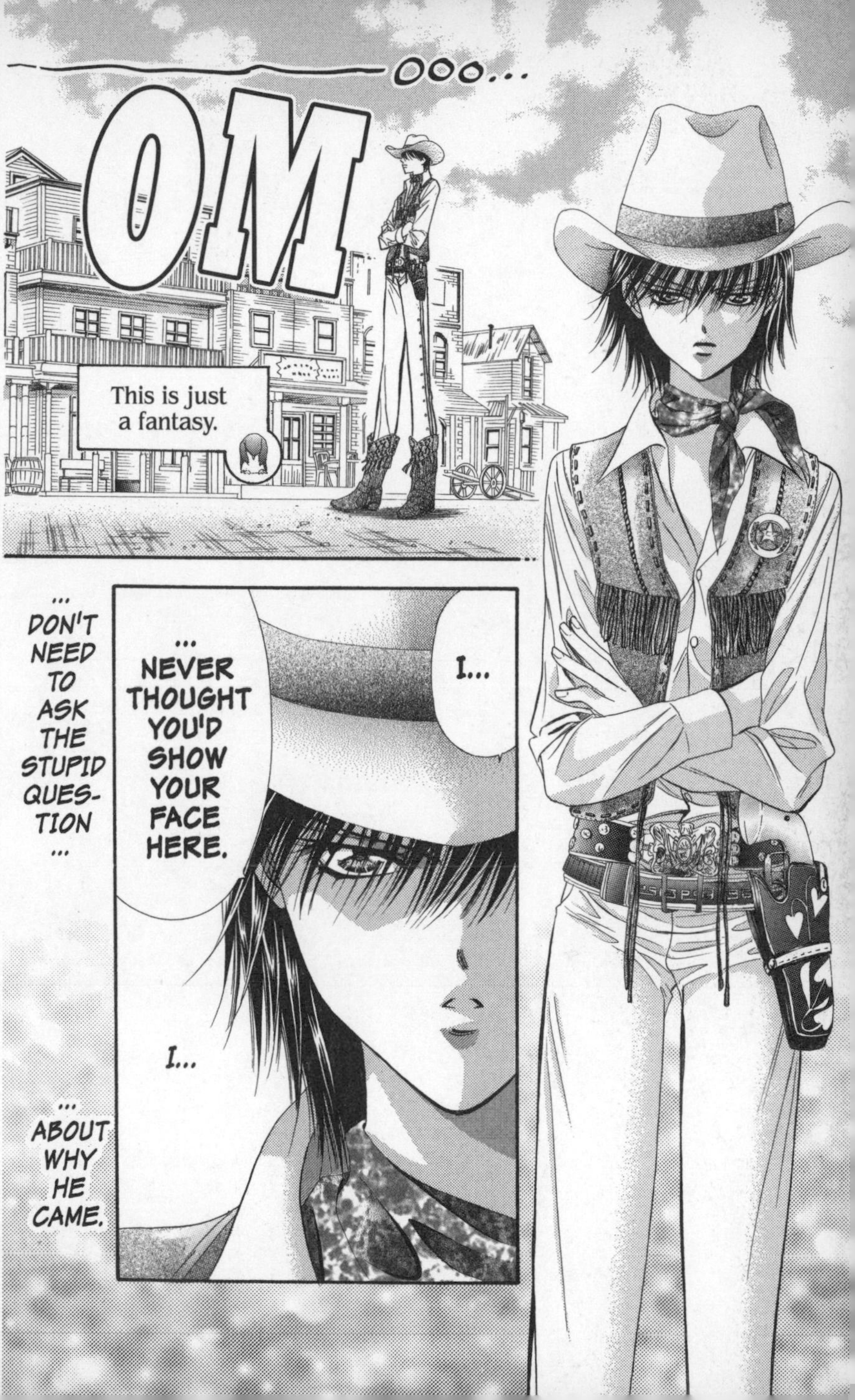
———OOO...
OM
This is just a fantasy.
I...
... NEVER THOUGHT YOU'D SHOW YOUR FACE HERE.
I...
... DON'T NEED TO ASK THE STUPID QUES- TION ...
... ABOUT WHY HE CAME.

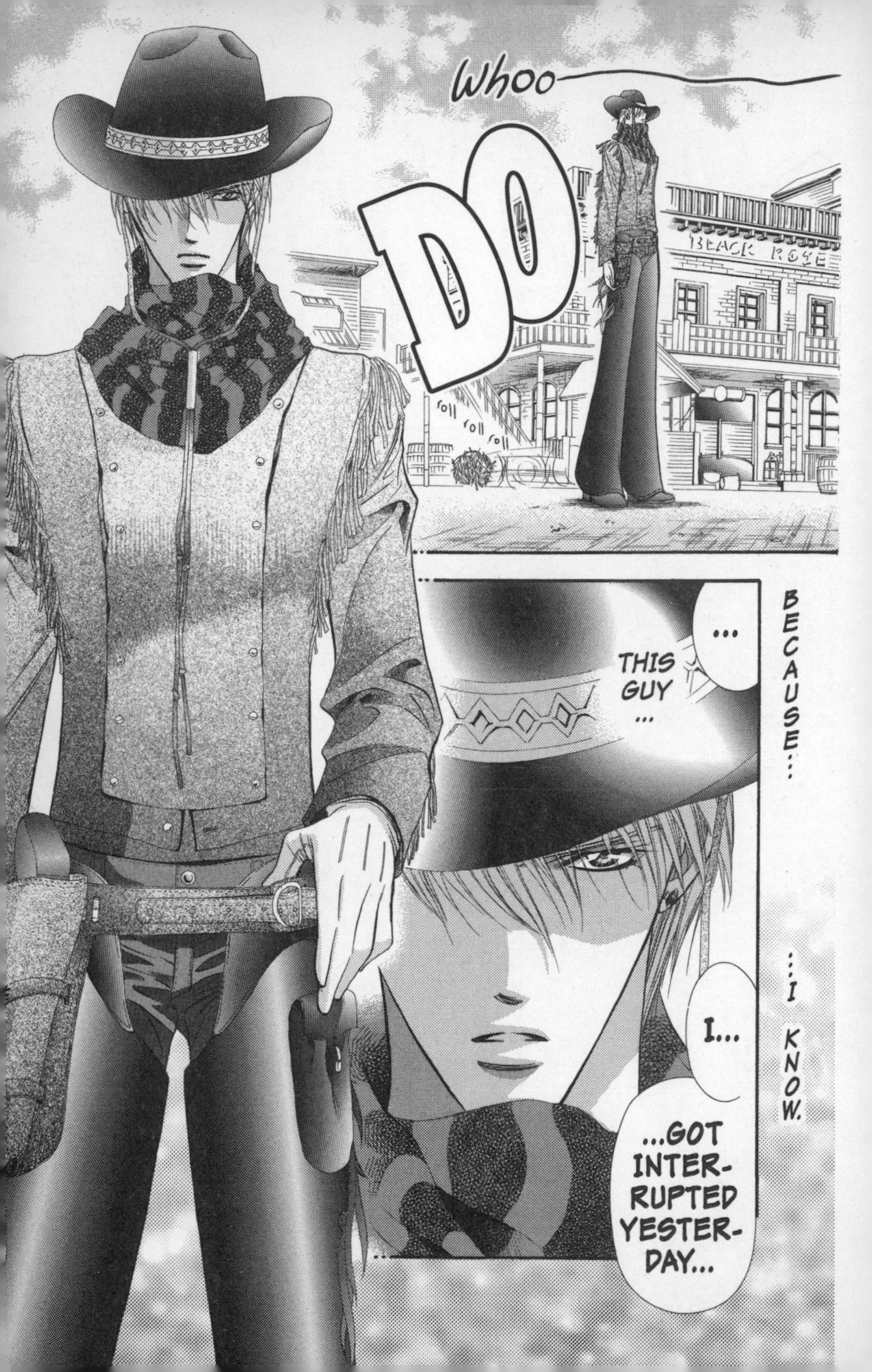
Whoo
DO
BLACK ROSE
roll roll roll
BECAUSE...
...
THIS GUY ...
...I KNOW.
I...
...GOT INTER-RUPTED YESTER-DAY...

...DOES NOT USE "COMMON SENSE" WHEN DEALING WITH ME!
heh
I KNEW IT...
Back to normal.
A LITTLE THING LIKE WHETHER IT'S INCON-VENIENT FOR ME...
...BECAUSE I'M ABOUT TO START WORK NEVER OCCURS TO HIM!
WHAT'S IMPORTANT TO HIM IS THAT SOMEONE LIKE ME HURT HIS PRIDE, SO THERE'S FURY STILL BURNING INSIDE HIM.
AND HE WANTS TO LET IT ALL OUT!
SO...
...YOU CAME TO SETTLE THINGS...
FINE ...
Actually...
I want to settle things too!
I'LL MAKE "GRUDGE"-SHAPED WELTS ALL OVER YOUR HAND-SOME FACE!
I'LL KEEP WRITING "RESENT" ON IT!
THEN!
GRUDGE
RESENT
RESENT

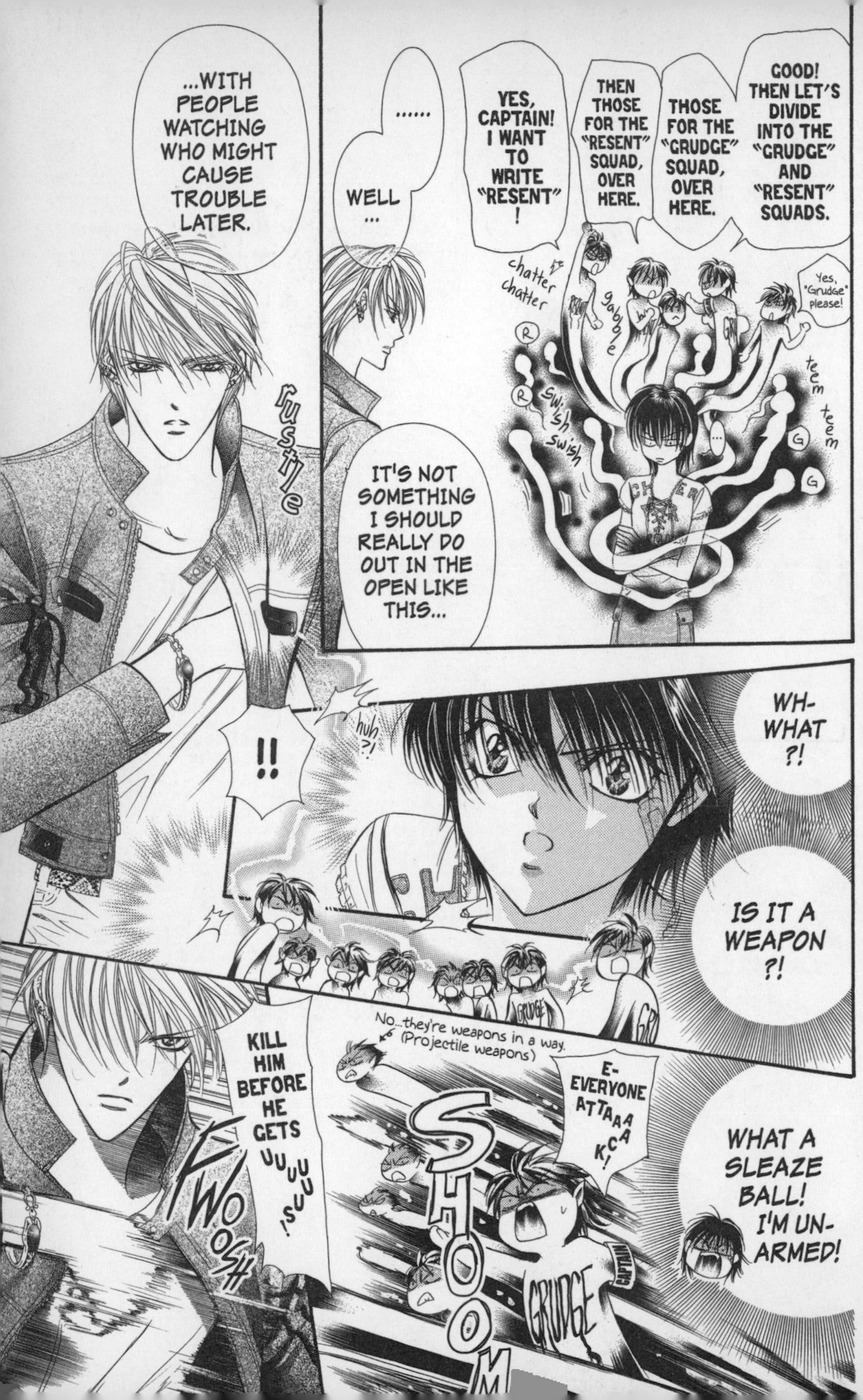
GOOD! THEN LET'S DIVIDE INTO THE "GRUDGE" AND "RESENT" SQUADS.
THOSE FOR THE "GRUDGE" SQUAD, OVER HERE.
THEN THOSE FOR THE "RESENT" SQUAD, OVER HERE.
YES, CAPTAIN! I WANT TO WRITE "RESENT"!
Yes, "Grudge" please!
chatter chatter
gabble
teem teem
swish swish
......
WELL ...
IT'S NOT SOMETHING I SHOULD REALLY DO OUT IN THE OPEN LIKE THIS...
...WITH PEOPLE WATCHING WHO MIGHT CAUSE TROUBLE LATER.
rustle
!!
WH- WHAT?!
huh?!
IS IT A WEAPON?!
WHAT A SLEAZE BALL! I'M UN-ARMED!
E- EVERYONE ATTAAAACK!
No...they're weapons in a way. (Projectile weapons)
SHOOOM
GRUDGE
CAPTAIN
KILL HIM BEFORE HE GETS UUUUUS!
FWOOSH

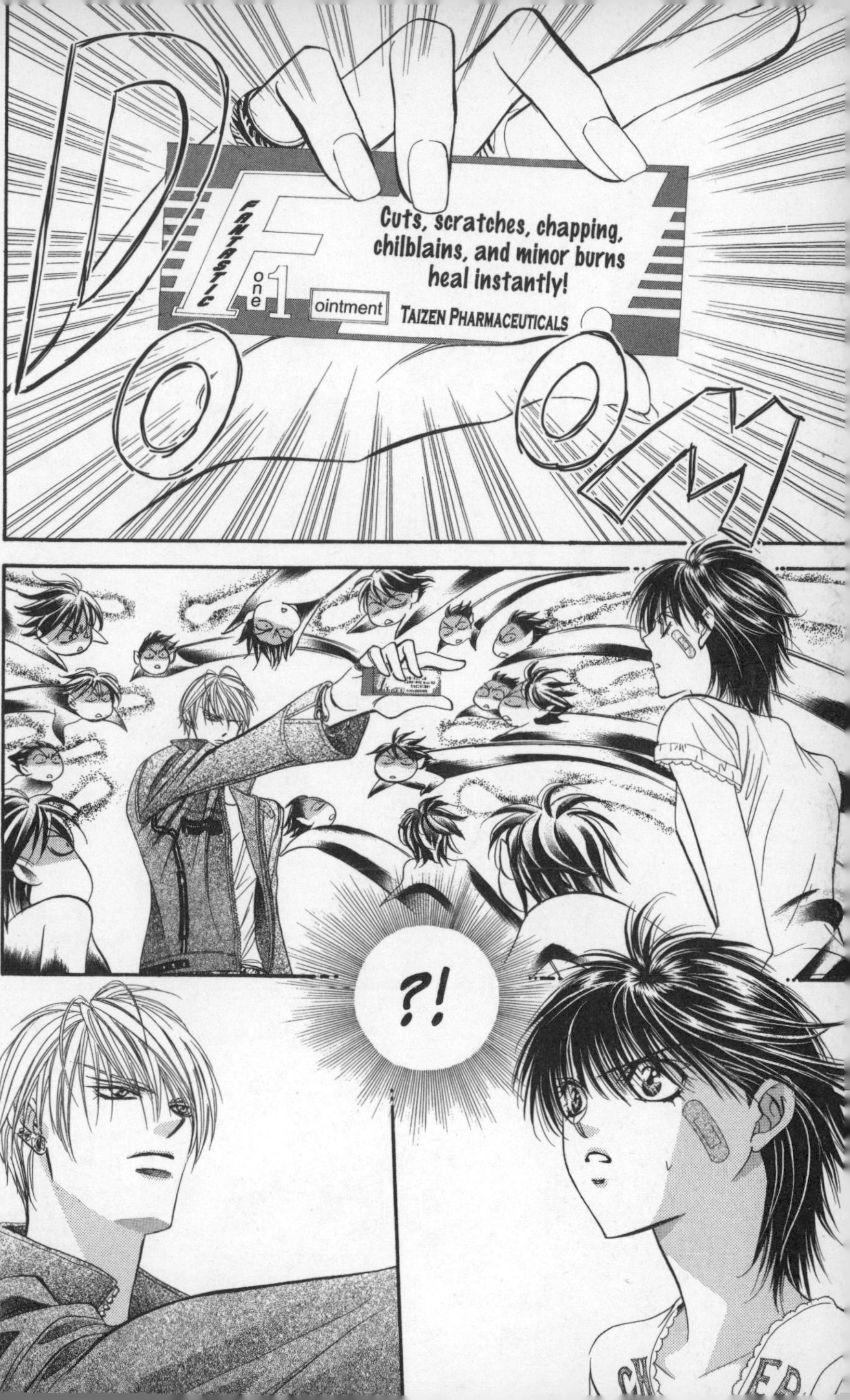
DOOM
FANTASTIC one 1 ointment
Cuts, scratches, chapping, chilblains, and minor burns heal instantly!
TAIZEN PHARMACEUTICALS
?!

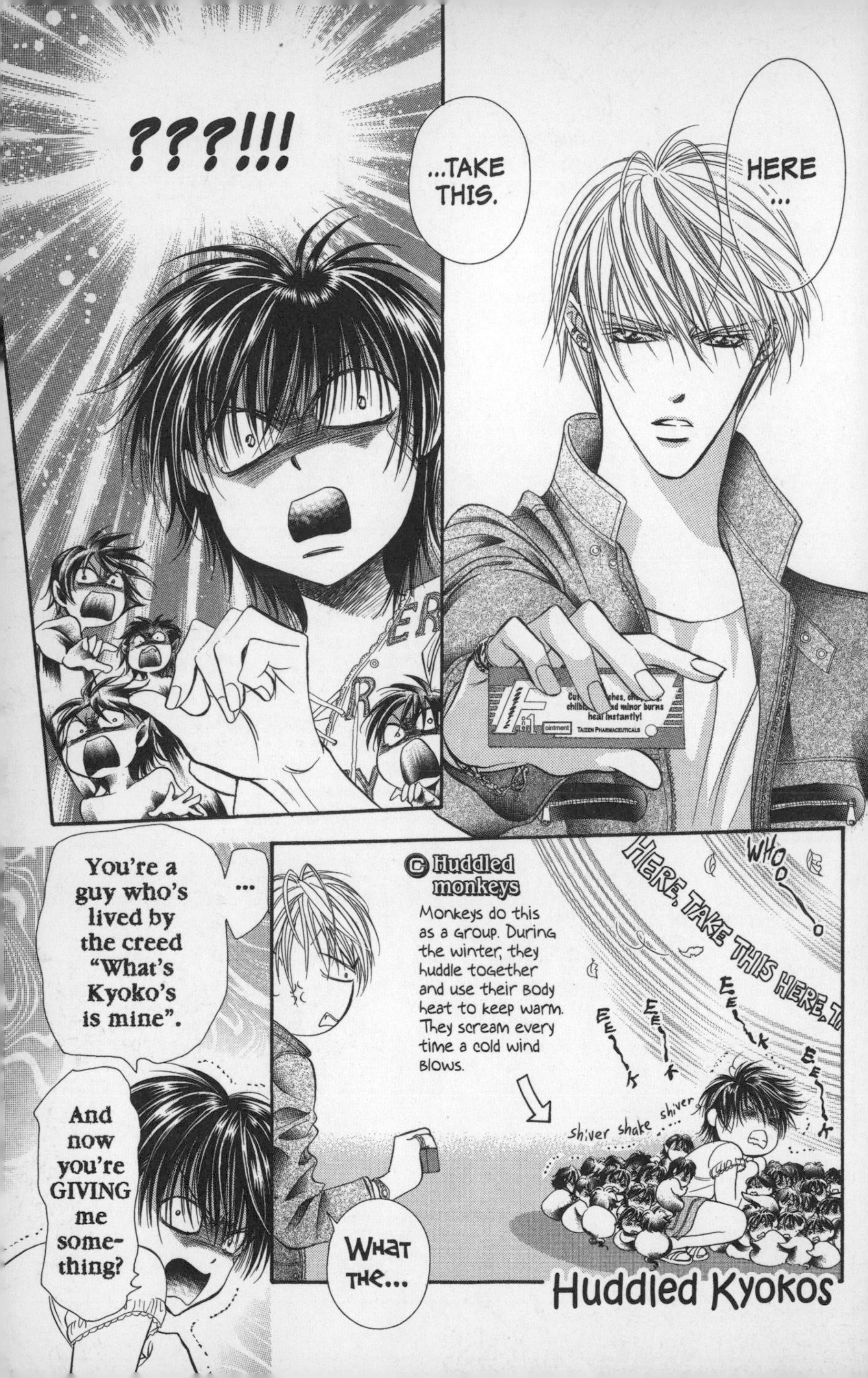
HERE ...
...TAKE THIS.
ointment
TAIZEN PHARMACEUTICALS
heal instantly!
???!!!
WHOOO
HERE, TAKE THIS HERE, T
EEEK
EEEK
EEEK
EEEK
Huddled monkeys
Monkeys do this as a group. During the winter, they huddle together and use their body heat to keep warm. They scream every time a cold wind blows.
shiver shake shiver
Huddled Kyokos
What the...
...
You're a guy who's lived by the creed "What's Kyoko's is mine".
And now you're GIVING me some-thing?

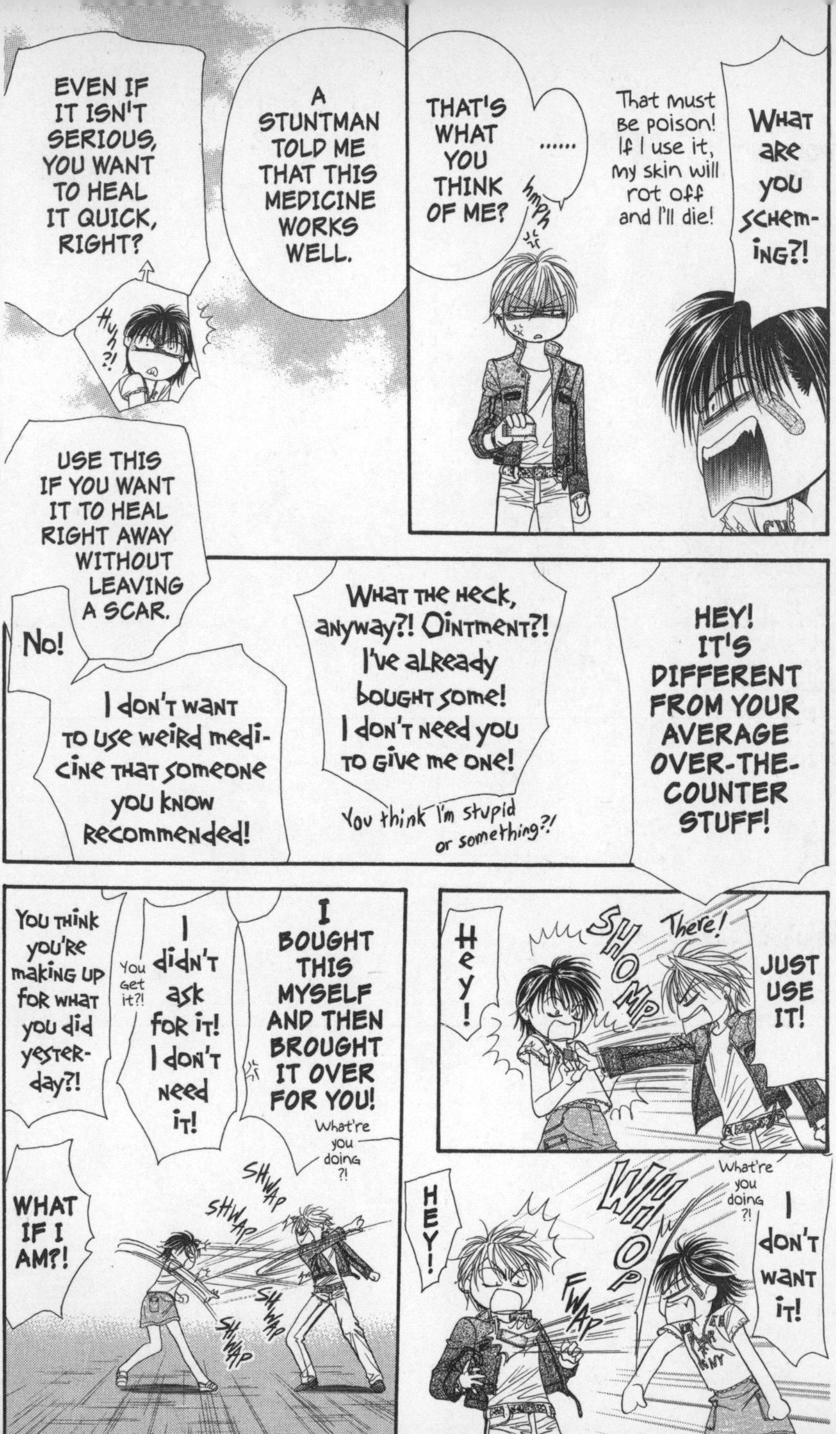
What are you scheming?!
That must be poison! If I use it, my skin will rot off and I'll die!
THAT'S WHAT YOU THINK OF ME?
......
hmph
A STUNTMAN TOLD ME THAT THIS MEDICINE WORKS WELL.
EVEN IF IT ISN'T SERIOUS, YOU WANT TO HEAL IT QUICK, RIGHT?
Huh?!
USE THIS IF YOU WANT IT TO HEAL RIGHT AWAY WITHOUT LEAVING A SCAR.
HEY! IT'S DIFFERENT FROM YOUR AVERAGE OVER-THE-COUNTER STUFF!
What the heck, anyway?! Ointment?! I've already bought some! I don't need you to give me one!
You think I'm stupid or something?!
No!
I don't want to use weird medicine that someone you know recommended!
There!
JUST USE IT!
SHOMP
Hey!
I BOUGHT THIS MYSELF AND THEN BROUGHT IT OVER FOR YOU!
I didn't ask for it! I don't need it!
You get it?!
You think you're making up for what you did yesterday?!
I don't want it!
What're you doing?!
WHOOP
FWAP
HEY!
What're you doing?!
WHAT IF I AM?!
SHWAP
SHWAP
SHWAP
SHWAP

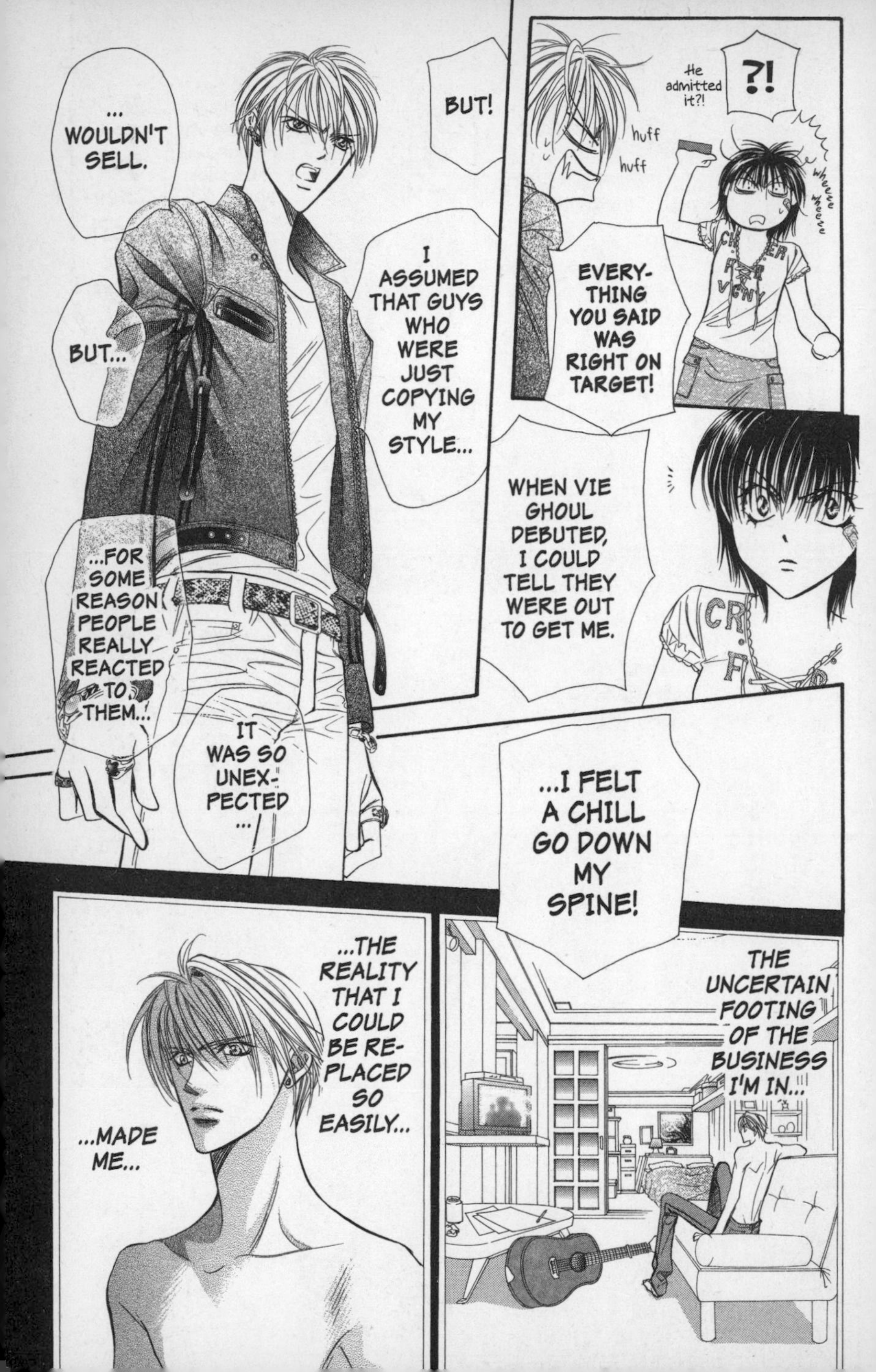
I ASSUMED THAT GUYS WHO WERE JUST COPYING MY STYLE...
... WOULDN'T SELL.
BUT...
...FOR SOME REASON PEOPLE REALLY REACTED TO THEM...
IT WAS SO UNEXPECTED...
BUT!
huff
huff
He admitted it?!
?!
wheeze wheeze
EVERYTHING YOU SAID WAS RIGHT ON TARGET!
WHEN VIE GHOUL DEBUTED, I COULD TELL THEY WERE OUT TO GET ME.
...I FELT A CHILL GO DOWN MY SPINE!
THE UNCERTAIN FOOTING OF THE BUSINESS I'M IN...
...THE REALITY THAT I COULD BE REPLACED SO EASILY...
...MADE ME...

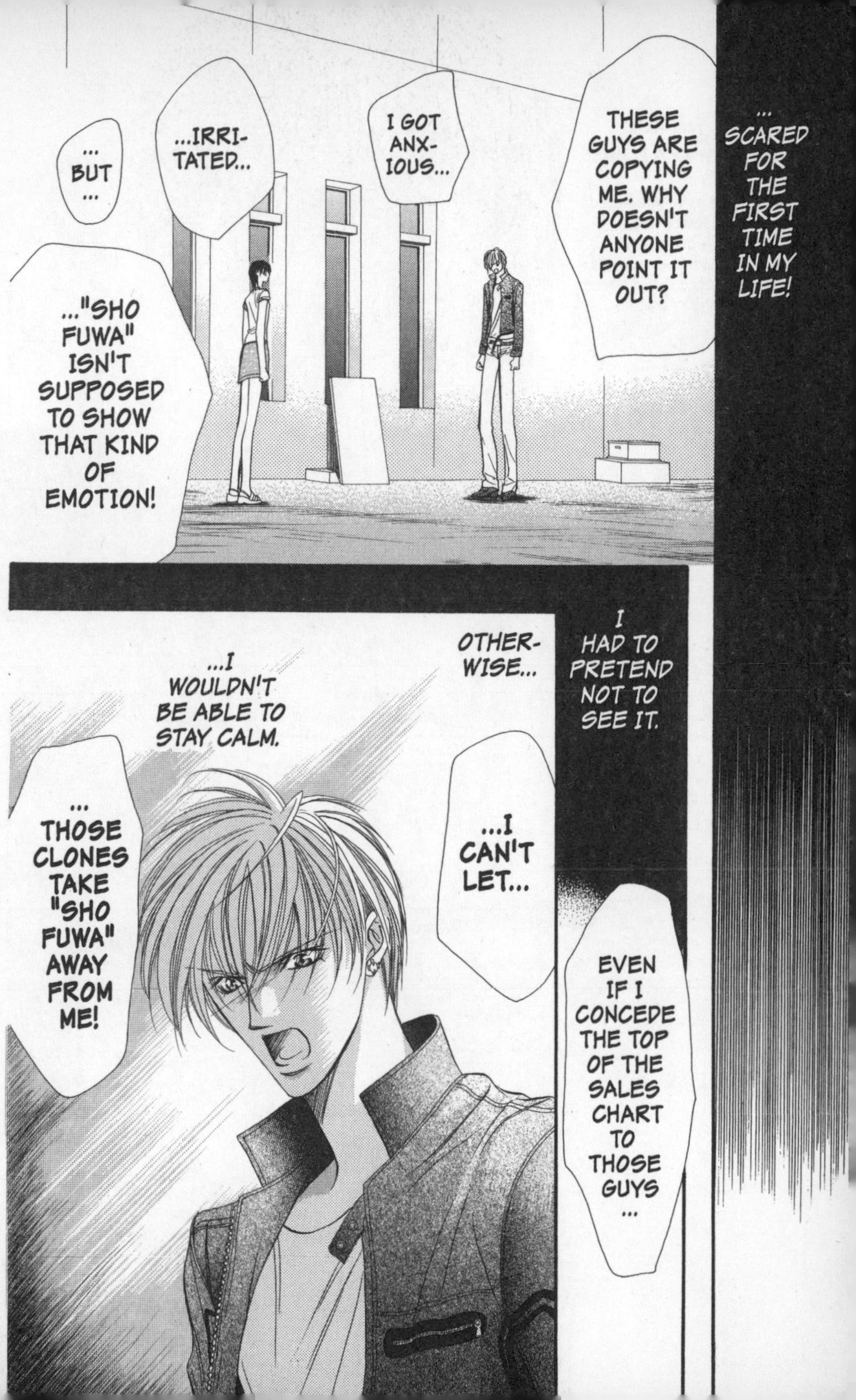
...SCARED FOR THE FIRST TIME IN MY LIFE!
THESE GUYS ARE COPYING ME. WHY DOESN'T ANYONE POINT IT OUT?
I GOT ANXIOUS...
...IRRITATED...
...BUT...
..."SHO FUWA" ISN'T SUPPOSED TO SHOW THAT KIND OF EMOTION!
I HAD TO PRETEND NOT TO SEE IT.
OTHERWISE...
...I WOULDN'T BE ABLE TO STAY CALM.
EVEN IF I CONCEDE THE TOP OF THE SALES CHART TO THOSE GUYS...
...I CAN'T LET...
...THOSE CLONES TAKE "SHO FUWA" AWAY FROM ME!

CD Jacket Before ⇨ After

And just as I'd predicted... Ren's reaction was apparently different from what the readers had expected. So despite the ardent requests, the readers' reactions to that scene were lukewarm...(Tahaha...) It's all right though. I dragged out "Prisoner" to draw the scene where Ren watches the angel Kyoko, but it wasn't just for that. I thought...I could also use "Prisoner" for Sho, who hadn't appeared in a while (yes, it has been quite a while). But... leaving that aside, I initially had no intention of re-using "Prisoner" even a bit, so I hadn't thought of how the CD jacket would look. Thus the jacket when it appeared in the magazine was a real hack job... ♪ I just drew something, anything. I drew what I associated with "Prisoner," and it turned out that way... ♪ ...tied up...? In the manga volume, the jacket illustration has been re-drawn (it's this volume's title page).

- Continued -

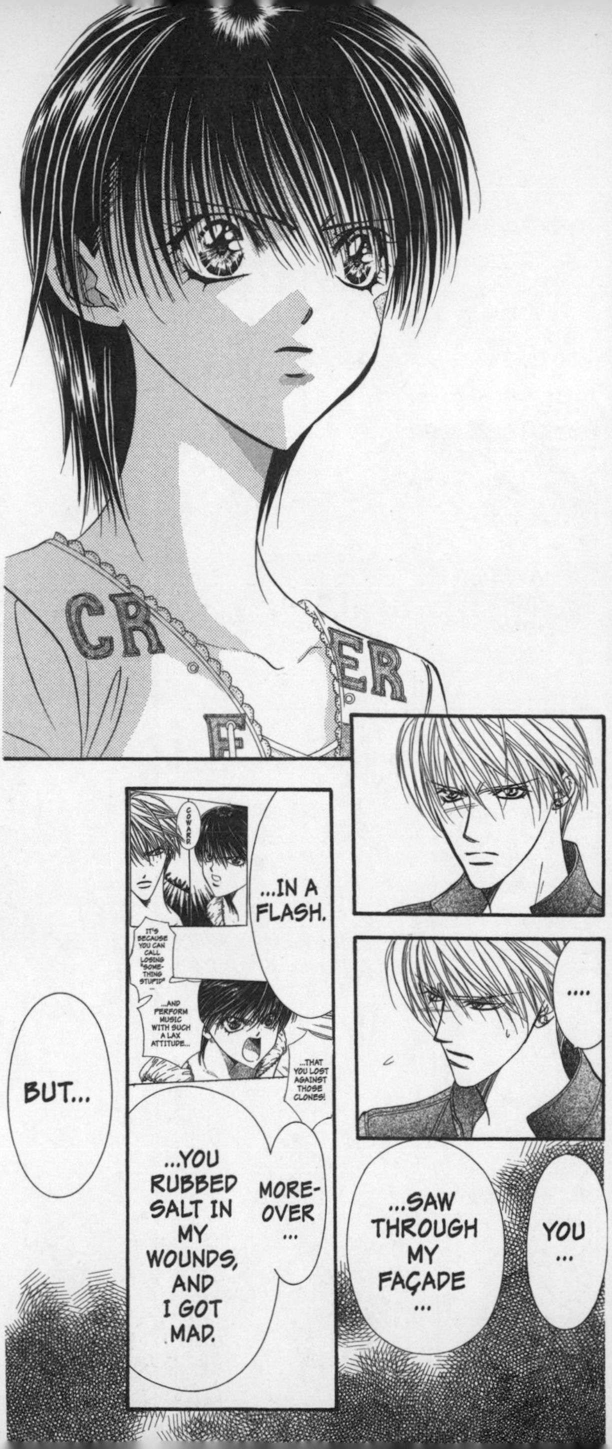
....
YOU...
...SAW THROUGH MY FAÇADE...
...IN A FLASH.
COWARD.
IT'S BECAUSE YOU CAN CALL LOSING "SOMETHING STUPID"...
...AND PERFORM MUSIC WITH SUCH A LAX ATTITUDE...
...THAT YOU LOST AGAINST THOSE CLONES!
BUT...
MORE-OVER...
...YOU RUBBED SALT IN MY WOUNDS, AND I GOT MAD.

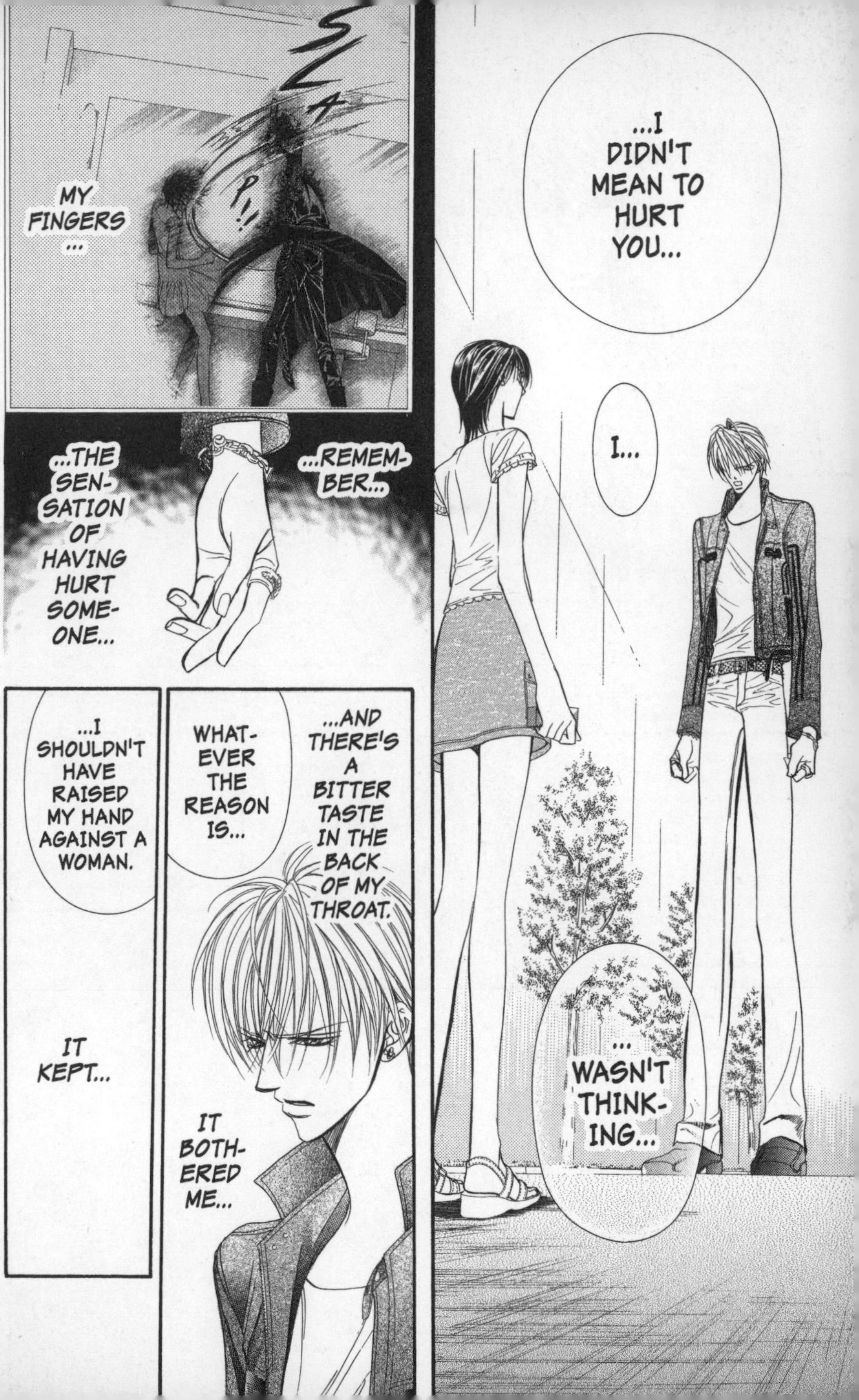
...I DIDN'T MEAN TO HURT YOU...
I...
...WASN'T THINKING...
SZAP!!
MY FINGERS ...
...REMEMBER...
...THE SENSATION OF HAVING HURT SOMEONE...
...AND THERE'S A BITTER TASTE IN THE BACK OF MY THROAT.
WHATEVER THE REASON IS...
IT BOTHERED ME...
...I SHOULDN'T HAVE RAISED MY HAND AGAINST A WOMAN.
IT KEPT...

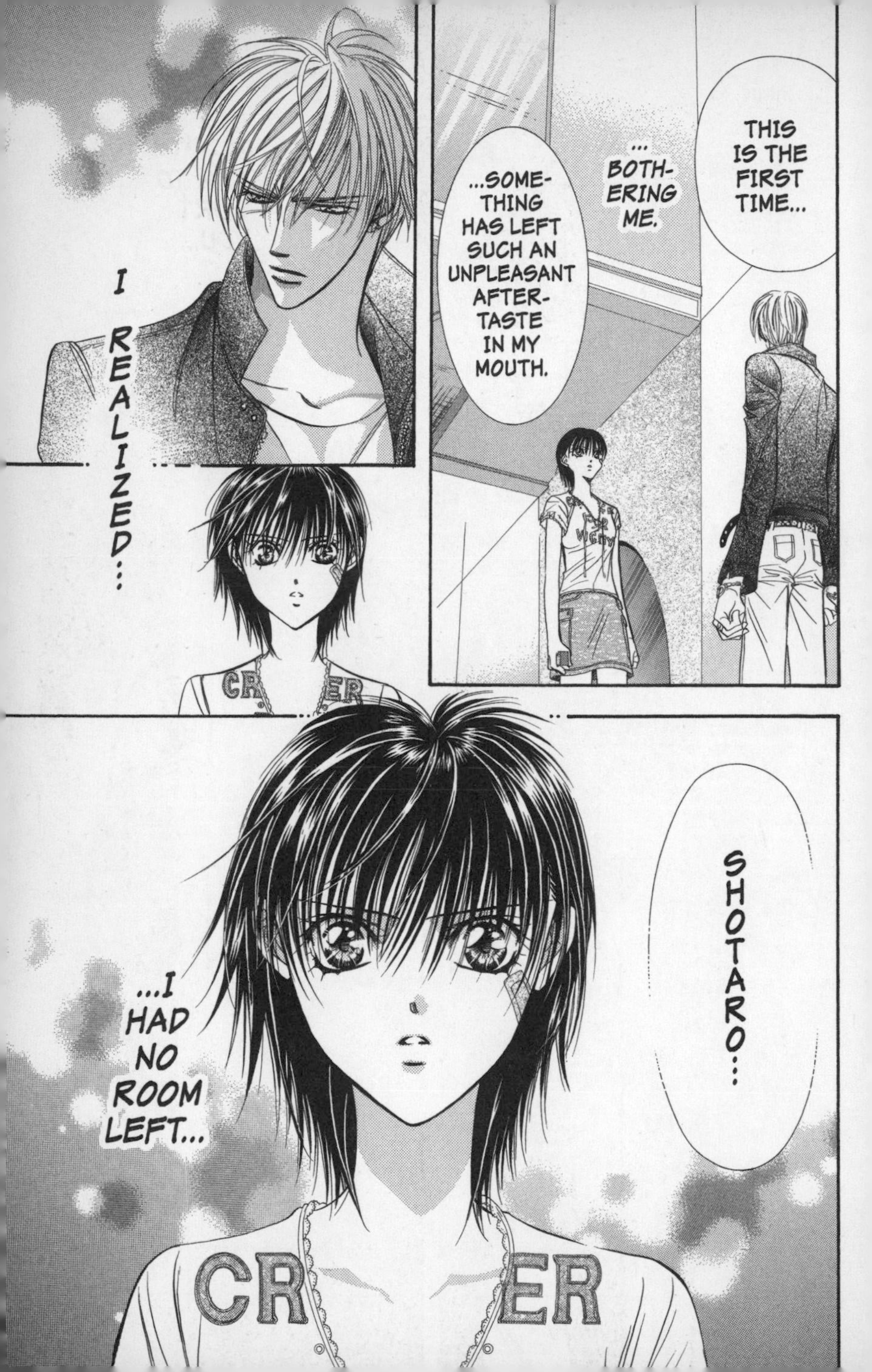
THIS IS THE FIRST TIME...
... BOTHERING ME.
...SOMETHING HAS LEFT SUCH AN UNPLEASANT AFTERTASTE IN MY MOUTH.
I REALIZED...
SHOTARO...
...I HAD NO ROOM LEFT...

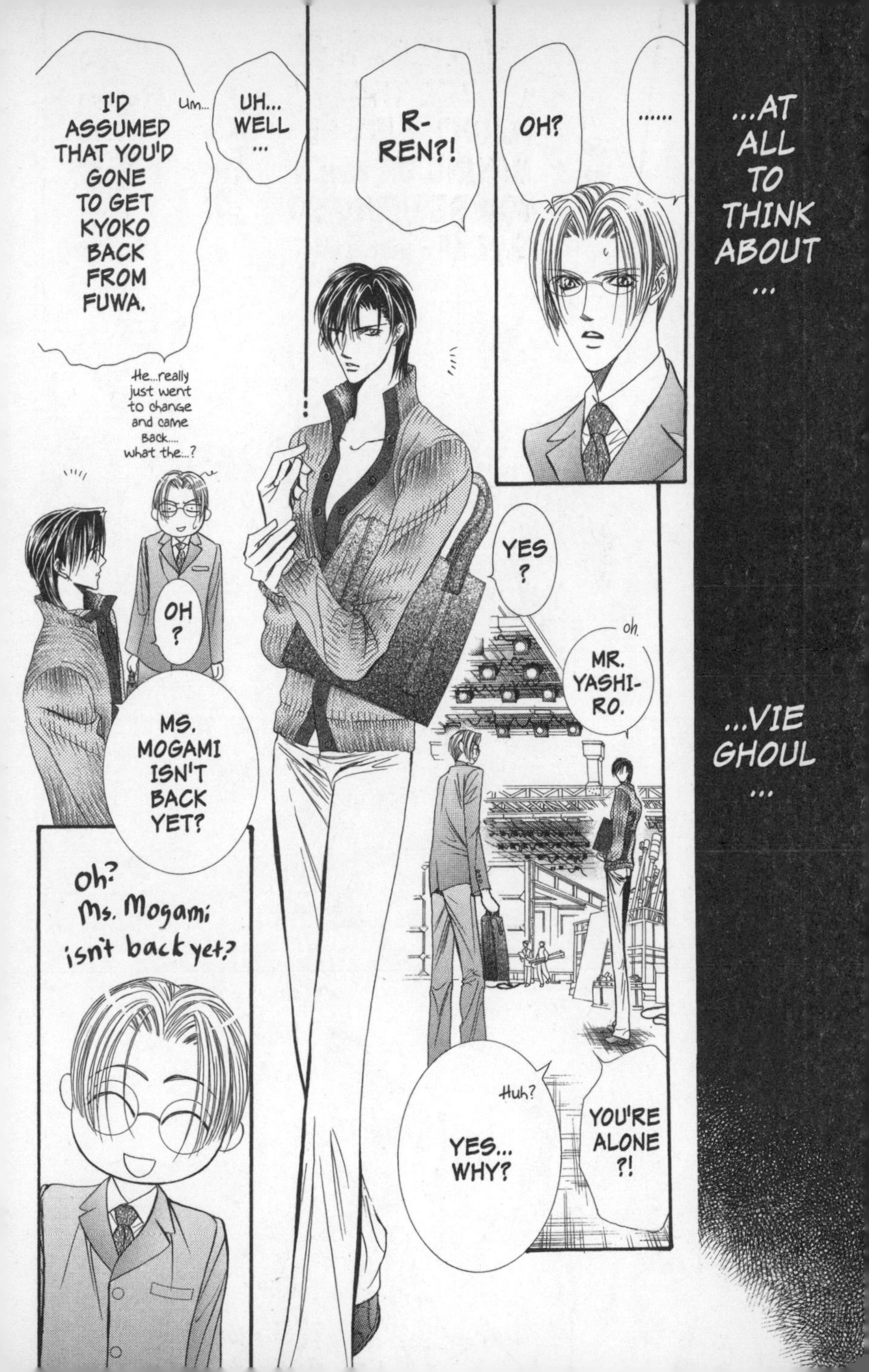
...AT ALL TO THINK ABOUT ...
...VIE GHOUL ...
......
OH?
R-REN?!
UH... WELL ...
Um...
I'D ASSUMED THAT YOU'D GONE TO GET KYOKO BACK FROM FUWA.
He...really just went to change and came back... what the...?
YES ?
oh.
MR. YASHIRO.
YOU'RE ALONE ?!
Huh?
YES... WHY?
OH ?
MS. MOGAMI ISN'T BACK YET?
Oh? Ms. Mogami isn't back yet?

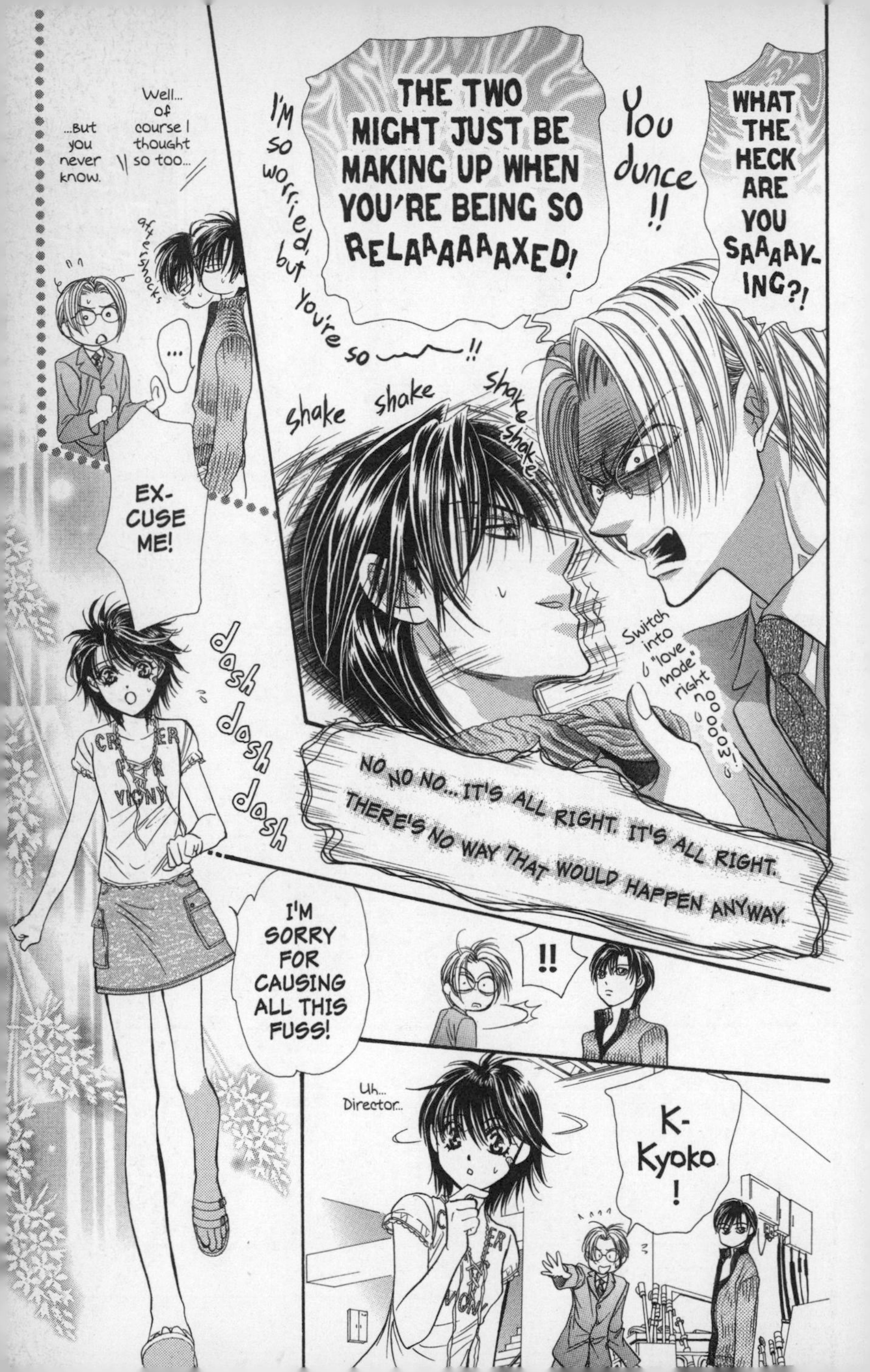
WHAT THE HECK ARE YOU SAAAAY-ING?!
You dunce!!
THE TWO MIGHT JUST BE MAKING UP WHEN YOU'RE BEING SO RELAAAAAAAXED!
I'M so worried, but you're so ~~~!!
shake shake shake shake shake
Switch into "love mode" right nooooow!
NO NO NO... IT'S ALL RIGHT. IT'S ALL RIGHT. THERE'S NO WAY THAT WOULD HAPPEN ANYWAY.
Well... of course I thought so too...
...but you never know.
aftershocks
...
EX-CUSE ME!
dosh dosh dosh
!!
I'M SORRY FOR CAUSING ALL THIS FUSS!
K-Kyoko!
Uh... Director...

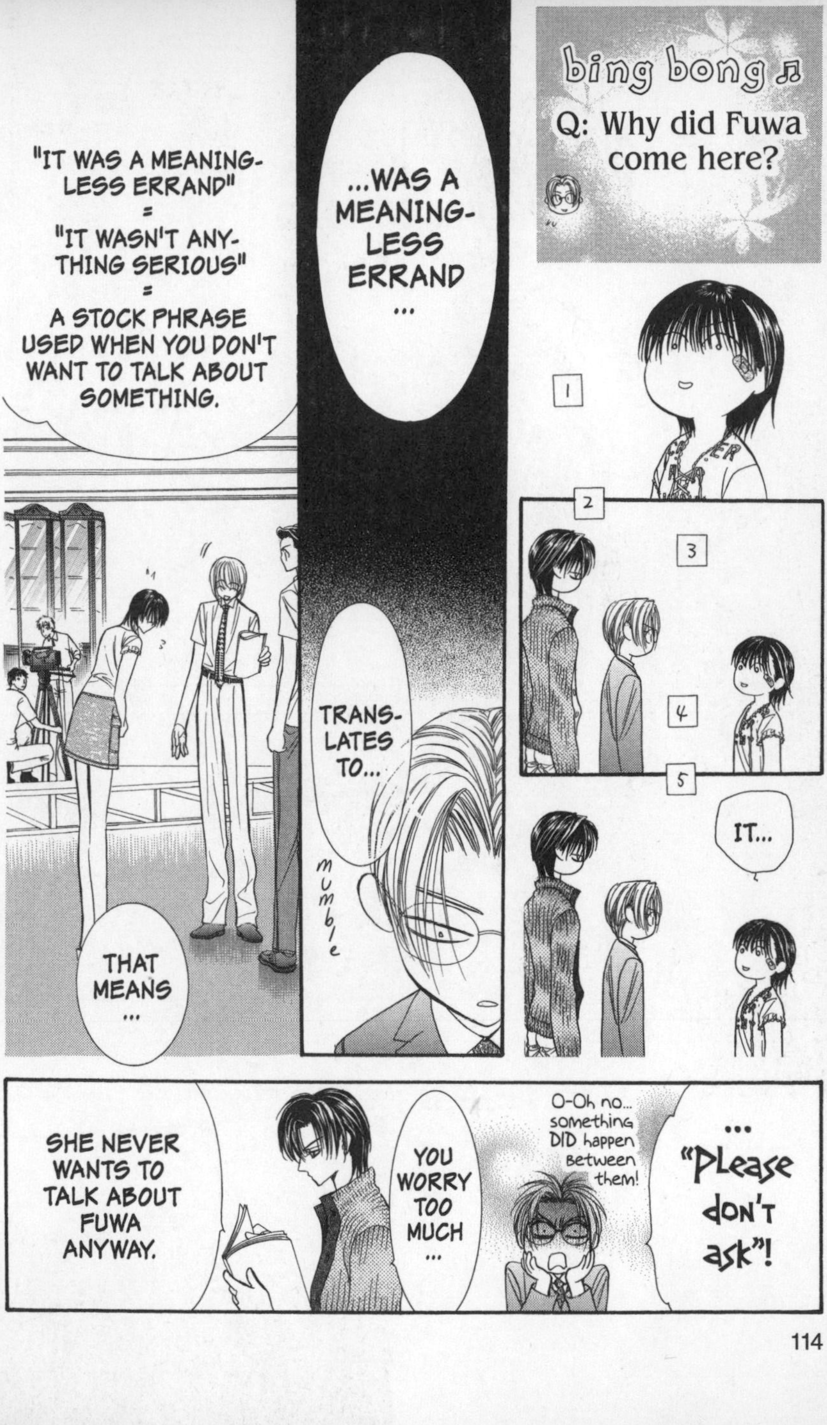
bing bong ♫
Q: Why did Fuwa come here?
1
2
3
4
5
IT...
...WAS A MEANING-LESS ERRAND ...
TRANS-LATES TO...
mumble
"IT WAS A MEANING-LESS ERRAND" = "IT WASN'T ANY-THING SERIOUS" = A STOCK PHRASE USED WHEN YOU DON'T WANT TO TALK ABOUT SOMETHING.
THAT MEANS ...
... "Please don't ask"!
O-Oh no... something DID happen between them!
YOU WORRY TOO MUCH ...
SHE NEVER WANTS TO TALK ABOUT FUWA ANYWAY.

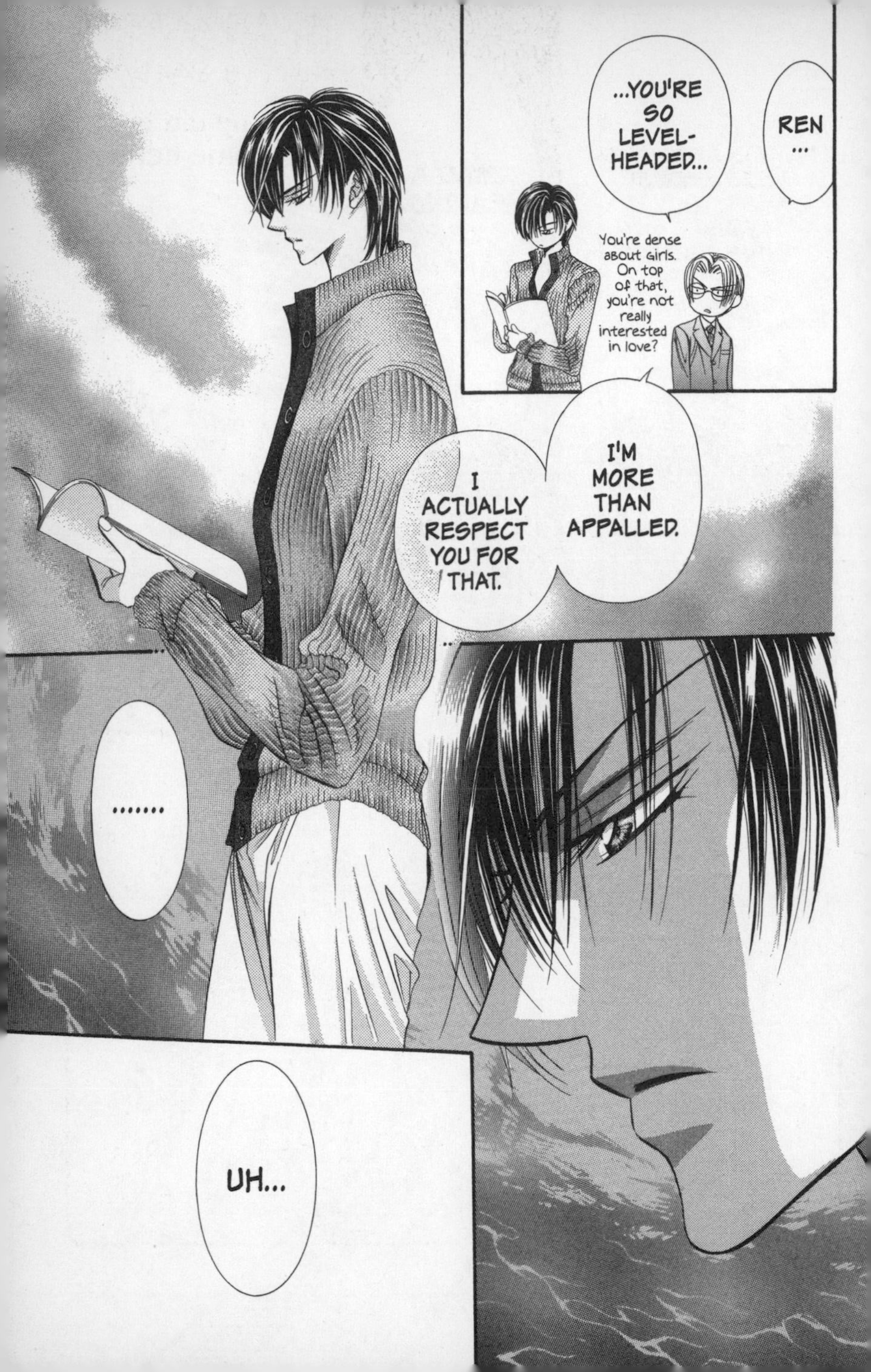
REN ...
...YOU'RE SO LEVEL-HEADED...
You're dense about girls. On top of that, you're not really interested in love?
I'M MORE THAN APPALLED.
I ACTUALLY RESPECT YOU FOR THAT.
....
UH...

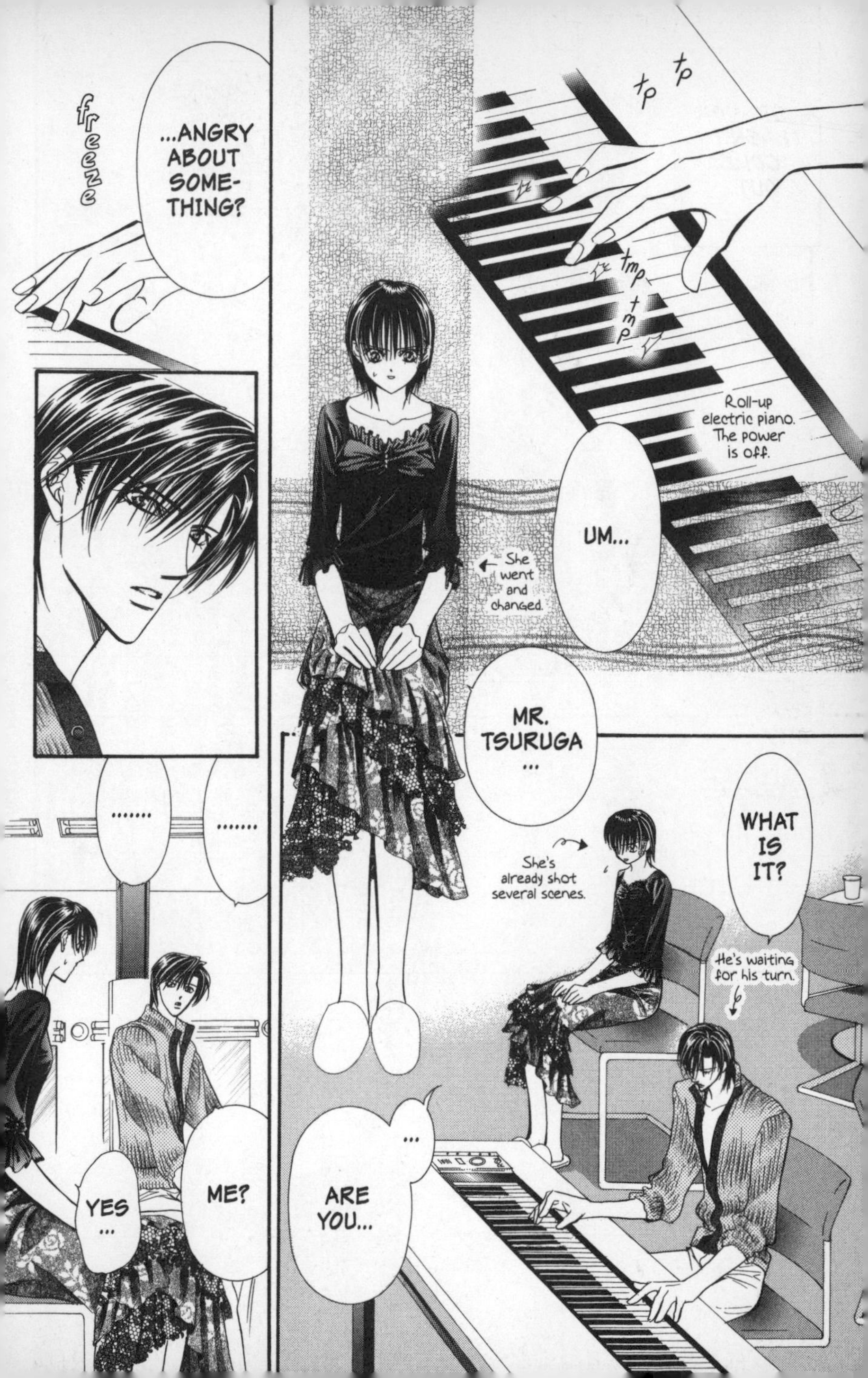
xp xp
tmp tmp
Roll-up electric piano. The power is off.
UM...
She went and changed.
MR. TSURUGA ...
WHAT IS IT?
She's already shot several scenes.
He's waiting for his turn.
...
ARE YOU...
...ANGRY ABOUT SOME-THING?
freeze
....
....
ME?
YES ...

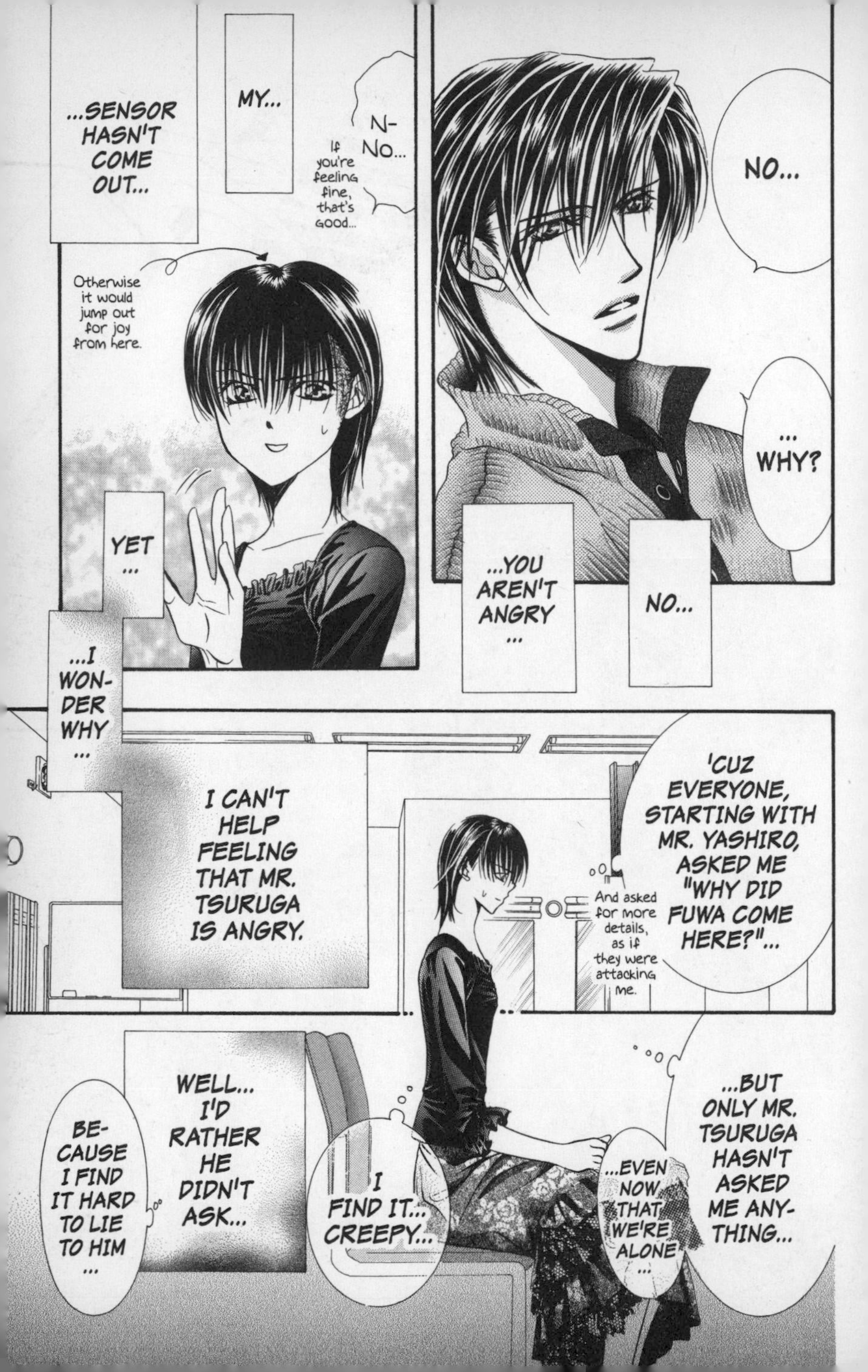
NO...
... WHY?
NO...
...YOU AREN'T ANGRY ...
N- NO...
If you're feeling fine, that's good...
MY...
...SENSOR HASN'T COME OUT...
Otherwise it would jump out for joy from here.
YET ...
...I WON-DER WHY ...
'CUZ EVERYONE, STARTING WITH MR. YASHIRO, ASKED ME "WHY DID FUWA COME HERE?"...
And asked for more details, as if they were attacking me.
I CAN'T HELP FEELING THAT MR. TSURUGA IS ANGRY.
...BUT ONLY MR. TSURUGA HASN'T ASKED ME ANY-THING...
...EVEN NOW THAT WE'RE ALONE ...
I FIND IT... CREEPY...
WELL... I'D RATHER HE DIDN'T ASK...
BE-CAUSE I FIND IT HARD TO LIE TO HIM ...

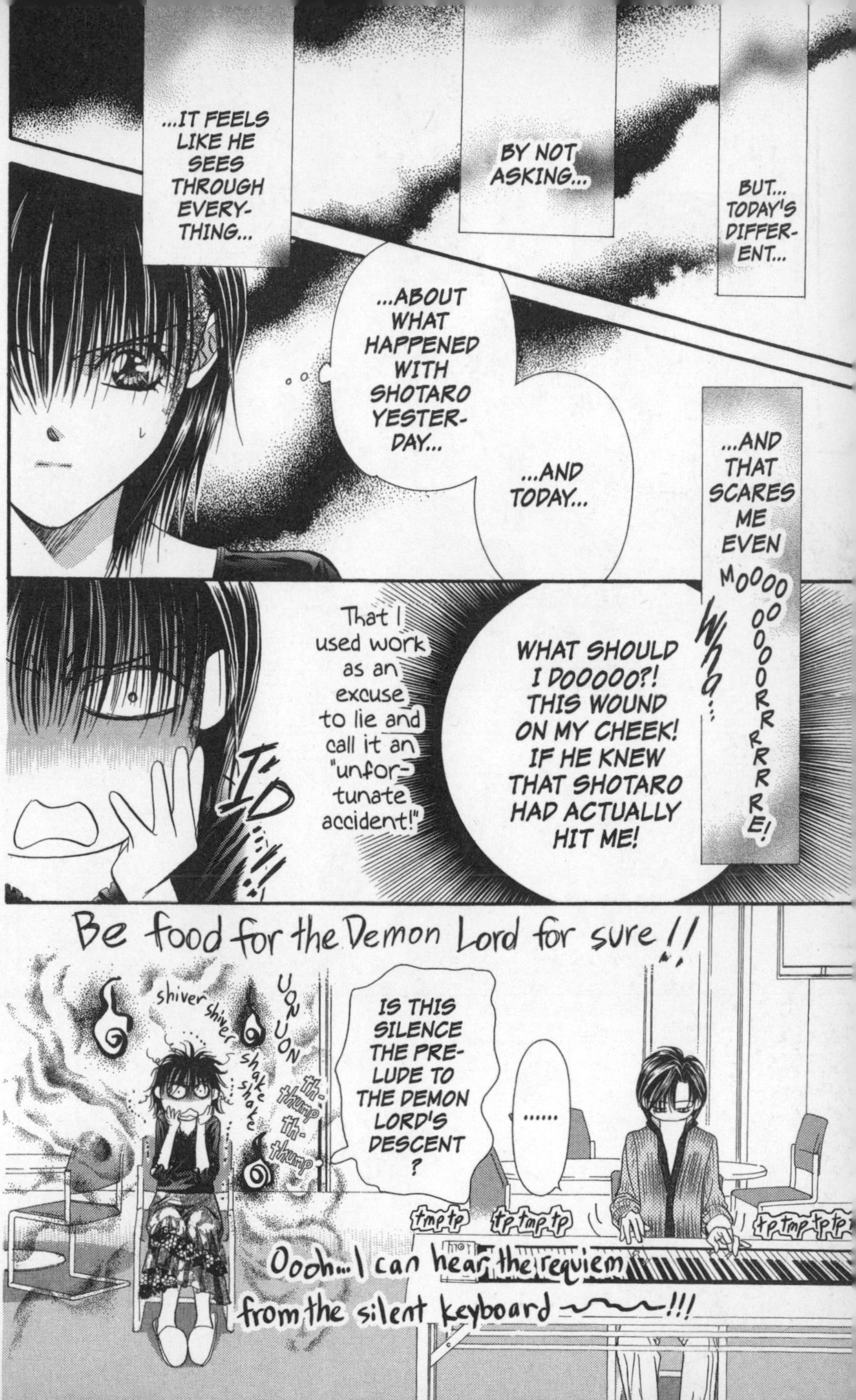
BUT... TODAY'S DIFFERENT...
BY NOT ASKING...
...IT FEELS LIKE HE SEES THROUGH EVERYTHING...
...ABOUT WHAT HAPPENED WITH SHOTARO YESTERDAY...
...AND TODAY...
...AND THAT SCARES ME EVEN MOOOOOOORRRRRE!
Whaa...
WHAT SHOULD I DOOOOO?! THIS WOUND ON MY CHEEK! IF HE KNEW THAT SHOTARO HAD ACTUALLY HIT ME!
That I used work as an excuse to lie and call it an "unfortunate accident!"
I'D...!!
Be food for the Demon Lord for sure!!
tp tmp tp tp
......
tp tmp tp
tmp tp
IS THIS SILENCE THE PRELUDE TO THE DEMON LORD'S DESCENT?
UON UON
th-thump th-thump
shiver shiver shake shake
Oooh... I can hear the requiem from the silent keyboard~~!!!

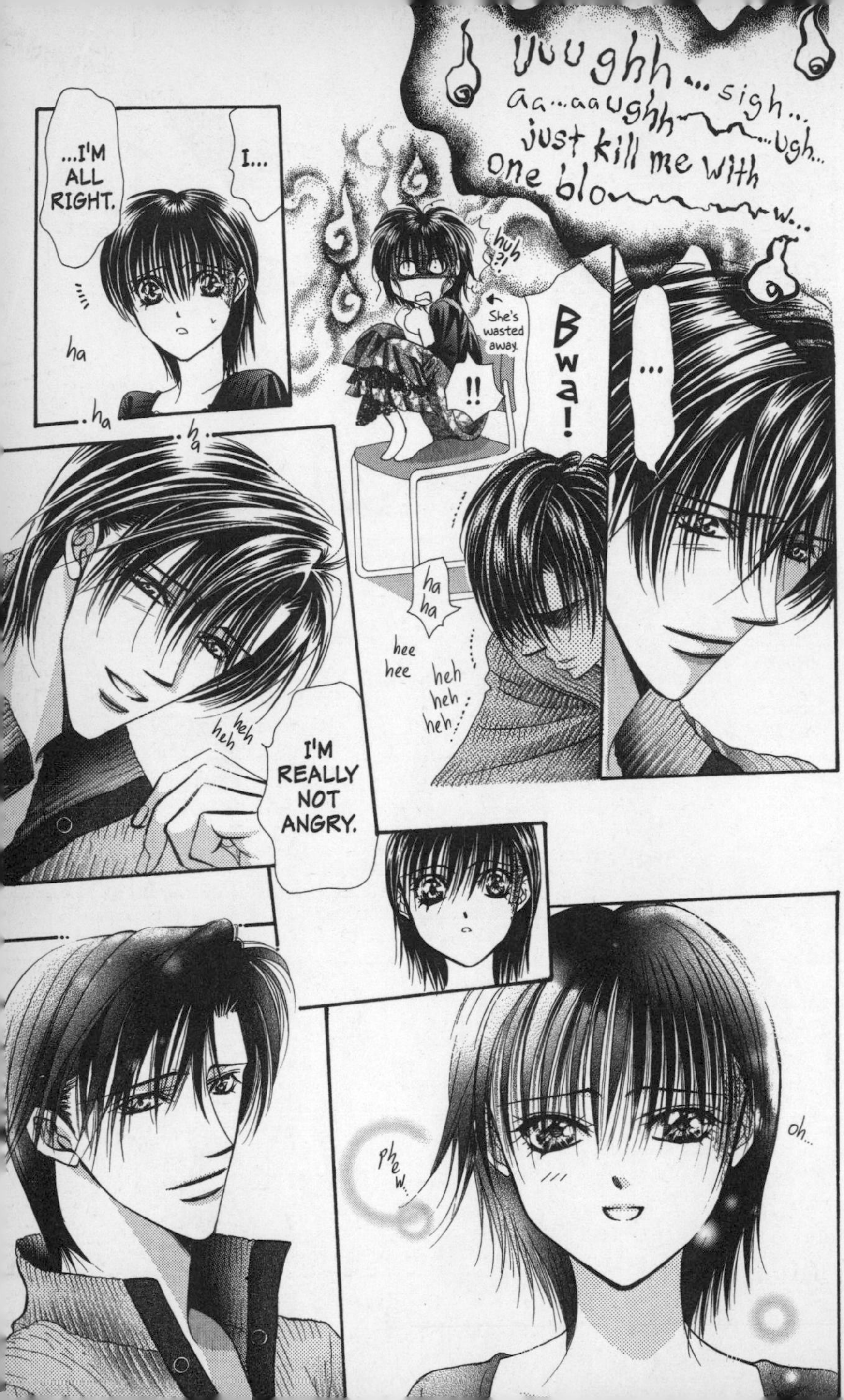
Uuughh... aa...aaughh... sigh... just kill me with one blowww... ugh...
...
Bwa!
huh?!
She's wasted away.
!!
ha ha
hee hee
heh heh heh
I...
...I'M ALL RIGHT.
ha ha ha
heh heh
I'M REALLY NOT ANGRY.
oh...
phew...

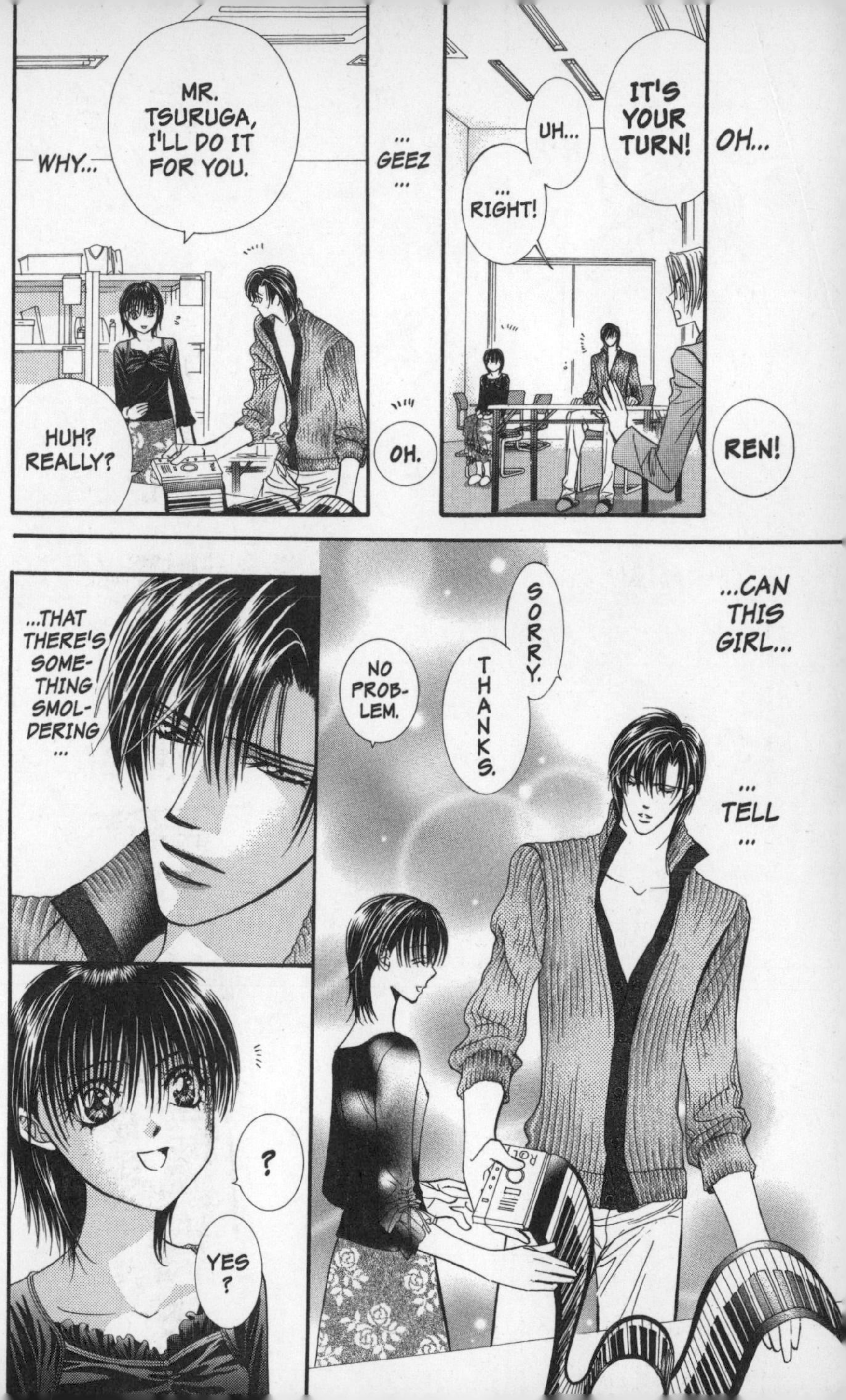
OH...
IT'S YOUR TURN!
UH...
...RIGHT!
REN!
...GEEZ...
MR. TSURUGA, I'LL DO IT FOR YOU.
WHY...
OH.
HUH? REALLY?
...CAN THIS GIRL...
SORRY.
THANKS.
NO PROB-LEM.
...TELL...
...THAT THERE'S SOME-THING SMOLDERING...
?
YES?

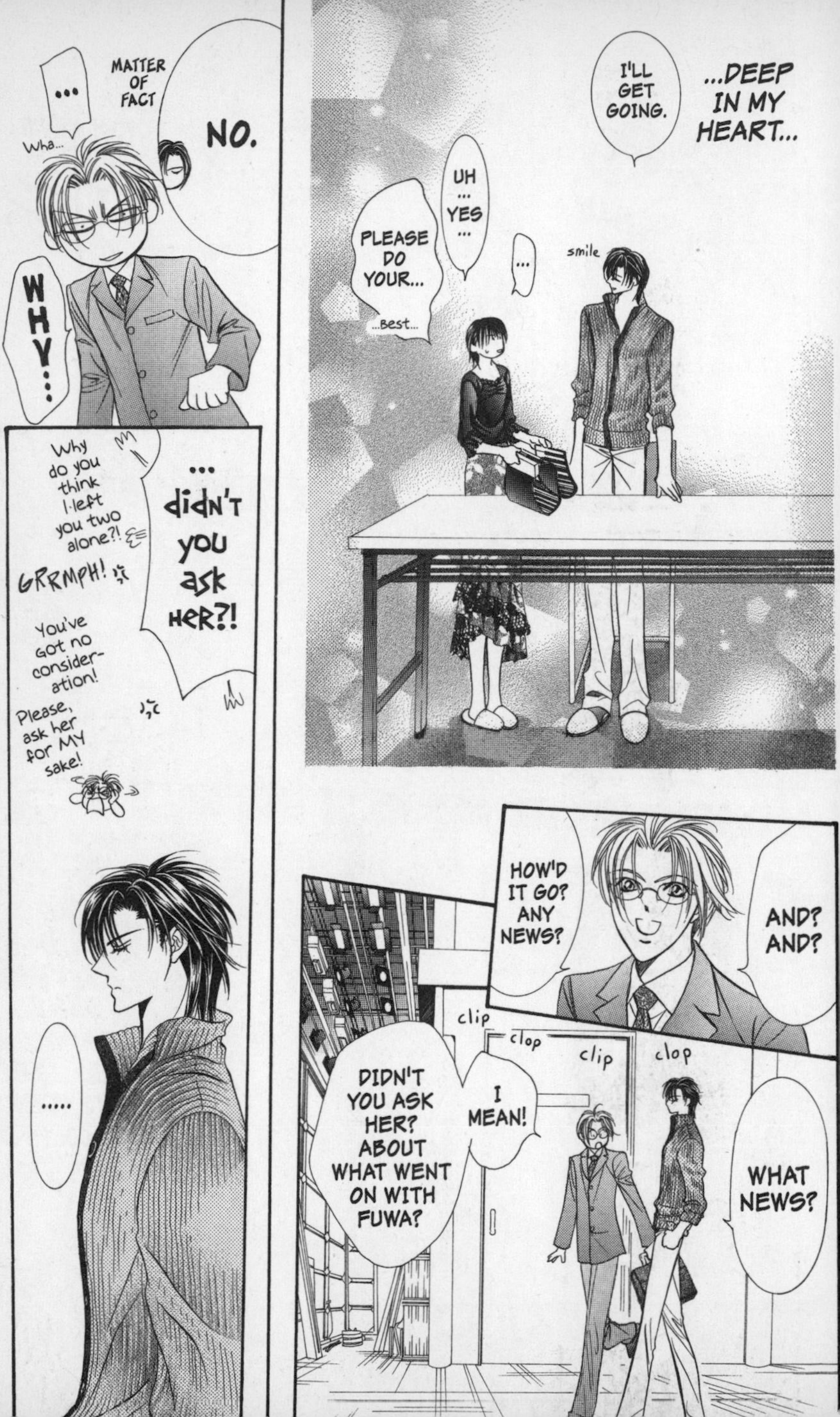
...DEEP IN MY HEART...
I'LL GET GOING.
UH ... YES ...
...
smile
PLEASE DO YOUR...
...best...
AND? AND?
HOW'D IT GO? ANY NEWS?
WHAT NEWS?
clop
clip
clop
clip
I MEAN!
DIDN'T YOU ASK HER? ABOUT WHAT WENT ON WITH FUWA?
NO.
MATTER OF FACT
...
Wha...
WHY...
...didn't you ask her?!
Why do you think I left you two alone?!
GRRMPH!
You've got no consider-ation!
Please, ask her for MY sake!
.....

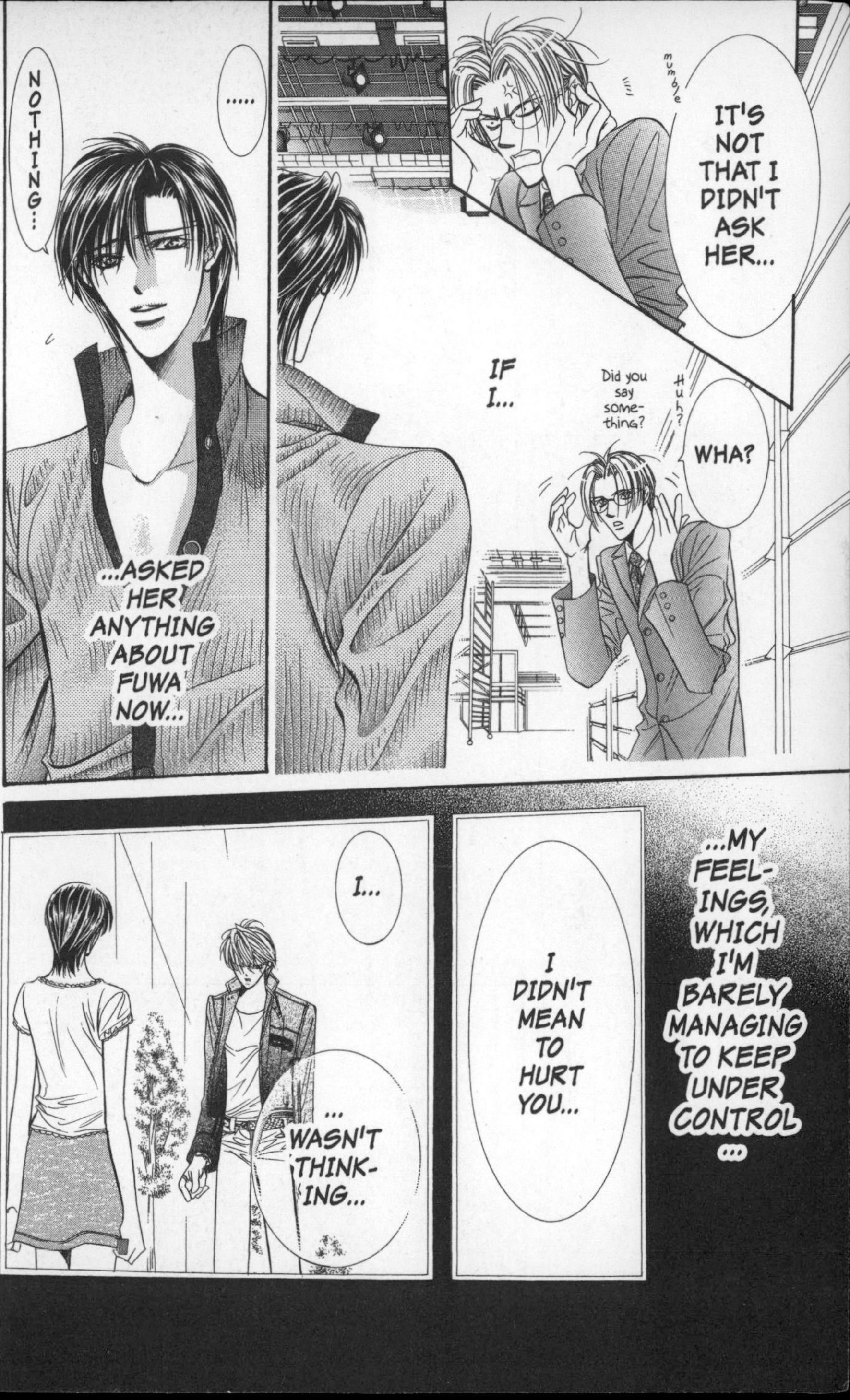

IT'S NOT THAT I DIDN'T ASK HER...
mumble
IF I...
WHA?
Huh?
Did you say something?
...ASKED HER ANYTHING ABOUT FUWA NOW...
.....
NOTHING...
...MY FEELINGS, WHICH I'M BARELY MANAGING TO KEEP UNDER CONTROL...
I DIDN'T MEAN TO HURT YOU...
I...
...WASN'T THINKING...

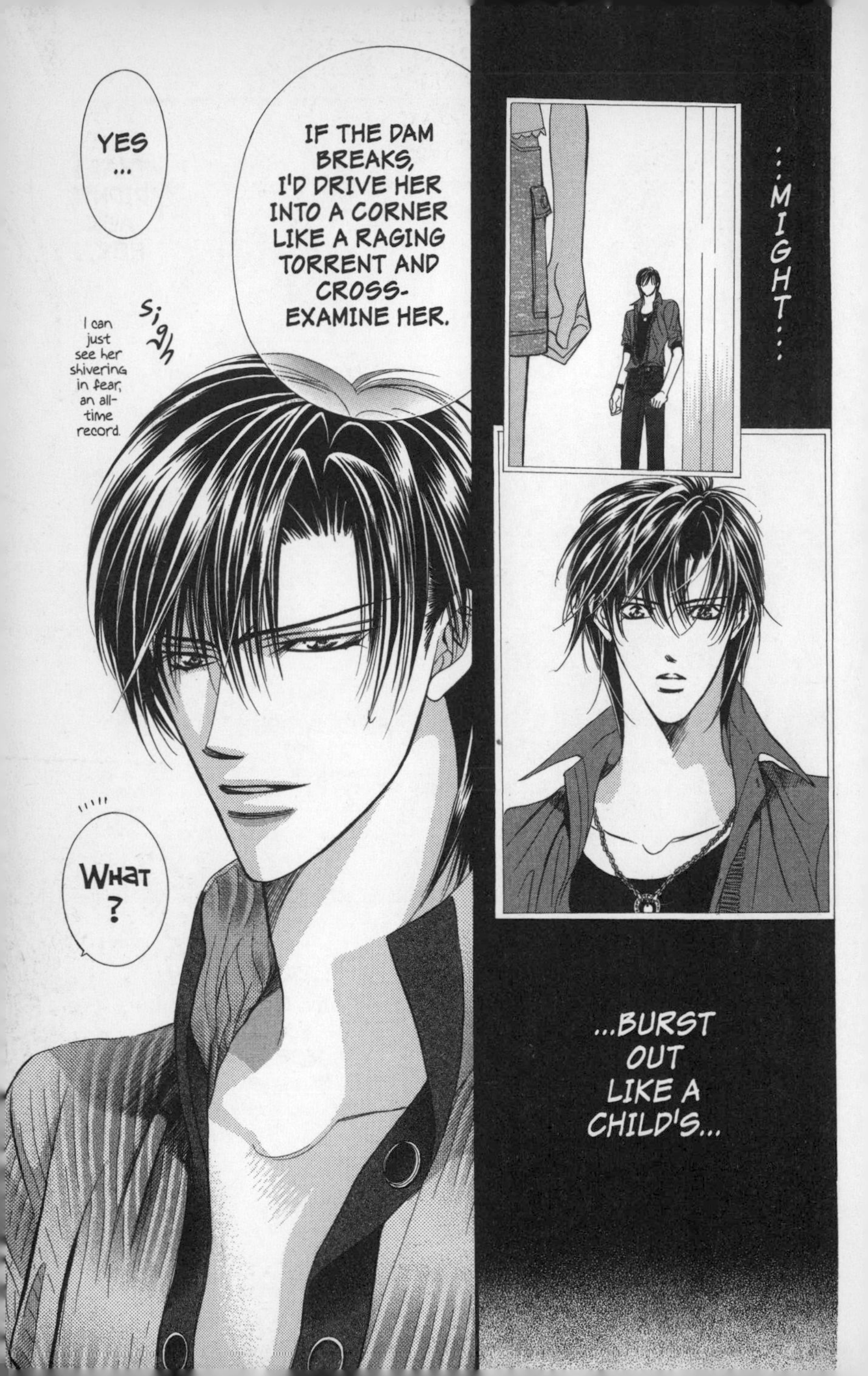
...MIGHT...
...BURST OUT LIKE A CHILD'S...
IF THE DAM BREAKS, I'D DRIVE HER INTO A CORNER LIKE A RAGING TORRENT AND CROSS-EXAMINE HER.
YES ...
sigh
I can just see her shivering in fear, an all-time record.
WHAT ?

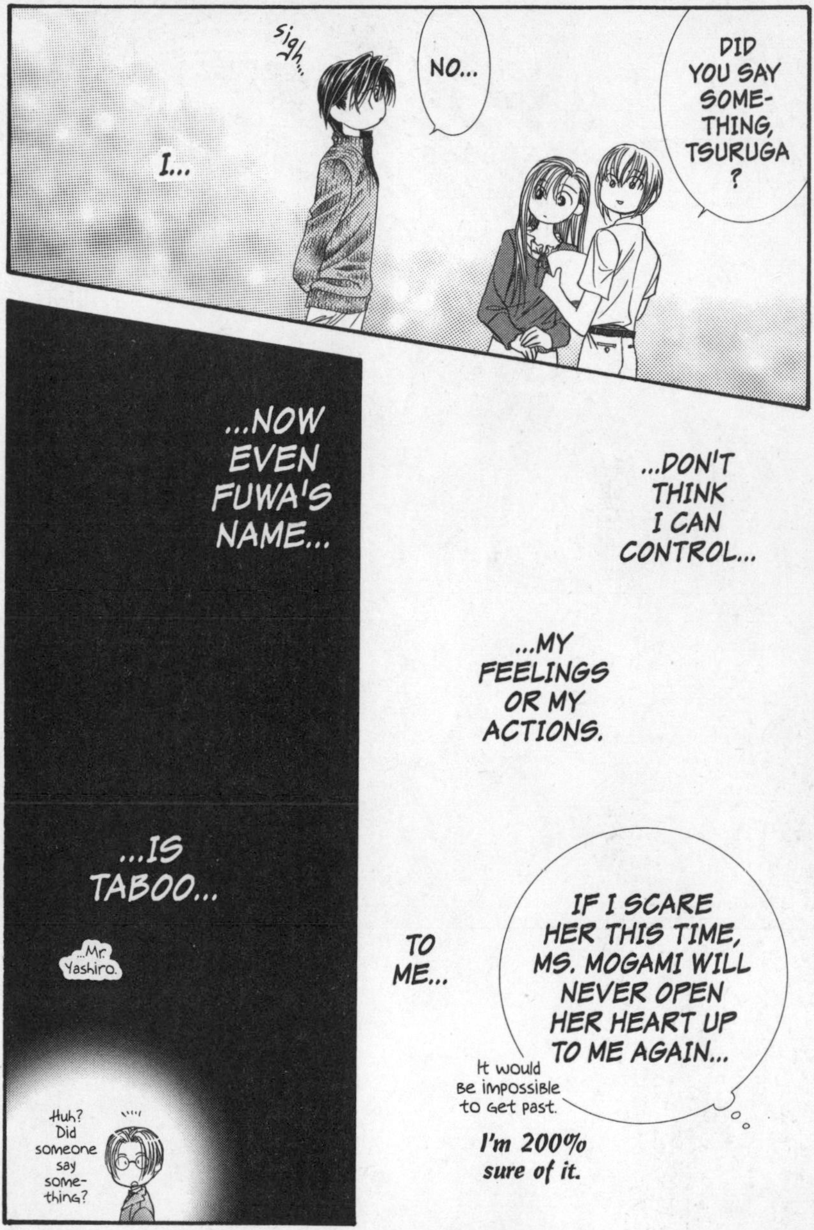
DID YOU SAY SOME- THING, TSURUGA ?
NO...
sigh...
I...
...DON'T THINK I CAN CONTROL...
...MY FEELINGS OR MY ACTIONS.
...NOW EVEN FUWA'S NAME...
...IS TABOO...
TO ME...
IF I SCARE HER THIS TIME, MS. MOGAMI WILL NEVER OPEN HER HEART UP TO ME AGAIN...
It would be impossible to get past.
I'm 200% sure of it.
...Mr. Yashiro.
Huh? Did someone say some- thing?

End of Act 82

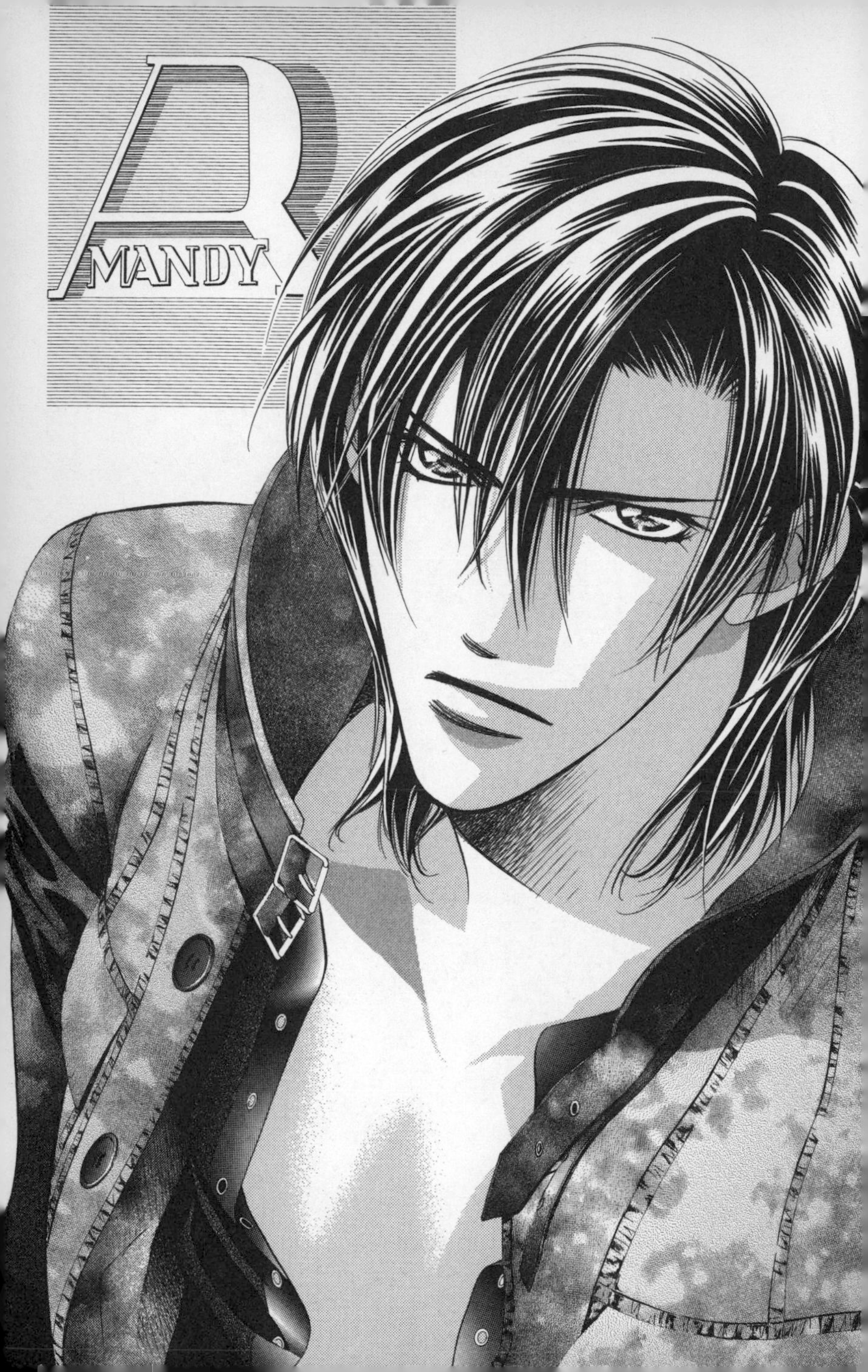

ARMANDY

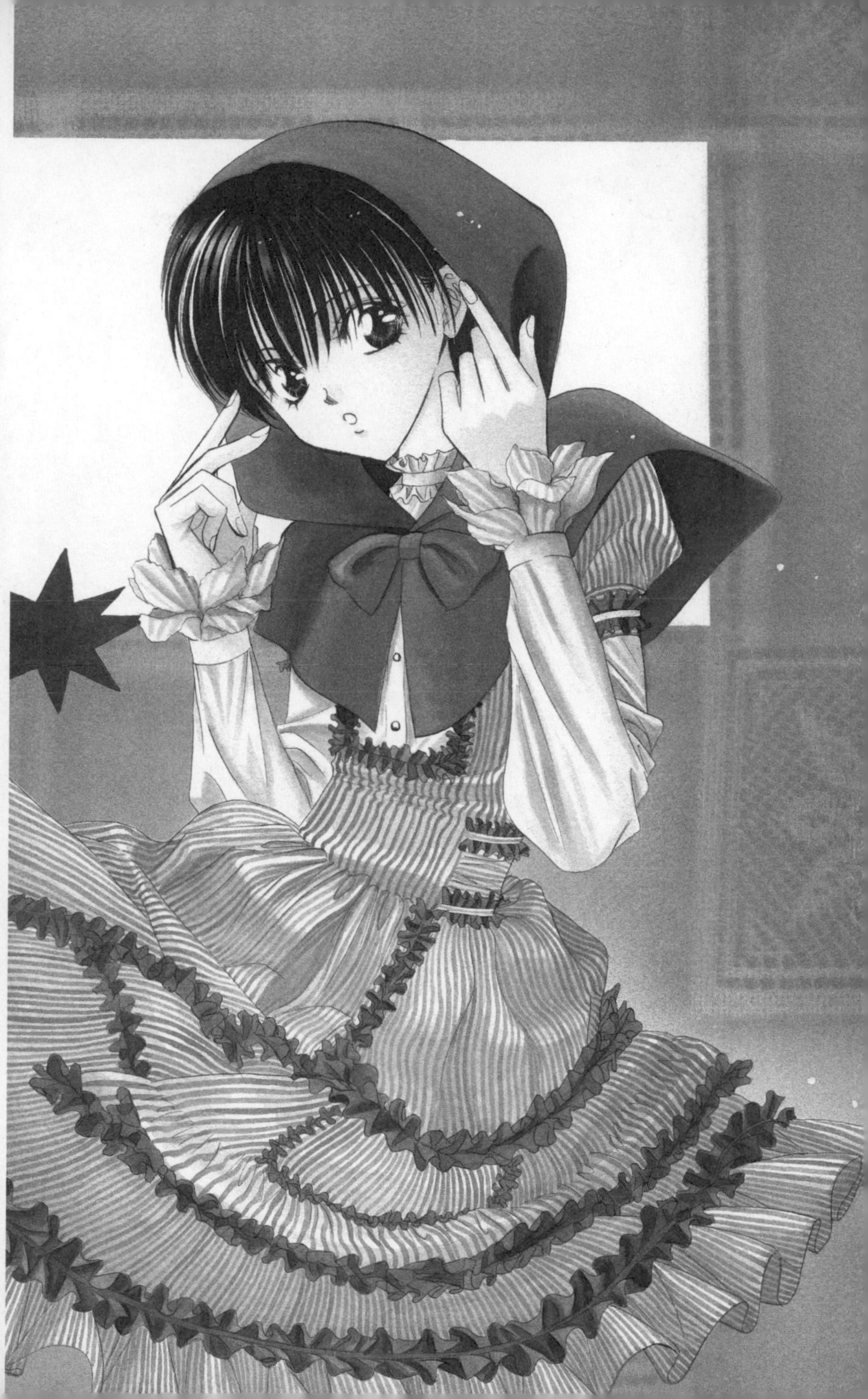

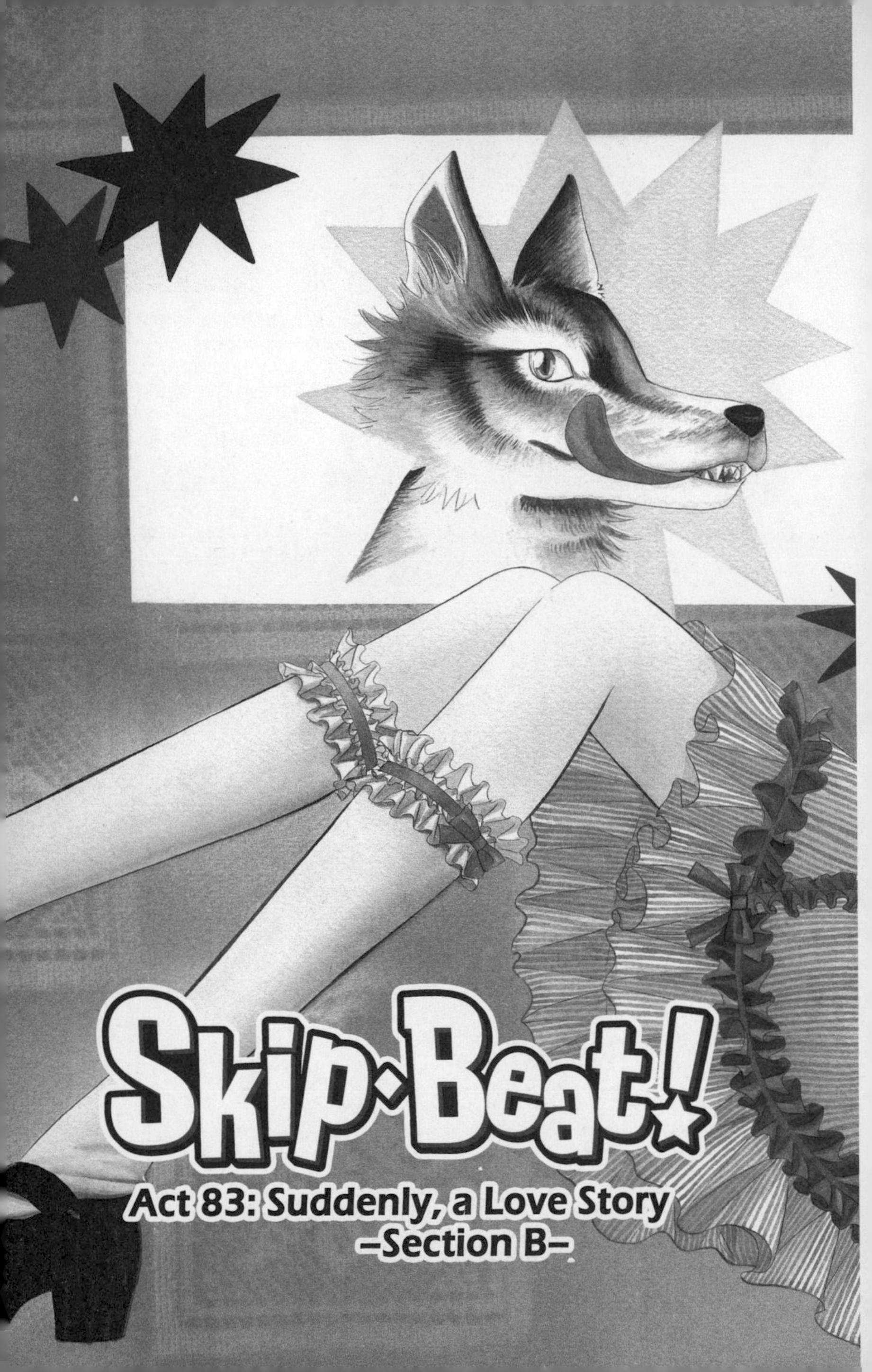
Skip·Beat!
Act 83: Suddenly, a Love Story
–Section B–

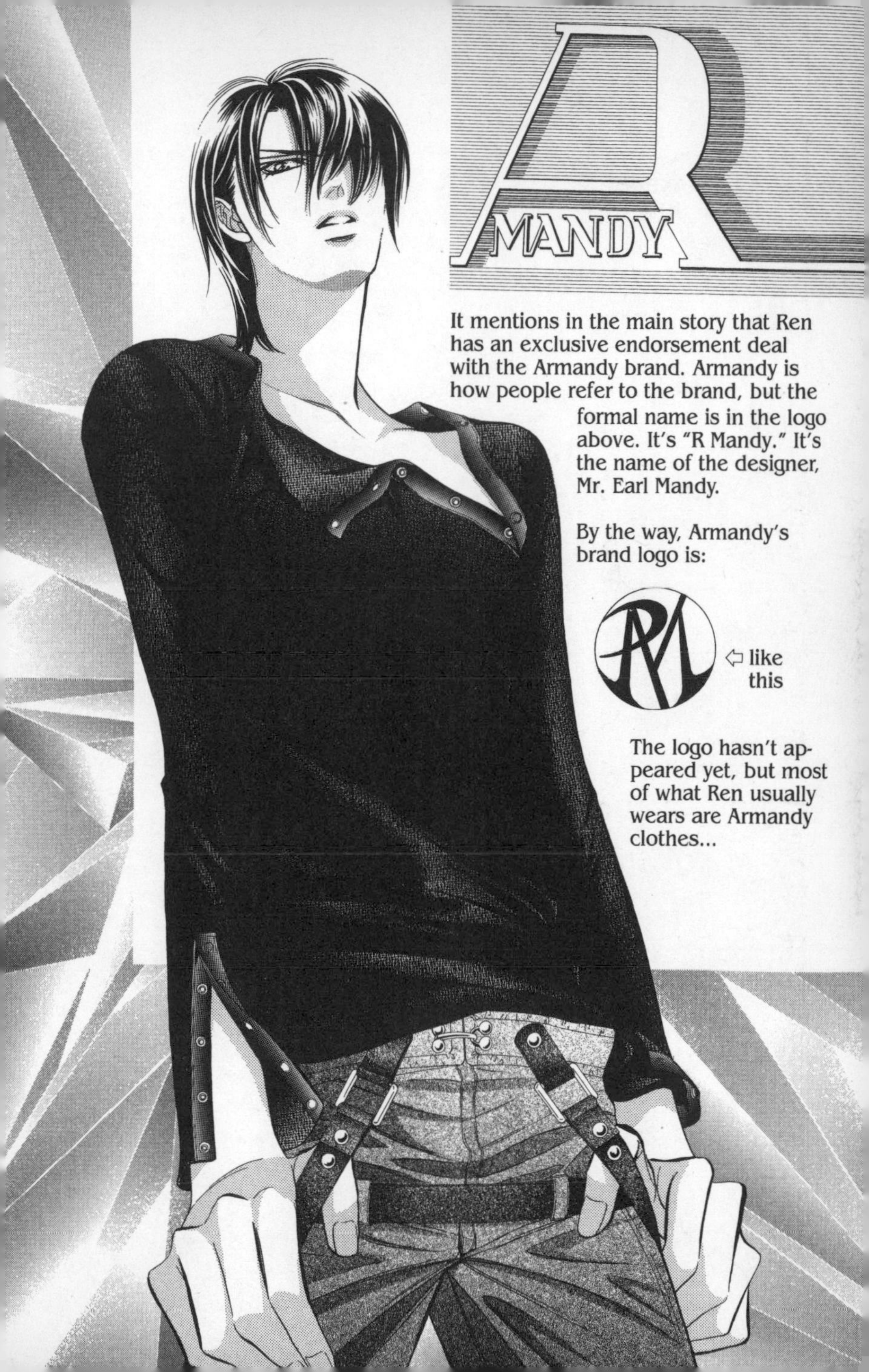

AR MANDY

It mentions in the main story that Ren has an exclusive endorsement deal with the Armandy brand. Armandy is how people refer to the brand, but the formal name is in the logo above. It's "R Mandy." It's the name of the designer, Mr. Earl Mandy.

By the way, Armandy's brand logo is:

⇦ like this

The logo hasn't appeared yet, but most of what Ren usually wears are Armandy clothes...

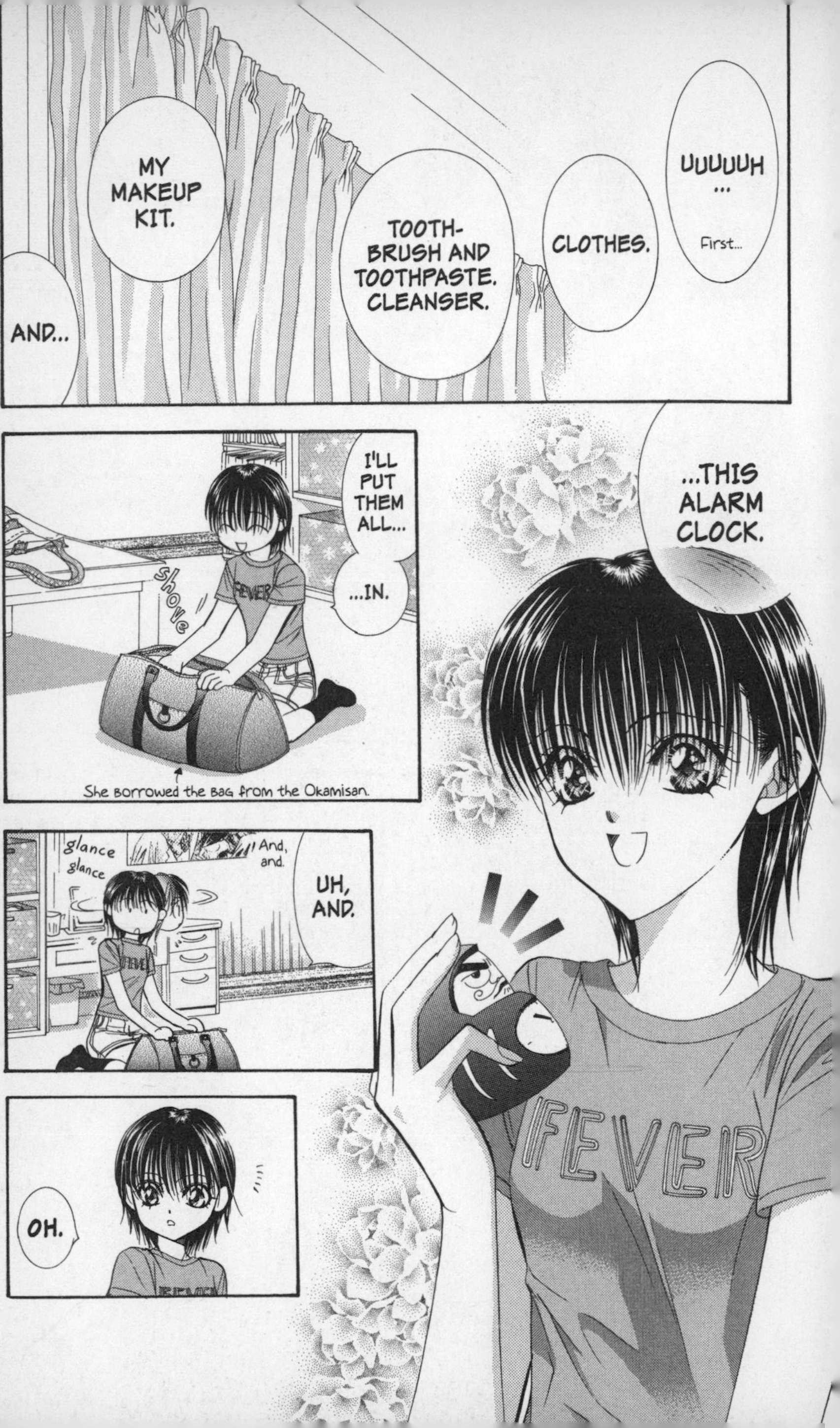
UUUUUH ...
First...
CLOTHES.
TOOTH-BRUSH AND TOOTHPASTE. CLEANSER.
MY MAKEUP KIT.
AND...
...THIS ALARM CLOCK.
FEVER
I'LL PUT THEM ALL...
...IN.
shove
FEVER
She borrowed the bag from the Okamisan.
UH, AND.
And, and.
glance
glance
OH.

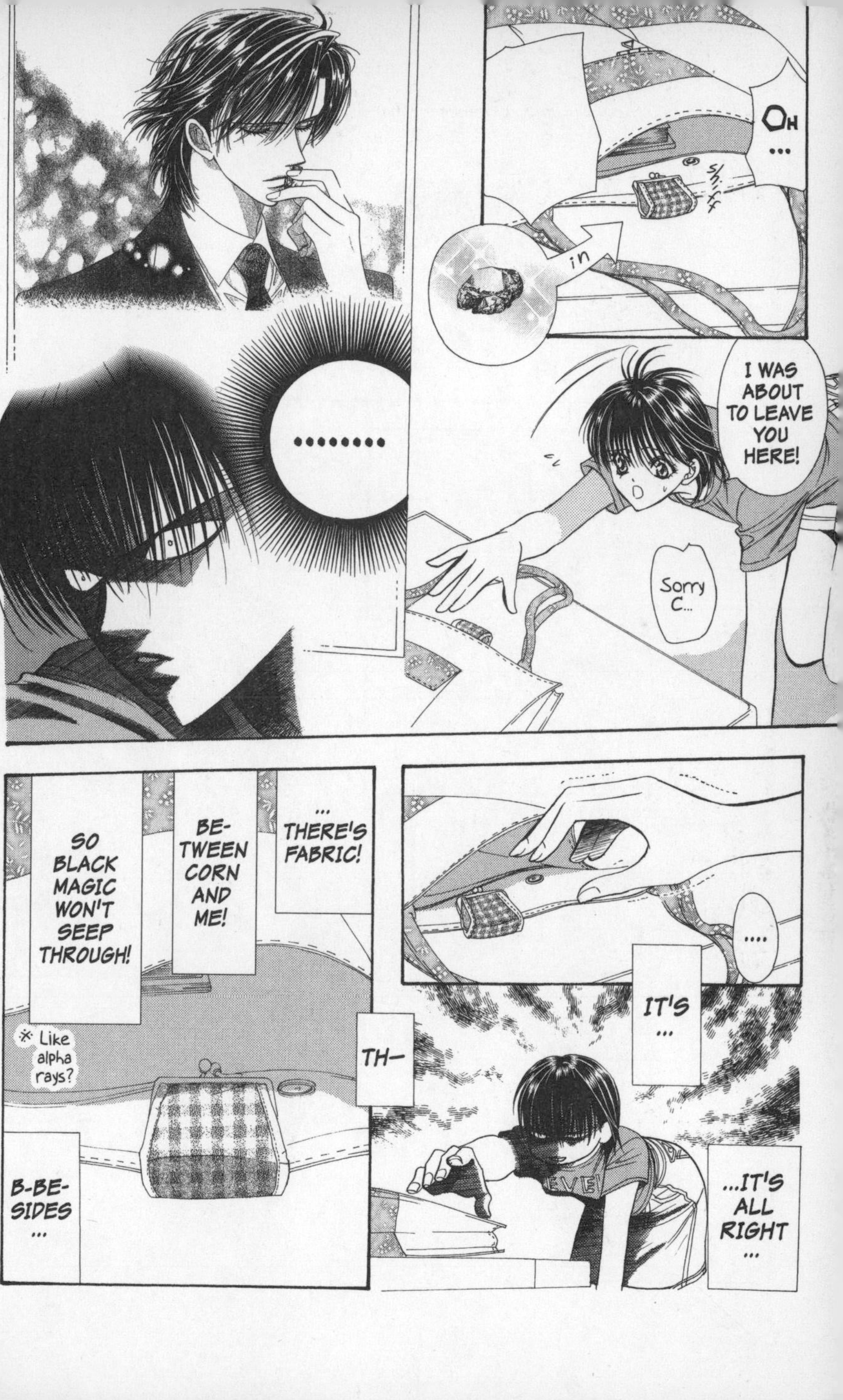
OH ...
shift
in
I WAS ABOUT TO LEAVE YOU HERE!
Sorry C...
....
....
IT'S ...
...IT'S ALL RIGHT ...
TH—
... THERE'S FABRIC!
BE-TWEEN CORN AND ME!
SO BLACK MAGIC WON'T SEEP THROUGH!
※ Like alpha rays?
B-BE-SIDES ...

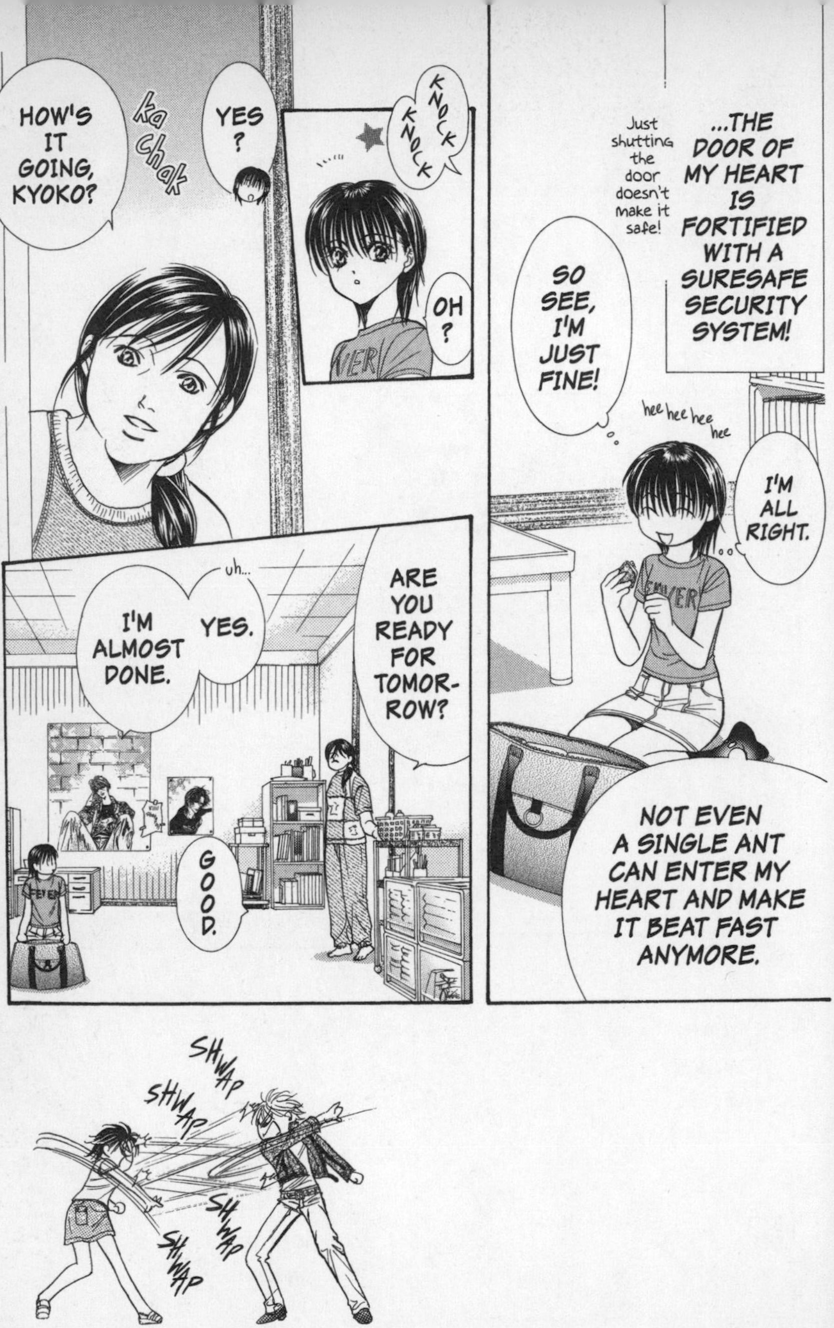
KNOCK KNOCK
OH?
YES?
ka chak
HOW'S IT GOING, KYOKO?
ARE YOU READY FOR TOMORROW?
uh...
YES.
I'M ALMOST DONE.
GOOD.
...THE DOOR OF MY HEART IS FORTIFIED WITH A SURESAFE SECURITY SYSTEM!
Just shutting the door doesn't make it safe!
SO SEE, I'M JUST FINE!
hee hee hee hee
I'M ALL RIGHT.
NOT EVEN A SINGLE ANT CAN ENTER MY HEART AND MAKE IT BEAT FAST ANYMORE.
SHWAP
SHWAP
SHWAP
SHWAP

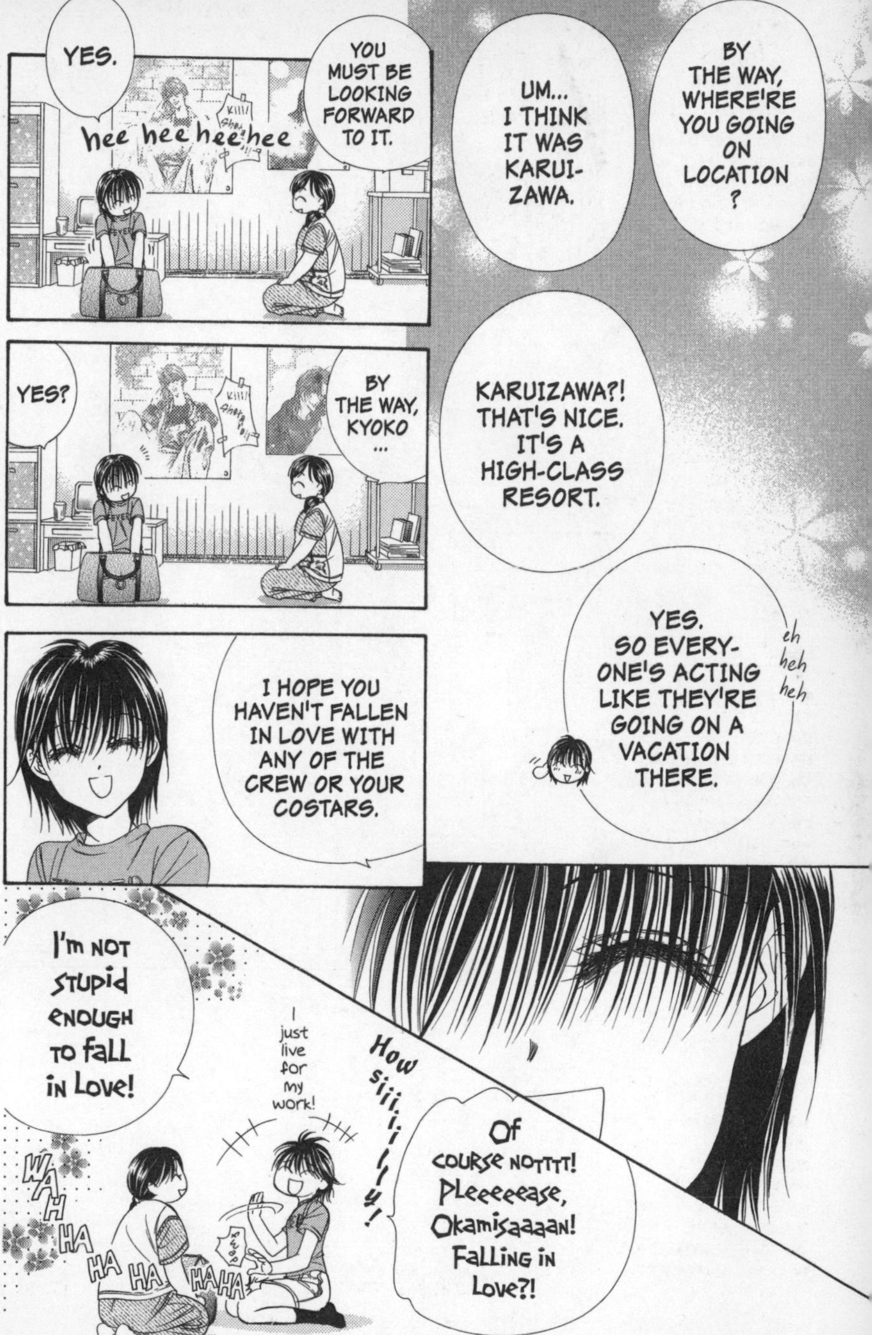
BY THE WAY, WHERE'RE YOU GOING ON LOCATION?
UM... I THINK IT WAS KARUI-ZAWA.
KARUIZAWA?! THAT'S NICE. IT'S A HIGH-CLASS RESORT.
YES. SO EVERY-ONE'S ACTING LIKE THEY'RE GOING ON A VACATION THERE.
eh heh heh
YOU MUST BE LOOKING FORWARD TO IT.
YES.
hee hee hee hee
BY THE WAY, KYOKO...
YES?
I HOPE YOU HAVEN'T FALLEN IN LOVE WITH ANY OF THE CREW OR YOUR COSTARS.
Of course nottttt! Pleeeeease, Okamisaaaan! Falling in Love?!
How siiiiiilly!
I just live for my work!
I'm NOT stupid enough to fall in Love!
WAH HA HA HA HA HAHA

It was printed in the magazine

The Truth about the Lyrics

It's the fruit of my assistants' labor, who took three days finishing it...! So I was disappointed that the top and bottom portions were cut off in the title page illustration...but if I used the cut to fill a page between two chapters, then a lot of the left and right portions would have been cut off, and I didn't want that either...so we decided to use it for the title page illustration, so people could see the parts that my assistants really worked hard on.

I would've written this in Volume 8 if I had the time. The revelation is that "Prisoner" is not a song with angels and devils as the theme. The lyrics are about a boy who didn't know why he was born, or the value of living his life. He always held emptiness inside and was trapped by his mad heart. One day he met a girl, fell in love, and as a result, both their lives changed. Therefore, it's a song about a boy in this modern era who's very sensitive. And in that song, the boy compares himself to the devil, and the girl to an angel. And the promo clip was simply made to visualize the devil and the angel as the main characters...

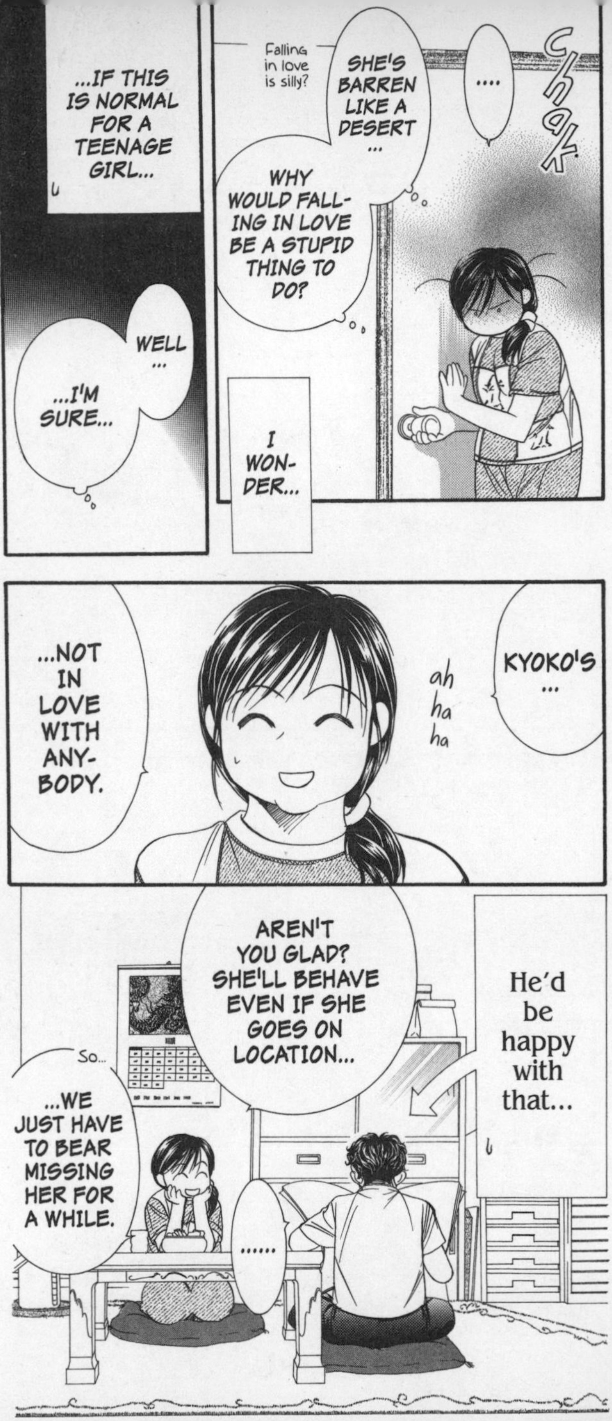

chak
....
SHE'S BARREN LIKE A DESERT ...
Falling in love is silly?
WHY WOULD FALLING IN LOVE BE A STUPID THING TO DO?
I WONDER...
...IF THIS IS NORMAL FOR A TEENAGE GIRL...
WELL ...
...I'M SURE...
KYOKO'S ...
ah ha ha
...NOT IN LOVE WITH ANYBODY.
He'd be happy with that...
AREN'T YOU GLAD? SHE'LL BEHAVE EVEN IF SHE GOES ON LOCATION...
......
So...
...WE JUST HAVE TO BEAR MISSING HER FOR A WHILE.

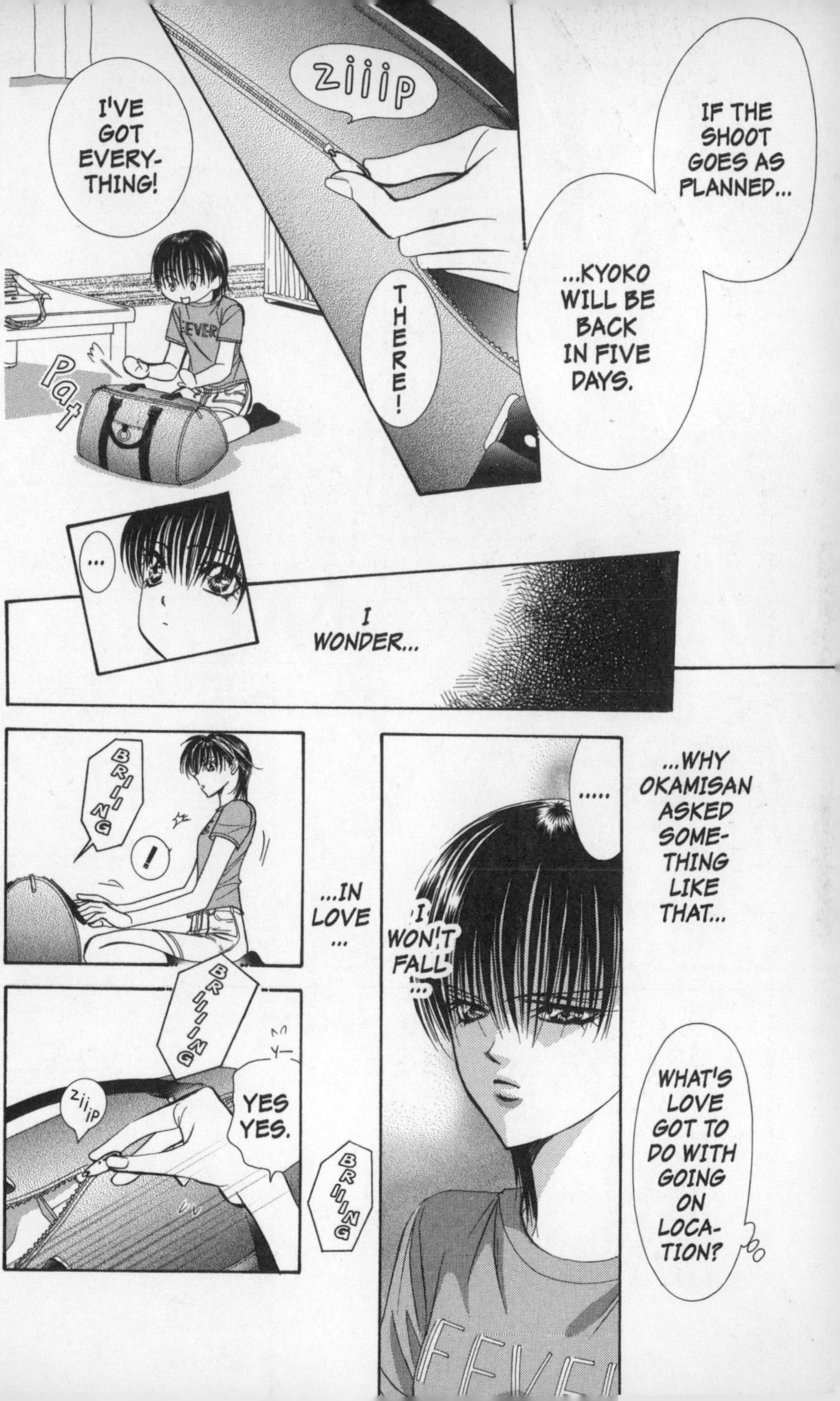
IF THE SHOOT GOES AS PLANNED...
...KYOKO WILL BE BACK IN FIVE DAYS.
ziiip
THERE!
I'VE GOT EVERY-THING!
Pat
I WONDER...
...
.....
...WHY OKAMISAN ASKED SOME-THING LIKE THAT...
I WON'T FALL ...
...IN LOVE ...
WHAT'S LOVE GOT TO DO WITH GOING ON LOCA-TION?
BRIIING
!
BRIIIING
YES YES.
ziiip
BRIIING

BRIIING
Incoming call
No Caller ID
......
I'LL NEVER...
BRIIING
...FALL IN LOVE...
BRIIING
...AGAIN...
Beep
YES?
HELLO.
Uh...
HMM?
.....
...
I... I KNEW IT...
Hello.
It's me.
UH...

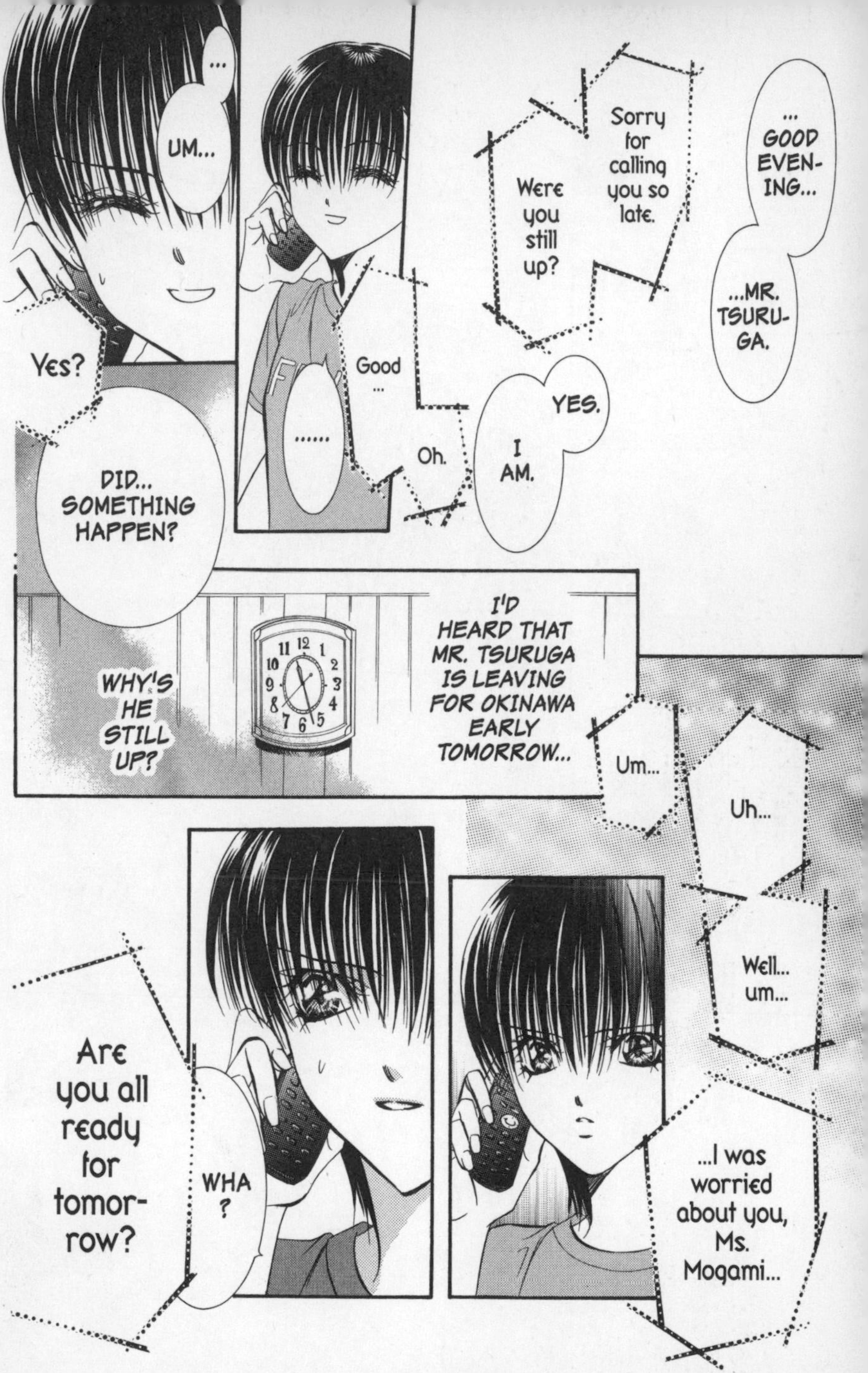
...GOOD EVENING...
...MR. TSURUGA.
Sorry for calling you so late.
Were you still up?
YES.
I AM.
Oh.
Good ...
......
...
UM...
Yes?
DID... SOMETHING HAPPEN?
I'D HEARD THAT MR. TSURUGA IS LEAVING FOR OKINAWA EARLY TOMORROW...
WHY'S HE STILL UP?
Um...
Uh...
Well... um...
...I was worried about you, Ms. Mogami...
WHA ?
Are you all ready for tomorrow?

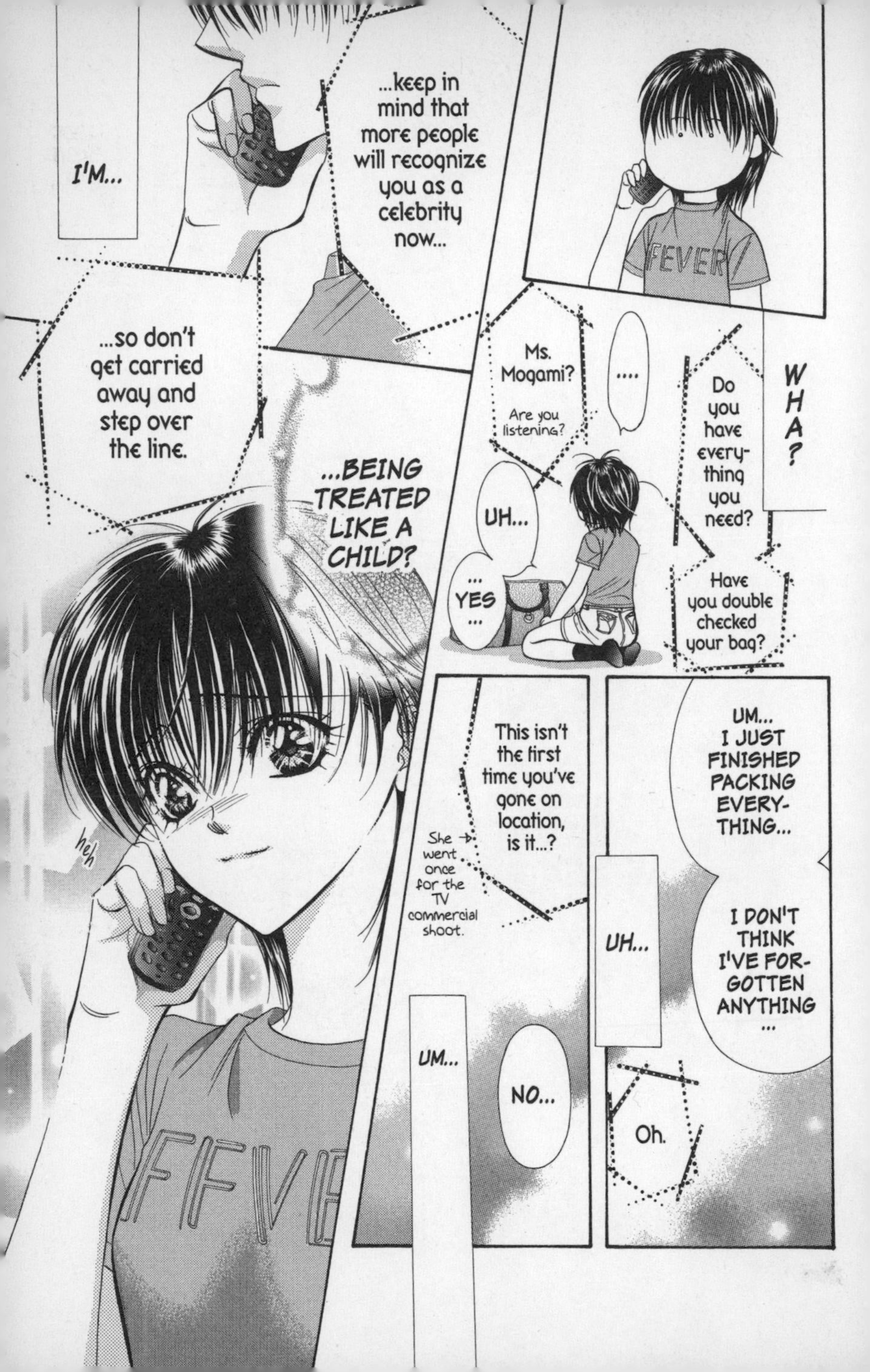
FEVER
...keep in mind that more people will recognize you as a celebrity now...
...so don't get carried away and step over the line.
WHA?
Do you have everything you need?
Have you double checked your bag?
....
Ms. Mogami?
Are you listening?
UH...
...YES...
UM... I JUST FINISHED PACKING EVERYTHING...
I DON'T THINK I'VE FORGOTTEN ANYTHING...
UH...
Oh.
This isn't the first time you've gone on location, is it...?
She went once for the TV commercial shoot.
NO...
UM...
I'M...
...BEING TREATED LIKE A CHILD?
heh
FEVE

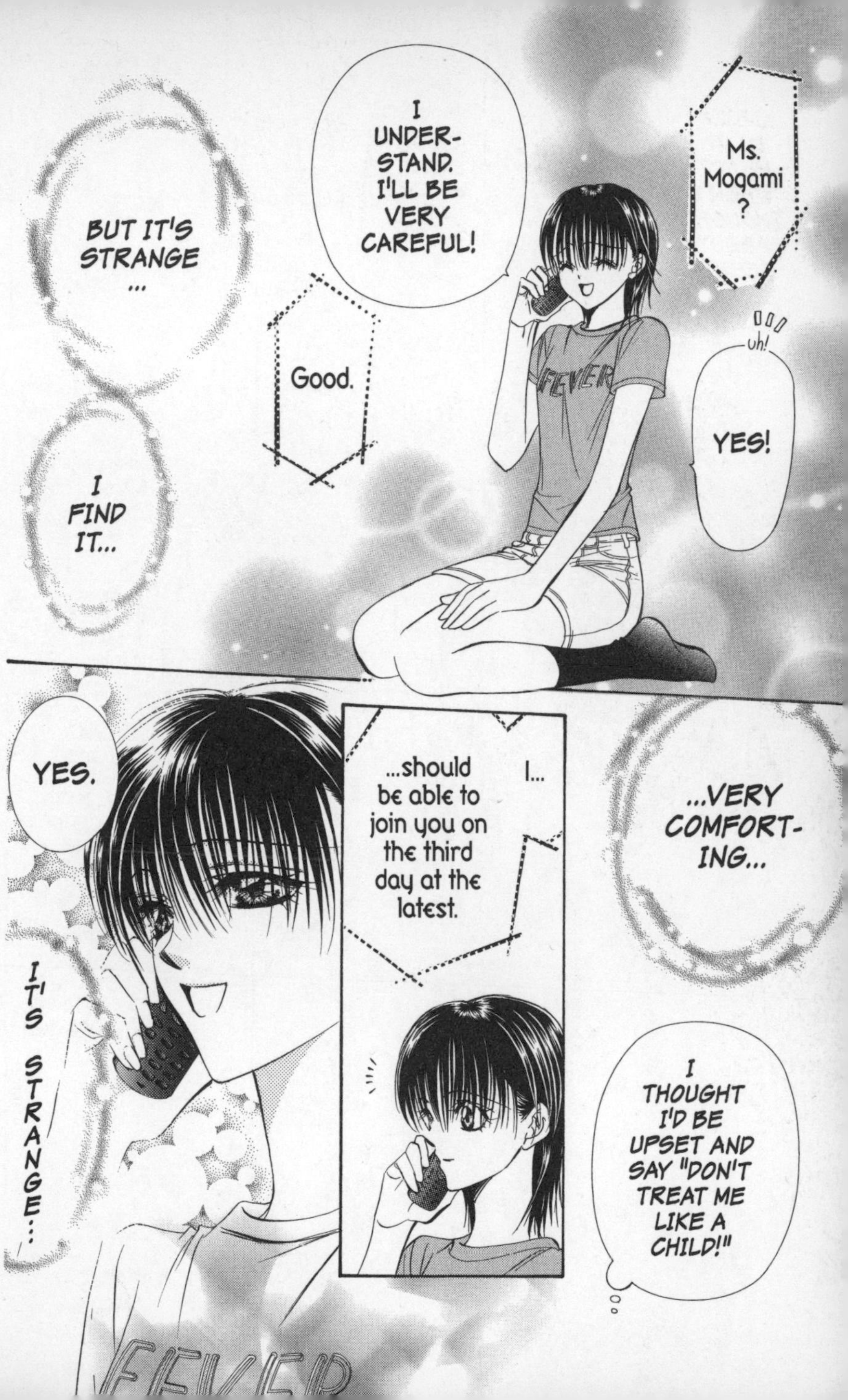
Ms. Mogami ?
uh!
YES!
I UNDER-STAND. I'LL BE VERY CAREFUL!
Good.
BUT IT'S STRANGE ...
I FIND IT...
...VERY COMFORT-ING...
I THOUGHT I'D BE UPSET AND SAY "DON'T TREAT ME LIKE A CHILD!"
I...
...should be able to join you on the third day at the latest.
YES.
IT'S STRANGE...

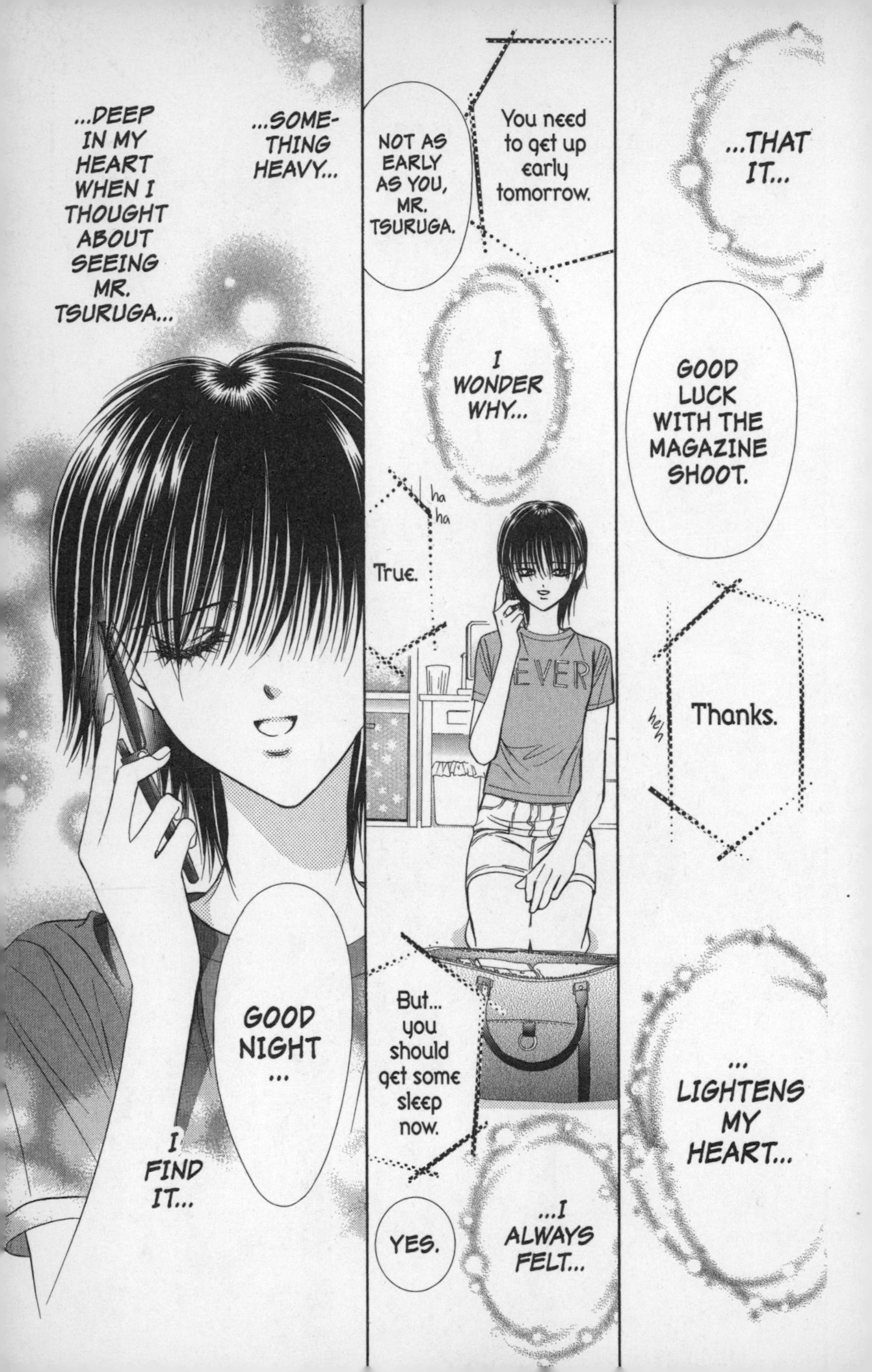
...THAT IT...
GOOD LUCK WITH THE MAGAZINE SHOOT.
heh
Thanks.
... LIGHTENS MY HEART...
You need to get up early tomorrow.
NOT AS EARLY AS YOU, MR. TSURUGA.
I WONDER WHY...
ha ha
True.
But... you should get some sleep now.
YES.
...I ALWAYS FELT...
...SOME-THING HEAVY...
...DEEP IN MY HEART WHEN I THOUGHT ABOUT SEEING MR. TSURUGA...
GOOD NIGHT ...
I FIND IT...

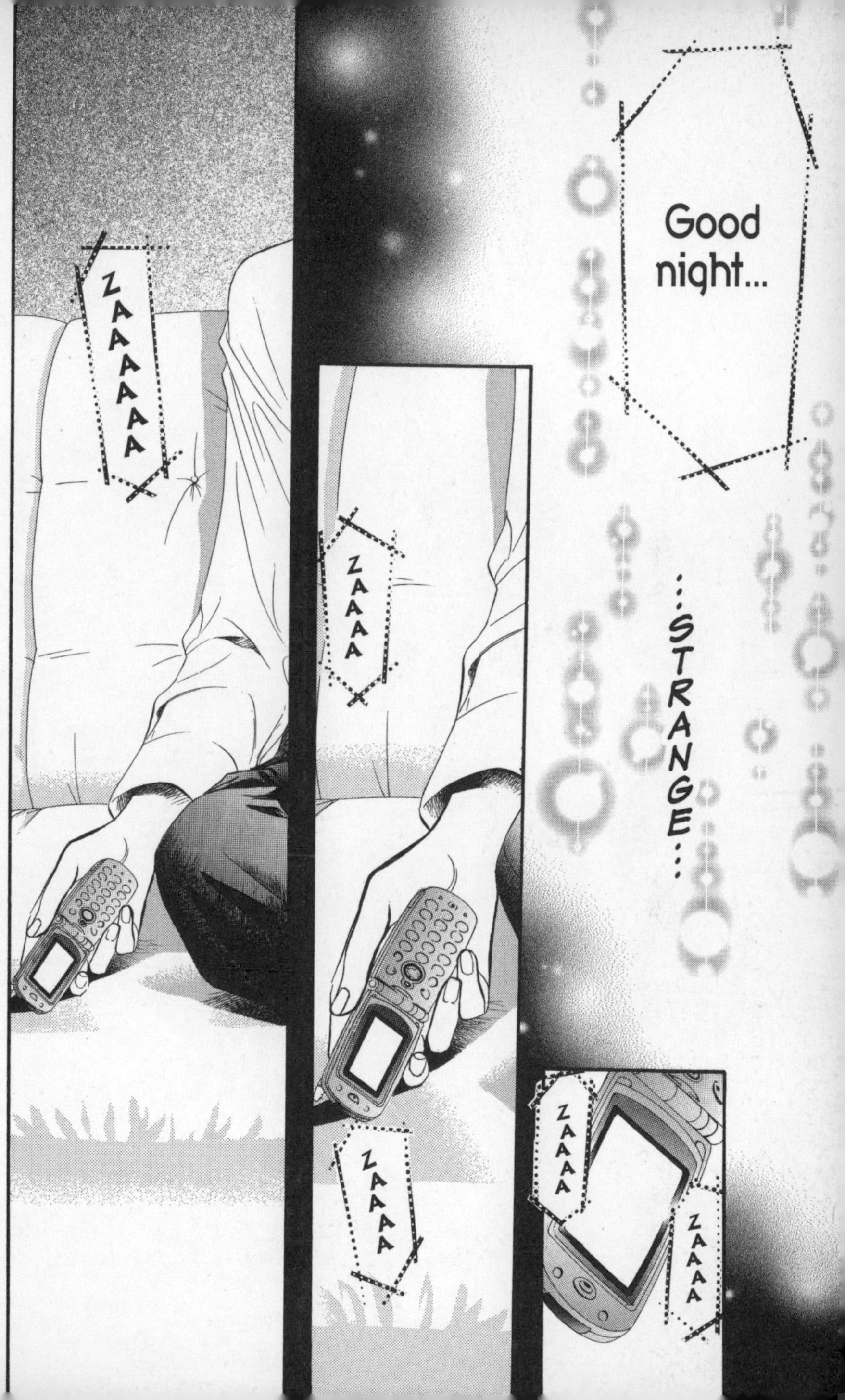
Good night...
...STRANGE...
ZAAAA
ZAAAA
ZAAAA
ZAAAA
ZAAAAAA

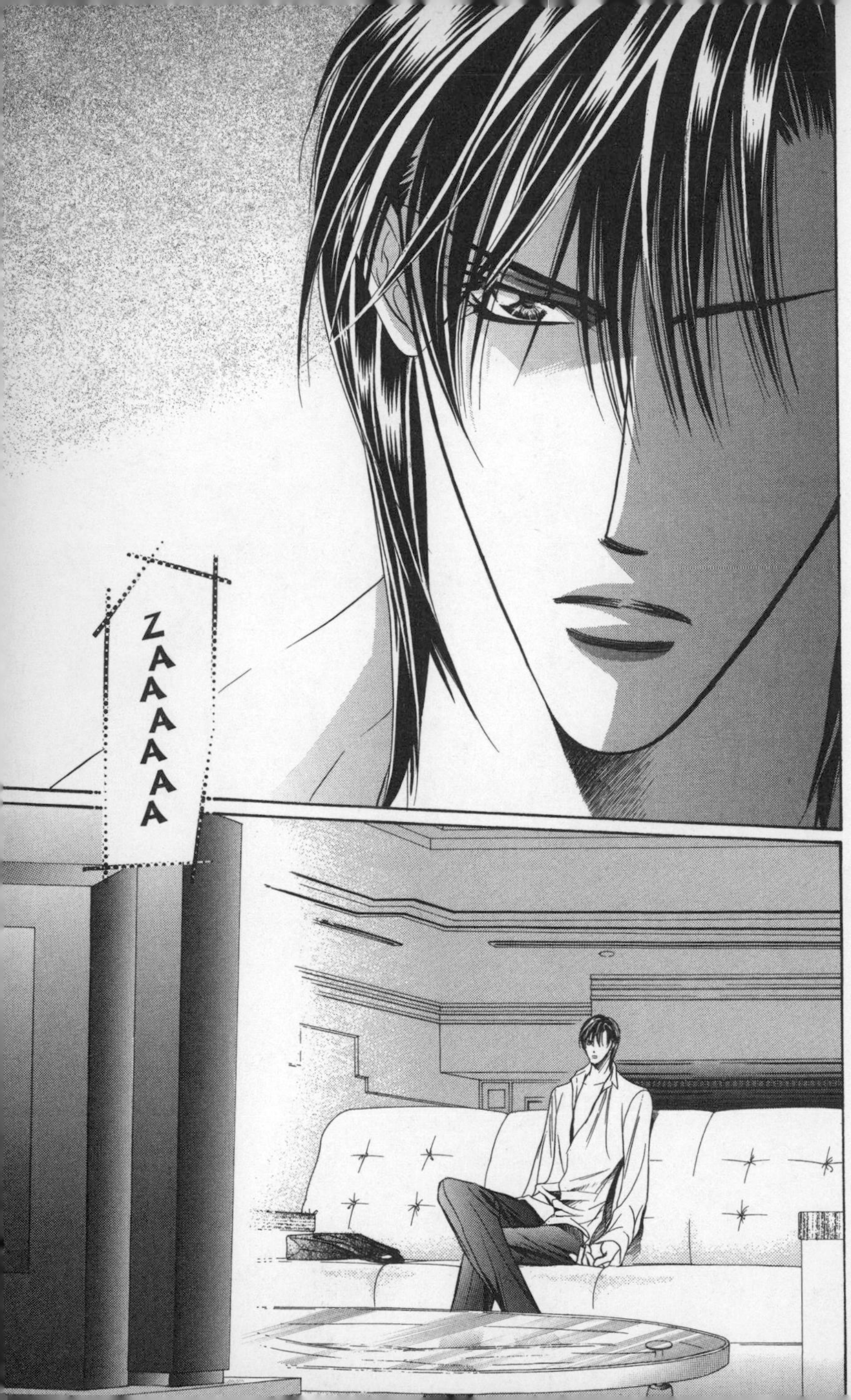
ZAAAAAA

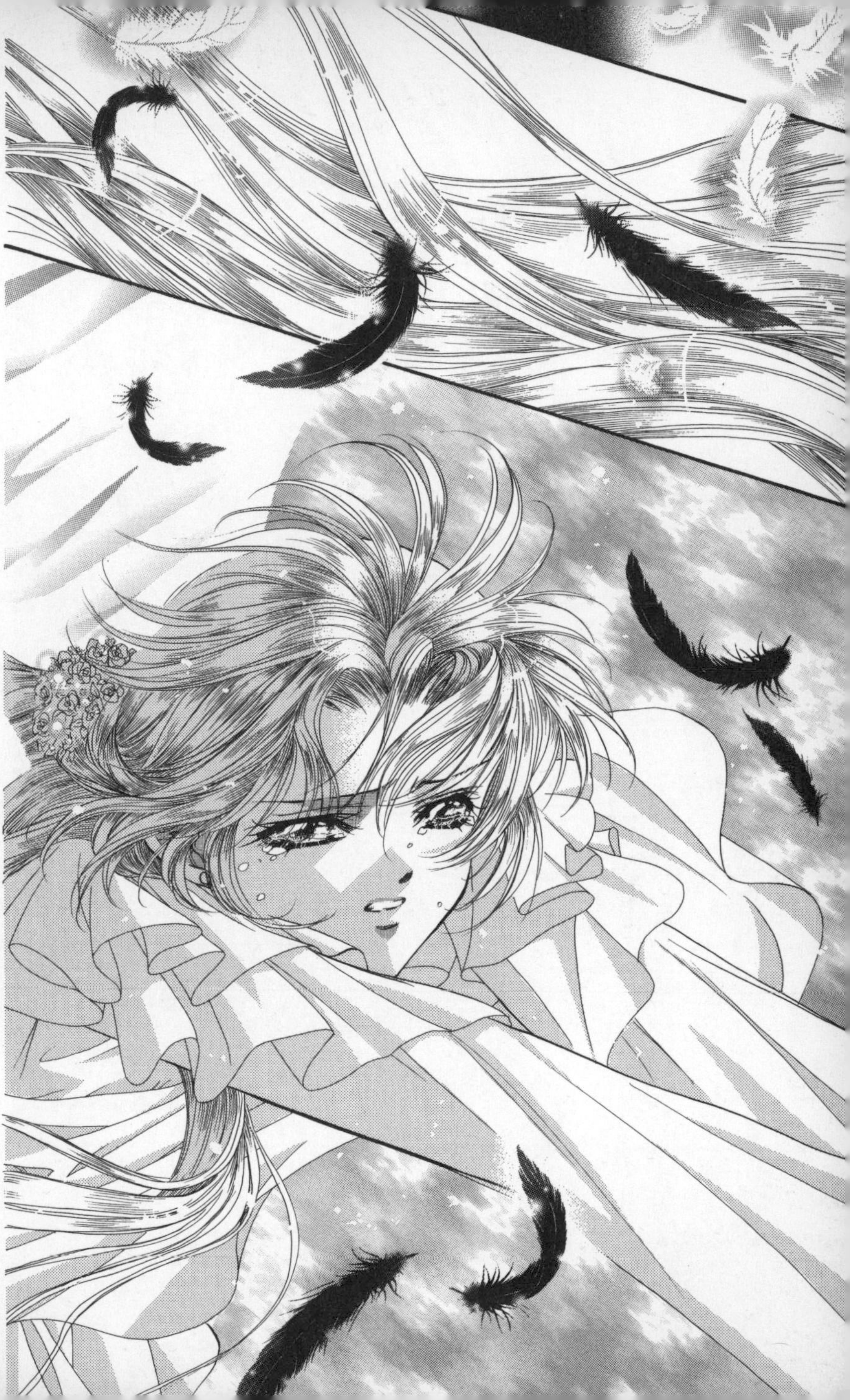

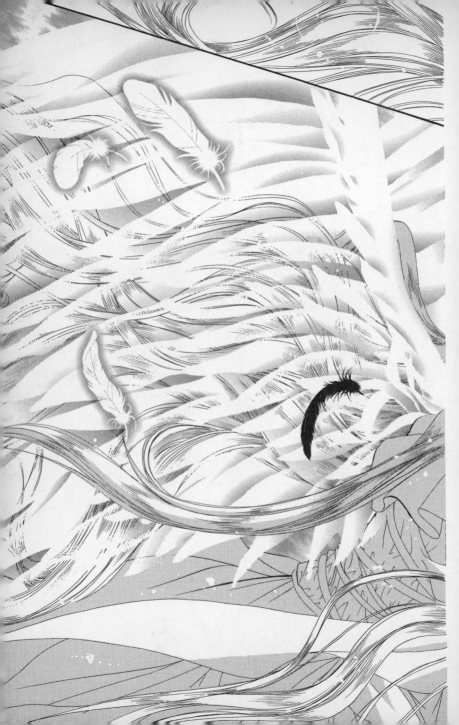

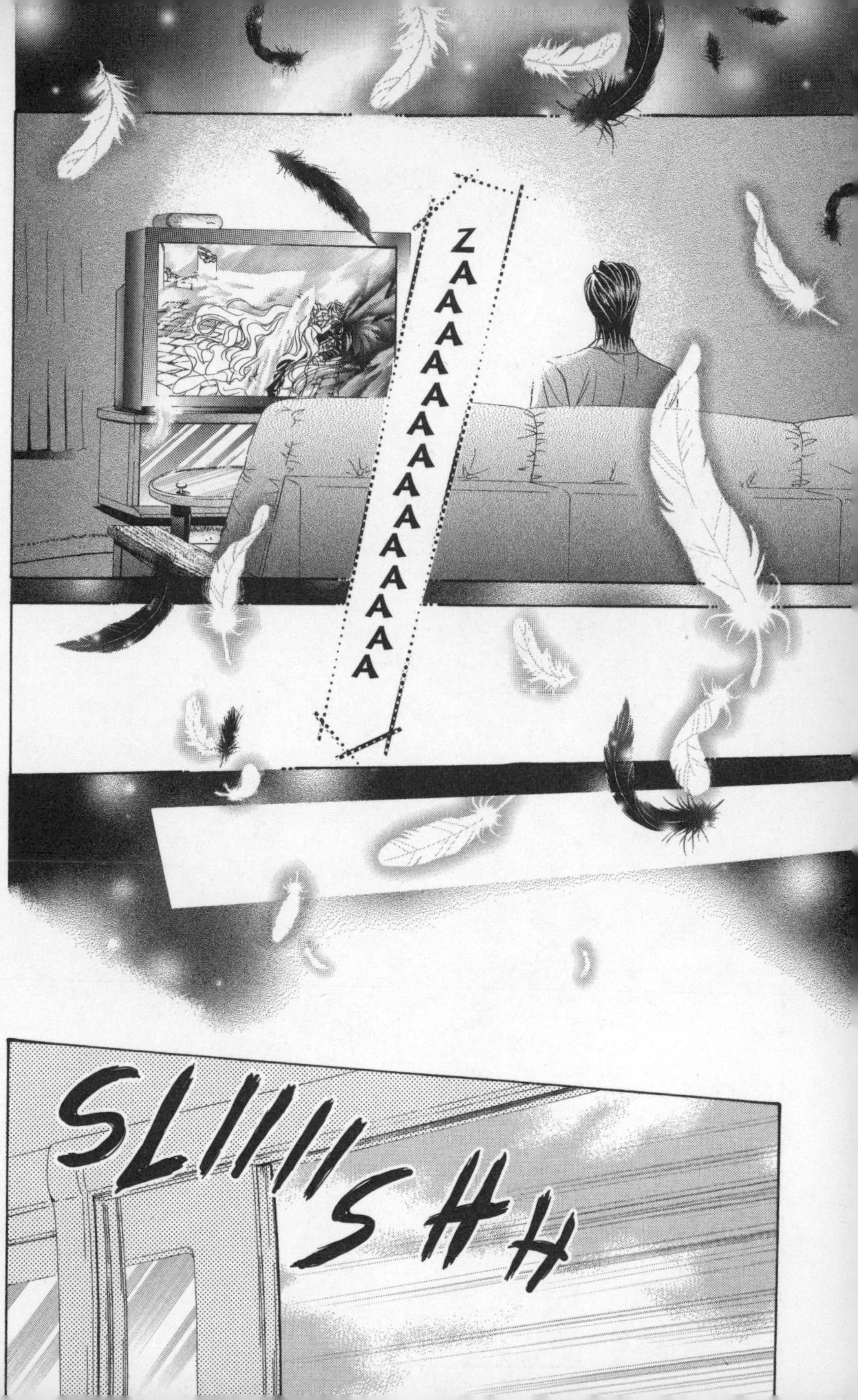
ZAAAAAAAAAAAAAA
SLIIIISHH

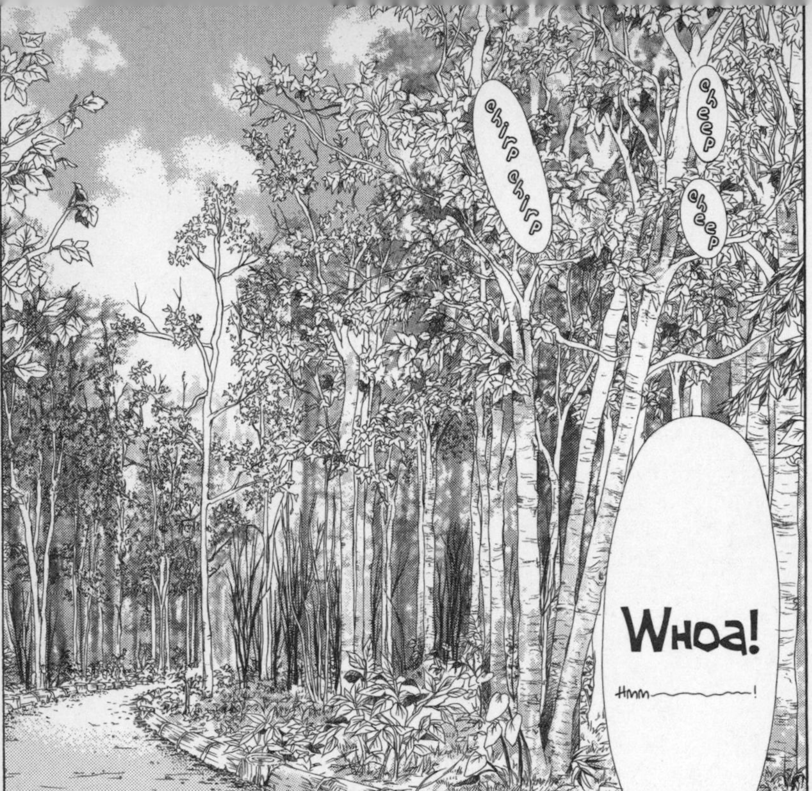
cheep cheep
chirp chirp
Whoa!
Hmm——!

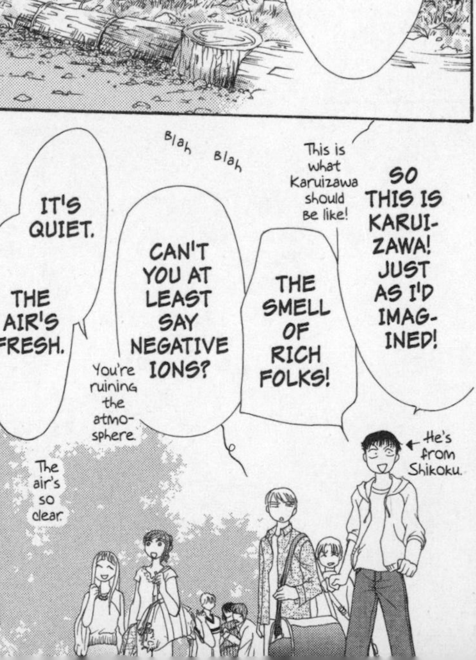
He's from Shikoku.
So this is Karui-zawa! Just as I'd imag-ined!
This is what Karuizawa should Be like!
Blah Blah
The smell of rich folks!
Can't you at least say negative ions?
You're ruining the atmo-sphere.
It's quiet.
The air's fresh.
The air's so clear.

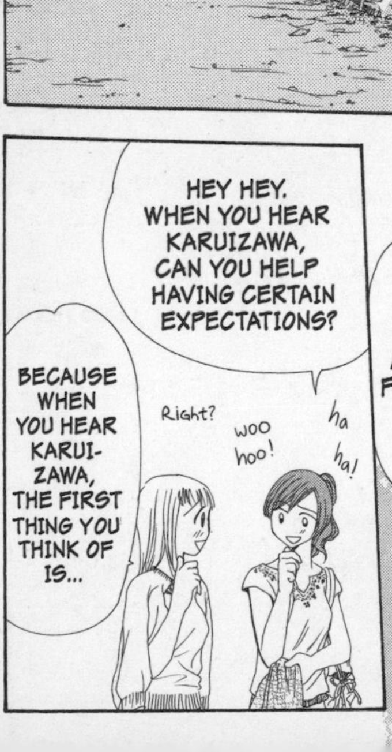
Hey hey. When you hear Karuizawa, can you help having certain expectations?
ha ha!
woo hoo!
Right?
Because when you hear Karui-zawa, the first thing you think of is...

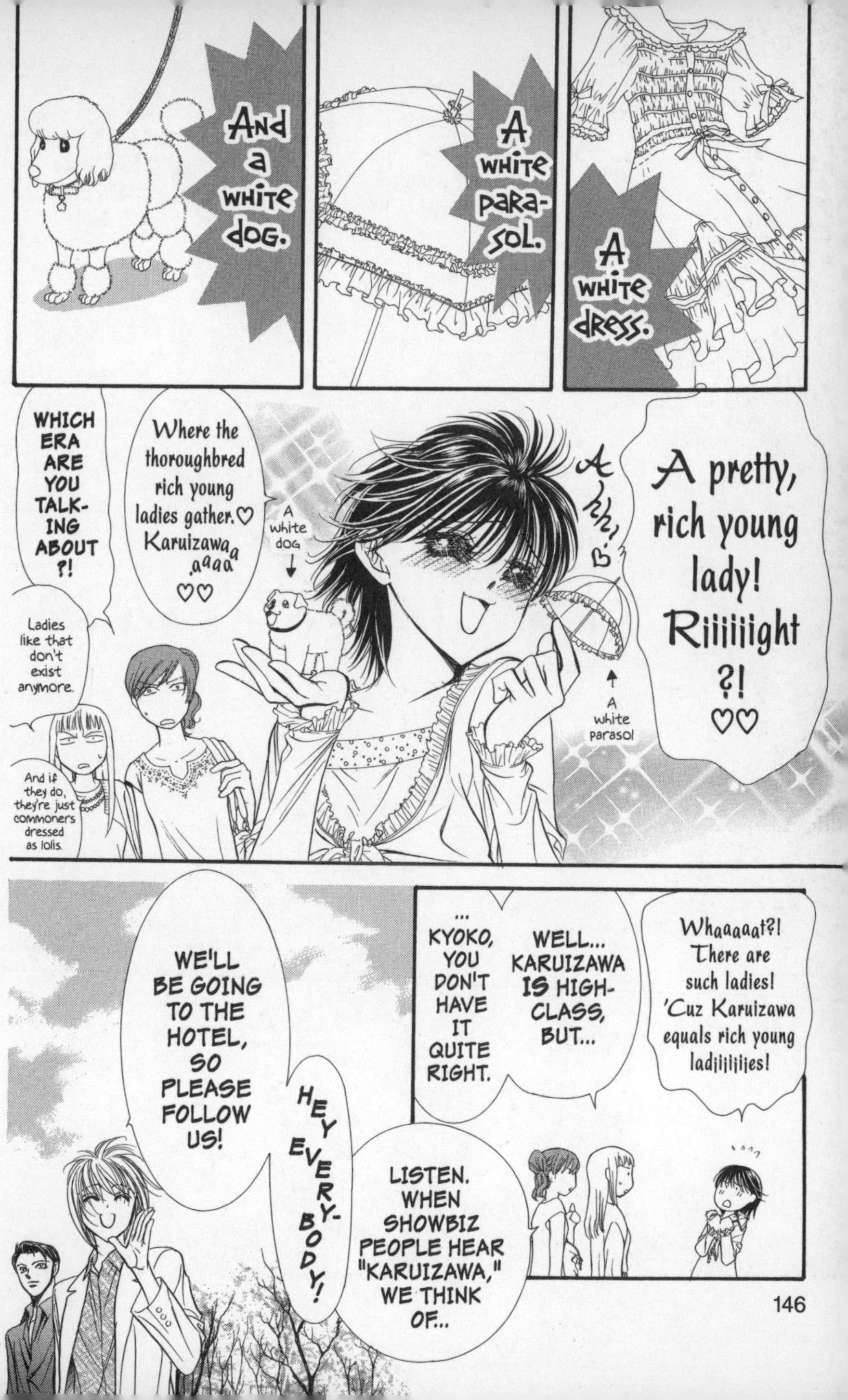
A white dress.
A white parasol.
And a white dog.
A pretty, rich young lady! Riiiiiight?! ♡♡
Ahh,!
A white parasol
A white dog
Where the thoroughbred rich young ladies gather.♡ Karuizawaaaaaa ♡♡
WHICH ERA ARE YOU TALKING ABOUT?!
Ladies like that don't exist anymore.
And if they do, they're just commoners dressed as lolis.
Whaaaaat?! There are such ladies! 'Cuz Karuizawa equals rich young ladiiiiiiies!
WELL... KARUIZAWA IS HIGH-CLASS, BUT...
...KYOKO, YOU DON'T HAVE IT QUITE RIGHT.
LISTEN. WHEN SHOWBIZ PEOPLE HEAR "KARUIZAWA," WE THINK OF...
HEY EVERYBODY!
WE'LL BE GOING TO THE HOTEL, SO PLEASE FOLLOW US!

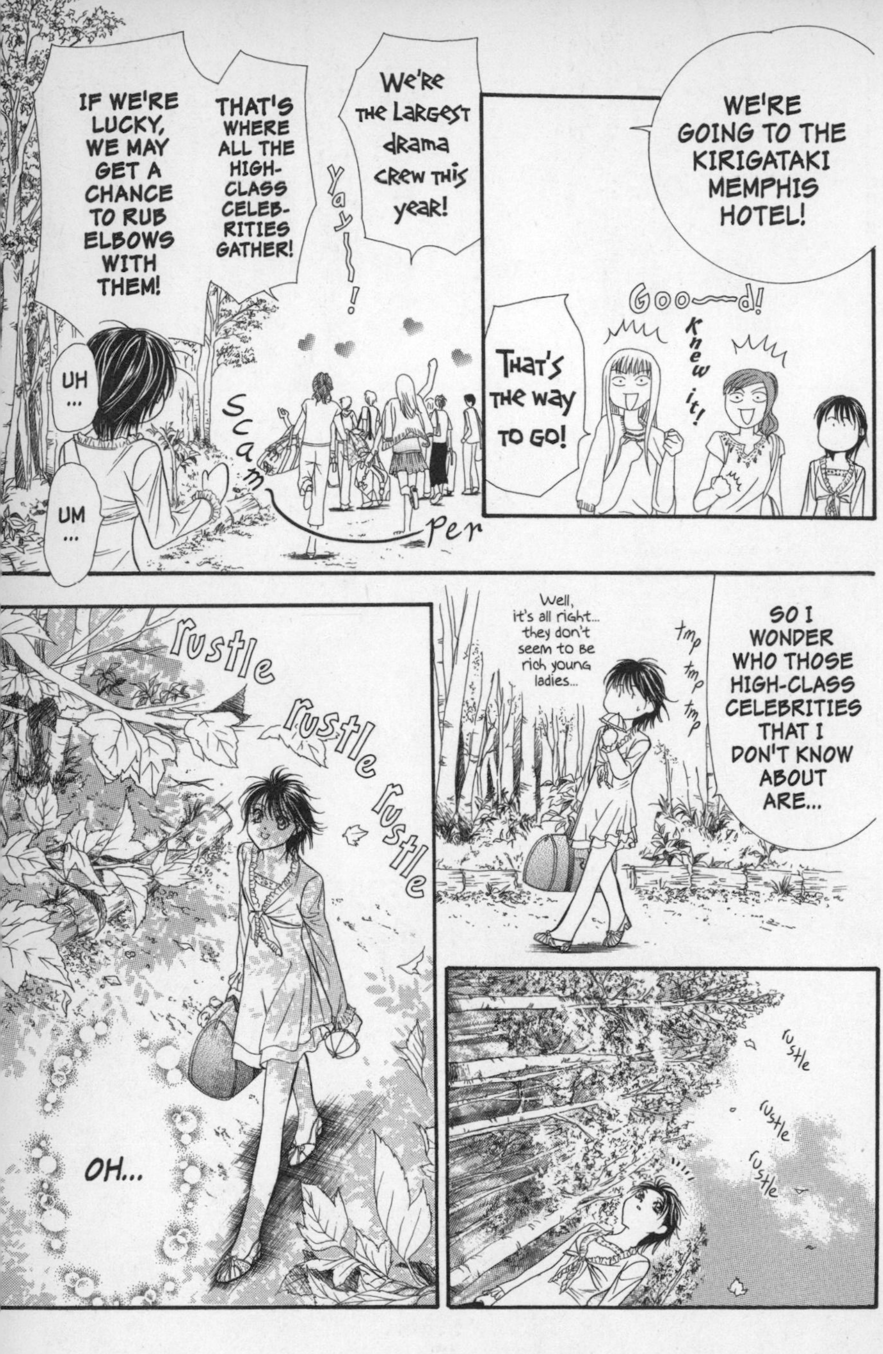
WE'RE GOING TO THE KIRIGATAKI MEMPHIS HOTEL!
Goo—d!
Knew it!
THAT'S THE WAY TO GO!
We're the largest drama crew this year!
Yay—!
THAT'S WHERE ALL THE HIGH-CLASS CELEBRITIES GATHER!
IF WE'RE LUCKY, WE MAY GET A CHANCE TO RUB ELBOWS WITH THEM!
Scamper
UH ...
UM ...
SO I WONDER WHO THOSE HIGH-CLASS CELEBRITIES THAT I DON'T KNOW ABOUT ARE...
tmp tmp tmp
Well, it's all right... they don't seem to be rich young ladies...
rustle
rustle
rustle
rustle
rustle
rustle
OH...

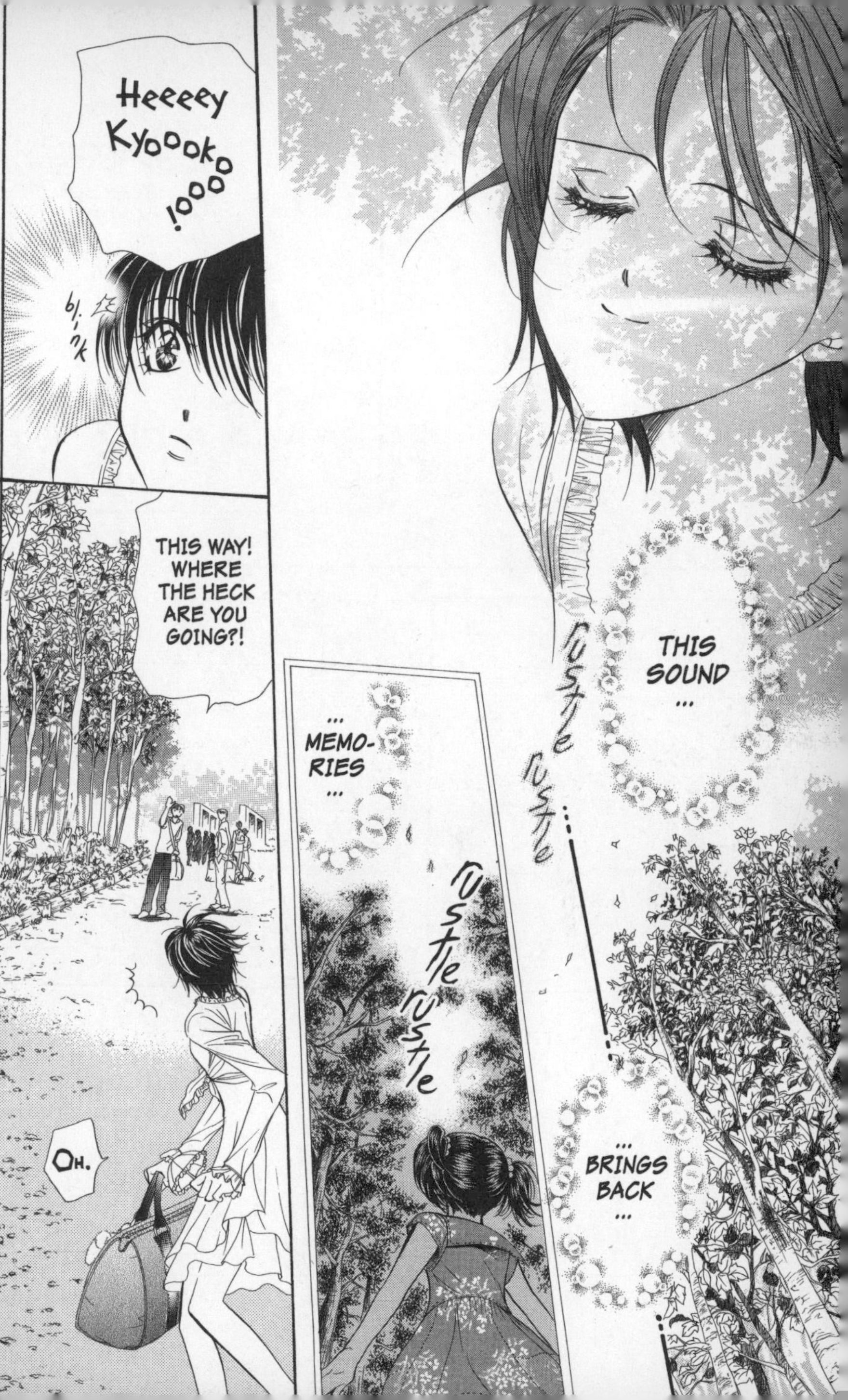
THIS SOUND ...
rustle rustle ...
... BRINGS BACK ...
... MEMORIES ...
rustle rustle
Heeeey Kyoookoooo!
blink
THIS WAY! WHERE THE HECK ARE YOU GOING?!
OH.

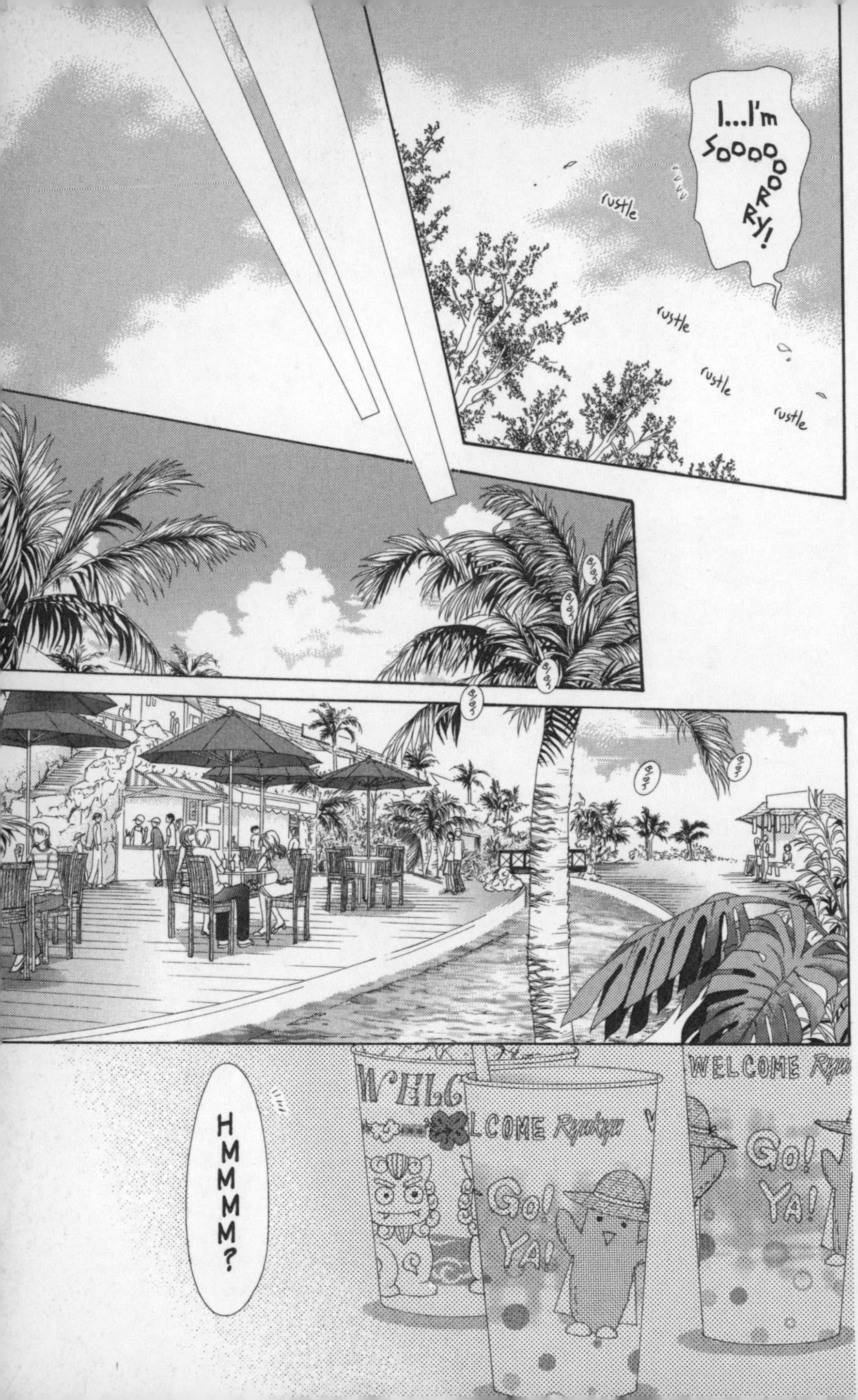
I...I'm SOOOOOORRY!
rustle
rustle
rustle
rustle
HMMMM?
WELCOME Ryukyu
Go! YA!

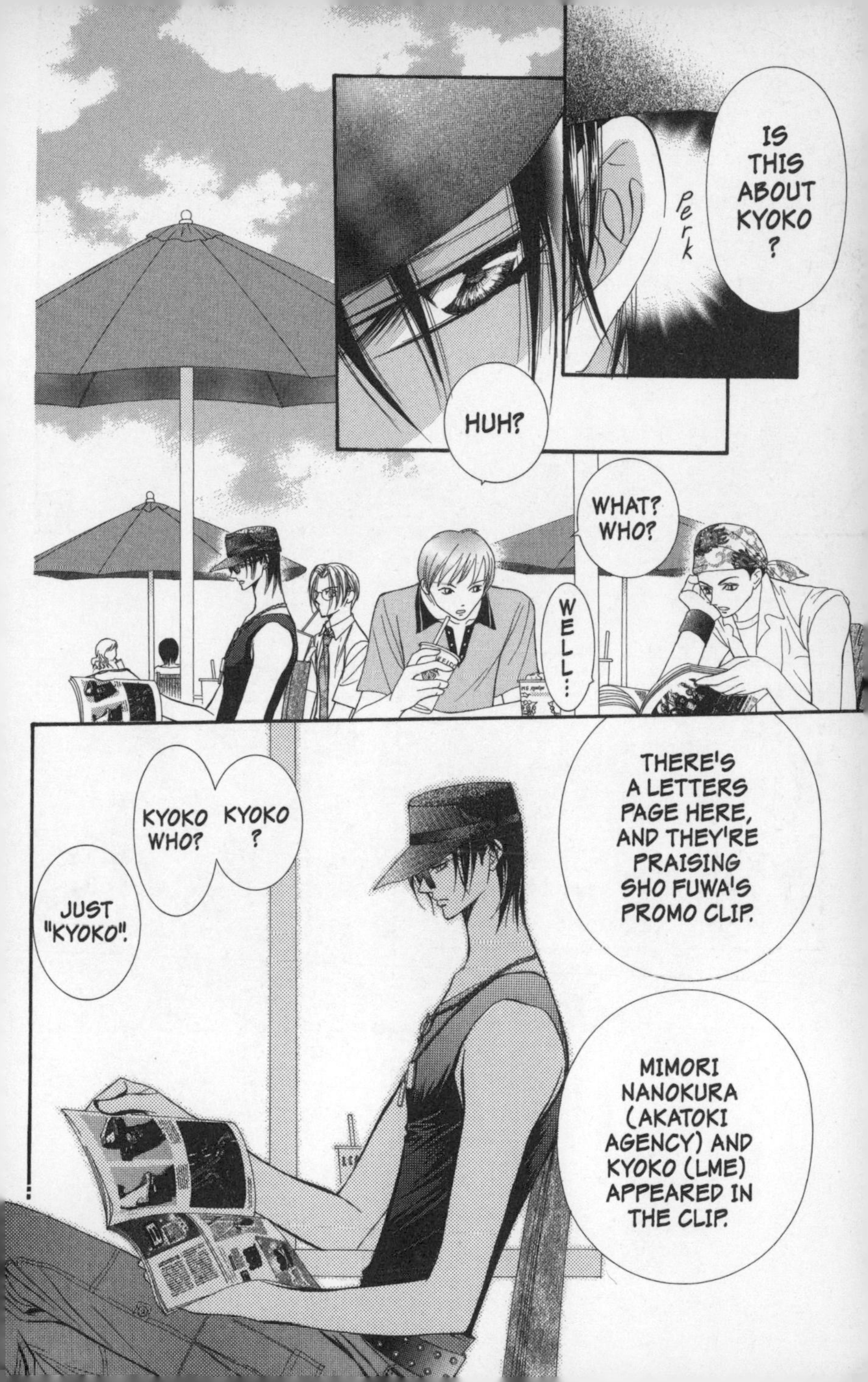
Perk
IS THIS ABOUT KYOKO?
HUH?
WHAT? WHO?
WELL...
THERE'S A LETTERS PAGE HERE, AND THEY'RE PRAISING SHO FUWA'S PROMO CLIP.
MIMORI NANOKURA (AKATOKI AGENCY) AND KYOKO (LME) APPEARED IN THE CLIP.
KYOKO?
KYOKO WHO?
JUST "KYOKO".

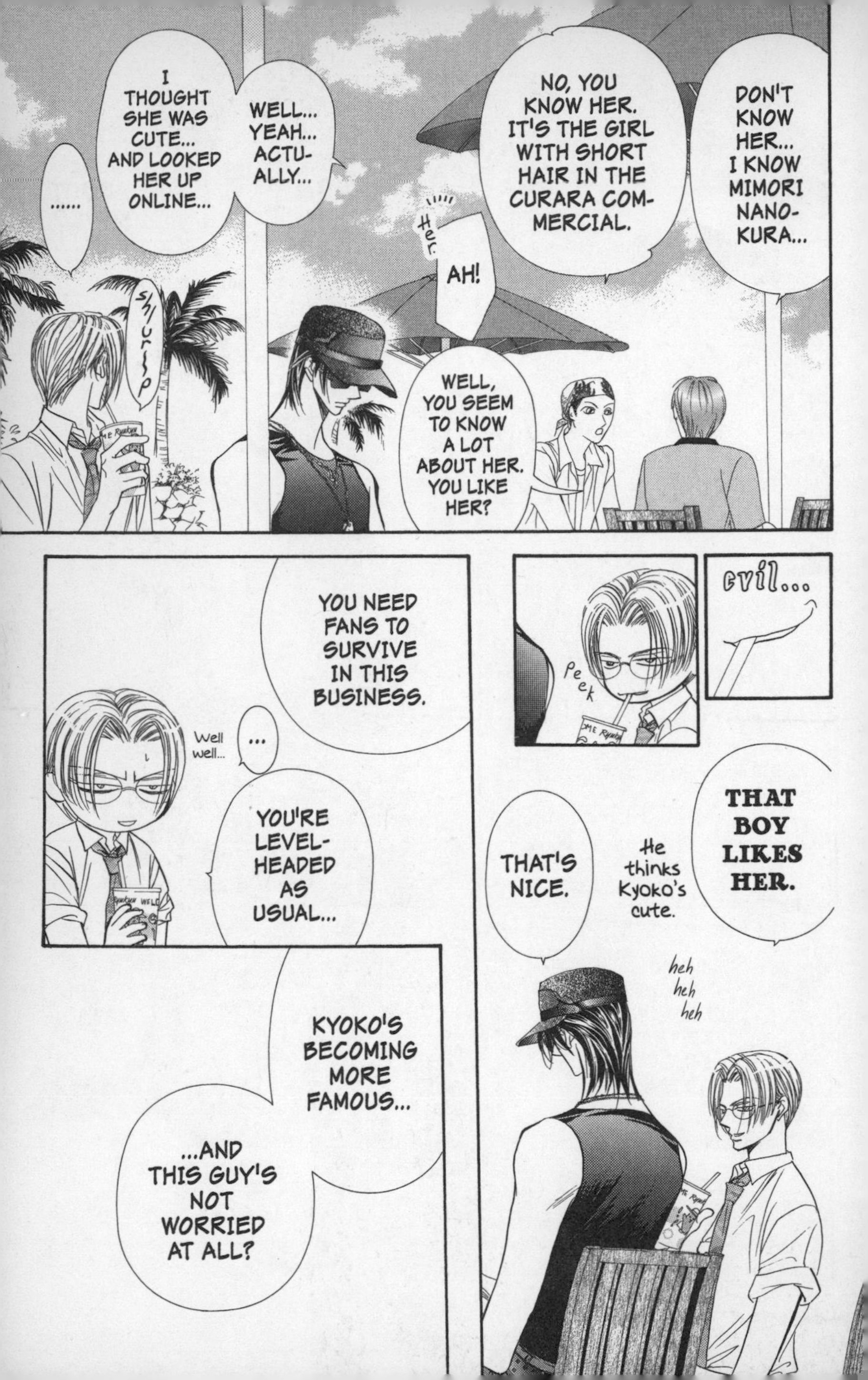
DON'T KNOW HER... I KNOW MIMORI NANOKURA...
NO, YOU KNOW HER. IT'S THE GIRL WITH SHORT HAIR IN THE CURARA COMMERCIAL.
Her.
AH!
WELL, YOU SEEM TO KNOW A LOT ABOUT HER. YOU LIKE HER?
WELL... YEAH... ACTUALLY...
I THOUGHT SHE WAS CUTE... AND LOOKED HER UP ONLINE...
......
shlurp
evil...
Peek
THAT BOY LIKES HER.
He thinks Kyoko's cute.
THAT'S NICE.
heh heh heh
YOU NEED FANS TO SURVIVE IN THIS BUSINESS.
...
Well well...
YOU'RE LEVEL-HEADED AS USUAL...
KYOKO'S BECOMING MORE FAMOUS...
...AND THIS GUY'S NOT WORRIED AT ALL?

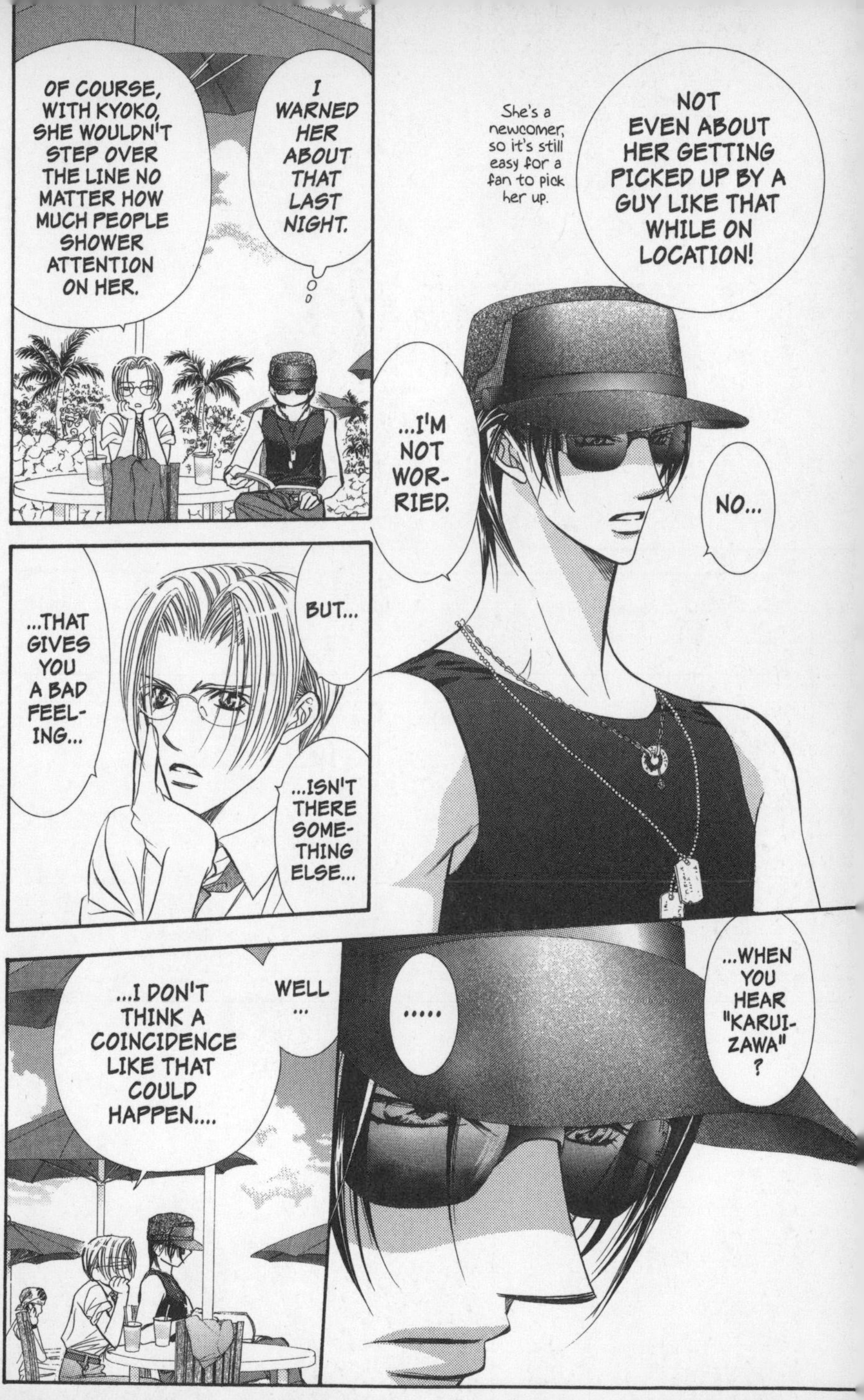
NOT EVEN ABOUT HER GETTING PICKED UP BY A GUY LIKE THAT WHILE ON LOCATION!
She's a newcomer, so it's still easy for a fan to pick her up.
NO...
...I'M NOT WOR-RIED.
I WARNED HER ABOUT THAT LAST NIGHT.
OF COURSE, WITH KYOKO, SHE WOULDN'T STEP OVER THE LINE NO MATTER HOW MUCH PEOPLE SHOWER ATTENTION ON HER.
BUT...
...ISN'T THERE SOME-THING ELSE...
...THAT GIVES YOU A BAD FEEL-ING...
...WHEN YOU HEAR "KARUI-ZAWA" ?
.....
WELL ...
...I DON'T THINK A COINCIDENCE LIKE THAT COULD HAPPEN....

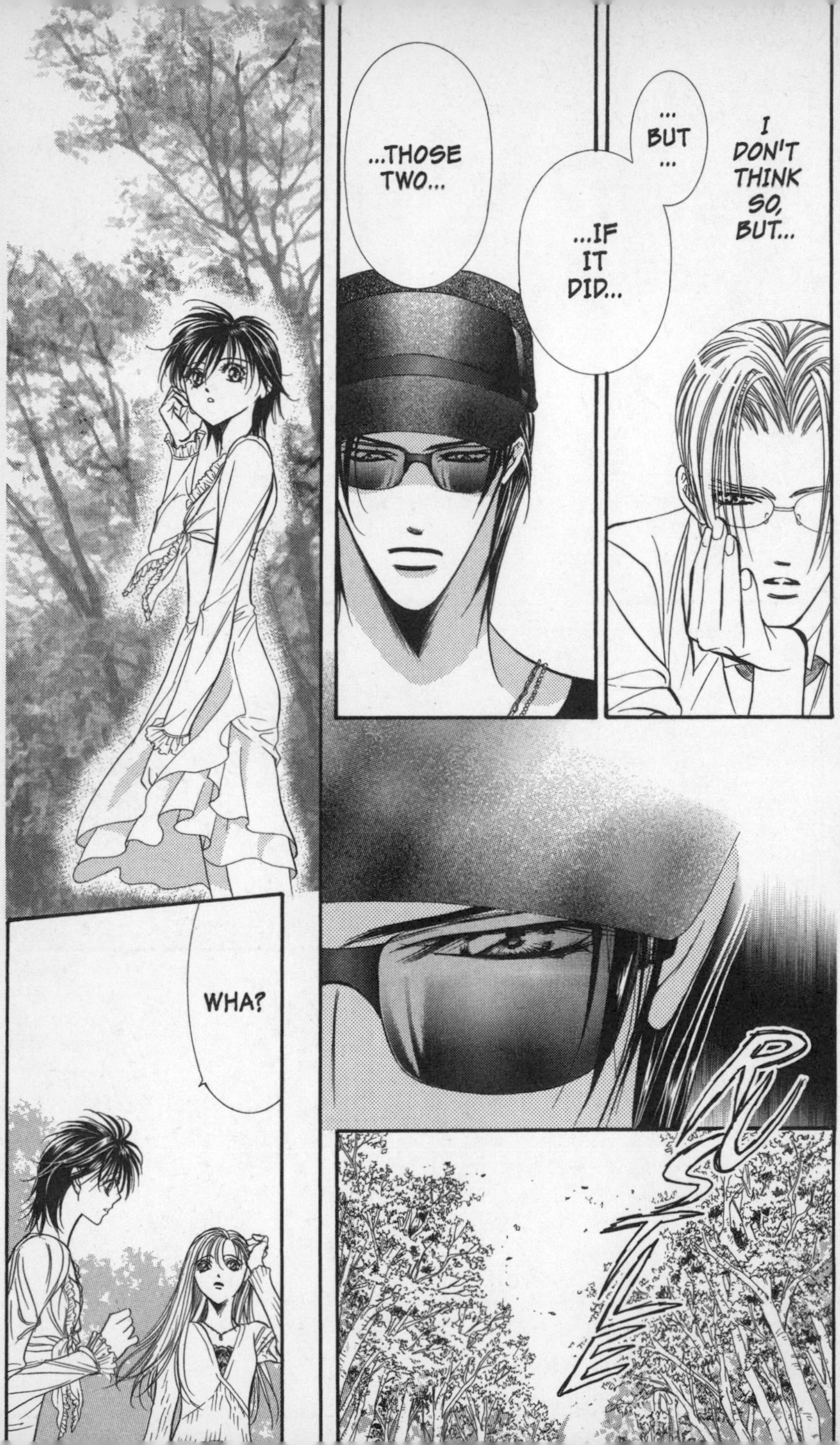

I DON'T THINK SO, BUT...
...BUT...
...IF IT DID...
...THOSE TWO...
RUSTLE
WHA?

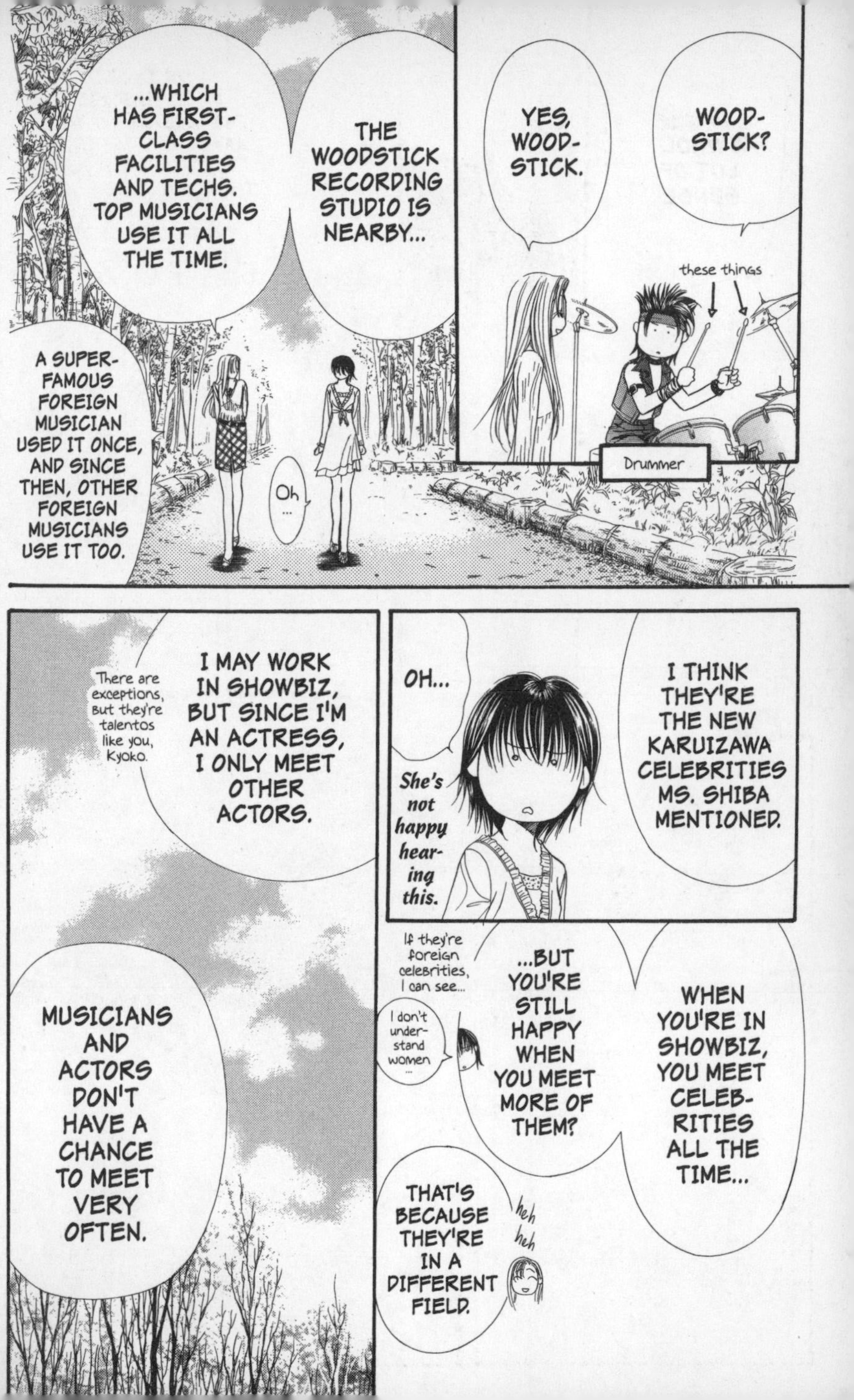
THE WOODSTICK RECORDING STUDIO IS NEARBY...
WOOD-STICK?
YES, WOOD-STICK.
these things
Drummer
...WHICH HAS FIRST-CLASS FACILITIES AND TECHS. TOP MUSICIANS USE IT ALL THE TIME.
A SUPER-FAMOUS FOREIGN MUSICIAN USED IT ONCE, AND SINCE THEN, OTHER FOREIGN MUSICIANS USE IT TOO.
Oh...
I THINK THEY'RE THE NEW KARUIZAWA CELEBRITIES MS. SHIBA MENTIONED.
OH...
She's not happy hearing this.
WHEN YOU'RE IN SHOWBIZ, YOU MEET CELEBRITIES ALL THE TIME...
...BUT YOU'RE STILL HAPPY WHEN YOU MEET MORE OF THEM?
If they're foreign celebrities, I can see...
I don't understand women...
THAT'S BECAUSE THEY'RE IN A DIFFERENT FIELD.
heh heh
I MAY WORK IN SHOWBIZ, BUT SINCE I'M AN ACTRESS, I ONLY MEET OTHER ACTORS.
There are exceptions, but they're talentos like you, Kyoko.
MUSICIANS AND ACTORS DON'T HAVE A CHANCE TO MEET VERY OFTEN.

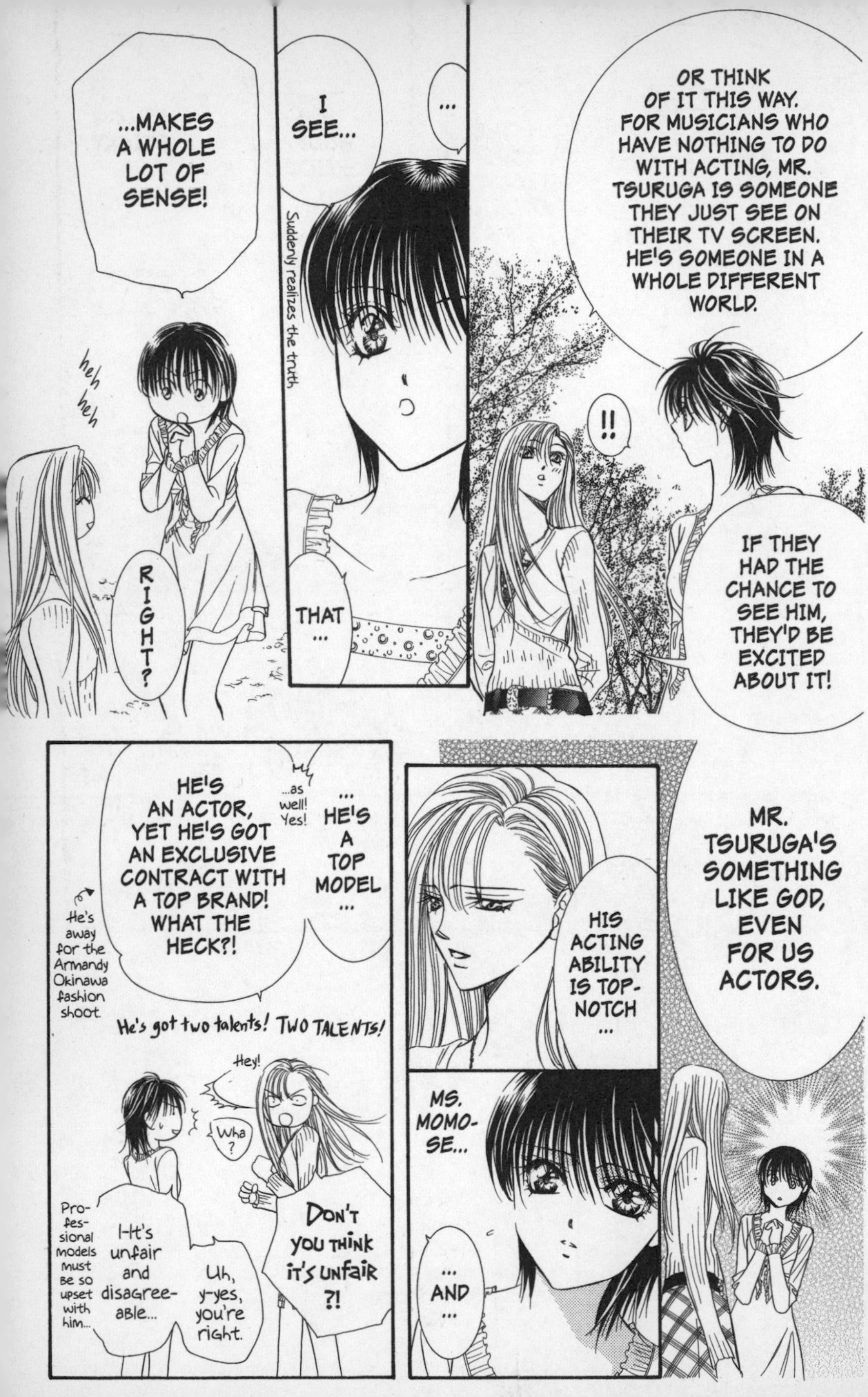
OR THINK OF IT THIS WAY. FOR MUSICIANS WHO HAVE NOTHING TO DO WITH ACTING, MR. TSURUGA IS SOMEONE THEY JUST SEE ON THEIR TV SCREEN. HE'S SOMEONE IN A WHOLE DIFFERENT WORLD.
!!
IF THEY HAD THE CHANCE TO SEE HIM, THEY'D BE EXCITED ABOUT IT!
...
I SEE...
Suddenly realizes the truth
THAT ...
...MAKES A WHOLE LOT OF SENSE!
heh heh
RIGHT?
MR. TSURUGA'S SOMETHING LIKE GOD, EVEN FOR US ACTORS.
HIS ACTING ABILITY IS TOP-NOTCH ...
MS. MOMOSE...
... AND ...
... HE'S A TOP MODEL ...
...as well! Yes!
HE'S AN ACTOR, YET HE'S GOT AN EXCLUSIVE CONTRACT WITH A TOP BRAND! WHAT THE HECK?!
He's away for the Armandy Okinawa fashion shoot.
He's got two talents! TWO TALENTS!
Hey!
Wha?
DON'T YOU THINK IT'S UNFAIR?!
Uh, y-yes, you're right.
I-It's unfair and disagreeable...
Professional models must be so upset with him...

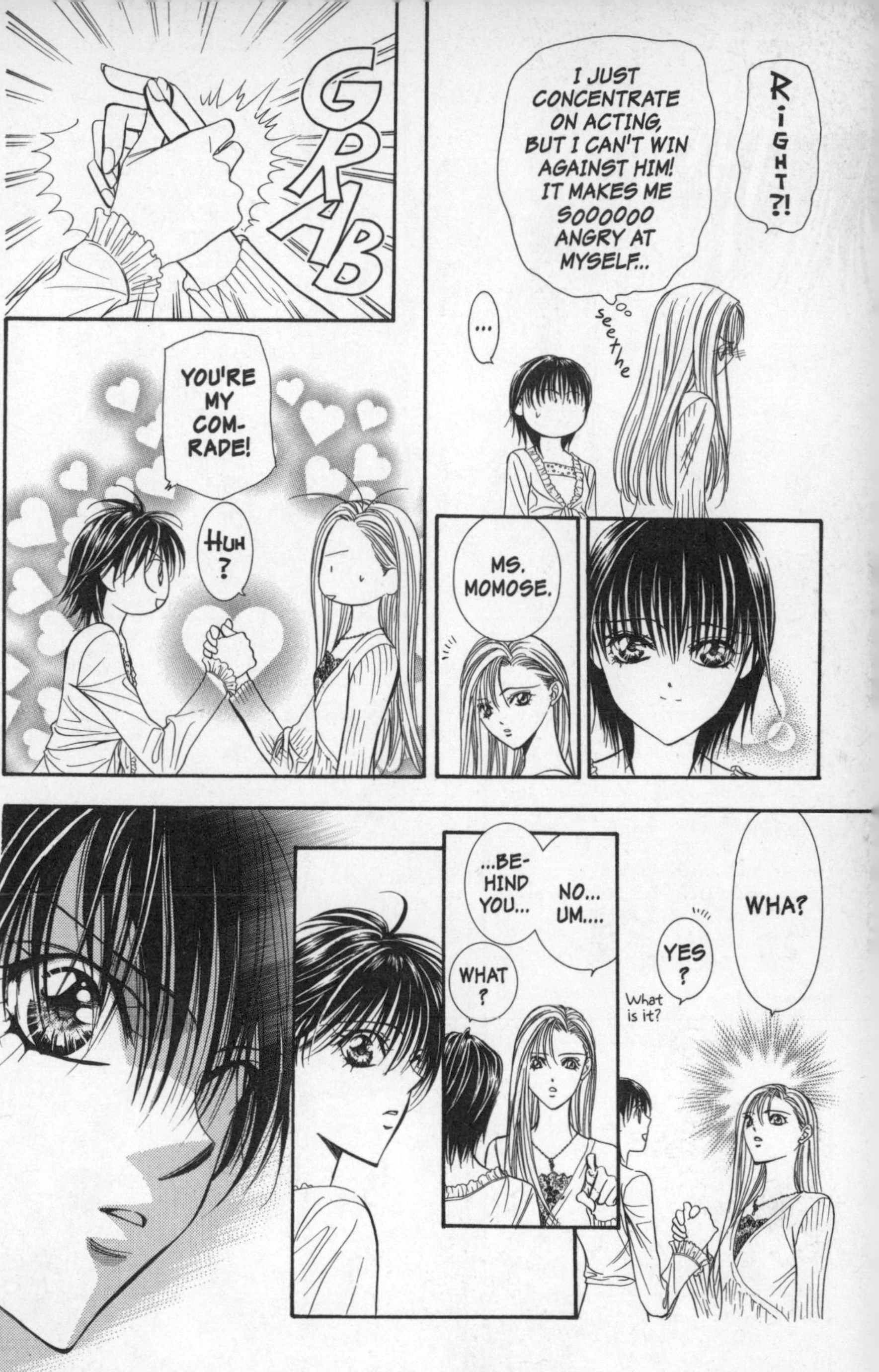
RIGHT?!
I JUST CONCENTRATE ON ACTING, BUT I CAN'T WIN AGAINST HIM! IT MAKES ME SOOOOOO ANGRY AT MYSELF...
seethe
...
GRAB
YOU'RE MY COM-RADE!
HUH?
MS. MOMOSE.
WHA?
YES?
What is it?
NO... UM....
...BE-HIND YOU...
WHAT?

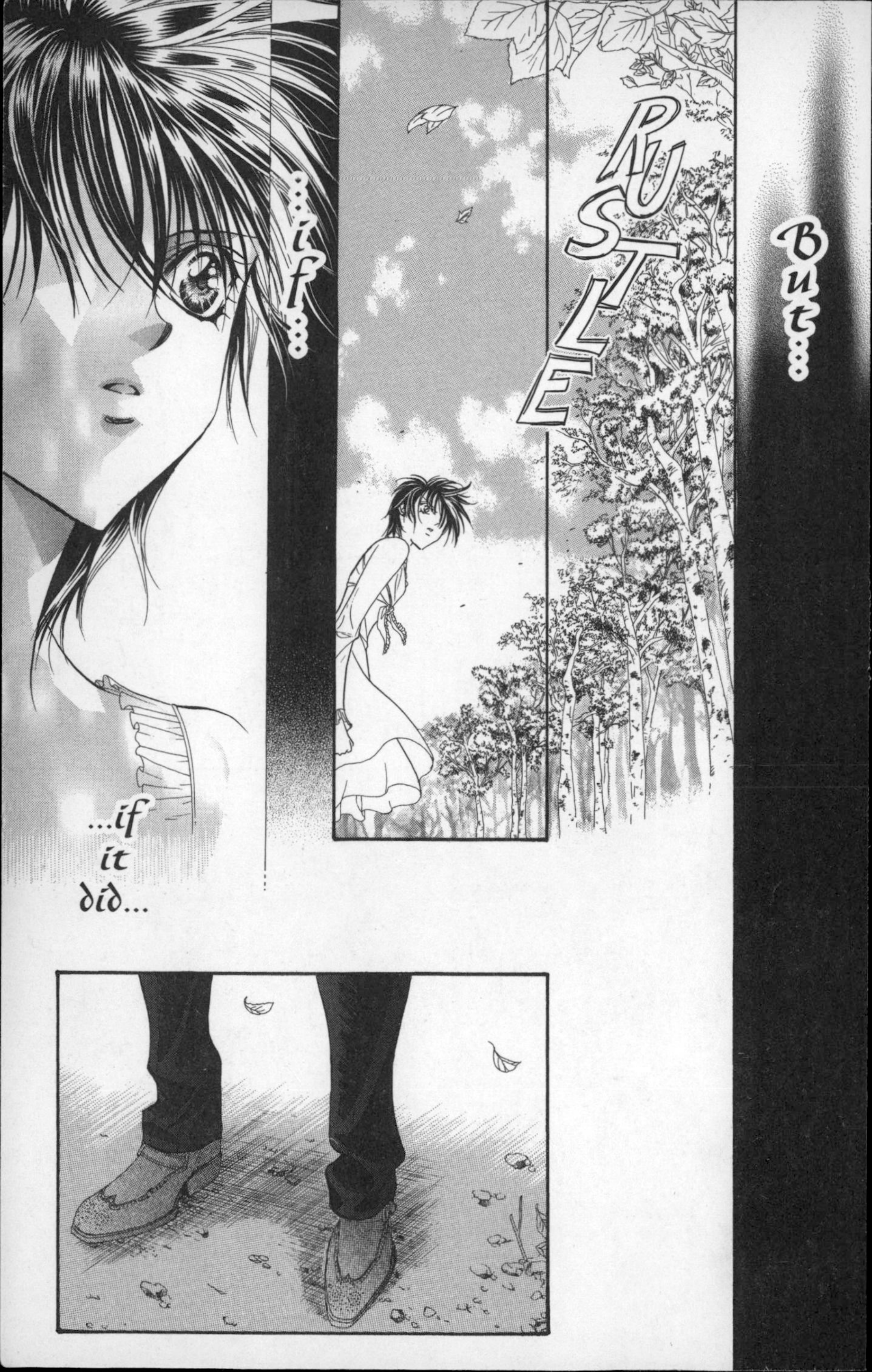

But...
RUSTLE
...if...
...if it did...

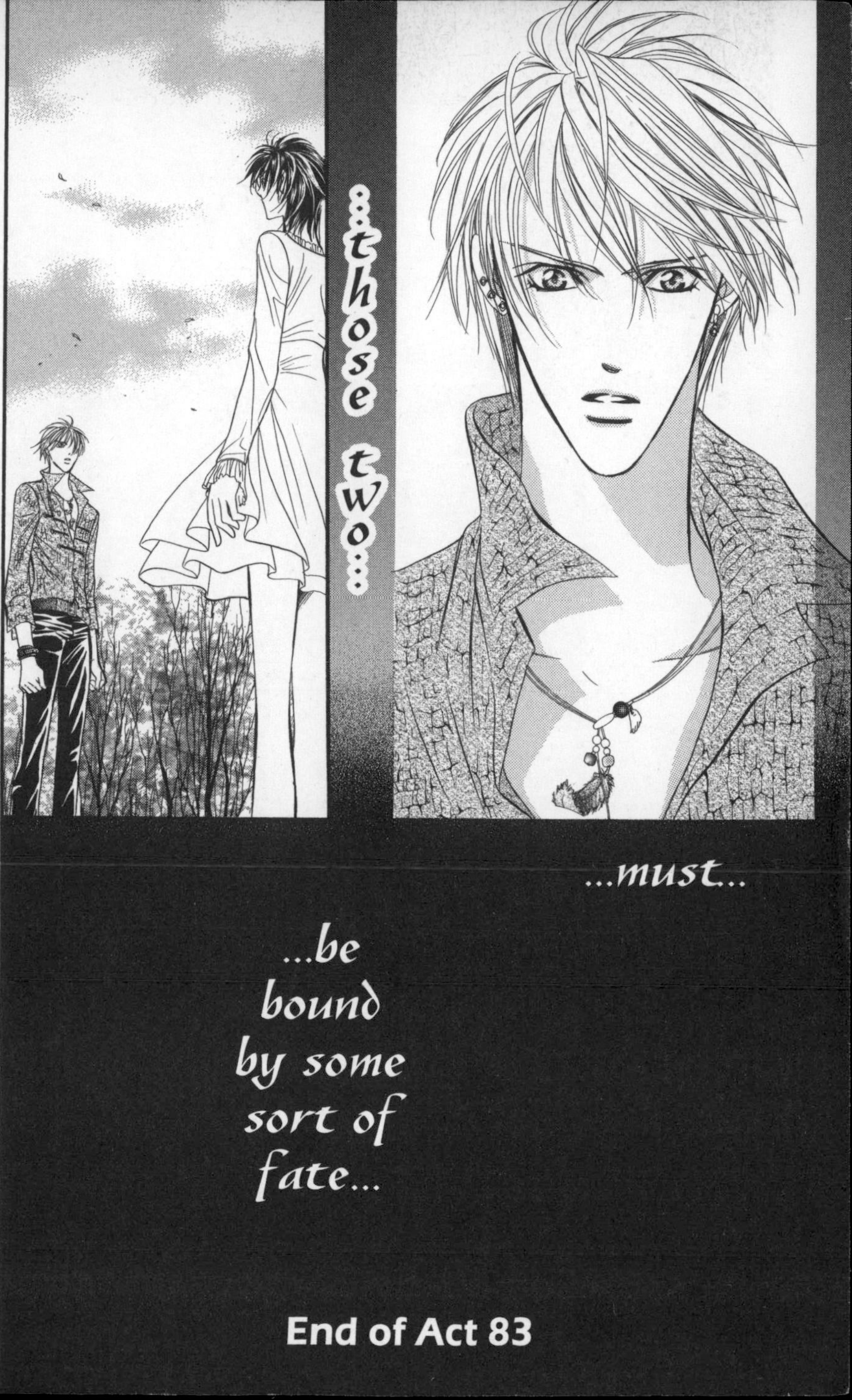
...those two...
...must...
...be bound by some sort of fate...
End of Act 83

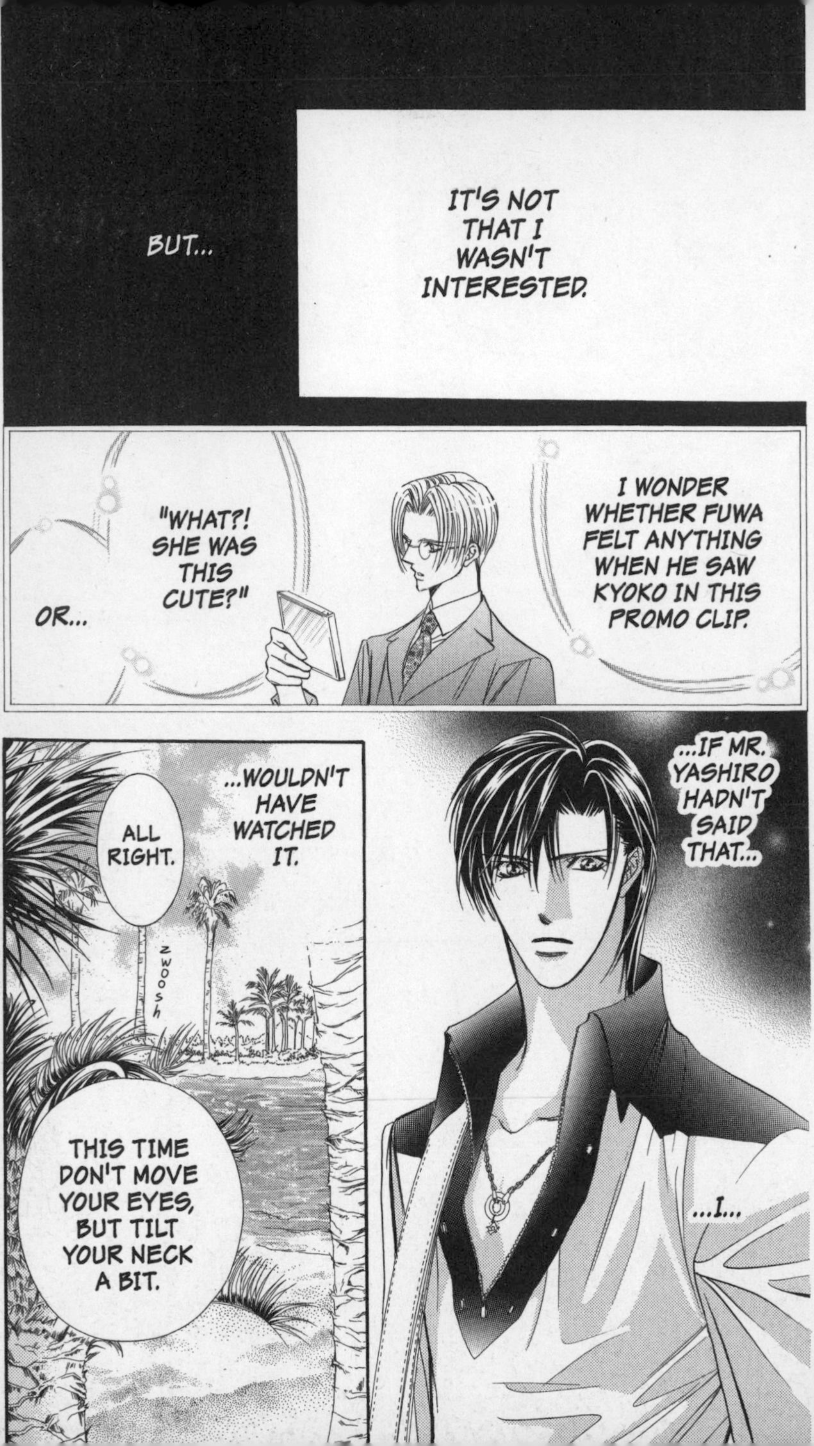
IT'S NOT THAT I WASN'T INTERESTED.
BUT...
I WONDER WHETHER FUWA FELT ANYTHING WHEN HE SAW KYOKO IN THIS PROMO CLIP.
"WHAT?! SHE WAS THIS CUTE?"
OR...
...IF MR. YASHIRO HADN'T SAID THAT...
...I...
...WOULDN'T HAVE WATCHED IT.
ALL RIGHT.
ZWOOSH
THIS TIME DON'T MOVE YOUR EYES, BUT TILT YOUR NECK A BIT.

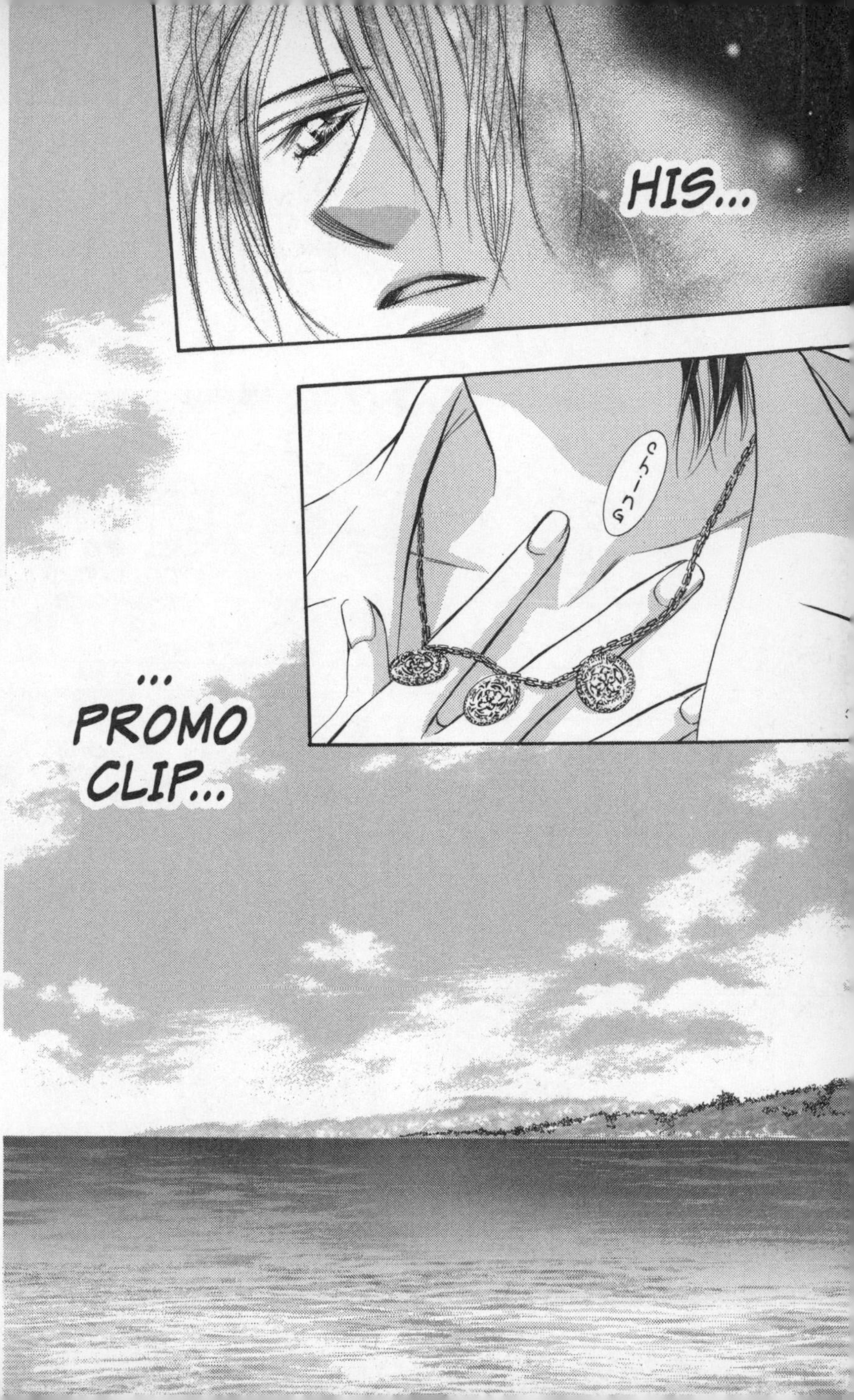
HIS...
CHING
... PROMO CLIP...

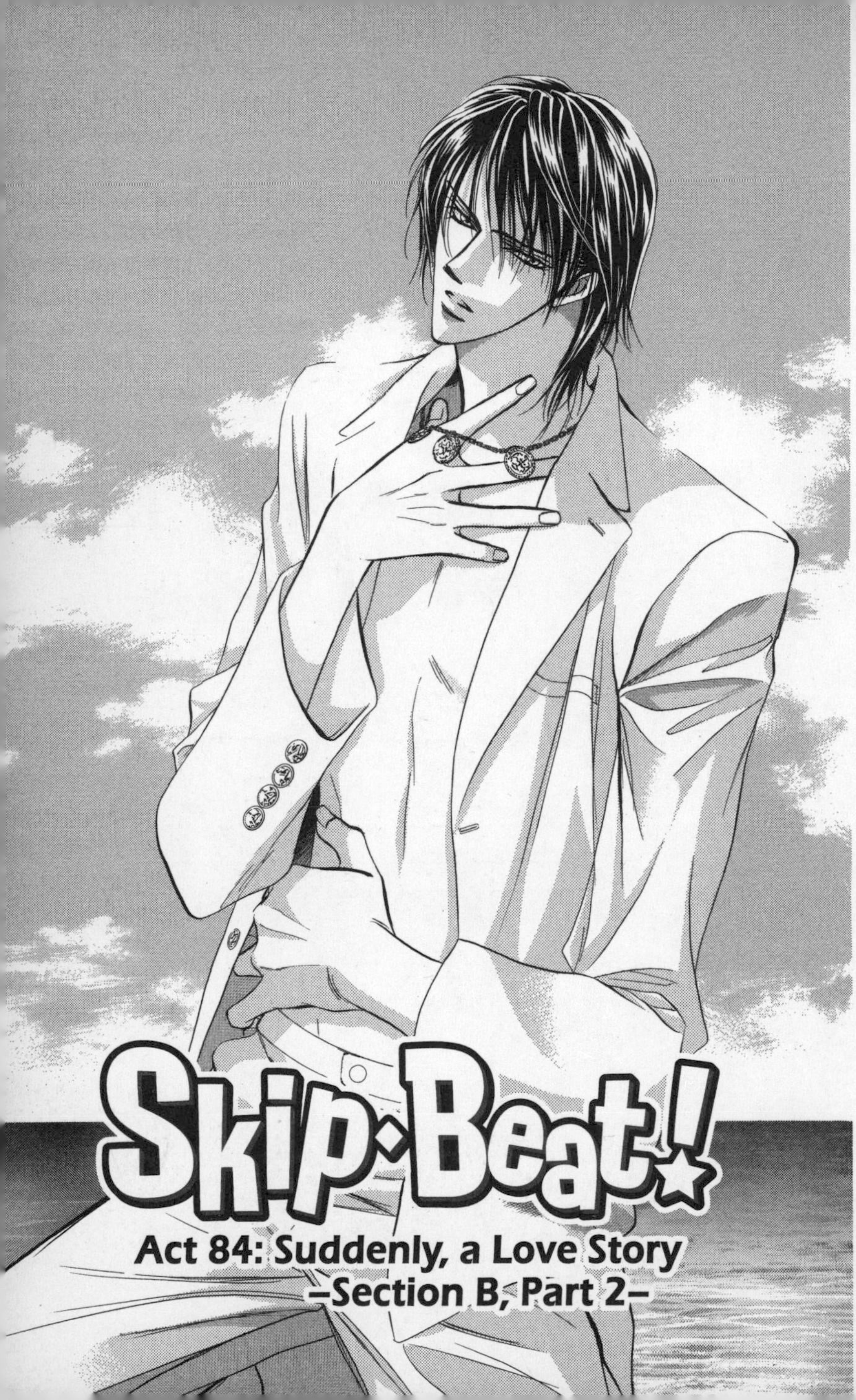
Skip·Beat!
Act 84: Suddenly, a Love Story
–Section B, Part 2–

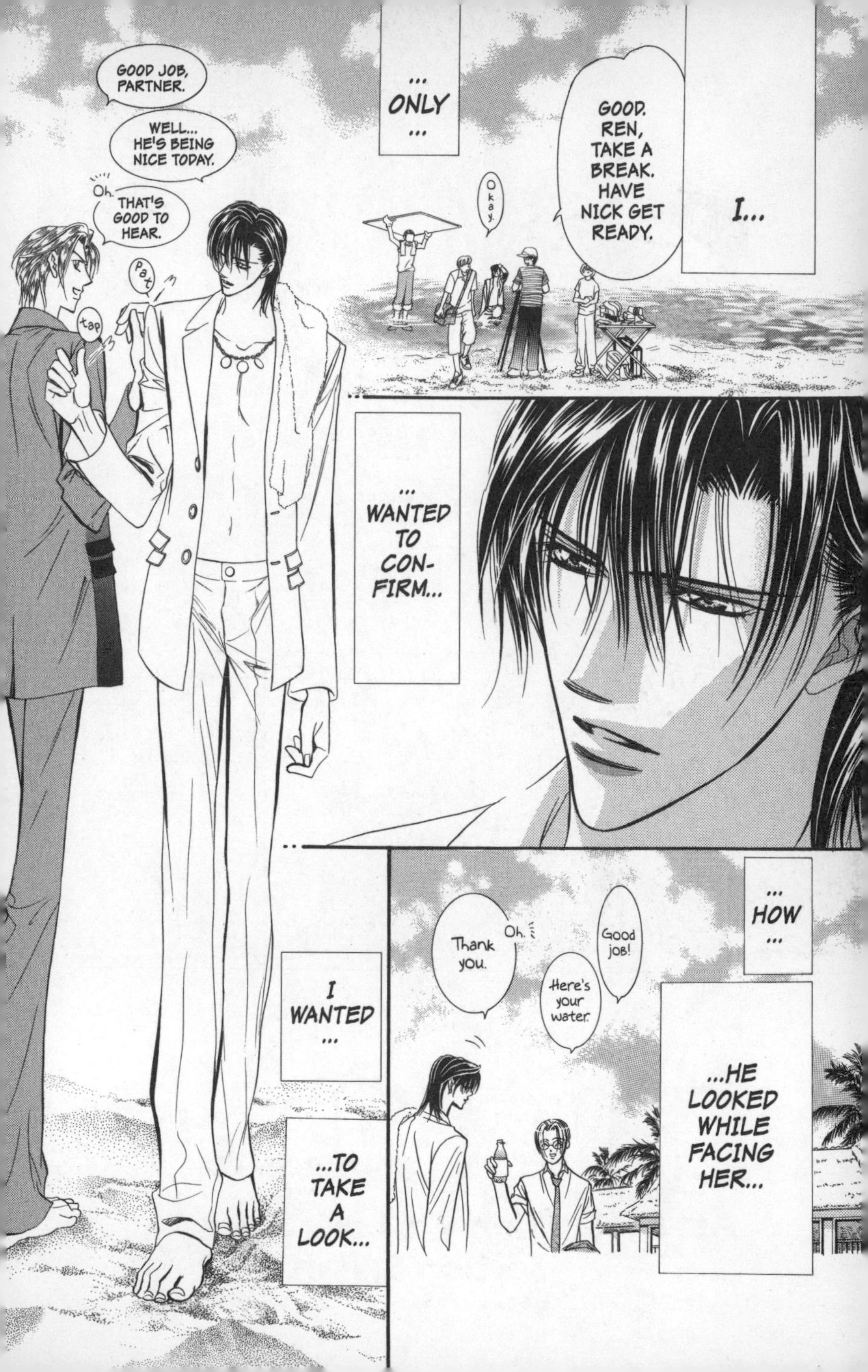
I...
GOOD. REN, TAKE A BREAK. HAVE NICK GET READY.
Okay.
...ONLY...
...WANTED TO CONFIRM...
...HOW...
...HE LOOKED WHILE FACING HER...
Good job!
Here's your water.
Oh.
Thank you.
I WANTED...
...TO TAKE A LOOK...
GOOD JOB, PARTNER.
WELL... HE'S BEING NICE TODAY.
Oh.
THAT'S GOOD TO HEAR.
Pat
tap

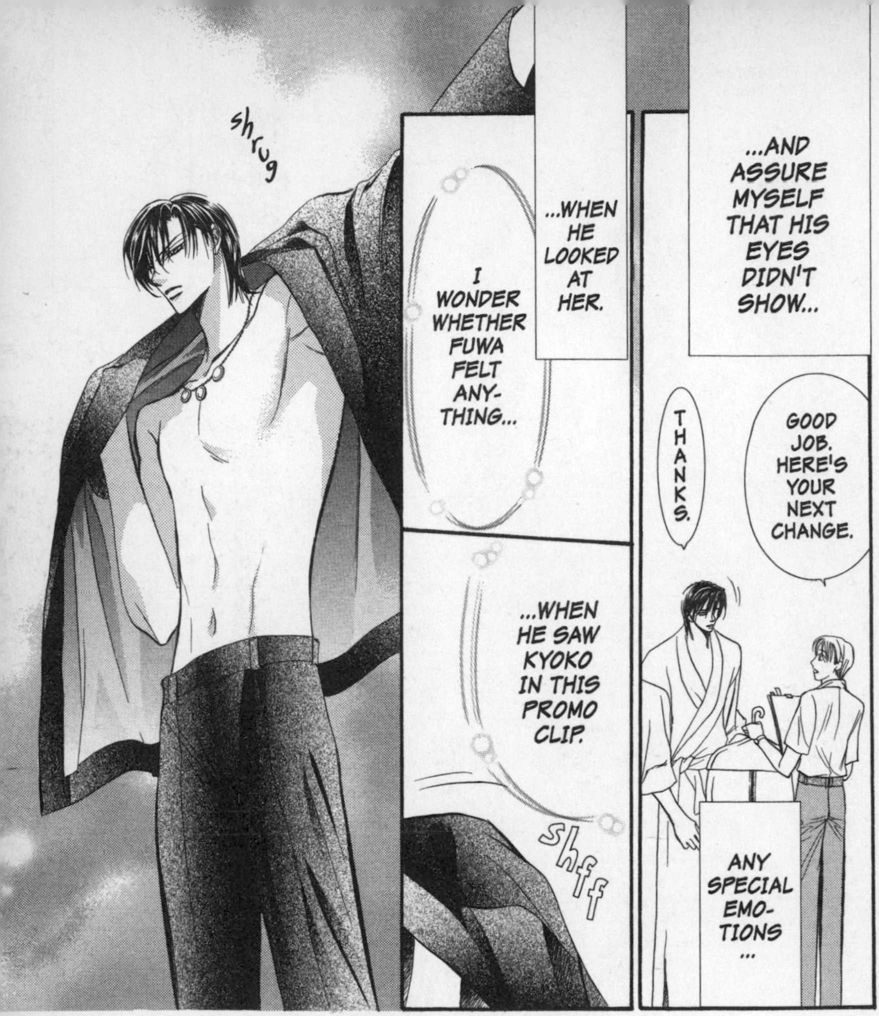
...AND ASSURE MYSELF THAT HIS EYES DIDN'T SHOW...
GOOD JOB. HERE'S YOUR NEXT CHANGE.
THANKS.
ANY SPECIAL EMOTIONS ...
...WHEN HE LOOKED AT HER.
I WONDER WHETHER FUWA FELT ANYTHING...
...WHEN HE SAW KYOKO IN THIS PROMO CLIP.
shff
shrug

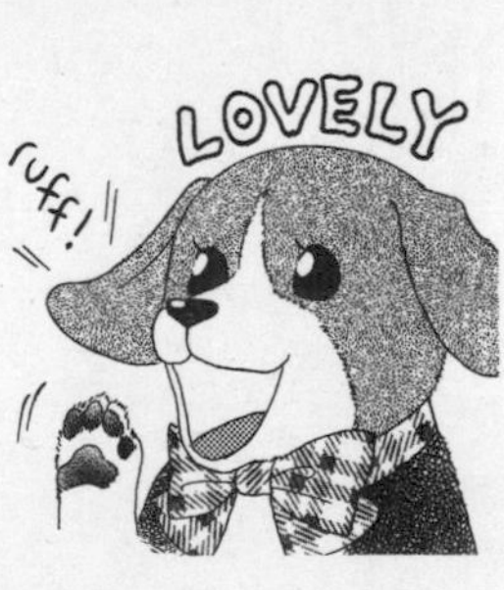
LOVELY
ruff!

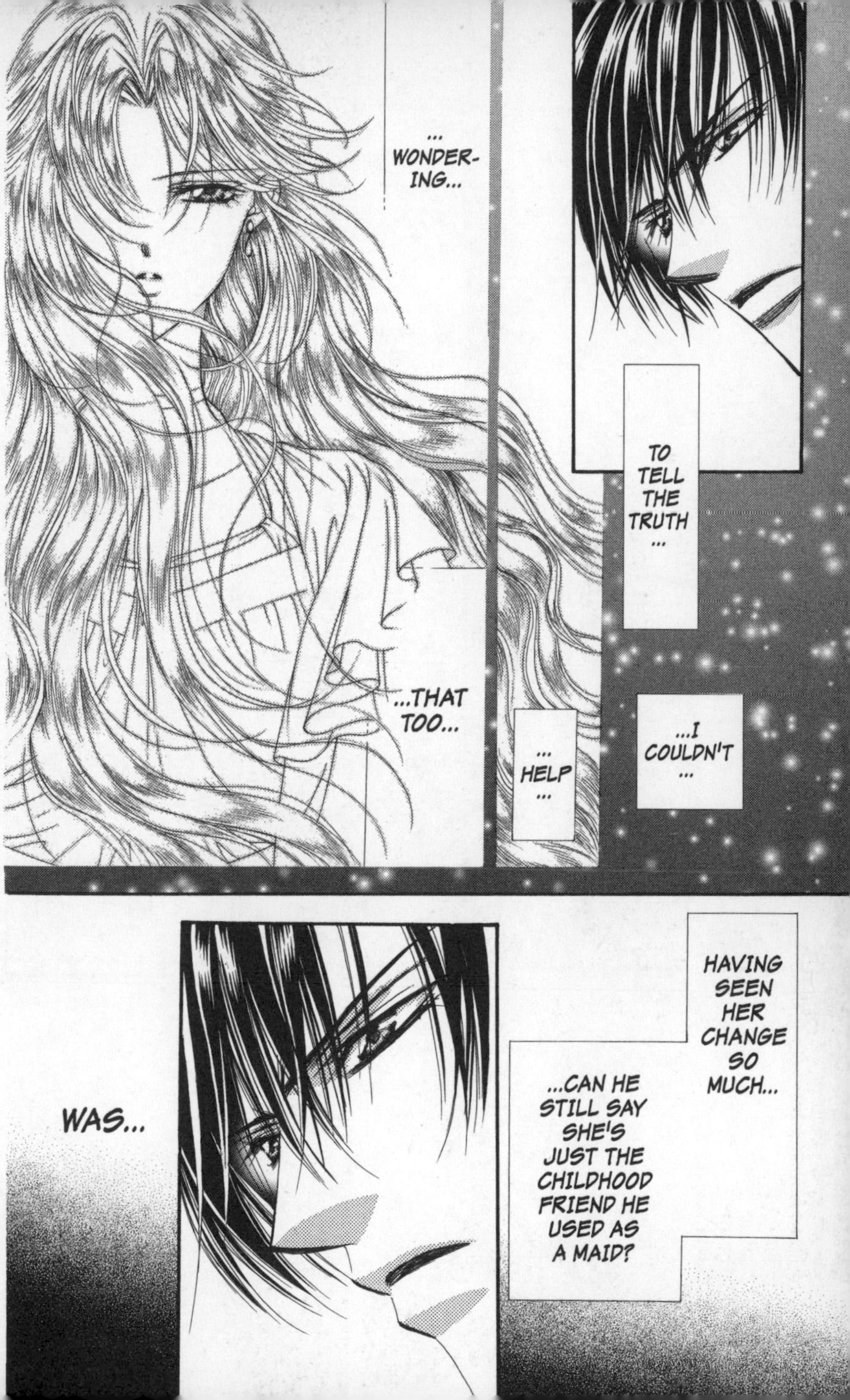
TO TELL THE TRUTH...
...I COULDN'T...
...HELP...
...WONDERING...
...THAT TOO...
HAVING SEEN HER CHANGE SO MUCH...
...CAN HE STILL SAY SHE'S JUST THE CHILDHOOD FRIEND HE USED AS A MAID?
WAS...

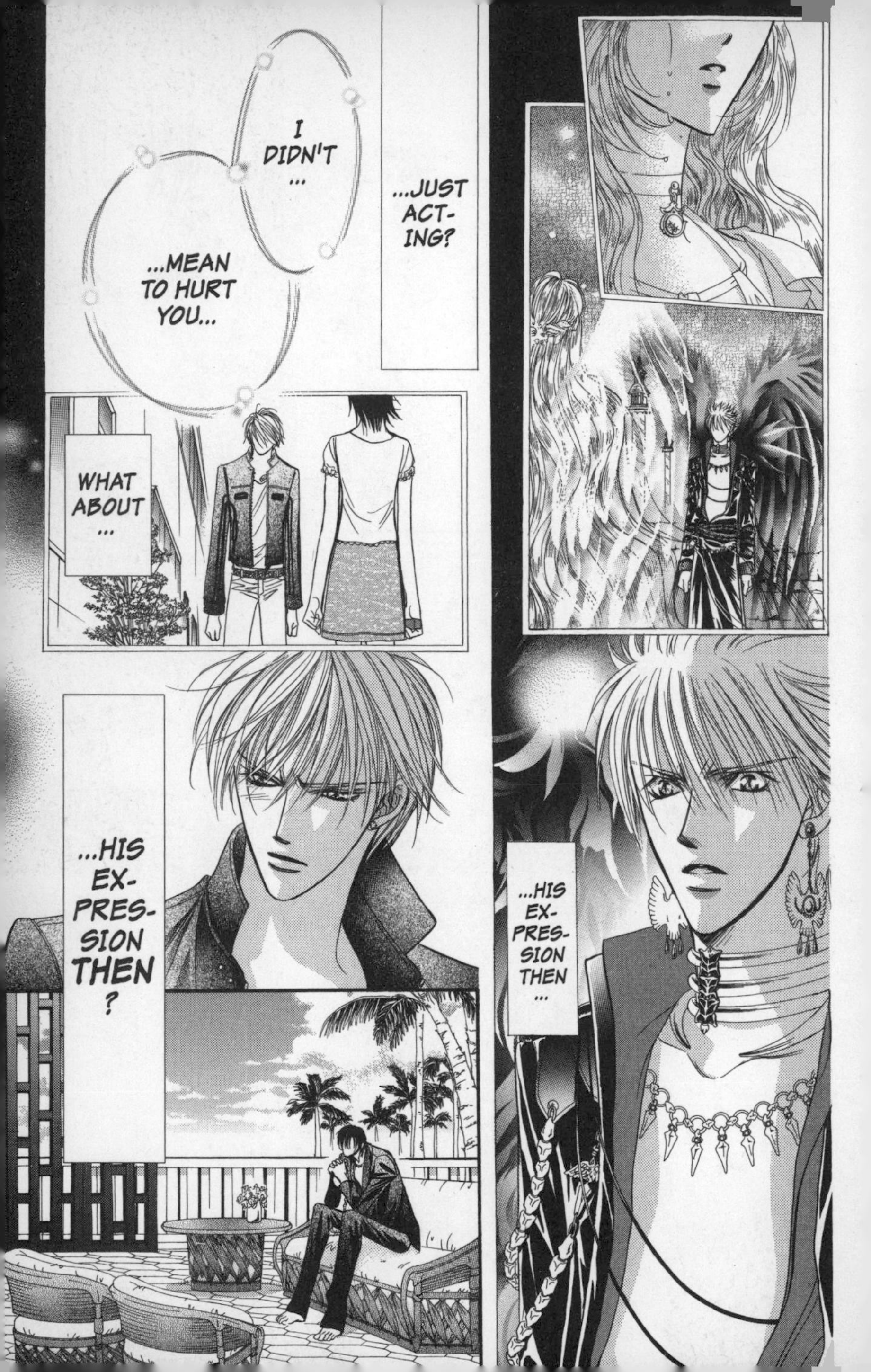
...HIS EX-PRES-SION THEN ...
...JUST ACT-ING?
I DIDN'T ...
...MEAN TO HURT YOU...
WHAT ABOUT ...
...HIS EX-PRES-SION THEN ?

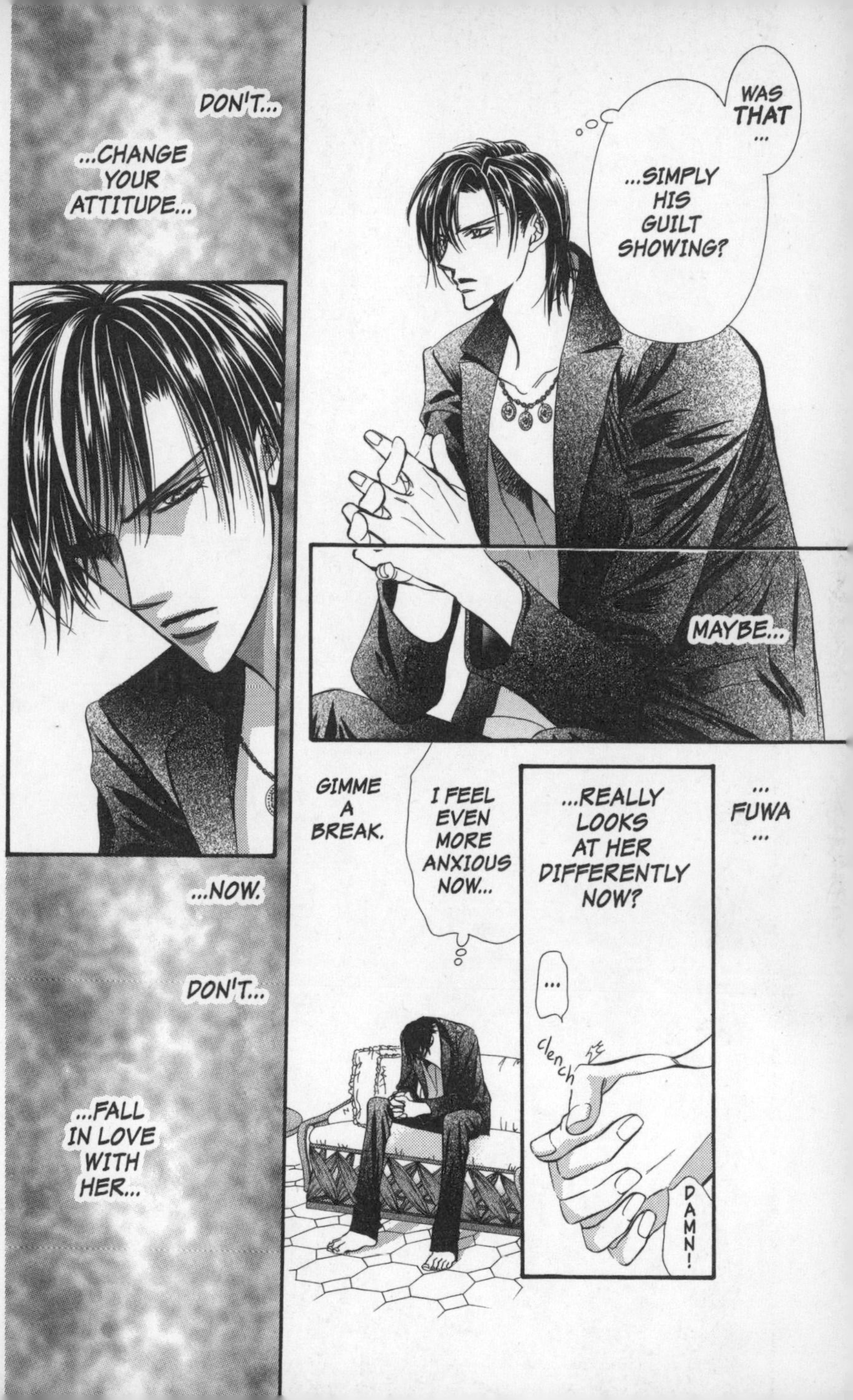
WAS THAT ...
...SIMPLY HIS GUILT SHOWING?
MAYBE...
... FUWA ...
...REALLY LOOKS AT HER DIFFERENTLY NOW?
I FEEL EVEN MORE ANXIOUS NOW...
GIMME A BREAK.
...
clench
DAMN!
DON'T...
...CHANGE YOUR ATTITUDE...
...NOW.
DON'T...
...FALL IN LOVE WITH HER...

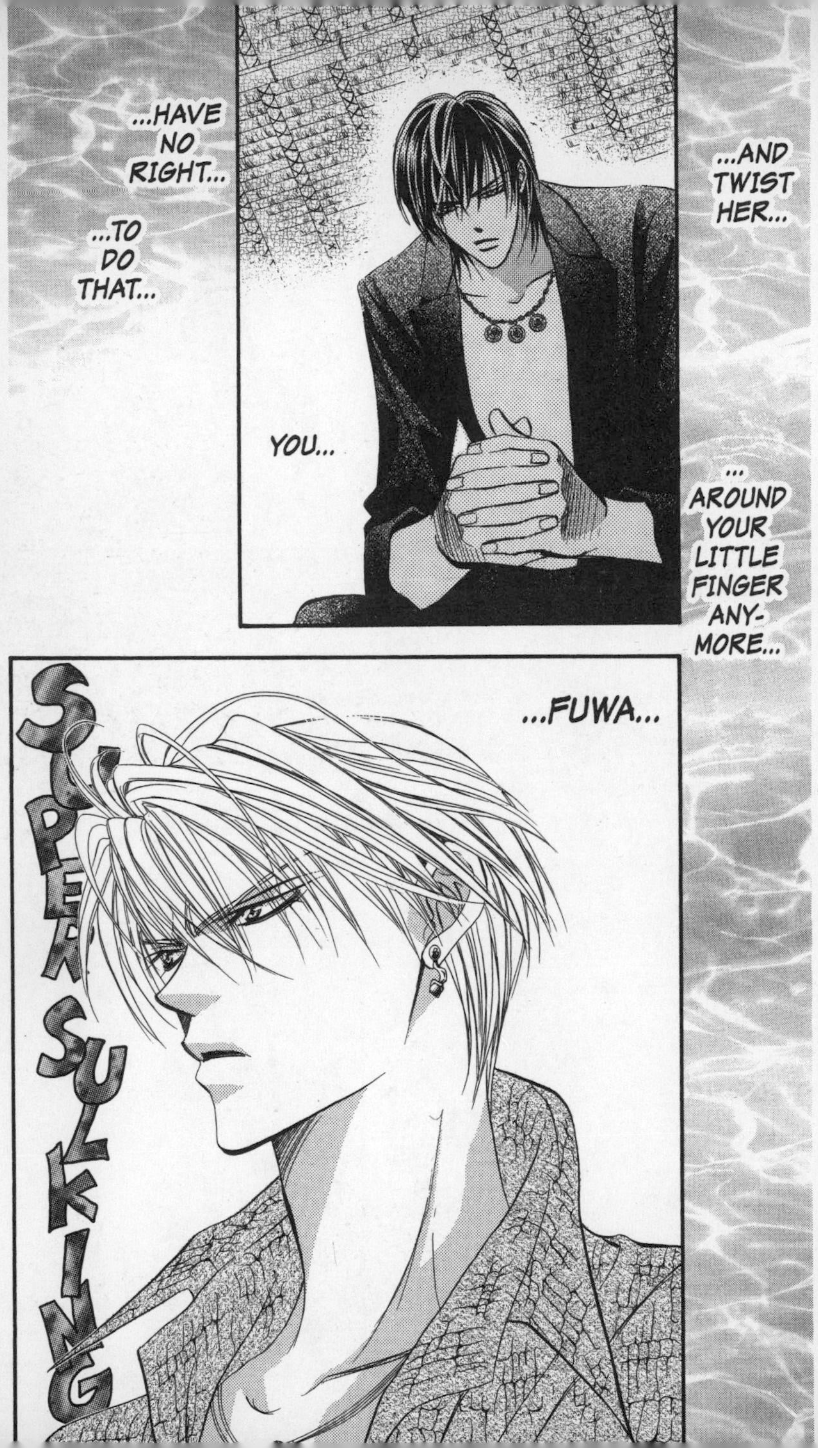
YOU...
...HAVE NO RIGHT...
...TO DO THAT...
...AND TWIST HER...
...AROUND YOUR LITTLE FINGER ANYMORE...
...FUWA...
SUPER SULKING

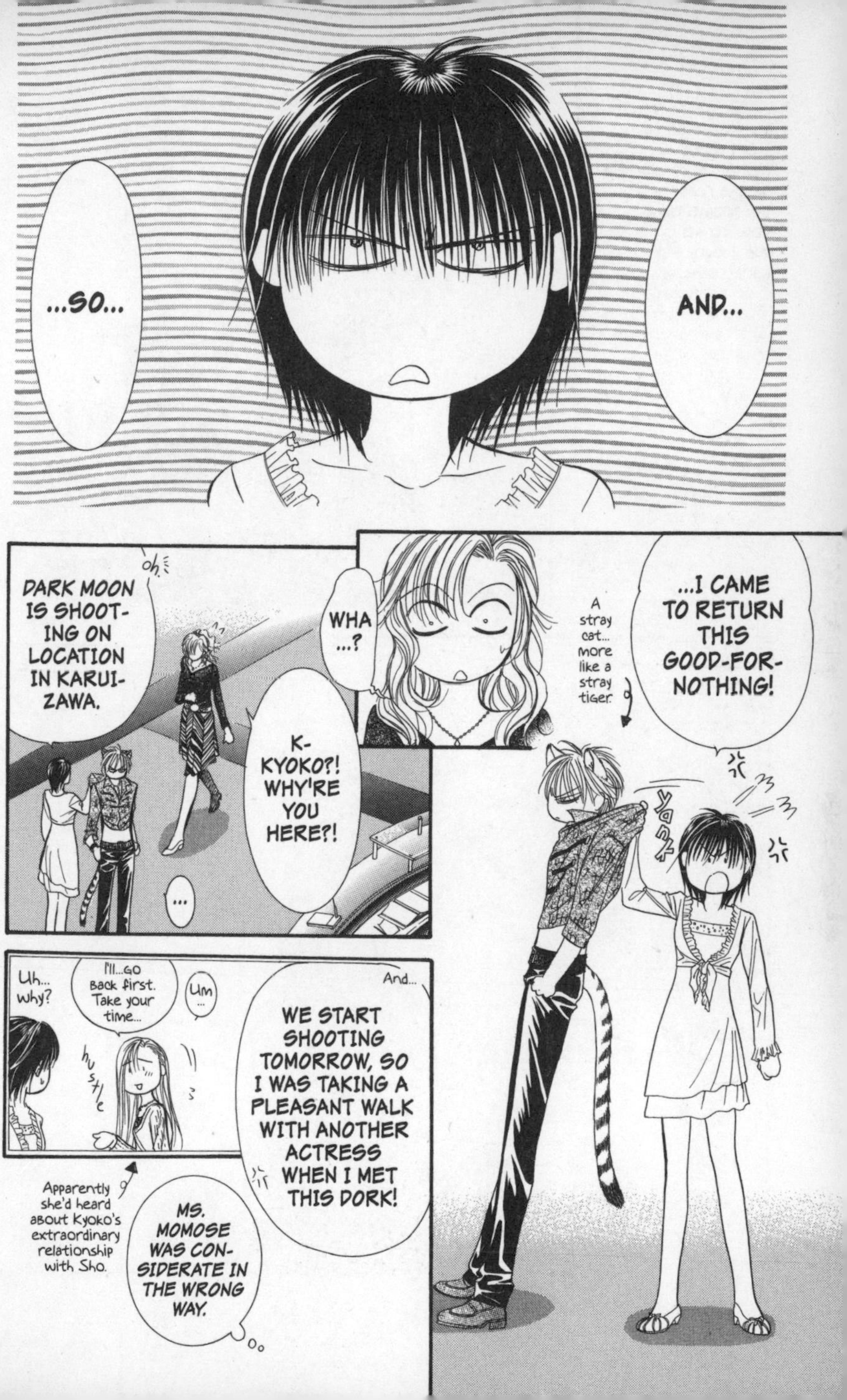
AND...
...SO...
WHA ...?
K-KYOKO?! WHY'RE YOU HERE?!
...
oh
DARK MOON IS SHOOTING ON LOCATION IN KARUIZAWA.
...I CAME TO RETURN THIS GOOD-FOR-NOTHING!
A stray cat... more like a stray tiger.
yank
Um...
I'll...GO back first. Take your time...
Uh... why?
hustle
And...
WE START SHOOTING TOMORROW, SO I WAS TAKING A PLEASANT WALK WITH ANOTHER ACTRESS WHEN I MET THIS DORK!
MS. MOMOSE WAS CONSIDERATE IN THE WRONG WAY.
Apparently she'd heard about Kyoko's extraordinary relationship with Sho.

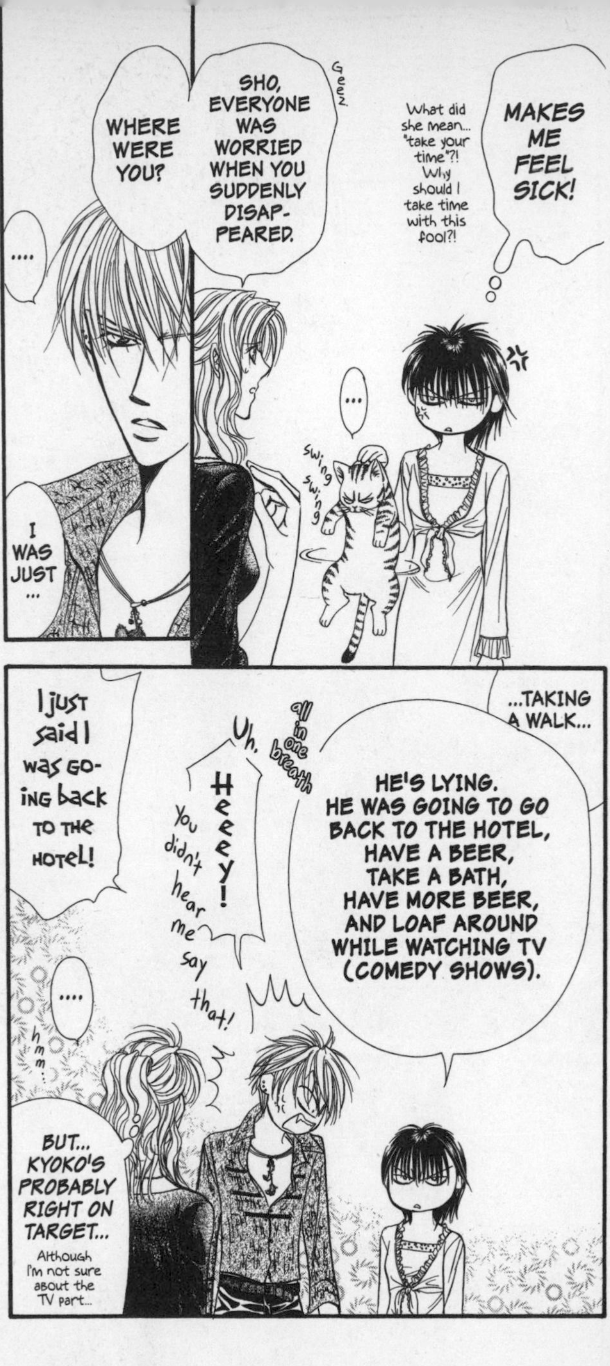
MAKES ME FEEL SICK!
What did she mean... "take your time"?! Why should I take time with this fool?!
Geez
SHO, EVERYONE WAS WORRIED WHEN YOU SUDDENLY DISAP-PEARED.
...
swing swing
WHERE WERE YOU?
....
I WAS JUST ...
...TAKING A WALK...
HE'S LYING. HE WAS GOING TO GO BACK TO THE HOTEL, HAVE A BEER, TAKE A BATH, HAVE MORE BEER, AND LOAF AROUND WHILE WATCHING TV (COMEDY SHOWS).
all in one breath
Uh,
Heeey!
You didn't hear me say that!
I just said I was go-ing back to the hotel!
....
hmm...
BUT... KYOKO'S PROBABLY RIGHT ON TARGET...
Although I'm not sure about the TV part...

When the promo clip arc was over, the story didn't mention the clip at all, so some of the readers felt the promo clip was slow to go on sale... But...I think that it took some time for it to be released... That's because "Prisoner"'s promo clip used powerful and beautiful computer graphics like in a Hollywood movie...although in the manga, it is difficult to realistically portray the beauty of the images...♪ But still, my assistants did their best so that my outrageous requests actually became images on paper. Thank you so much always. Correcting things for this manga volume was a tough job, but corrections for the next volume will be tough again too (is there no time when corrections aren't tough?)...♪ Please do your best the next time around too.

...And before I knew it, the sidebars were all filled with talking about "Prisoner"...♪ Well...the "Suddenly" arc has just begun, so I'll talk about the other things next time...

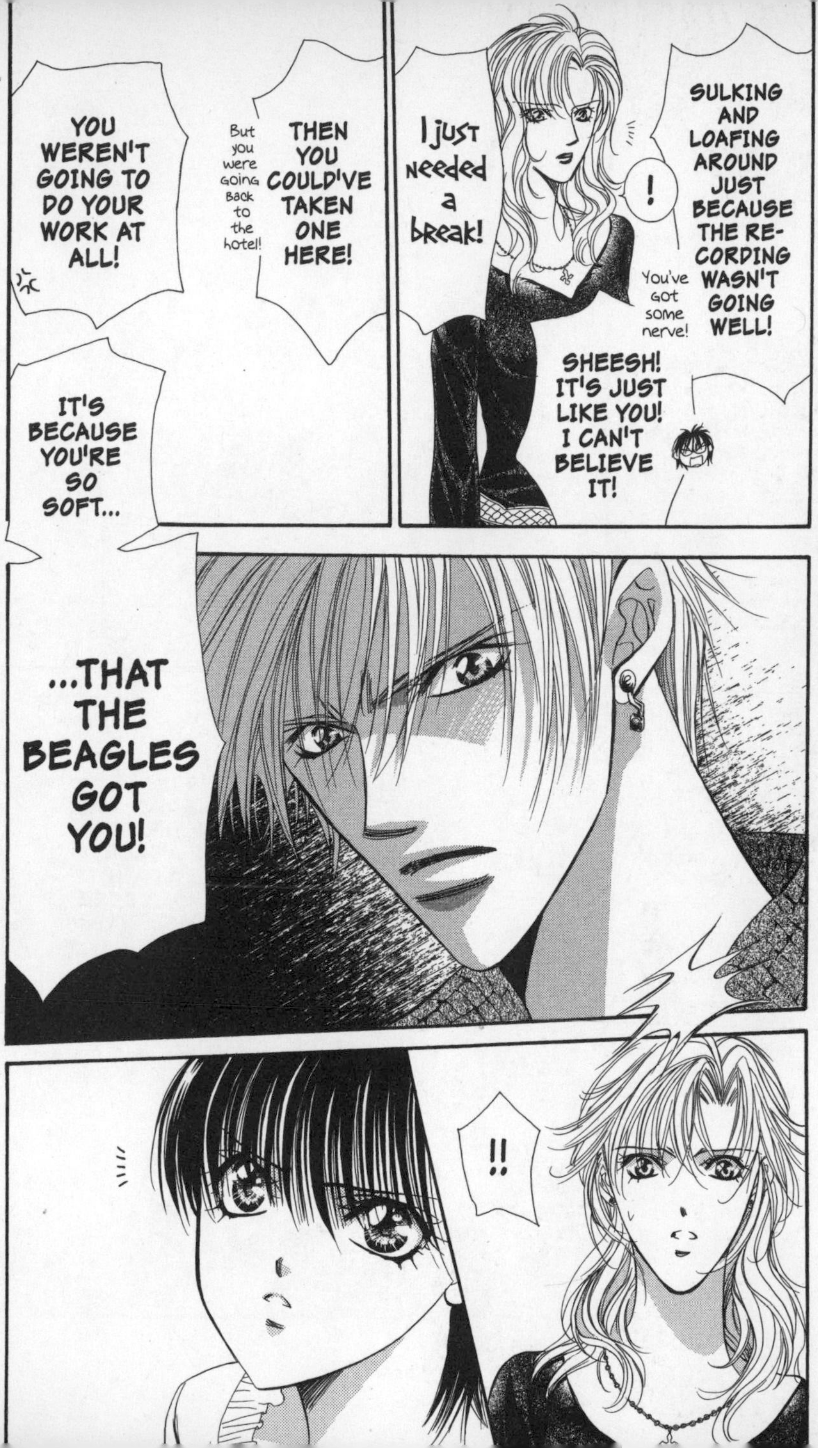
SULKING AND LOAFING AROUND JUST BECAUSE THE RE-CORDING WASN'T GOING WELL!
You've got some nerve!
!
I just needed a break!
SHEESH! IT'S JUST LIKE YOU! I CAN'T BELIEVE IT!
THEN YOU COULD'VE TAKEN ONE HERE!
But you were going back to the hotel!
YOU WEREN'T GOING TO DO YOUR WORK AT ALL!
IT'S BECAUSE YOU'RE SO SOFT...
...THAT THE BEAGLES GOT YOU!
!!

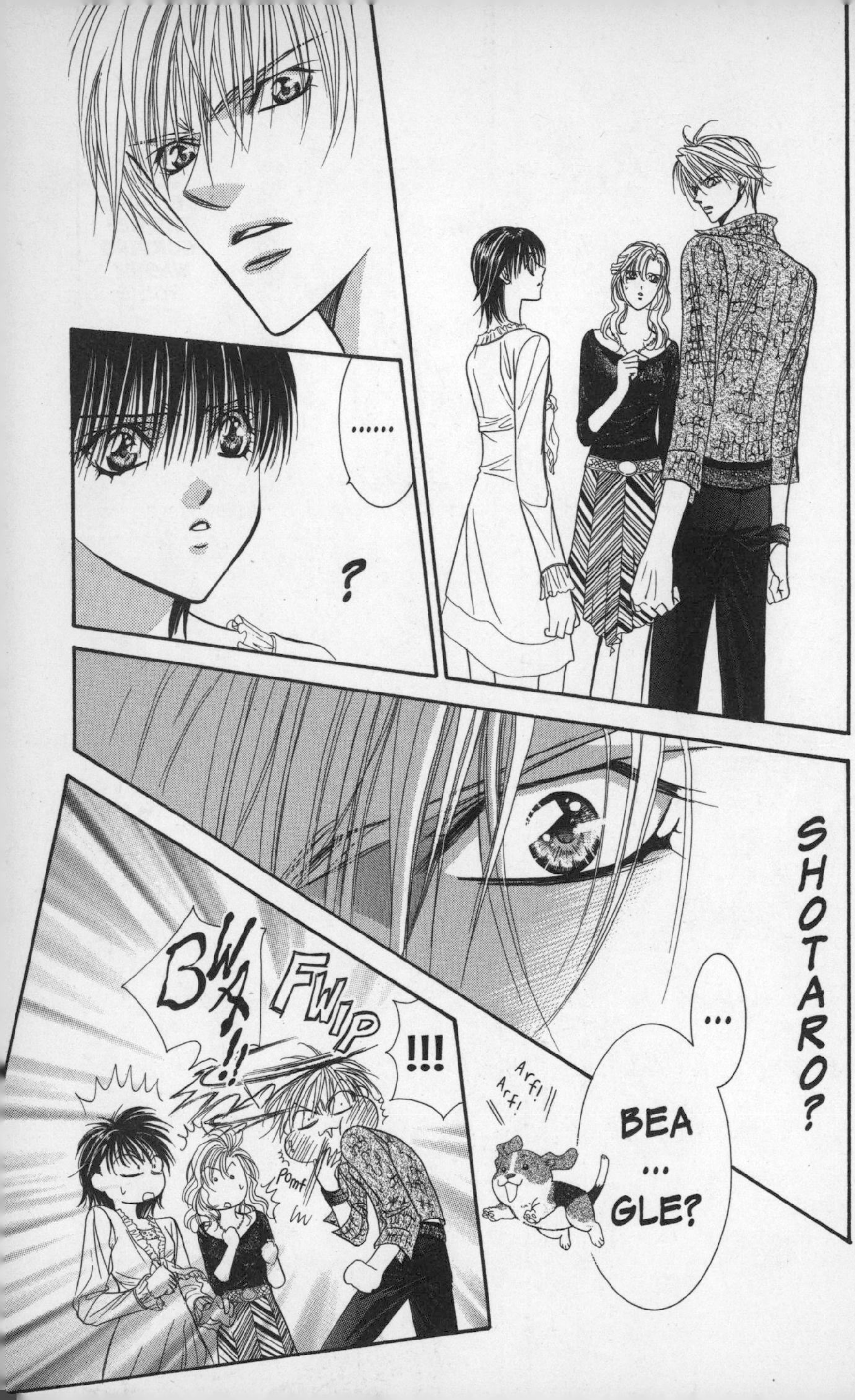
......
?
SHOTARO?
...
BEA ... GLE?
Arf! Arf!
!!!
FWIP
BWA!!
pomf

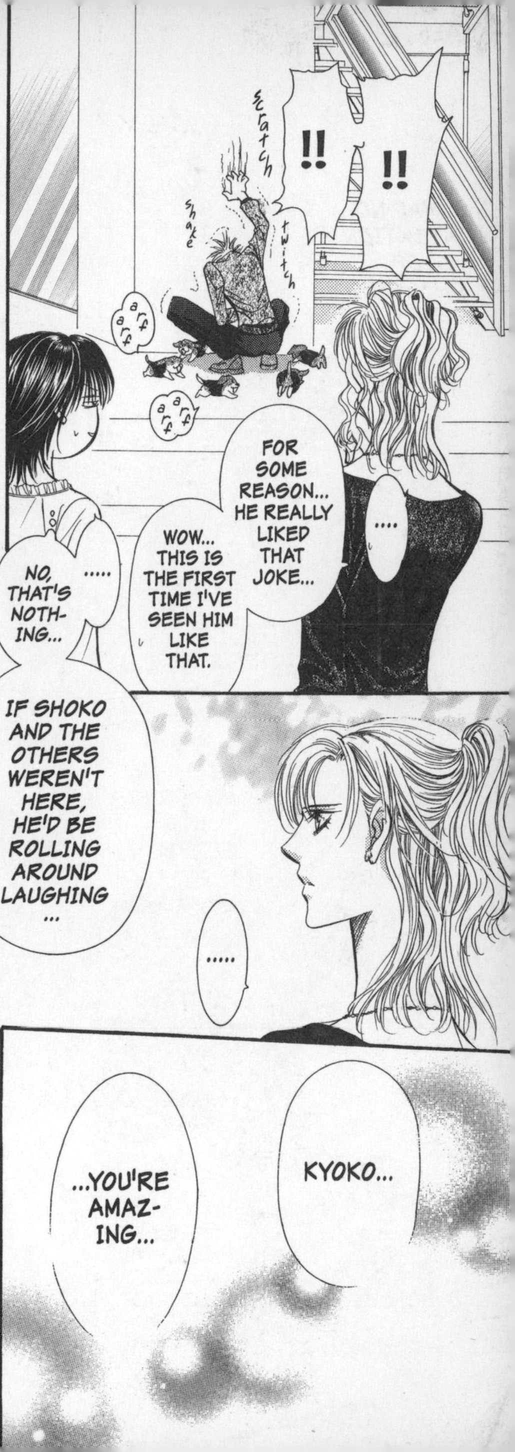
!!
!!
scratch
shake
twitch
arf arf
arf arf
FOR SOME REASON... HE REALLY LIKED THAT JOKE...
....
WOW... THIS IS THE FIRST TIME I'VE SEEN HIM LIKE THAT.
.....
NO, THAT'S NOTHING...
IF SHOKO AND THE OTHERS WEREN'T HERE, HE'D BE ROLLING AROUND LAUGHING...
.....
KYOKO...
...YOU'RE AMAZ-ING...
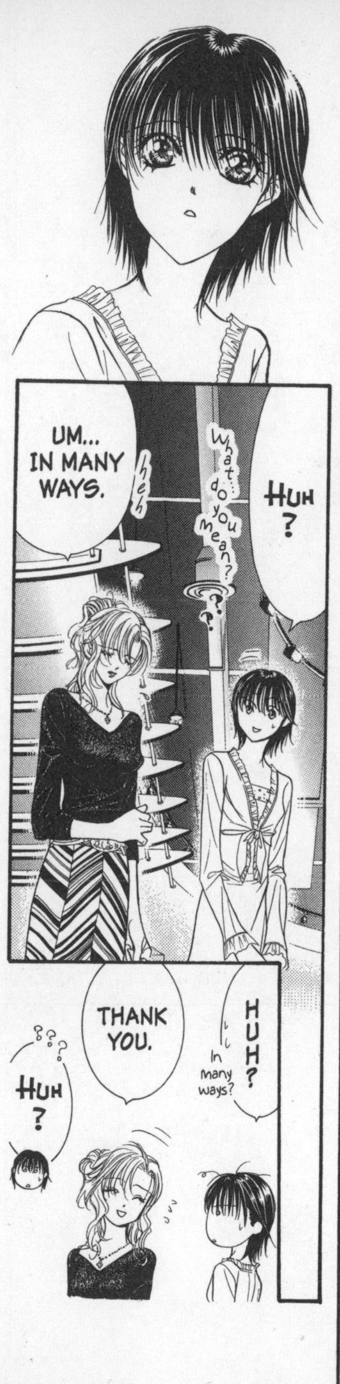
HUH?
What do you mean??
heh
UM... IN MANY WAYS.
HUH?
In many ways?
THANK YOU.
HUH?

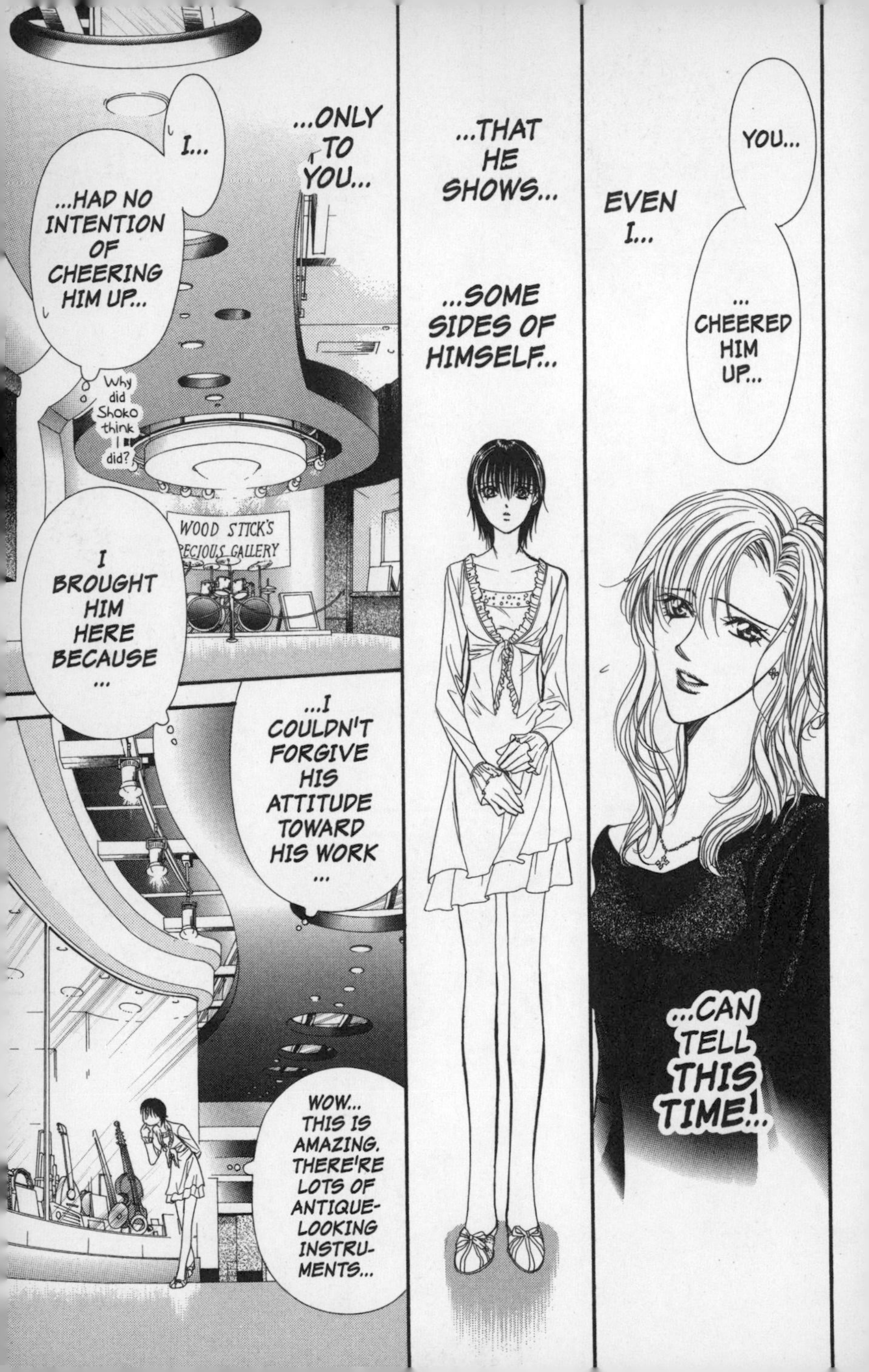

YOU...
EVEN I...
...CHEERED HIM UP...
...CAN TELL THIS TIME!...
...THAT HE SHOWS...
...SOME SIDES OF HIMSELF...
...ONLY TO YOU...
I...
...HAD NO INTENTION OF CHEERING HIM UP...
Why did Shoko think I did?
WOOD STICK'S PRECIOUS GALLERY
I BROUGHT HIM HERE BECAUSE...
...I COULDN'T FORGIVE HIS ATTITUDE TOWARD HIS WORK...
WOW... THIS IS AMAZING. THERE'RE LOTS OF ANTIQUE-LOOKING INSTRUMENTS...

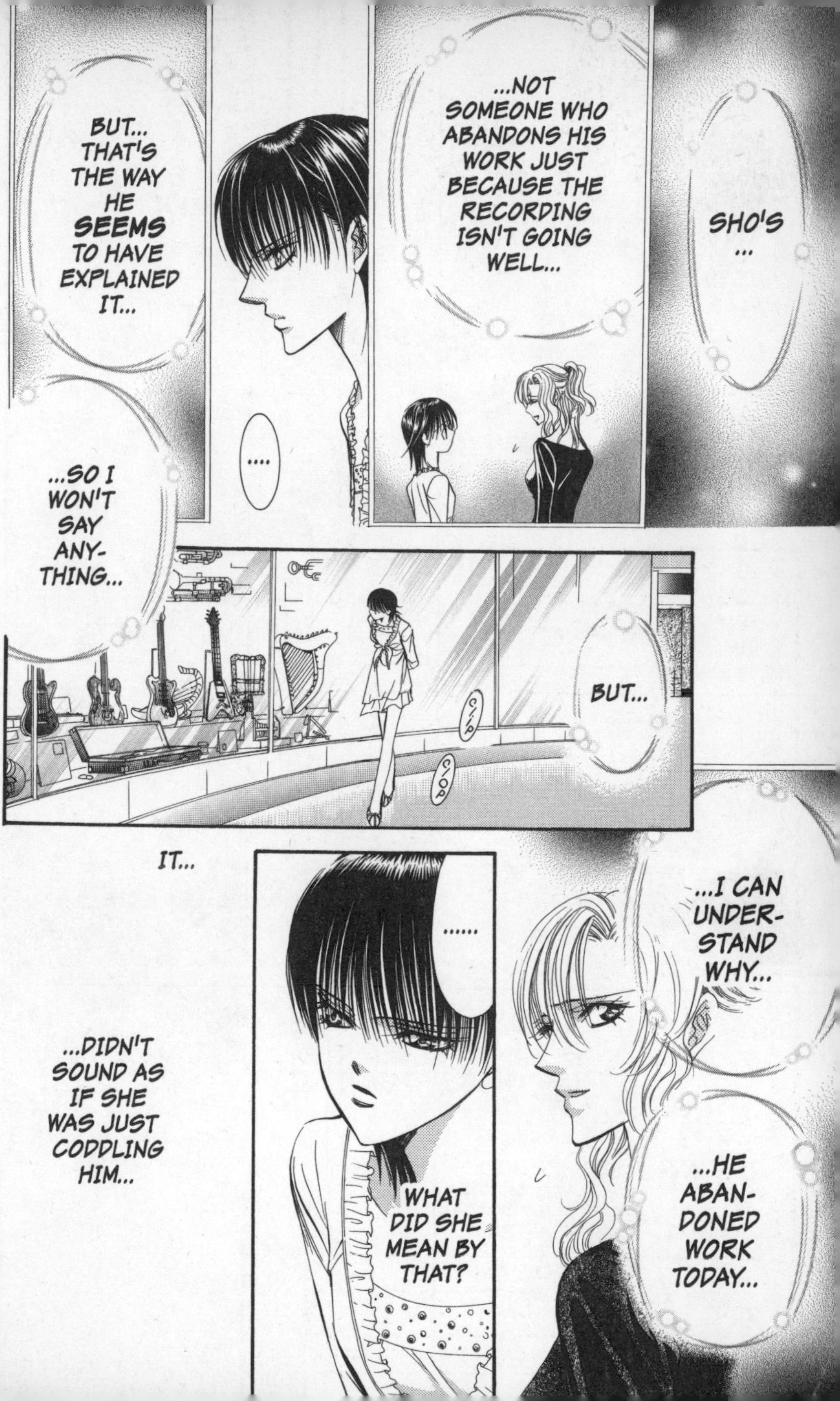
SHO'S...
...NOT SOMEONE WHO ABANDONS HIS WORK JUST BECAUSE THE RECORDING ISN'T GOING WELL...
BUT... THAT'S THE WAY HE SEEMS TO HAVE EXPLAINED IT...
....
...SO I WON'T SAY ANYTHING...
BUT...
CLIP
CLOP
...I CAN UNDERSTAND WHY...
...HE ABANDONED WORK TODAY...
......
WHAT DID SHE MEAN BY THAT?
IT...
...DIDN'T SOUND AS IF SHE WAS JUST CODDLING HIM...

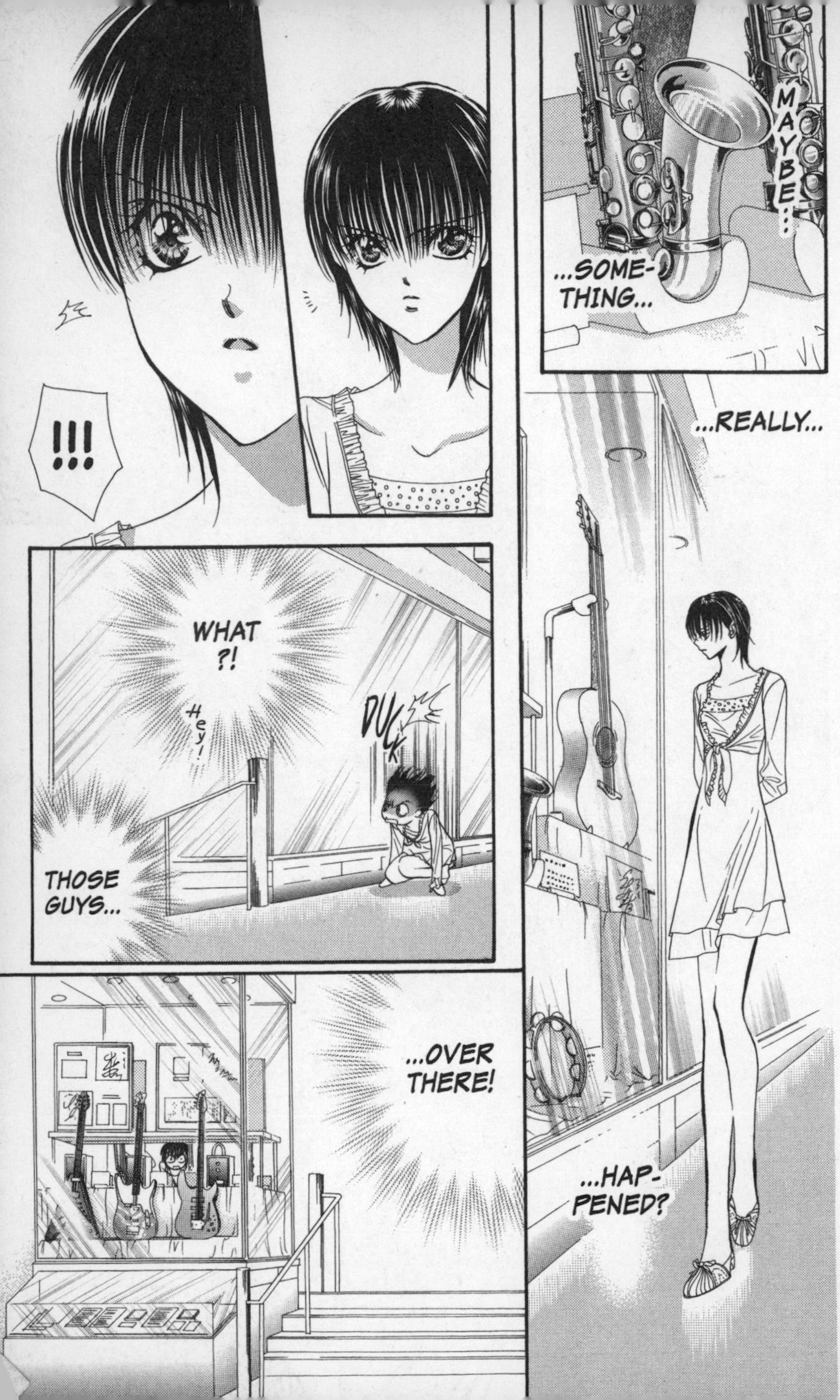
MAYBE...
...SOME-THING...
...REALLY...
...HAP-PENED?
!!!
WHAT ?!
Hey!
DUCK
THOSE GUYS...
...OVER THERE!

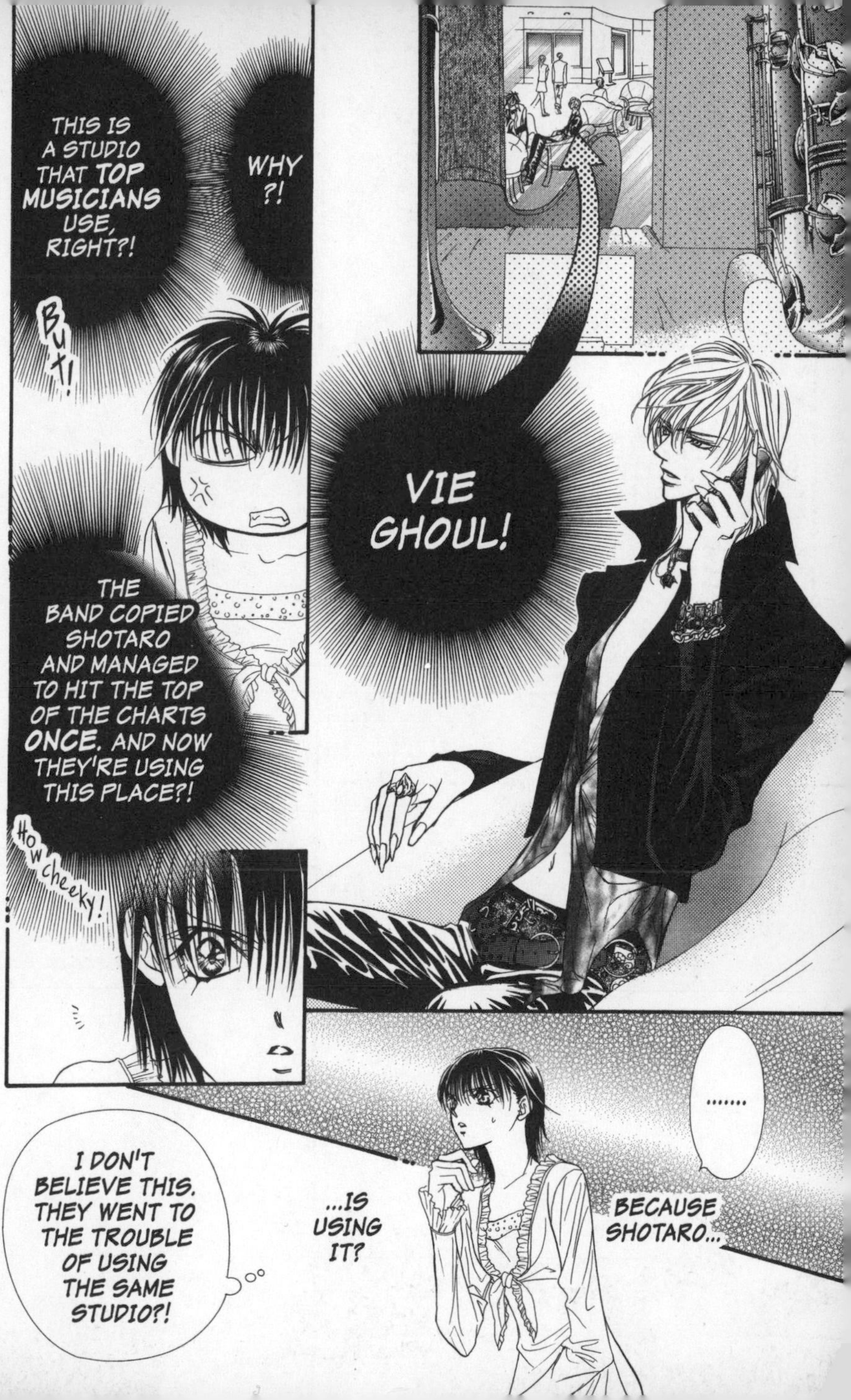
VIE GHOUL!
WHY?!
THIS IS A STUDIO THAT TOP MUSICIANS USE, RIGHT?!
But!
THE BAND COPIED SHOTARO AND MANAGED TO HIT THE TOP OF THE CHARTS ONCE. AND NOW THEY'RE USING THIS PLACE?!
How cheeky!
....
BECAUSE SHOTARO...
...IS USING IT?
I DON'T BELIEVE THIS. THEY WENT TO THE TROUBLE OF USING THE SAME STUDIO?!

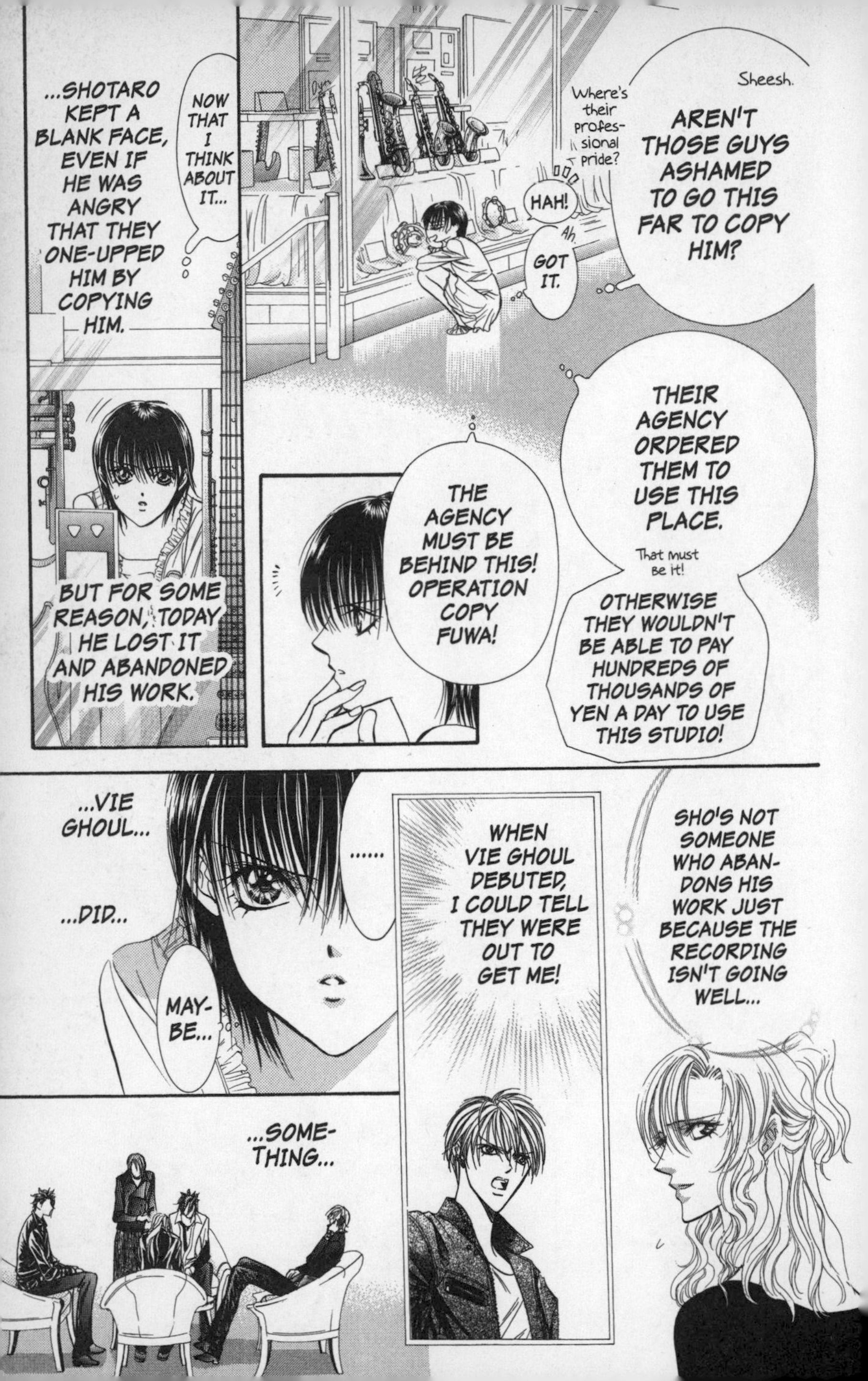
Sheesh.
AREN'T THOSE GUYS ASHAMED TO GO THIS FAR TO COPY HIM?
Where's their profes-sional pride?
HAH!
Ah.
GOT IT.
THEIR AGENCY ORDERED THEM TO USE THIS PLACE.
That must be it!
OTHERWISE THEY WOULDN'T BE ABLE TO PAY HUNDREDS OF THOUSANDS OF YEN A DAY TO USE THIS STUDIO!
THE AGENCY MUST BE BEHIND THIS! OPERATION COPY FUWA!
NOW THAT I THINK ABOUT IT...
...SHOTARO KEPT A BLANK FACE, EVEN IF HE WAS ANGRY THAT THEY ONE-UPPED HIM BY COPYING HIM.
BUT FOR SOME REASON, TODAY HE LOST IT AND ABANDONED HIS WORK.
SHO'S NOT SOMEONE WHO ABAN-DONS HIS WORK JUST BECAUSE THE RECORDING ISN'T GOING WELL...
WHEN VIE GHOUL DEBUTED, I COULD TELL THEY WERE OUT TO GET ME!
......
...VIE GHOUL...
...DID...
MAY-BE...
...SOME-THING...

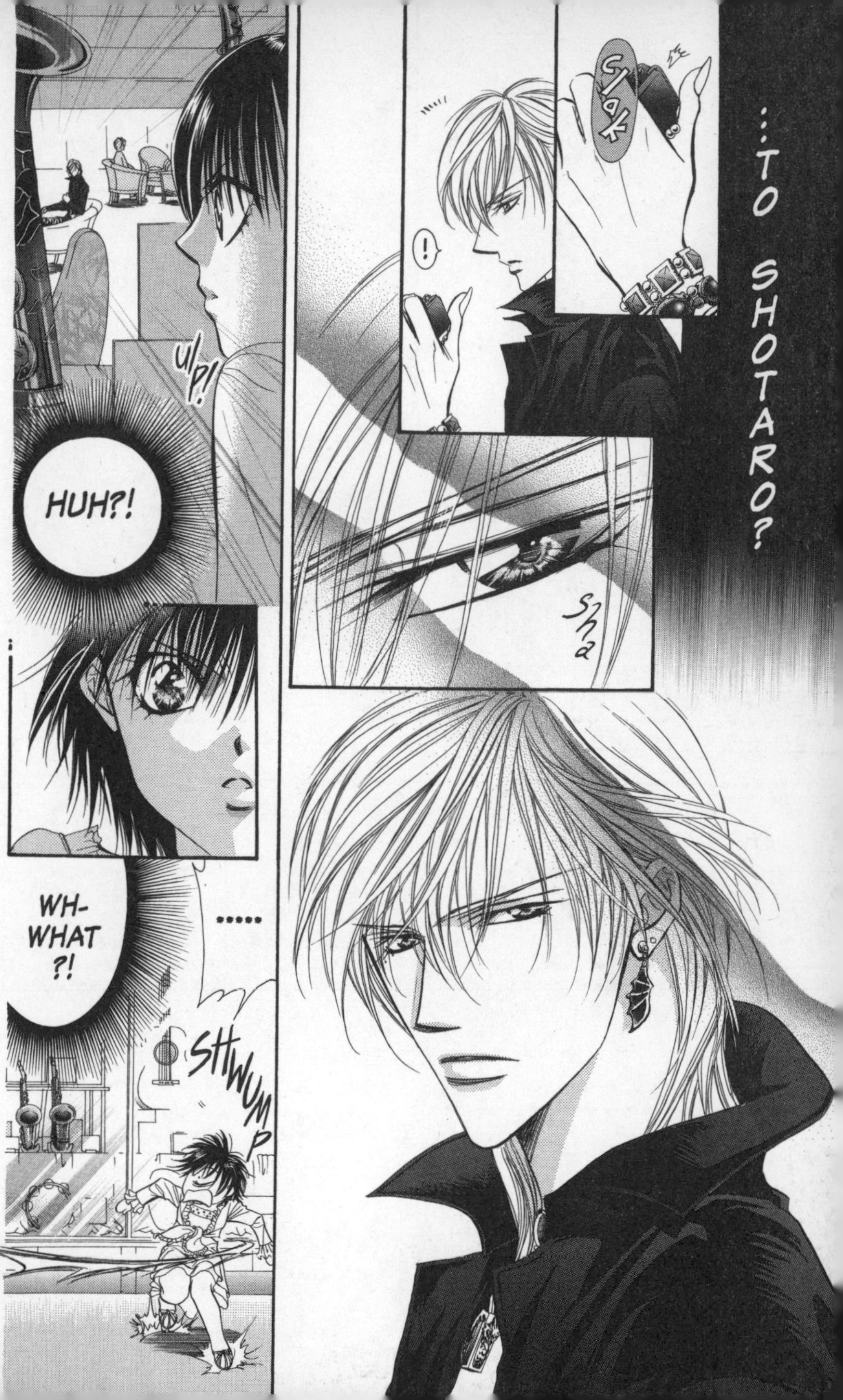
...TO SHOTARO?
clak
!
sha
ulp!
HUH?!
WH-WHAT?!
.....
SHWUMP

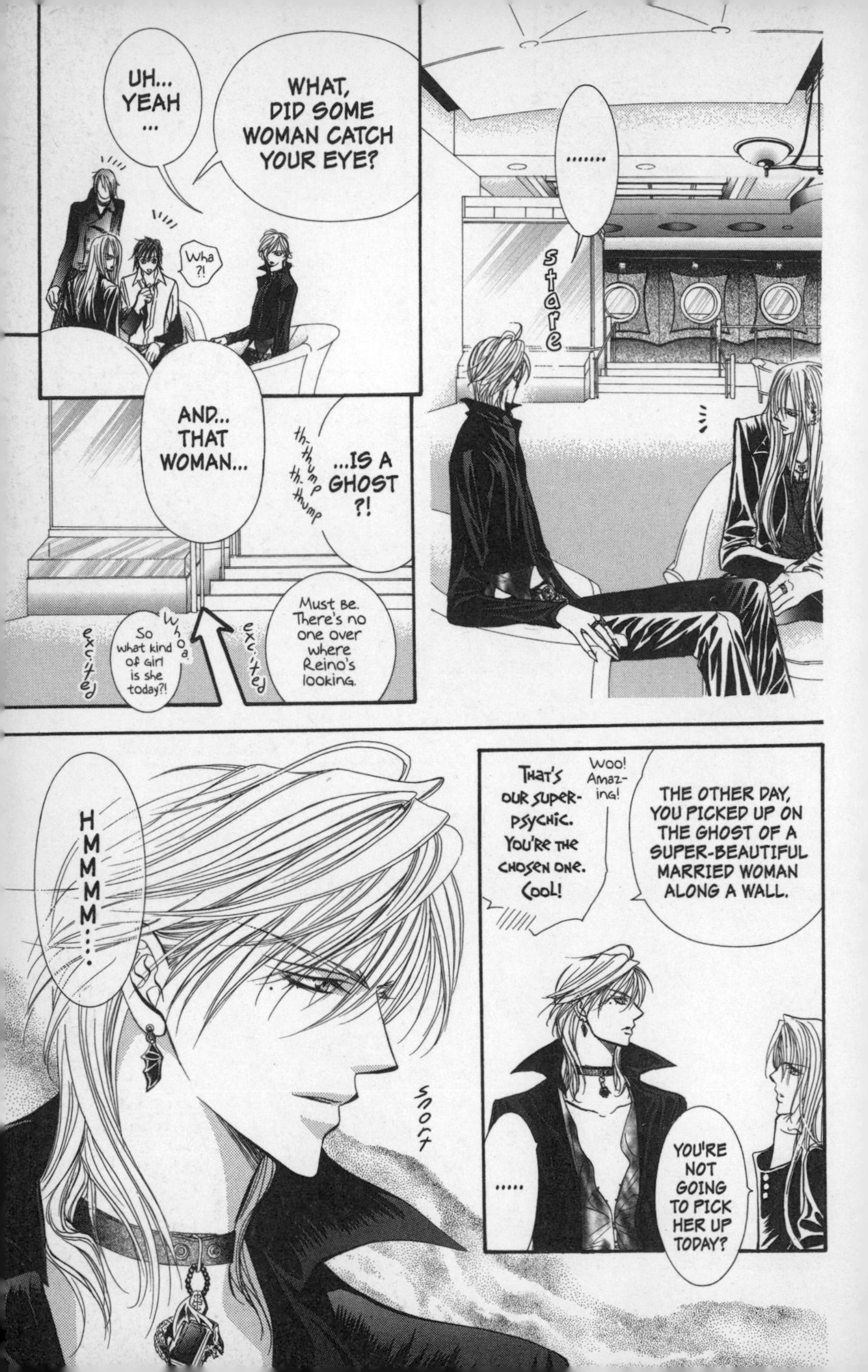

......
stare
WHAT, DID SOME WOMAN CATCH YOUR EYE?
UH... YEAH ...
Wha ?!
...IS A GHOST ?!
th-thump th-thump
AND... THAT WOMAN...
Must be. There's no one over where Reino's looking.
excited
Whoa
So what kind of girl is she today?!
excited
THE OTHER DAY, YOU PICKED UP ON THE GHOST OF A SUPER-BEAUTIFUL MARRIED WOMAN ALONG A WALL.
Woo! Amaz-ing!
That's our super-psychic. You're the chosen one. Cool!
YOU'RE NOT GOING TO PICK HER UP TODAY?
......
HMMMM....
snort

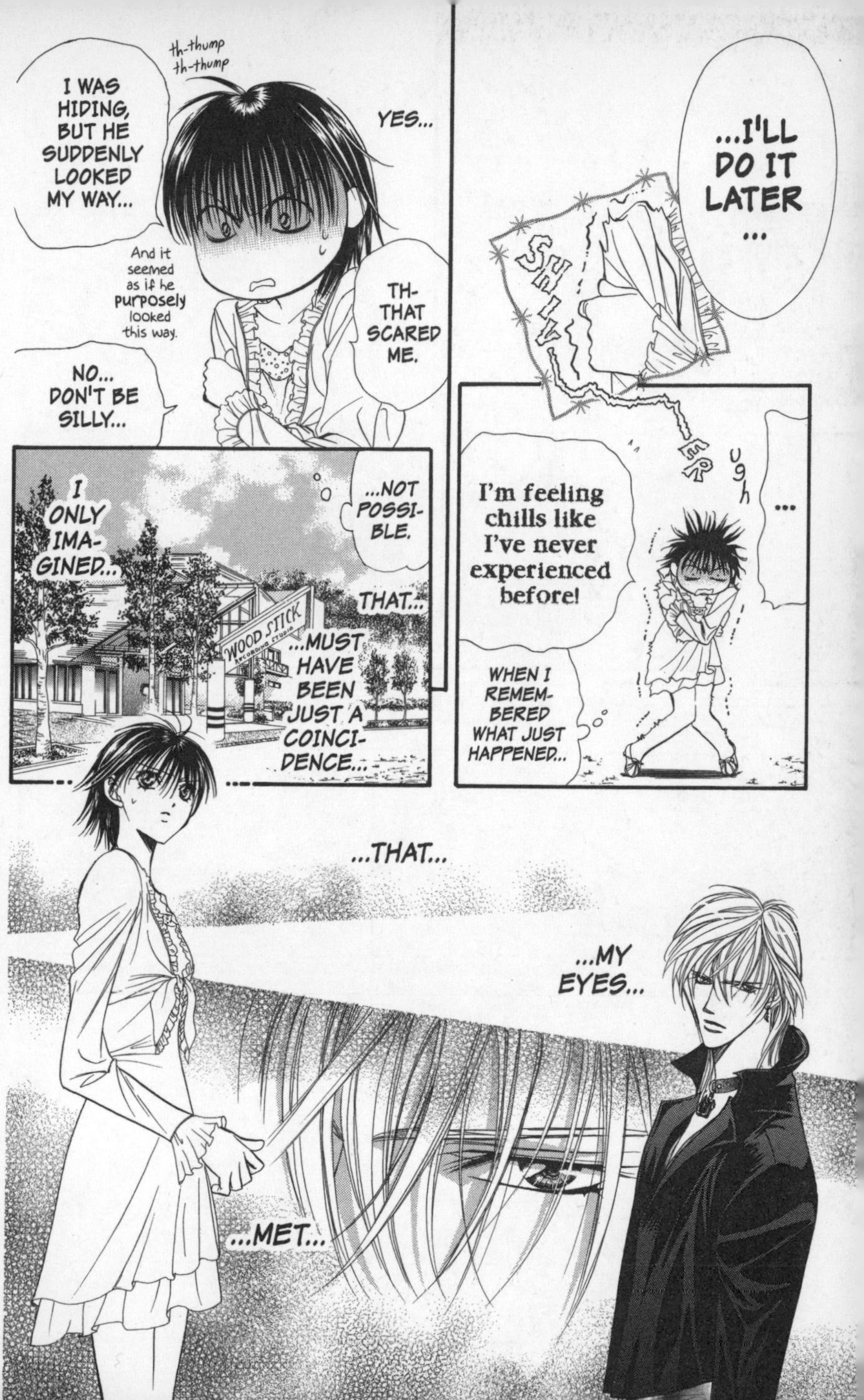
...I'LL DO IT LATER...
SHIVER
YES...
th-thump th-thump
I WAS HIDING, BUT HE SUDDENLY LOOKED MY WAY...
TH-THAT SCARED ME.
And it seemed as if he purposely looked this way.
NO... DON'T BE SILLY...
...
ugh
I'm feeling chills like I've never experienced before!
WHEN I REMEMBERED WHAT JUST HAPPENED...
...NOT POSSIBLE.
I ONLY IMAGINED...
THAT...
...MUST HAVE BEEN JUST A COINCIDENCE...
WOOD STICK RECORDING STUDIO
...THAT...
...MY EYES...
...MET...

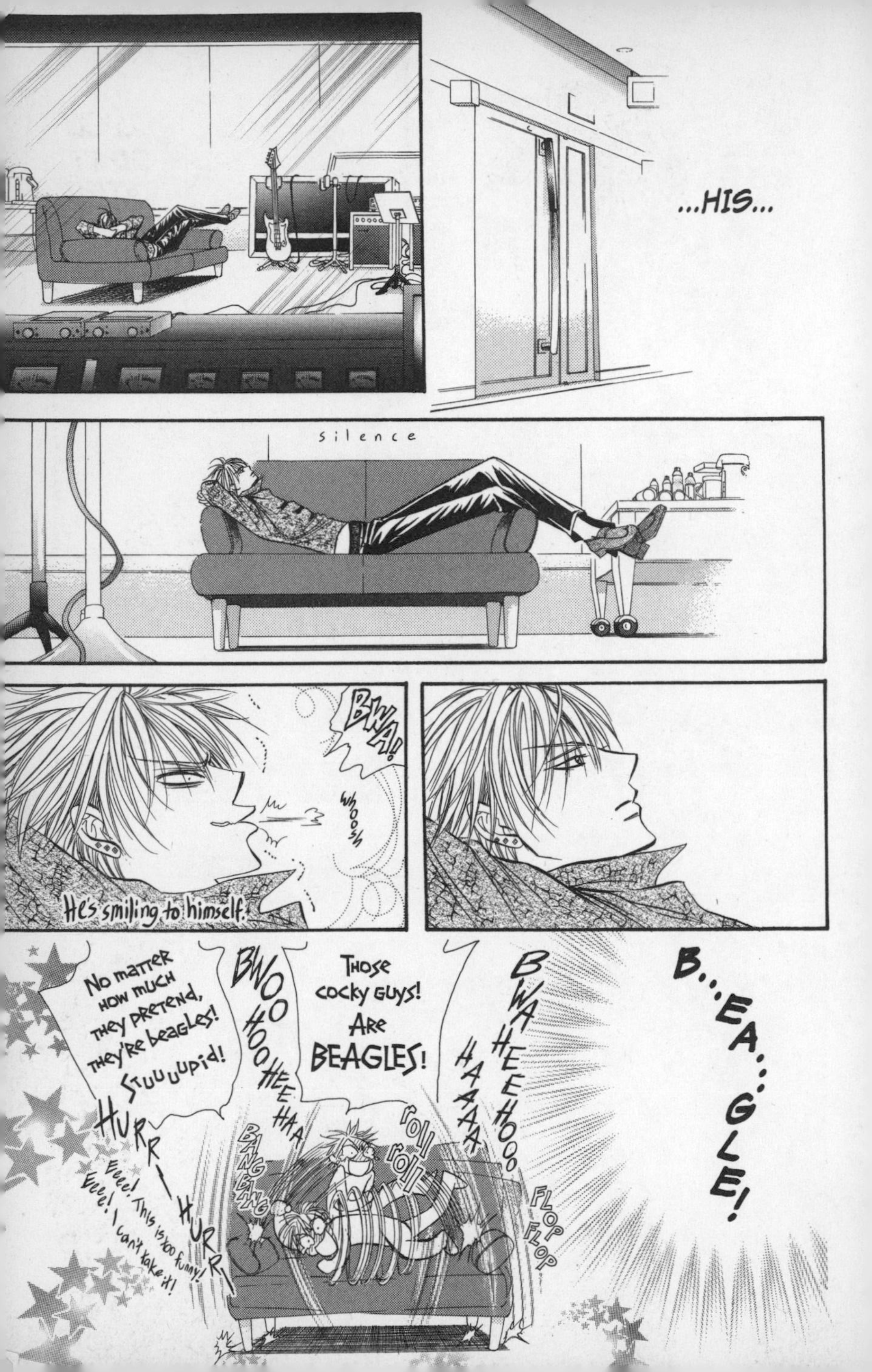
...HIS...
silence
BWA!
whoosh
He's smiling to himself.
B...EA...GLE!
BWA HEE HOOO HAAAAA
FLOP FLOP
roll roll
Those cocky guys! Are BEAGLES!
BWOO HOO HEE HAA
BANG BANG
No matter how much they pretend, they're beagles! Stuuuupid!
HURR HURR
Eeee! This is too funny!
Eeee! I can't take it!

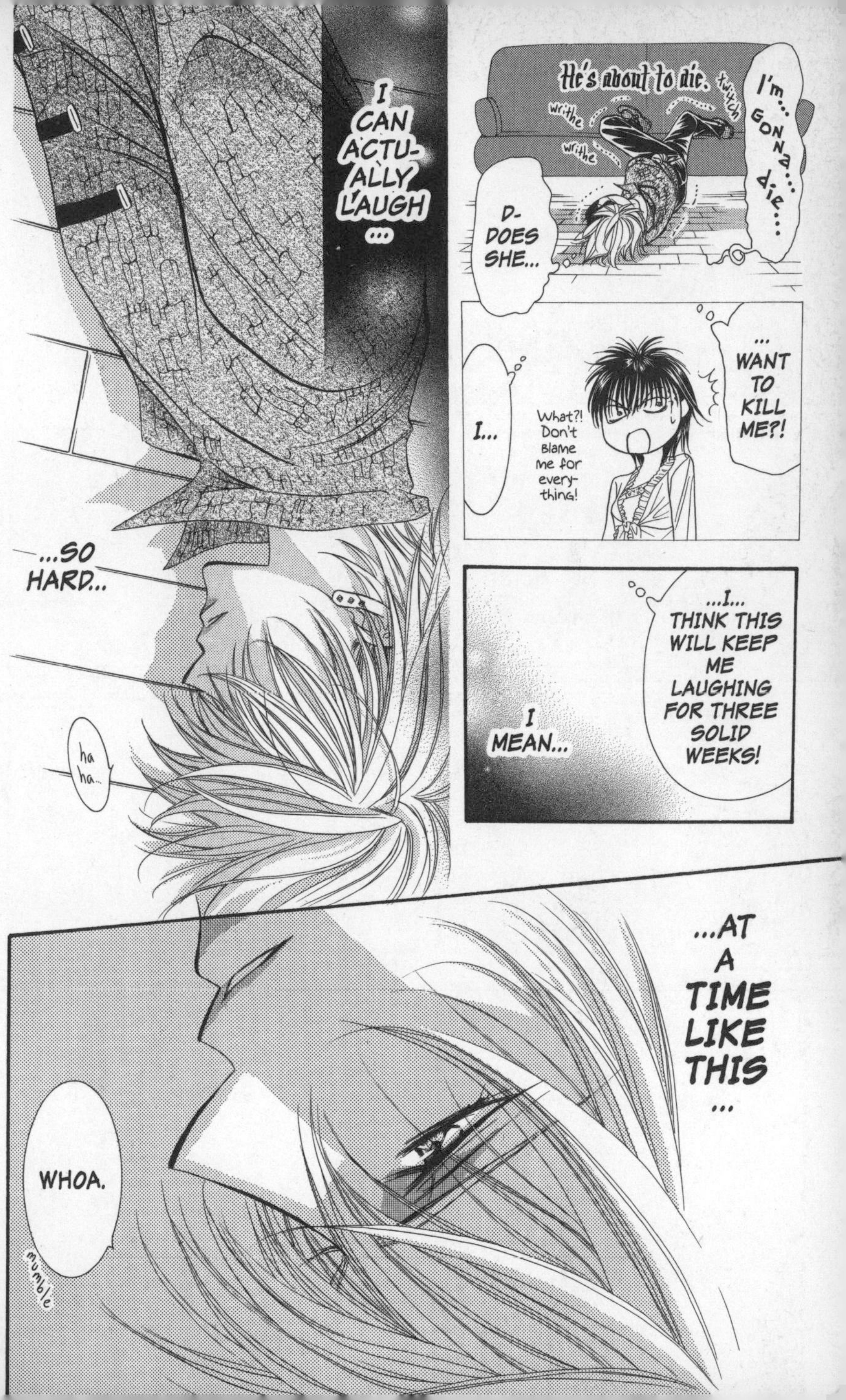
I'm... GONNA... die...
He's about to die.
twitch
writhe
writhe
D-DOES SHE...
...WANT TO KILL ME?!
What?! Don't blame me for every-thing!
I...
...I... THINK THIS WILL KEEP ME LAUGHING FOR THREE SOLID WEEKS!
I MEAN...
I CAN ACTUALLY LAUGH...
...SO HARD...
ha ha...
...AT A TIME LIKE THIS...
WHOA.
mumble

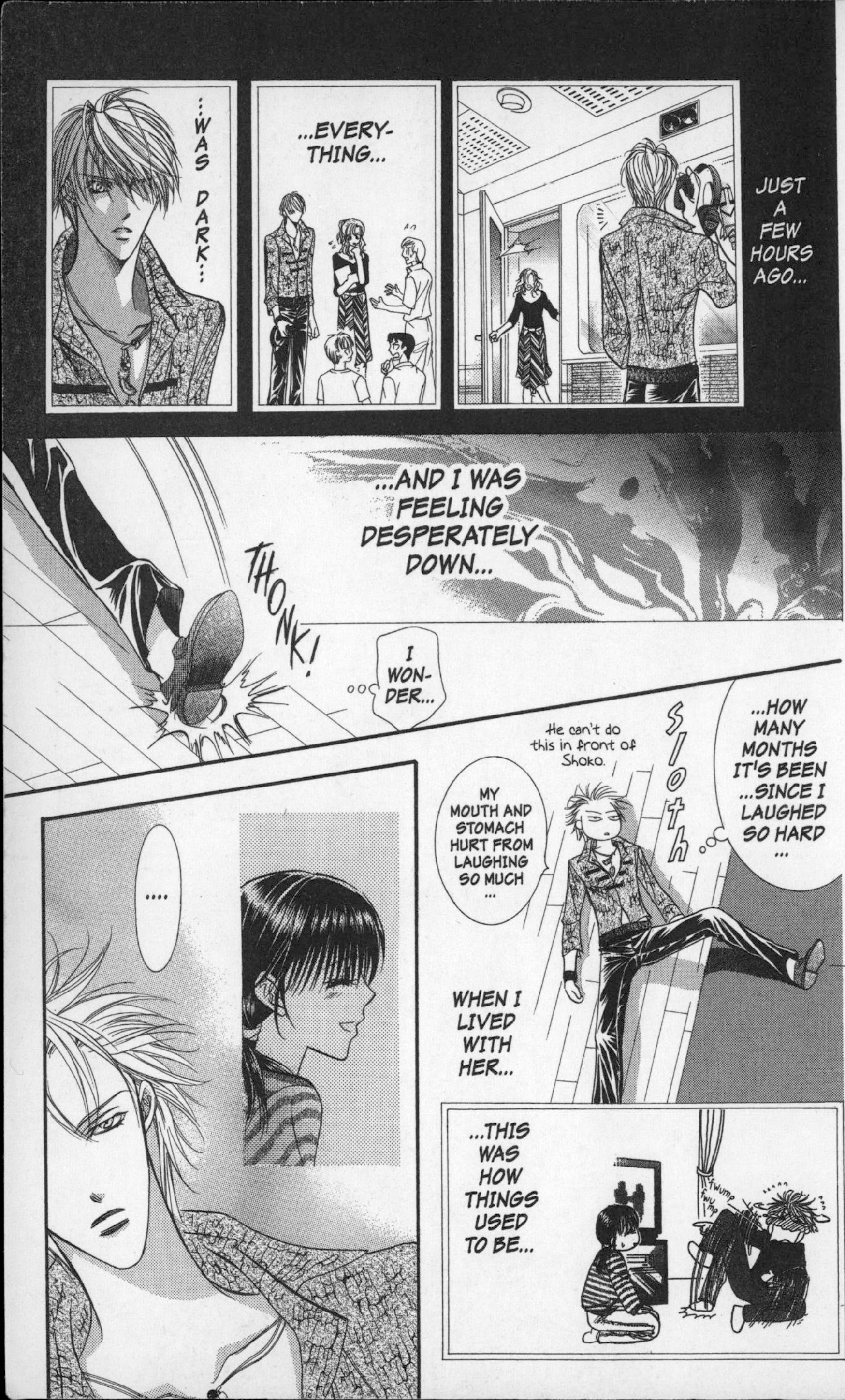

JUST A FEW HOURS AGO...
...EVERY-THING...
...WAS DARK...
...AND I WAS FEELING DESPERATELY DOWN...
THONK!
I WON-DER...
...HOW MANY MONTHS IT'S BEEN ...SINCE I LAUGHED SO HARD ...
Sloth
He can't do this in front of Shoko.
MY MOUTH AND STOMACH HURT FROM LAUGHING SO MUCH ...
WHEN I LIVED WITH HER...
...THIS WAS HOW THINGS USED TO BE...
fwump fwump
....

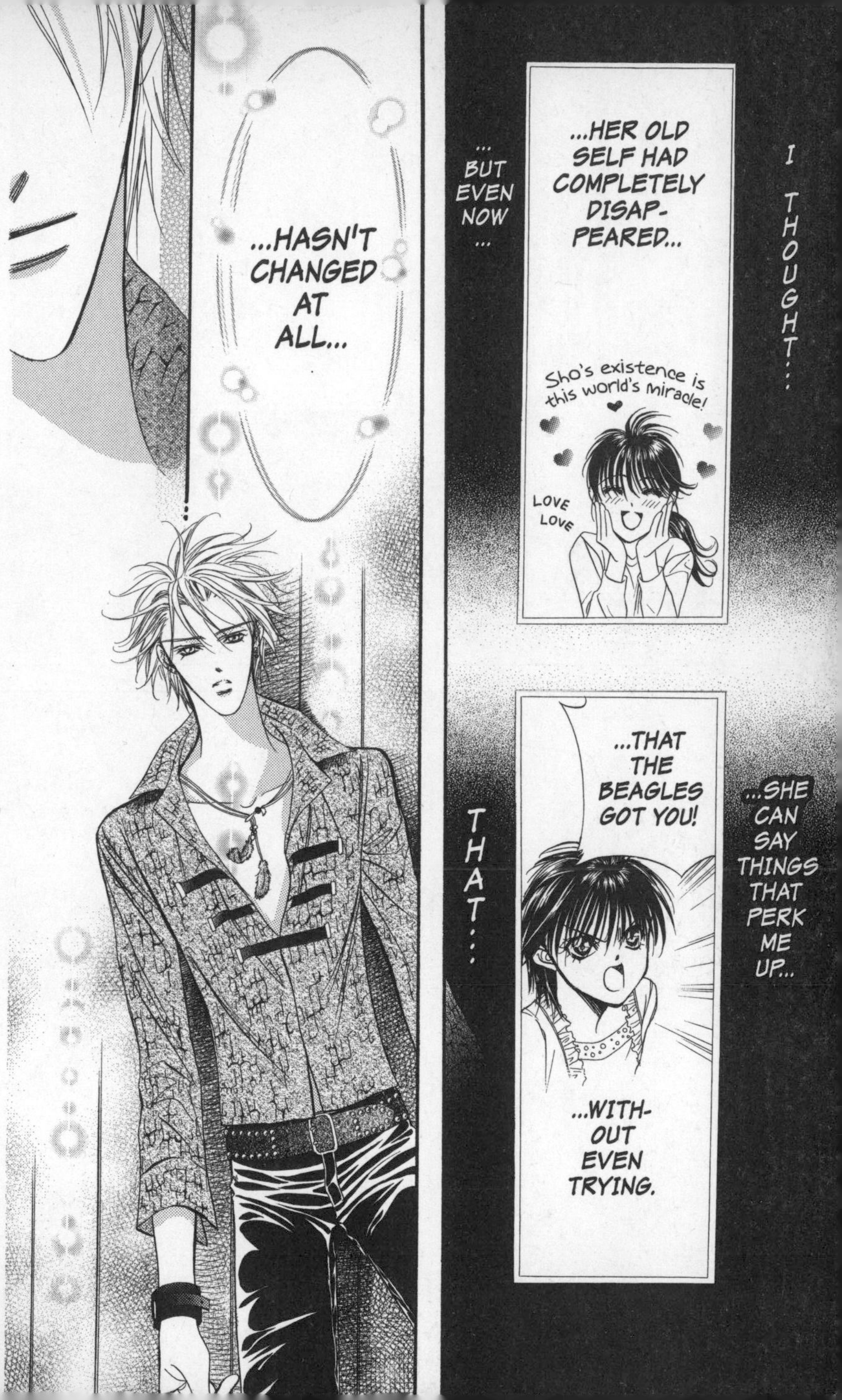
I THOUGHT...
...HER OLD SELF HAD COMPLETELY DISAP-PEARED...
Sho's existence is this world's miracle!
LOVE LOVE
...BUT EVEN NOW...
...SHE CAN SAY THINGS THAT PERK ME UP...
...THAT THE BEAGLES GOT YOU!
...WITH-OUT EVEN TRYING.
THAT...
...HASN'T CHANGED AT ALL...

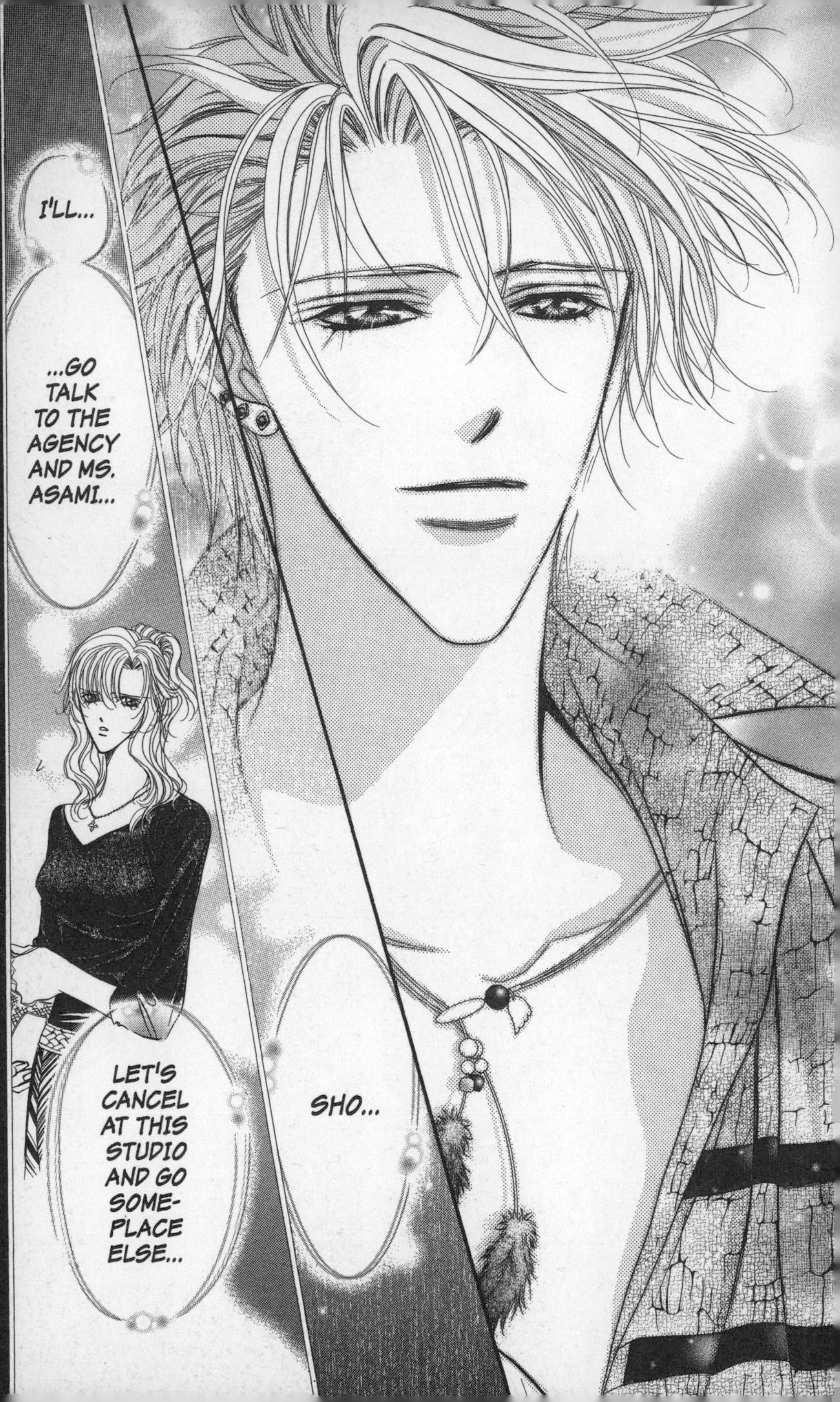
SHO...
I'LL...
...GO TALK TO THE AGENCY AND MS. ASAMI...
LET'S CANCEL AT THIS STUDIO AND GO SOME-PLACE ELSE...

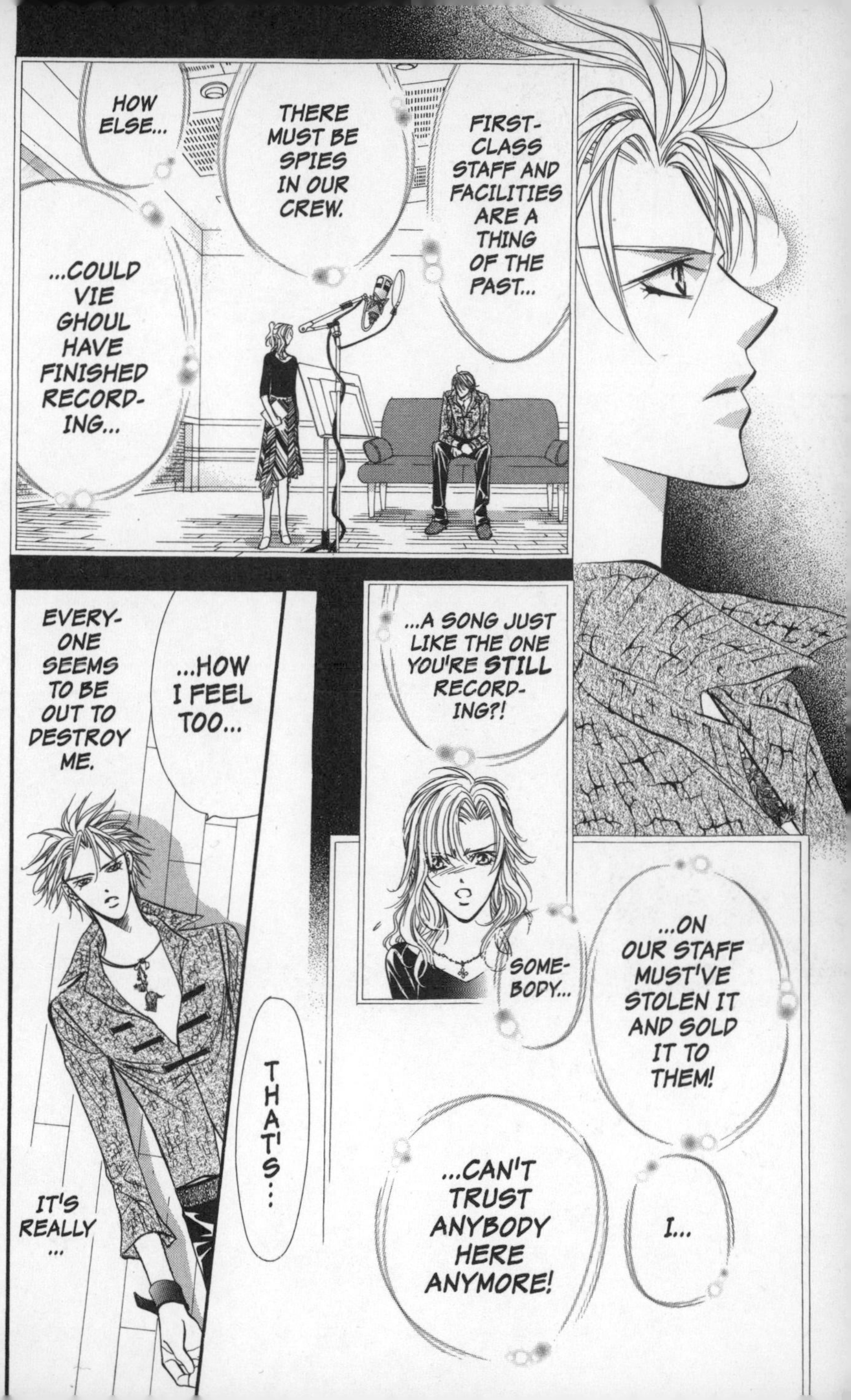
FIRST-CLASS STAFF AND FACILITIES ARE A THING OF THE PAST...
THERE MUST BE SPIES IN OUR CREW.
HOW ELSE...
...COULD VIE GHOUL HAVE FINISHED RECORDING...
...A SONG JUST LIKE THE ONE YOU'RE STILL RECORDING?!
SOMEBODY...
...ON OUR STAFF MUST'VE STOLEN IT AND SOLD IT TO THEM!
I...
...CAN'T TRUST ANYBODY HERE ANYMORE!
THAT'S...
IT'S REALLY...
...HOW I FEEL TOO...
EVERYONE SEEMS TO BE OUT TO DESTROY ME.

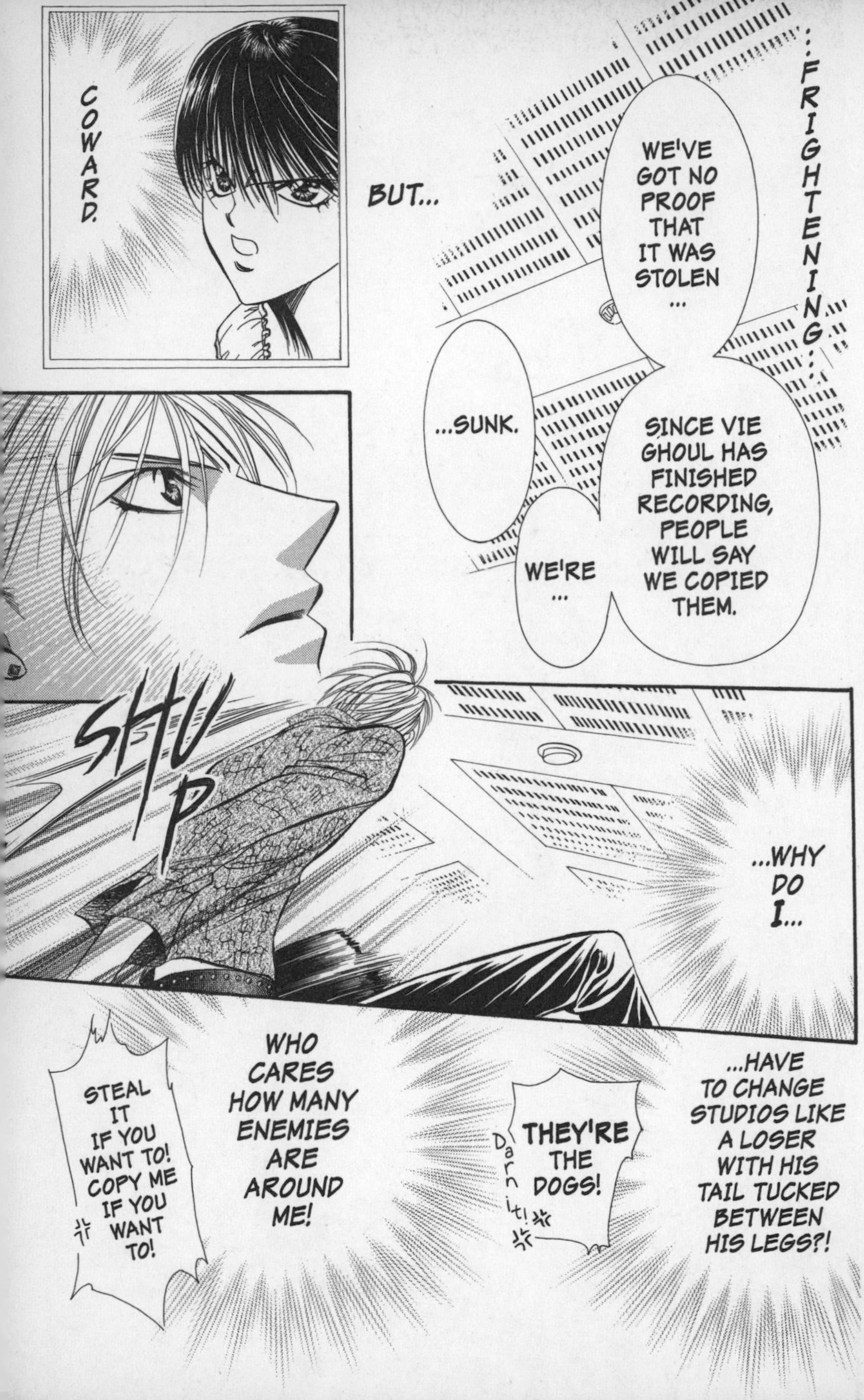
...FRIGHTENING...
WE'VE GOT NO PROOF THAT IT WAS STOLEN...
SINCE VIE GHOUL HAS FINISHED RECORDING, PEOPLE WILL SAY WE COPIED THEM.
WE'RE...
...SUNK.
BUT...
COWARD.
SHUT UP
...WHY DO I...
...HAVE TO CHANGE STUDIOS LIKE A LOSER WITH HIS TAIL TUCKED BETWEEN HIS LEGS?!
THEY'RE THE DOGS!
Darn it!
WHO CARES HOW MANY ENEMIES ARE AROUND ME!
STEAL IT IF YOU WANT TO! COPY ME IF YOU WANT TO!

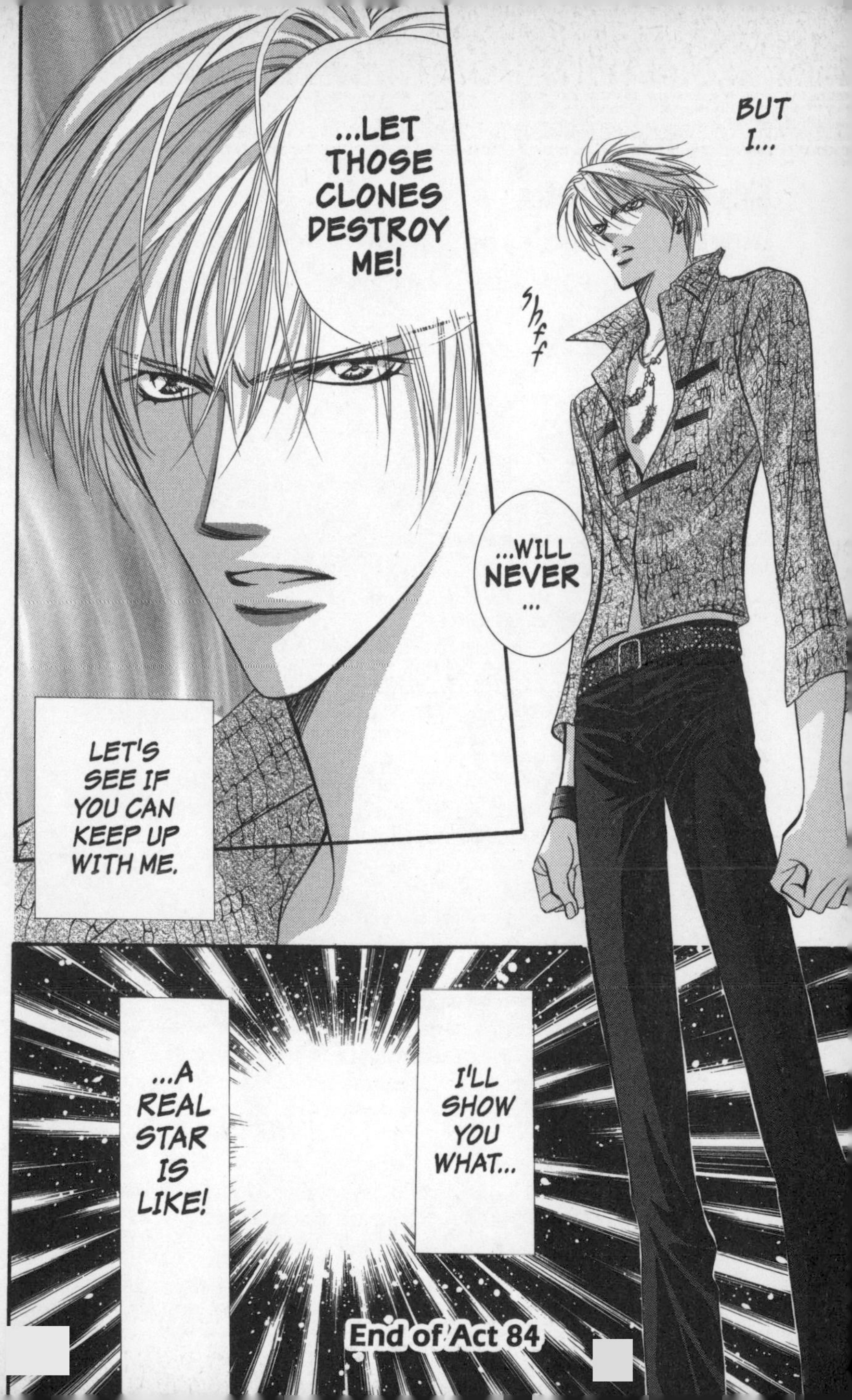
BUT I...
shff
...WILL NEVER ...
...LET THOSE CLONES DESTROY ME!
LET'S SEE IF YOU CAN KEEP UP WITH ME.
I'LL SHOW YOU WHAT...
...A REAL STAR IS LIKE!
End of Act 84

Skip·Beat! End Notes
Everyone knows how to be a fan, but sometimes cool things
from other cultures need a little help crossing the language barrier.

Page 5, title: Suddenly, a Love Story
The Japanese title "Love Story wa Totsuzen ni" was the theme song for the hit
TV drama *Tokyo Love Story*, based on the manga by Fumi Saimon.

Page 12, panel 6: Itadakimasu
Similar to a blessing, it means to give thanks for what you are receiving.

Page 13, panel 3: Vienna Sausage Coffee
In Japanese *winna* (ウィンナー) sounds like both Vienna and wiener.

Page 129, panel 3: Okamisan
The proprietress of a traditional Japanese restaurant. It is typical for the
employees and customers alike to call her by this term. The Okamisan's
husband is called *Taisho*.

Page 132, panel 1: Karuizawa
A town in Nagano prefecture that lies partially within the boundaries of two
national parks. It is known for its lovely scenery, and was established as a
summer resort in 1886 by English missionary Alexander Croft Shaw.

Page 145, panel 2: Shikoku
The smallest and least populated of the Japanese islands. The Meiji period
activist Ryoma Sakamoto was born on Shikoku.

Page 145, panel 2: Negative Ions
Popular belief says that negative ions, found in the air in natural habitats like
forest and beaches, enter your bloodstream and revitalize you. This theory is
very popular in Japan, where manufacturers produce ion generators marketed
to alleviate everything from asthma to depression.

Panel 146, panel 4: Loli
The short name for "Lolita," a style of dress originated in Japan that is inspired
by Victorian and Rococo fashions. There are different versions of Lolita style,
such as Sweet Loli, Goth Loli, and Punk Loli.

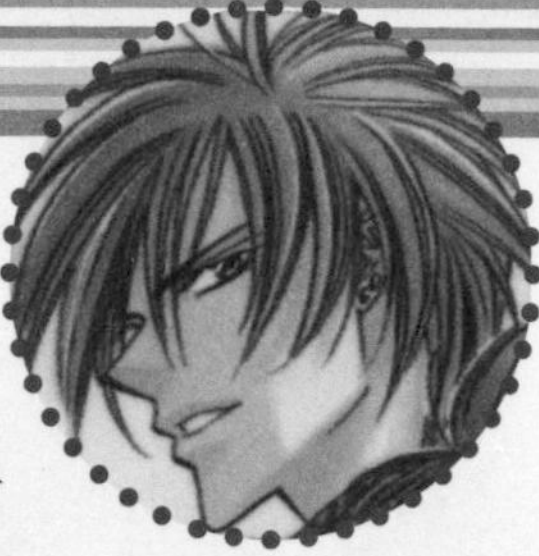

Yoshiki Nakamura is originally from Tokushima prefecture. She started drawing manga in elementary school, which eventually led to her 1993 debut of *Yume de Au yori Suteki* (Better than Seeing in a Dream) in *Hana to Yume* magazine. Her other works include the basketball series *Saint Love, MVP wa Yuzurenai* (Can't Give Up MVP), *Blue Wars*, and *Tokyo Crazy Paradise*, a series about a female bodyguard in 2020 Tokyo.

SKIP·BEAT!
Vol. 14
The Shojo Beat Manga Edition

STORY AND ART BY YOSHIKI NAKAMURA

English Translation & Adaptation/Tomo Kimura
Touch-up Art & Lettering/Sabrina Heep
Design/Izumi Evers
Editor/Pancha Diaz

Editor in Chief, Books/Alvin Lu
Editor in Chief, Magazines/Marc Weidenbaum
VP of Publishing Licensing/Rika Inouye
VP of Sales/Gonzalo Ferreyra
Sr. VP of Marketing/Liza Coppola
Publisher/Hyoe Narita

Printed in Canada

Published by VIZ Media, LLC
P.O. Box 77010
San Francisco, CA 94107

Shojo Beat Manga Edition
10 9 8 7 6 5 4 3 2 1
First printing, September 2008

PARENTAL ADVISORY
SKIP·BEAT! is rated T for Teen and is recommended for ages 13 and up. This volume contains a grudge.
ratings.viz.com

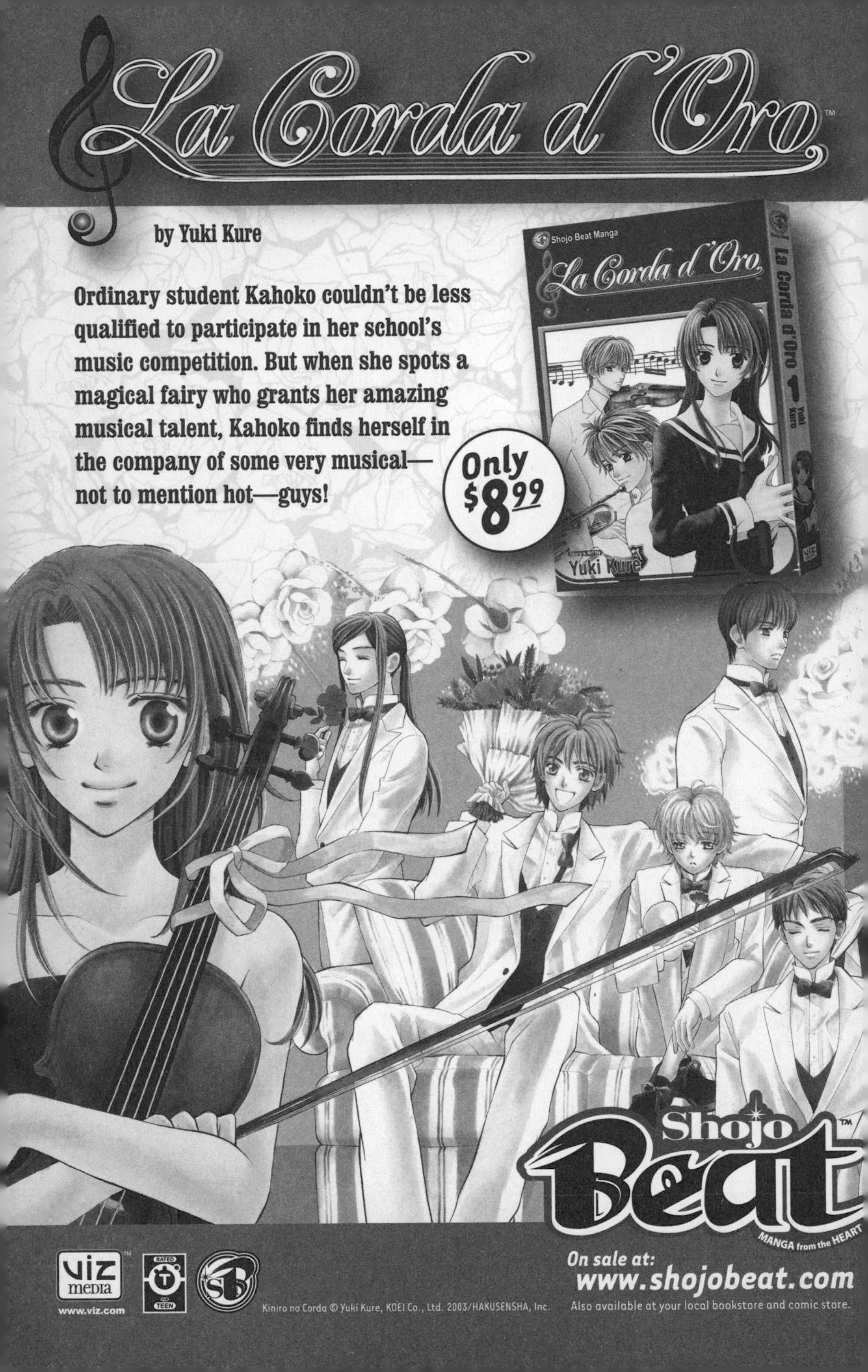
La Corda d'Oro™
by Yuki Kure
Ordinary student Kahoko couldn't be less qualified to participate in her school's music competition. But when she spots a magical fairy who grants her amazing musical talent, Kahoko finds herself in the company of some very musical—not to mention hot—guys!
Only $8.99
Shojo Beat Manga
La Corda d'Oro
Yuki Kure
Shojo Beat™
MANGA from the HEART
On sale at:
www.shojobeat.com
Also available at your local bookstore and comic store.
viz media
www.viz.com
RATED T TEEN
Kiniro no Corda © Yuki Kure, KOEI Co., Ltd. 2003/HAKUSENSHA, Inc.

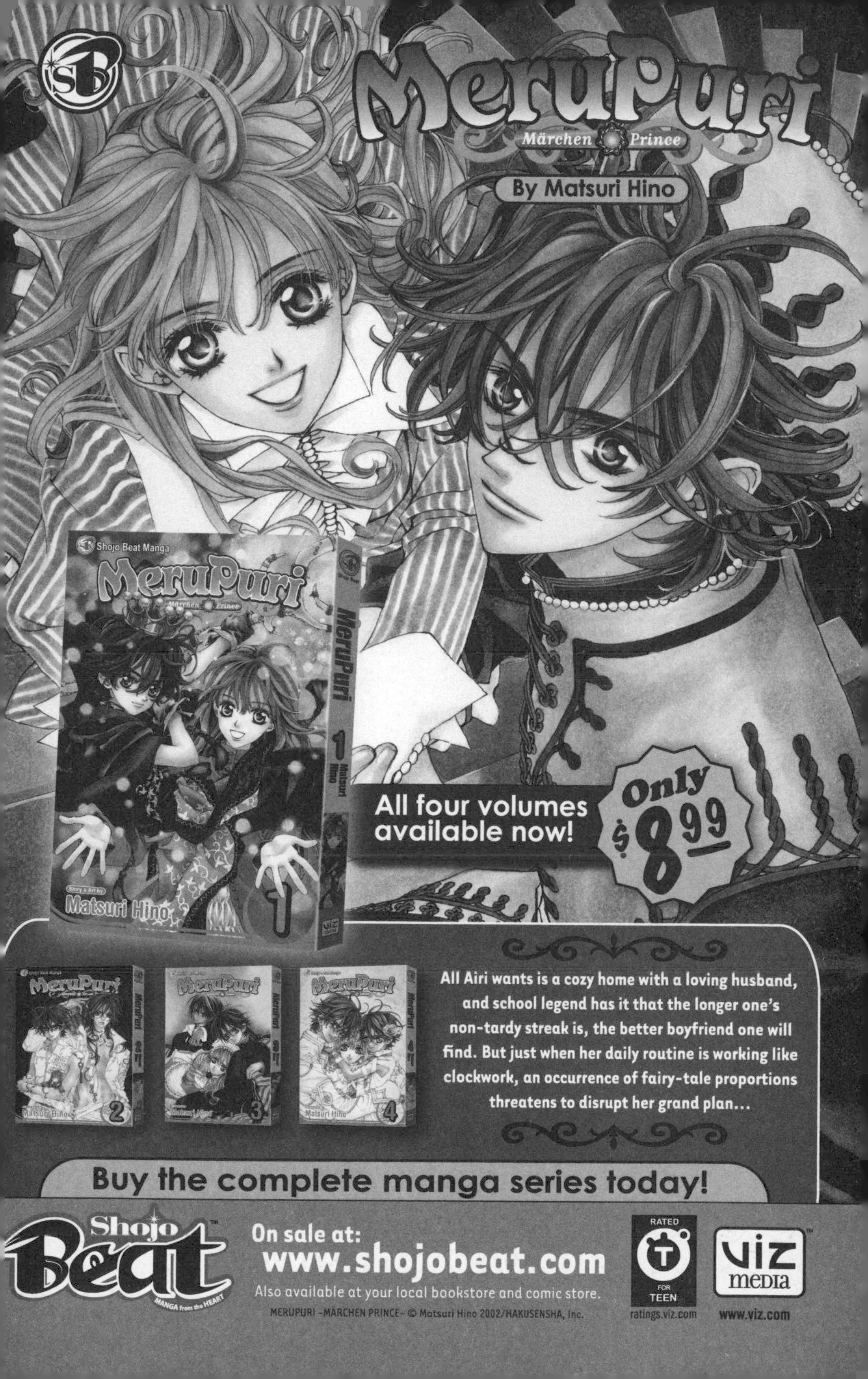
MeruPuri
Märchen Prince
By Matsuri Hino
Shojo Beat Manga
MeruPuri
Märchen Prince
Story & Art by
Matsuri Hino
All four volumes available now!
Only $8.99
MeruPuri
Matsuri Hino 2
Matsuri Hino 3
Matsuri Hino 4
All Airi wants is a cozy home with a loving husband, and school legend has it that the longer one's non-tardy streak is, the better boyfriend one will find. But just when her daily routine is working like clockwork, an occurrence of fairy-tale proportions threatens to disrupt her grand plan...
Buy the complete manga series today!
Shojo Beat
MANGA from the HEART
On sale at:
www.shojobeat.com
Also available at your local bookstore and comic store.
MERUPURI -MARCHEN PRINCE- © Matsuri Hino 2002/HAKUSENSHA, Inc.
RATED T FOR TEEN
ratings.viz.com
VIZ MEDIA
www.viz.com

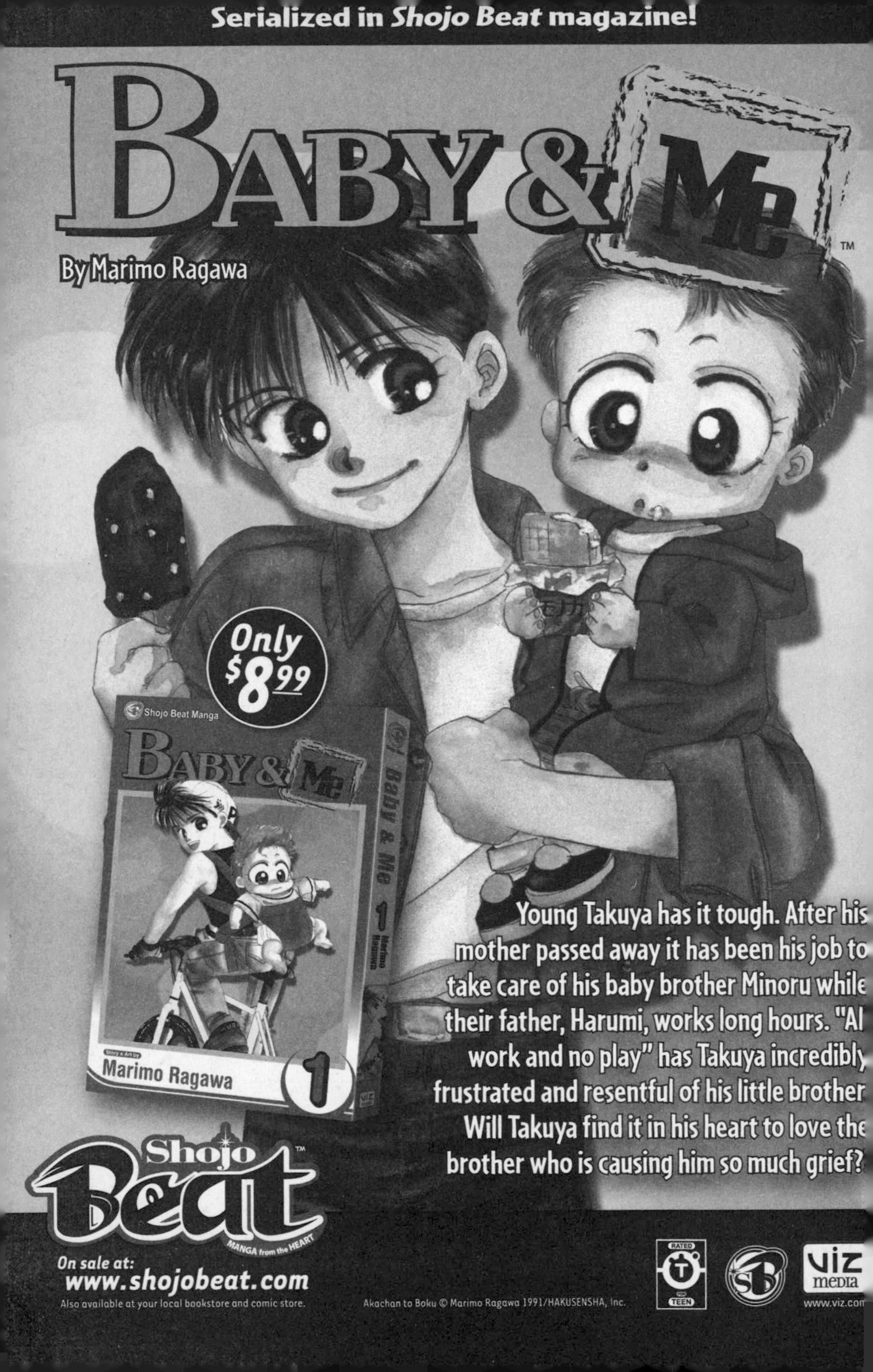
Serialized in Shojo Beat magazine!
BABY & ME™
By Marimo Ragawa
Only $8.99
Shojo Beat Manga
BABY & ME
Baby & Me 1
Story & Art by
Marimo Ragawa
1
Young Takuya has it tough. After his mother passed away it has been his job to take care of his baby brother Minoru while their father, Harumi, works long hours. "Al work and no play" has Takuya incredibl frustrated and resentful of his little brother Will Takuya find it in his heart to love the brother who is causing him so much grief?
Shojo Beat™
MANGA from the HEART
On sale at:
www.shojobeat.com
Also available at your local bookstore and comic store.
Akachan to Boku © Marimo Ragawa 1991/HAKUSENSHA, Inc.
RATED T FOR TEEN
VIZ media
www.viz.com

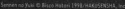

Tell us what about Shojo Beat Manga!

Our survey is now available online. Go to:

shojobeat.com/mangasurvey

Help us make our product offerings better!

THE REAL DRAMA BEGINS IN...

Shojo Beat MANGA from the HEART

Save OVER 50% off!

P9-DDM-504

Shojo Beat

MANGA from the HEART

The Shojo Manga Authority

This monthly magazine is injected with the most **ADDICTIVE** shojo manga stories from Japan. PLUS, unique editorial coverage on the arts, music, culture, fashion, and much more!

☑ **YES!** Please enter my one-year subscription (12 GIANT issues) to *Shojo Beat* at the LOW SUBSCRIPTION RATE of **$34.99!**

Over **300 pages** *per issue!*

NAME

ADDRESS

CITY   STATE   ZIP

E-MAIL ADDRESS   CHASE BRANCH LIBRARY

☐ MY CHECK IS ENCLOSED (PAYABLE TO *Shojo Beat*)   ☐ BILL ME LATER

17731 W. SEVEN MILE RD.

CREDIT CARD: ☐ VISA   ☐ MASTERCARD   DETROIT, MI 48235

ACCOUNT #   578-8002   EXP. DATE

SIGNATURE

CLIP AND MAIL TO →

SHOJO BEAT
Subscriptions Service Dept.
P.O. Box 438
Mount Morris, IL 61054-0438